Two Evenings in Saramaka

Two Evenings in Saramaka

Richard Price and Sally Price

with musical transcriptions by Kenneth M. Bilby

The University of Chicago Press ■ Chicago and London

Richard and Sally Price have been learning and writing about Afro-Caribbean life for nearly thirty years. Richard Price's most recent books include *First-Time* and *Alabi's World;* Sally Price's include *Co-wives and Calabashes* and *Primitive Art in Civilized Places;* together they wrote *Afro-American Arts of the Suriname Rain Forest* and edited John Gabriel Stedman's *Narrative of a Five Years Expedition.* They have taught at Yale, Johns Hopkins, Minnesota, Stanford, and the University of Paris and now live in rural Martinique.

The University of Chicago Press, Chicago 60637
The University of Chicago Press, Ltd., London

© 1991 by The University of Chicago
All rights reserved. Published 1991
Printed in the United States of America
99 98 97 96 95 94 93 92 91   54321

Library of Congress Cataloging-in-Publication Data
Price, Richard, 1941–
    Two evenings in Saramaka / Richard Price and Sally Price.
       p.   cm.
    Includes bibliographical references.
    ISBN 0-226-68061-4 (alk. paper).—ISBN 0-226-68062-2 (pbk. :
alk. paper)
       1. Saramacca (Surinam people)—Folklore.   2. Tales—Surinam.
    3. Saramacca (Surinam people)—Funeral customs and rites.
    4. Folklore—Performance.   I. Price, Sally.   II. Title.
    GR133.S753S277   1991
    398'.09883'3—dc20   90-35941
                                                                   CIP

⊗ The paper used in this publication meets the minimum requirements of the American National Standard for Information Sciences—Permanence of Paper for Printed Library Materials, ANSI Z39.48-1984.

The textile featured on the cover was photographed in 1978 at the request of Saramaka Chief Agbagó (Abóikóni) as part of his contribution to the traveling museum exhibition called Afro-American Arts from the Suriname Rain Forest. He later told us that this shoulder cape was made by Apúmba (ca. 1890–1978), one of his wives, or possibly by his mother, Bo, during the first decade of this century. Although he offered us other textiles for the exhibition, this one he preferred to keep: for use, he explained, at his funeral. He died early in 1989, at the age of 102.

Dedicated to the memory of

Apaasú, Apênti, Asipéi, Asópi, Dooté, Faánsisónu, Fansiêti, Kandámma, Kasindó, Konoi, Sakuíma, Takité, and Tianên,

who participated with us in these two evenings and who have since been honored with tale-telling evenings of their own

Contents

The Saramaka, today some 22,000 people, are one of six Maroon (or "Bush Negro") groups in Suriname that together constitute well over 10 percent of the national population. Their ancestors were among those Africans sold into slavery in the late seventeenth and early eighteenth centuries to work Suriname's sugar plantations. They soon escaped into the dense rain forest—individually, in small groups, sometimes in great collective rebellions—where for nearly one hundred years they fought a war of liberation. In 1762, a full century before the general emancipation of slaves in Suriname, they won their freedom. The very great majority of present-day Saramakas, who continue to live in their traditional riverine villages deep in the rain forest, are heirs to a way of life forged two centuries ago. And until the 1980s, when Suriname's civil war brutally disrupted many aspects of that life, it had changed less radically through time than that of many peoples on the periphery of the Western world. (For locations of villages mentioned in this book, see R. Price 1983 : 16–17.)

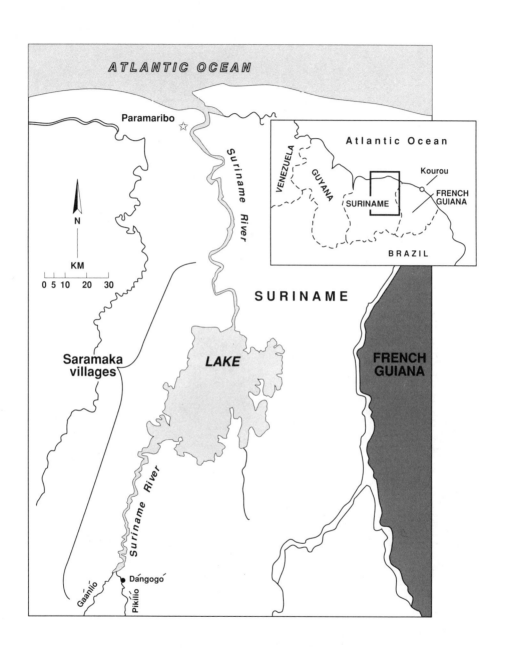

Preface

"Have you seen this ad for a book of folktales from Suriname? Whatever has gotten into the Prices?" asked Professor Goodfellow, the noted anthropologist. "After all those books on history and ethnography," he mused, "why are they now turning to children's stories and nonsense songs—mere folklore? Must be their move to Martinique. A touch of that Caribbean sun or too much rum, I dare say!" Professor Jefferson, his distinguished colleague in comparative religions, puffed thoughtfully at his pipe before replying. "My dear James, I beg to differ. Sun and rum there may be. But in my view it's only with this volume that they've tackled a subject of any depth. After all, myth is the very heart of a culture. He who ignores myth ignores cosmology, and he who ignores cosmology . . ."

But as so often in academic contestations, both professors were a bit off the mark. For in Saramaka, folktales are neither children's stories nor cosmological charters. Rather, they combine for Saramakas many of the rewards that Americans, Germans, or Brazilians find in television, novels, movies, and the theater. They are—albeit oral—adult imaginative literature par excellence, with all the emotional and moral depth of a long cultural tradition that remains alive and vibrant, constantly renewed but always reflecting its links with the past.[1] Neither a peripheral frill nor some mystical key to the essence of Saramaka life, folktales and their telling constitute one of many possible entrées into the Saramaka world. Accordingly, this book is offered as another in our series of experiments in evoking and recording Saramaka lifeways—alongside *Afro-American Arts of the Suriname Rain Forest, First-Time, Co-wives and Calabashes, Alabi's World,* and others.[2] In our view—pace Professor Goodfellow—it matches in "seriousness" any work we have yet produced. Yet it is also intended to permit even such as he to have a good read, in the company of the Saramaka raconteurs who made the experience so much of a pleasure for us and the others privileged to be present in the cool of those long-ago Dángogó evenings.

During the past two decades, the study of expressive culture has witnessed a reorientation, aptly glossed by Dell Hymes as a "breakthrough into performance" (1975). Art objects (from Africa, Oceania, and native America) that had been gathering dust in museum cases began to be recontextualized "in motion," with the help of contemporary ethnography and of video and multimedia presentations (see, for an early example, Thompson 1974). Folktales that had been silenced on the printed page were given new life, not just through structuralism, deconstruction and other new textual modes of analysis, but by ethnographic recontextualization and attention to the performative dimension of their telling (see, for example, Abrahams 1983; Basso 1987; Cosentino 1982; Crowley 1966; Falassi 1980; Hymes 1981; Seitel 1980; Sherzer and Woodbury 1987; Tanna 1984; Tedlock 1972). Visual and verbal arts, previously analyzed largely in static, normative modalities (almost as *langue* rather than *parole*) began to be examined in their quotidian settings, as lively arts within the context of ongoing expressive cultures. Folklore studies among the Suriname Maroons have not yet caught up with these scholarly trends.[3] The available published collections (by Herskovits and Herskovits 1936; Hurault 1961; members of the Summer Institute of Linguistics, who have produced numerous pamphlets; and others) continue to privilege written over oral communication. Frequently "informants" have been asked to tell a tale (in artificial and often ritually prohibited circumstances) in an investigator's temporary quarters, phrase by slow phrase, to an interpreter who, phrase by slow phrase, has rendered a version to the investigator who then wrote "it" down. Or in the case of the Summer Institute of Linguistics, potential Christian converts (usually children) learning to read and write have been given the exercise of writing out a tale in their own language. Although a faithful Lévi-Straussian might argue that none of this matters (since the "structure" of the tale would in theory be recoverable by the analyst even from corrupt texts like these), it is our experience as ethnographers that there is little relationship between such tales (which are ultimately little more than artifacts of their elicitation) and those that form such an integral part of the Maroon moral and aesthetic universe.[4]

Furthermore, for various reasons (among which racism and ethnocentrism predominate), Suriname Maroons have had a consistently bad press in regard to language and speech. Otherwise perceptive visitors (like V. S. Naipaul or John Walsh) conclude that they speak a kind of "baby talk" (Naipaul 1962; Walsh 1967); and the 1971 *Guinness Book of World Records* awarded their language the palm for being the world's "least complex," allegedly possessing "only 340 words." In fact, however, the Saramaccan language may well be the world's oldest extant Afro-American creole.[5] It is a rich and complex communicative vehicle, enabling tales like those translated here to express central cultural values and to serve as a medium for sophisticated verbal artistry.

The rationale and organization of this book relate to these concerns. Our goal is at once to place Saramaka folktales within the broader context of modern folklore scholarship and to make them accessible to anyone interested in the verbal arts more generally. Saramaka folktales bear witness to a lively, creative culture and form part of a vibrant Afro-American verbal tradition. Presented here in English translation, they may be read from any of several perspectives. But whatever else they may represent in their present form, we intend them—as did the tellers—above all as collective entertainment, a communal theater to honor the dead and bring pleasure, as well as instruction, to the living.

This folktale project, however modest, has spanned most of our professional careers and has involved the generosity of numerous institutions and individuals. The 1966–68 fieldwork during which we recorded most of our corpus of tales was based in Dángogó (a village of some two hundred people on the Pikílío) and funded by a predoctoral grant (to RP) from the National Institute of Mental Health. The Concilium on International and Area Studies of Yale University and the Oral Data Committee of the African Studies Association provided support for the preparation of preliminary transcriptions during the early 1970s. The staff of the Archives of Traditional Music (the Folklore Institute, Indiana University) has been consistently helpful regarding the original tapes we have entrusted to their care. Further fieldwork on other subjects in Suriname during the mid-1970s (especially history and the visual arts), which also permitted us to deepen our knowledge of tales and their telling, was funded by a grant (to RP) from the National Science Foundation. Additional work on the tales was made possible by a NATO Postdoctoral Fellowship in Science (to SP) during 1981–82. But our most important support for the project, specifically for the production of translations for this book (including final fieldwork with Saramakas in French Guiana and the Netherlands to refine our understandings), came from a grant (to SP) from the Editions Program of the National Endowment for the Humanities. To all these agencies, we express our gratitude.

Among the many individuals who either participated in the two evenings or otherwise helped us at some point on this project, we would like to single out for special thanks Abátelí, Aduêngi, Akúndumíni, Asipéi, Elimá, Kandámma, Kasindó, Peléki, and Tandó (all of whom provided us special insights into folktales during the 1960s and 1970s in Dángogó); the enthusiastic group of Saramaka men in Kourou, French Guiana—Amoída, Antonísi, Kasólu, Lodí, Samsón, and Sinêli—who spent a number of memorable afternoons with us in 1987, after they had already put in a hard day's work at the French missile base, listening over and over to folktale tapes, eating watermelon and drinking beer, and helping us refine our transcriptions and notes; Gálimo and Kalusé, who also helped us with our transcriptions during that summer in Cayenne; Michel Sauvain and Arthur Othily, who through ORSTOM Cayenne generously made available to us lodging and transportation during our stay; and Rudi Wooje (to whom Bonno Thoden van Velzen kindly introduced us), who worked on the recordings with us in 1986 in the unlikely modernistic setting of Nieuwegein, Netherlands; and Harry and Ligia Hoetink, who helped make that Dutch visit so pleasant.

Kourou, 1987. From left to right: Kasólu, Antonísi, Amoída, SP,

Terry Agerkop took the photo on page 49 (bottom); Antonia Graeber took the photo on page 242; and the *apínti* shown, now in the Schomburg Center for Research in Black Culture, Melville J. and Frances S. Herskovits Collection, is reproduced here with the kind permission of Jean Herskovits. All other photos are our own.

Two colleagues, Roger Abrahams and Dennis Tedlock, read a penultimate draft of this book and, drawing on their long experience with the spoken word, made a number of important suggestions. Roger helped us more fully situate our tales, as well as various features of Saramaka performance, within the broader context of Afro-American folkways. Dennis not only helped us understand better how to describe in the Introduction what we were actually doing in our transla-

RP, Lodí, Sinêli.

Ken Bilby and Adiante Franszoon, Baltimore, 1990.

tions, but also inspired us to bring the translations themselves into closer correspondence with the flow of Saramaka speech. We are very

grateful to both for making this a much better book.

We would like to express special thanks to Adiante Franszoon, who sat for much of two years in a basement language lab at Yale during the early 1970s, patiently transcribing from our field tapes what became some 1,030 typescript pages of Saramaccan; though in the course of time, working with these materials in the field, we have extensively modified many of these transcriptions, this whole project would not have been possible without Adi's conscientiousness. Kenneth Bilby, who has carried out extensive fieldwork with Aluku Maroons, generously undertook the complex task of transcribing the nearly sixty musical examples of Saramaka songs and chants/shouts that are scattered throughout the text. We are very grateful for his collaboration.

We wish also to thank Christina T. Davidson, music copyist, for rendering Bilby's transcriptions with considerable grace.

Introduction

Collective Fabulation

$\int$ aramaka folktales (*kóntu*) are closely associated with funeral cele-
brations. The immediate goal of every Saramaka funeral (which
serves ultimately to usher a recently deceased member of the community into the world of the ancestors) is "to bury the deceased
with celebration [*pizíi*]." Amid the hectic weeks of drumming, dancing,
singing, feasting, and complex rituals that contribute to these festivities, the telling of folktales—which takes place during the night after
the actual burial (and for some deaths, on subsequent nights)—consti-
tutes a special moment for people of all ages. The setting is more intimate than other funeral-related gatherings, typically involving thirty
to forty kinsfolk and neighbors, sitting on stools before the deceased's
doorstep. Together they in effect agree to transport themselves into a
separate reality that they collectively create and maintain: *kóntu-kôndè*
("folktale-land," an earlier time as well as a distant place), where animals speak, the social order is often inverted, Saramaka customs have
been only partially worked out, and the weak and clever tend to triumph over the strong and arrogant. For Saramakas, folktales are
sharply distinguished from history; *kóntus* are fictions with deep moral
lessons for the present, not accounts of "what really happened."[6] Sitting by torchlight or the light of the moon, the participants at a tale-
telling wake come face to face with age-old metaphysical problems and
conundrums; by turns frightened by the antics of a villainous monster,
doubled over with laughter at a lascivious song, or touched by a character's sentimental farewell, they experience an intellectually and emotionally rich evening of multimedia entertainment.

An evening of *kóntus* begins with riddling, a long string of witty
prompts and responses performed by two people at a rapid pace,
ideally without pause, prefaced by the conventional exchange "*Hílíti*"/
"*Dáiti*." People memorize the answers they hear others giving to riddles
(*kísi kóntu*) rather than figuring them out on the spot when they take
part in the verbal performance, and it is not uncommon for a person
to know the answer to a riddle without being able to explain the rationale behind it.[7] Riddles tend to be told in clusters that share a common form—those based on imitation of particular sounds, those that
refer to the speaker's father, and so forth. The two wakes we have
translated for this book had already passed from riddling to tale-
telling by the time we showed up with our tape recorder, but a record-

1

ing made in Dángogó on another night gives something of the flavor of Saramaka riddles:

—*Híliti.*
 —*Dáiti.*
—A creek splits into twelve tributaries.
 —Silk-cotton tree [which has a long trunk topped with a complex branch formation].

—*Híliti.*
 —*Dáiti.*
—A single man at the prow of a ship headed out to sea.
 —Needle.

—*Híliti.*
 —*Dáiti.*
—I make a house for myself. I paint the outside with green paint. I paint the inside with red paint. All the people who are inside wear black jackets.
 —Watermelon.

—*Híliti.*
 —*Dáiti.*
—Indian up high.
 —Awara [a tall palm tree with bright orange fruit]. . . .

—*Híliti.*
 —*Dáiti.*
—Two brothers go hunting. They see a tapir behind a stone. One takes a gun and shoots the stone, pierces it, and kills the tapir. The younger one walks through the hole and takes the tapir away. The sister is back in the village boiling its liver and has it ready for them to eat when they return. Who is the cleverest one?
 —The sister. . . .

—*Híliti.*
 —*Dáiti.*
—"*Kolólo kolólo.*"
 —Okra's gone from the plate [the sound of the spoon scraping an empty plate].

—*Híliti.*
 —*Dáiti.*
—"*Tjobó tjobó.*"

   —Dog swimming.
—*Híliti.*
   —*Dáiti.*
—*"Kalala kom."*
   —Poling stick [of a canoe] hits a rock. . . .
—*Híliti.*
   —*Dáiti.*
—My father has a dog that barks from morning to night. It's
never silent.
   —Rapids.
—*Híliti.*
   —*Dáiti.*
—My father has a jug. He loads it with water again and again. It
never gets full.
   —Ants' nest.

After a few minutes of riddling, someone calls out "*Mató!*" the
opening formula for tales, and another responds vigorously, "*Tòngôni!*"[8] At this signal, everyone present steps over the invisible barrier
into folktale-land.

By calling out "*Mató!*" a person appropriates center stage as the
narrator of the first tale. By answering "*Tòngôni!*" another person
assumes the role of *píkima* ("responder" or "whatsayer"), thereby
agreeing to punctuate the narration at frequent intervals, usually with
the conventional "*íya,*" but occasionally varying with "That's true,"
"Really!" or "Right!" and shifting to the negative ("Certainly not!"
"Not at all," or simply "No") at appropriate points in the story. All
present informally monitor the conscientiousness of this responder,
whose performance is essential to the proper telling of the tale, com-
plaining when the responses are too widely spaced or weakly delivered
and collectively insisting that the telling maintain a clear call-and-
response pattern. The teller and responder are often close friends or
relatives, and they play out their interaction with joking, teasing, and
collegial criticism that heighten the pleasure of the session.

   Another way a teller can "frame" a narrative involves the explicit
suspension of everyday etiquette. For example, before launching into
a ribald nugget, one man pleaded for understanding, arguing with
mock seriousness that "When you're doing tale-telling like this, there
are certain things you say, so everybody please excuse me. If fathers-
in-law are present. . . . If mothers-in-law are present, we're not doing

that kind of [polite] talking. Today is for Anasi stories, not for father-in-law or mother-in-law matters! We mustn't take offense."

Once under way, a tale should be interrupted periodically by tale nuggets; Saramakas use the word *kóti* ("to cut [into, across, off]") in talking about this interruptive pattern. Each nugget briefly evokes a longer tale, often simply through a song that plays a pivotal role when fuller versions of that folktale are told. There is a presumption that most people present will be able to grasp the allusion, and this lends further force to the complicitous character of the tale-telling event. The announcement of such a nugget comes without warning, in many cases interrupting the narrator in midphrase: "Just as such-and-such was happening [referring to the action currently under way in the main story], I was there." "Really?" the narrator may ask. "And what did you see?" The nugget unfolds in a combination of speech and song (often enhanced by dance and mime), with the narrator of the main tale temporarily taking on the role of responder (and usually providing more varied responses than those punctuating the main tale). The end is signaled with the remark "Go on with your story." The person offering a tale nugget stitches it into the fabric of the tale it is interrupting in some more-or-less imaginative fashion—by selecting a nugget that has some intrinsic parallel with the plot or characters of the main tale, by singing a song associated with a character or musical instrument from the main tale, by altering the usual plot of the nugget to blend it into the current action in the main tale, by inserting characters from the main tale into the plot of the nugget, and so forth.

The aesthetic success of an evening of tale-telling depends explicitly on listeners' cutting into longer narratives. When a tale goes on too long without interruption, people chide one another until someone cuts in and restores the evening's rhythmic momentum. One late-night contribution by Kandámma, for example (p. 153), was accompanied by frequent criticisms and excuses about the lack of interruptions, as listeners began to feel sleepy and think about dispersing. "Won't somebody cut this tale, my god?" pleads Asabôsi. Akóbo seconds her concern: "You men should cut it. Those machetes you carry around with you, what about using them?" Kasólu pleads a lack of options: "All I could do would be to make something up," and Akóbo quickly pins him: "Well, make it up then, and let's hear it!" But Kasólu (a prolific narrator but a reluctant singer in tale-telling) still begs off: "I always forget the songs when I sing and it ends up being a half-assed thing." There follows a prolonged silence, broken finally when Asabôsi calls out to Kandámma: "'Mmá, at that time, I was already there. . . ." At other times the synergistic effect of frequent interruptions by tale nuggets builds dramatically, and people almost queue up to make their contributions. When Kódji interrupted a tale by Aduêngi with a particularly sweet tale nugget, Aduêngi jumped right back in with a tale nugget of his own—in effect "interrupting" his own tale and stepping up the rhythmic pace of the session—loudly defending his unconventional move by saying, "If a man kicks you, you have to kick him back" (p. 327).

The narrator of a tale ends it by any one of several conventions. It might be a simple "That's where my story ends" or "That's as far as my story goes"; it might be a moral lesson, perhaps prefaced by a several-phrase synopsis of the plot; or if the tale began by noting the once-upon-a-time absence of a particular feature of Saramaka life (polygyny, drumming, all-night dancing, etc.), it might be an expression of gratitude to one of the tale's characters for having carved out this aspect of current custom. A tale's "moral" may bear only tangentially on its content or may be ironic or humorous, and listeners sometimes volunteer humorous "morals" of their own invention. When the tale ends there usually follows some mix of compliments on its telling, animated discussion of its content and style, and extraneous conversation—but more or less quickly someone in the gathering calls out "*Mató!*" a second person responds with "*Tòngôni!*" and the next tale is already under way.

Many of the striking performative, stylistic, and expressive features that characterize an evening of tale-telling belong to a broader pattern of Saramaka speech and verbal play. Saramakas display a lively attentiveness to the art of speech (as they do to visual artistry as well).[9] Even in the comparative context of Afro-American societies (where performative and expressive events play such a central role), Saramakas exhibit an unusually keen appreciation of nuance in voice, phrasing, accent, gesture, and posture. Playfulness, creativity, and improvisation permeate conversation, and spontaneously invented elliptical phrases frequently substitute for standard words; for example, a watch may become a "back-of-the-wrist motor," food "under-the-nose material," a stool "the rump's rejoicing," and—as in one of the folktales in this book—swimming "underwater work." Speech play assumes other forms as well: verbal dueling by young men (involving the improvisation and recital of run-on strings of wittily phrased insults); the casual insertion of foreign-language expressions (e.g., from French Guiana creole, coastal Suriname creole, Dutch, or English);

and elaborate secret play languages (usually developed by groups of young men). Saramakas' interest in individual mannerisms inspires frequent verbal and gestural mimicry. We once saw two friends, separated by roaring rapids, silently greet each other: one began with a humorous imitation of the dance style of a fellow villager, and the second—who had no trouble identifying the subject of the mime—countered with his own rendition of another man's performance of the same dance. Saramaka women are especially adept at ridiculing their co-wives through comic impersonations. The expressive, dramatic quality of Saramaka life also comes through in the spontaneous songs and dances that are sparked by mundane but happy events. We once saw an elderly woman, who had been fishing without success for over an hour, catch a tiny fish; dropping into a sitting position in the shallow water, she broke into a sinuous dance of celebration with her upper torso. Another time, a woman noticed SP passing her door with a new enamel bucket on her head and sang out a spontaneous little song: "The red bucket suits my 'sister-in-law,' look how the red bucket suits my 'sister-in-law.'"

Saramakas are also masters of indirection and ellipsis: the art of allusion through proverbs or other condensed verbal and gestural forms, as well as other spontaneous and conventional means of avoiding direct reference. Although the use of such devices intensifies in formal contexts (prayer, council meetings, and so forth), even everyday ways of addressing or referring to people are treated as a complex and subtle art. We have heard people manage to avoid uttering any of a person's names, for example, by substituting kin terms, official titles, references to kinship ("so-and-so's mother"), residence ("the man up the hill"), physical characteristics ("the dark one"), temporary states ("the woman who was sick"), recent actions ("the man who killed the tapir"), and so forth. Often reference becomes a kind of sophisticated wordplay in which the speaker uses progressively less ambiguous terms seriatim until the identity of the referent becomes clear to the listener. This same kind of ellipsis appears in many of the folktales in this book; for example, Anaconda is sometimes referred to as "the long one," Elephant as "the big guy," and Jaguar as "the old man."

From a Saramaka perspective, the ability to use proverbs—or, more frequently, cryptic proverbial allusions—represents the ultimate achievement in the verbal arts. Proverbs form a central repository of moral wisdom and values and play an important role in almost any formal conversation. As people grow older they tend to use proverbs with greater frequency and skill—which in Saramaka terms means more elliptically and more often in esoteric ritual languages. Proverbs are also "spoken" on the *apínti* (talking) drum, for example, as a running commentary on the debates in a tribal council meeting. Proverbs are occasionally spoken as full sentences ("If you don't poke around in a hole, you won't know what's in it"), and such statements are often preceded by a reference to the person, animal, or other being conventionally credited with the observation ("The elders say, 'Spider monkeys don't beget howler monkeys'" [Like father, like son]; or "Lizard says, 'Speed is good, but so is caution'"). But more frequently the proverb is left half-finished ("If you don't poke around in a hole . . ."), in the expectation that listeners will complete it mentally. And in many cases one or two key words from a proverb are cited in isolation, or an allusion is made to its characters or to the being credited with its invention. To mention "the one about River Grass" communicates the moral of a proverb expressed, in its full version, in terms of a conversation between a certain fish and the vegetation in a rapids; and "the talk of Chicken" represents the wisdom of a proverb introduced as originally spoken by that fowl. Such condensed allusions in everyday speech are not always to proverbs: they may be made to folktales, to "dilemma tales," to well-known proclamations or favorite aphorisms of living Saramaka elders, or to any philosophical fragment that a speaker can expect a listener to have heard. The mere mention of "*nóuna*," for example, can serve as an effective warning, from one Saramaka to another, to be on guard about revealing information to an outsider—since in a well-known folktale that nonsense word is used to protect secret knowledge from discovery (see p. 18 below). In tale-telling, the Saramaka art of allusion reaches a high point in the "tale nuggets" that interrupt longer narratives. Here, as in proverbial allusions, a part is artfully offered for the whole, and the communicative process takes on a fully dialogic form as listeners are called on to fill in, silently, a whole folktale on the basis of a few cryptic phrases of narrative or, often, of song.

More generally, Saramaka expressive events at all levels of formality are characterized by total participation and the highly structured (though at the same time fluid) interplay among participants, rendering inappropriate the analytical use of Western distinctions between "audience" and "performer." There are, for example, certain stylized contrapuntal patterns that recur in everyday speech and gossip, the formal rhetoric of ritual and judicial sessions, public song/dance/drum performances, and the telling of tales. Normal conversations are punctuated by supportive comments such as "That's right," "Yes indeed," or "Not at all." Even when men living on the coast send tape-recorded messages back to their villages, they leave pauses after each phrase so that the "conversation" may assume its proper two-party form once the tape is played. In formal settings stylized responses become more frequent, and a particular individual assumes responsibility for providing them. Discussions involving the tribal chief, for example, are always conducted with the rhetorical aid of a third party, who explicitly represents "the public." Prayers also assume an antiphonal structure as participants support the speaker's words at intervals with slow handclapping and a specially intoned declaration of "Great thanks." Solo work songs are interrupted by the comments of others present, and popular songs involve the alternation of a soloist and a responsive chorus. Whatever the specific context, this fundamental dialogic pattern—which characterizes folktales as well—privileges the ongoing, active engagement of those who are not the "principal" speaker or performer of the moment.

A closely related feature of Saramaka performance is role switching between (temporary) soloist and other participants. For example, song/dance/drum "plays" are characterized by the emergence of a succession of individual soloists, each of whom briefly enjoys center stage and then yields to another. In other words, Saramaka "performances" resemble a jam session rather than the playing of a piano concerto.

Many cultural events in Saramaka, including tale-telling, exhibit a common diachronic structure characterized by repeated interruptions. An initial exposition is interrupted by another, which in turn may be interrupted by a third, with subsequent portions of each unfolding—often with further interruptions—throughout the performance. For example, a divinatory seance with an oracle or a formal court session might proceed from A (the first case) to B, to a continuation of A, to the end of B, to a continuation of A, to the beginning of C, to the whole of D, to another continuation of A, to the end of C, and finally to the end of A. This practice of interrupting and overlaying segments strung out through time is closely related to central features of Saramaka musical performance—for example, drummers' or singers' staggered points of entry and the pervasiveness of polyrhythms.

These very general features (which are paralleled by fundamental Saramaka concepts about the unfolding of events through time) are part of the historical synthesis that the original maroons and their immediate descendants forged during the late seventeenth and early eighteenth centuries. Ethnohistorical evidence makes clear that many of them were already firmly established by the second half of the eighteenth century—antiphonal speech and song, "interruption" as a syntagmatic principle, interactive participation in performative events, and verbal indirection, ellipsis, and play. On the plantations of coastal Suriname, slave songs were described from a European viewpoint as "melodious but without Time; in Other respects not unlike that of some Clarks reading to the Congregation, One Person Pronouncing a Sentence Extemporary, which he next hums or Whistles, when all the others Repeat the Same in Chorus, another sentence is then Spoke and the Chorus is Renew'd a Second time & So ad perpetuum" (Stedman 1988:516). Eighteenth-century German missionaries complained that their sermons were frequently disrupted: "One [Saramaka] said, 'Teacher, today we understand your words.' Another, 'What you say is the truth.' A third, 'I see that our Obia men have deceived us.' A fourth, 'I believe that the Great God is the one and only God'" (cited in R. Price 1990:254).

Viewing Afro-American folktales within a historical, comparative context, Roger Abrahams has written that "together, they demonstrate a wholeness in this folk literature, an integrity of theme, a consistency of style and pattern that owes much to its African origins, even while it breathes with a life of its own" (1985:18). A comprehensive analysis of the historical continuities in Saramaka (and other Afro-American) tale-telling remains to be undertaken. The pioneering pages of the Herskovitses (1936:117–48) are still unmatched in pointing toward some of the paths that might be followed.[10] But what is certain is that such an analysis would uncover both remarkable continuities with tale-telling in the African homelands and significant dynamism and change. As we have argued elsewhere, the arts of Saramaka—visual and musical as well as verbal—are strongly marked

> by continuity-in-change, by what Amiri Baraka, writing of Afro-American music, called "the changing same" (Jones 1967). In building creatively upon their collective past, the early Maroons synthesized African aesthetic principles and adapted, played with, and reshaped artistic forms into arts that were quite new yet still organically related to that past. The arts of the [Saramaka], forged in an inhospitable rain forest by people under constant threat of annihilation, stand as enduring testimony to Afro-American resilience and creativity and to the remarkable exuberance of the Maroon artistic imagination working itself out within the rich, broad framework of African cultural ideas (S. Price and R. Price 1980:215).

And as Abrahams suggests (1985:20), it is often in focusing on the ways Afro-Americans have reshaped African or European patterns to their own ends that the deeper meaning and significance of New World tale-telling emerges.

Unfortunately, we have little specific information about eighteenth-century Saramaka folktales, since neither the missionaries nor the Dutch civil servants who lived among these Maroons seem to have been interested in such matters. One tale, however, was written out by these missionaries (in German), undoubtedly because it "explained" why whites and blacks had separate stations in life. Though it is somewhat difficult to plumb because of the corrupt form in which it was recorded, it appears to be more a part of Saramaka men's ironic "tomming" repertoire with whitefolks than the kind of folktale that would be told during an evening of *kóntus*.[11]

For Saramakas as for other Afro-Americans, folktales "both reflect and refract reality" (Abrahams 1985:9). What Cosentino claims for Mende (West African) tale-telling could equally well be said for Saramaka: "In the mundaneness of their thematic concerns and the fabulous contrivances of their plotting, [tales] seem related to the conventions of the modern 'soap opera.'. . . [The aim seems to be] to incapsulate the incredible within the believable in order to sustain both" (1982:8, 96). To participate in an evening of Saramaka tale-telling is to join speakers and listeners in the collective creation and maintenance of a fictional but richly significant separate reality.

But the creation and maintenance of this separate reality—no matter how many outrageous acts are perpetrated therein—does not require in Saramaka, as Abrahams suggests it does for Afro-American societies more generally, the suspension of "the kind of moral conscience that asks that we judge such doings on moral grounds" (1985:5). Although Saramakas listening to a folktale suspend *certain* expectations derived from everyday reality—everyone knows that in folktale-land animals talk, devils haunt the forests, and many "normal" social forms do not exist—they do not suspend moral standards. They judge Anasi's outrageous greed or a devil's lechery in much the same way they judge the behavior of their fellow villagers in everyday life, and much of their pleasure in participating in an evening of tale-telling derives from the animated, interactive discussion that focuses on moral judgments of action and character. Exclamations of approval and disapproval are frequent: "What a generous way to bury a parent!" or "How could anyone be so greedy?" And though once or twice we have heard some claim by a teller prompt an appreciative listener to exclaim "*Lègèdè f'i!*" (which translates literally as "You're lying!" and might be glossed as a complimentary "Bullshit!"), there is considerably less insistence in Saramaka than elsewhere in Afro-America on the "lies" and "nonsense" aspect of tale-telling (Abrahams 1985).[12] For Saramakas, in any case, the appreciation of fabulation seems largely independent of any notion of moral inversion or the suspension of moral standards.

A Saramaka tale-telling session is privileged in terms of the social solidarity it expresses. Individuals (whether neighbors or kin) whose daily lives include frequent and strongly felt frictions lay aside their differences for an evening to honor the dead. The enthusiasm for Asabôsi's contributions to her mother's wake, for example, overrode the gossip of the moment about her involvement in the dead woman's malevolent rituals; people responded to Kasindó's Anasi stories as if they had never been critical of his sluggish participation in earlier stages of the funeral rites; and hostile co-wives laughed together as Aduêngi performed a dance miming the founding father of polygynous marriages. When tales are being told, individuals who normally quarrel over moral issues can agree on what is right or wrong, justified or outrageous, cunning or foolish. And since people of all ages are present when tales are told, *kóntus* represent an important crucible for socialization.

Saramaka tale-tellers (and responders) draw on various rhetorical devices (and other expressive means) to enhance the persuasiveness of the fictional reality of folktale-land. They identify themselves as eye-witnesses to the action; they were "there" when it happened. A person begins a tale nugget by asserting formulaically that "when Cayman was carrying the boy across the river [or the two brothers were setting out to seek wives, or the devil was leering at the young girl], I was standing right there! And I saw Squirrel wrestling with Mouse [or Dog chasing Goat, or the Old Woman sweeping her doorstep with her breasts]." Other self-insertions are more active: "Well, just when Jaguar was drugging that stream for fish, I was standing there on the shore, and he asked me to help out." Similarly, current place-names and relationships are frequently injected into a tale to create verisimilitude and familiarity: "Anasi's wife lived pretty close by—about as far as from here to Akísiamáu [the next village downstream]." And listeners often insert themselves into the story by remarking on how *they* would have handled a particular dilemma or challenge. Speakers also use frequent shunts between perspectives or tenses to enhance a story's sense of immediacy. A narrator may move quickly, for example, from a description of what "people" used to do to get wage-labor jobs on the coast, to "You'd go and ask the white man," and this, in turn, might be complemented by some version of the "I was there" rhetoric. Similarly, speakers may move from the past tense to the present and back again—for example, "They were paddling along" to "The wind is coming up" to "And they said." Direct discourse serves as another concretizing device and permits a variety of effects. Speakers frequently mimic characters, sometimes with facial expressions and gestures as well as speech. Foreign words and accents crop up frequently (evoking, for example, the speech of urban bosses, French gendarmes, or Hindustani shopkeepers); and the devil characteristically speaks Sranan, the creole language of the coast. All active tale-tellers cultivate stylistic specialties. One male teller is especially appreciated for the sweet, innocent voice of an adolescent virgin about to be hoodwinked by a devil; another brings down the house with his nasalized, stuttering renditions of Anasi the spider as he engages in one or another mischievous trick; and one elderly woman is the undisputed master of onomatopoeic descriptions—such as the exquisitely innocent "*píí páá, píí páá*" of devils who are feigning sleep and the rambunctious "*a tiá gbéngbelen, a tiá gbéngbelen*" when they are *really* snoring, or the "*Hólo bigódo, hólo gwégede*" as plates of food are tossed into the devil's upturned asshole and clang downward to join the motley assortment of pots, human bones, and other detritus that rests in his belly.

Tale-telling sessions are supremely interactive. In addition to tellers, responders, and those who "cut into" the *kóntu* with tale nuggets, others frequently put in their own two cents, expressing a reaction, requesting a clarification, citing a parallel, and so on. The comments and questions of all of these contribute visibly to reality maintenance, to the persuasiveness of the fiction. Out of the ordinary characters and situations are constantly made to seem reasonable; what would be nonsensical outside folktale-land is repeatedly brought into the realm of logic. Like well-meaning tourists in a foreign country, participants at a *kóntu* session struggle to learn the rules of appropriateness in this other milieu. For example, we will see how a woman named Akóbo frequently interrupts to engage exotic events: "Imagine a husband who carries you on his back! And with your basket on your head!" or "[The boy] saw the [snake's] body with all those [twelve] heads and decided he *liked* him?" Some brief interjections place a listener right in the story, at least in an "as if" mode: "If I had been around, [the beautiful girls who had been refusing all suitors] certainly would have wanted me!" "I would have snuck off quietly instead of playing the drum like that." Or "*I* would have been happy to dig up the gold when that happened." Other such side comments tell the characters what to do (or not to do), much as someone identifying with a character in a horror film might gasp, "No! Don't open the door!" Still others simply express support for a seemingly unlikely part of the story: "Well, yes, Jaguar and Goat *would* have become friends, because when you live right next door to a person, you become friends."

The rapidity with which most tale nuggets follow upon the detail in the main tale that triggers them suggests that the most active listeners are constantly alert and ready to take the floor. Indeed, the great majority of nuggets are triggered by some such specific detail mentioned in the main tale rather than by general features of its plot or theme.[13] We list here, in order of their appearance in the two evenings, a number of examples of these rapid-fire interruptions and the associative links with the tales they cut into. Kasólu's incidental mention of the burial of women (in a tale about something else) sparks an immediate interruption by Kandámma, who tells about the burial of Jaguar's mother (p. 78). And Kasólu's description of ritual advice being offered to a boy inspires Kandámma's tale nugget about a boy who seeks ritual advice to slay a devil (p. 89). Kasólu's depiction of an underwater swimming scene prompts Asabôsi's nugget about Anasi summoning a god from the depths of the river (p. 97). Kandámma's reference to a boy chasing birds from a garden leads Antonísi to tell a story about Hummingbird (p. 113). Only a moment after Kandámma's detailed description of the contents of the devil's belly, Kasólu breaks in with a nugget about Shit (p. 116). Kasólu's mention that all the chickens fell down dead sparks Kandámma's nugget about the behavior of birds during a great famine that was destroying the world (p. 132). As soon as Kasólu mentions the twelve devils' twelve earthenware plates, Akóbo interrupts with a nugget about the twelve paddles that Anasi offered as a courtship gift (p. 171). And when Kasólu mimics the rumbling sound of devils snoring, Kandámma cuts in with a nugget centered on the (similar) sounds made by the shaking body of the old man who bore all the sicknesses in the whole world (p. 174). When Aduêngi mentions the girl who sings and dances at her father's funeral, Kasindó interrupts with a nugget about how Anasi gave a very unusual song and dance performance at a funeral (p. 224). Kasindó's allusion to a calabash salt container that a devil used to store the eyes of his victims inspires Agumiíi to tell how Housefly decided to salt Toad's meat for him (p. 257). A confrontation taking place under a tree, with Amáka rendering the dialogue in Sranan, triggers a tale nugget sung in Sranan about a shameless woman who seduced a man under a tree (p. 265). When Kódji mentions that a woman in his tale was loading up her basket, Aduêngi cuts in instantly with a nugget that includes a girl loading up her own basket (p. 268). Right after Kasindó's riotous song and mime of Anasi introducing a whole village of women to the joys of sex, Aduêngi cuts in with his own ribald rendition of how Sòkôtiláma succeeded in introducing polygyny to Saramaka by having simultaneous public sex with four women (p. 287). During Aduêngi's description of an acrimonious dispute between two women over the custody of a child, Kasindó interrupts with a nugget about a dispute between Piká-bird and Jaguar about the ownership of a garden (p. 320). And just a moment after Aduêngi describes the king's vain attempts to discover the identity of the man who has made his daughter pregnant, there are back-to-back tale nuggets by Kódji and by Aduêngi himself in which people try to discover the identity of mystery performers at two all-night dances (pp. 325 and 327).

The stock characters in Saramaka folktales number in the scores and have diverse proveniences. Some, like the "scrawny little kid" (usually the youngest sibling, who saves his sister from disaster), appear (albeit in different guise) throughout Afro-America; others, like the ubiquitous "devils," have at least partial Christian/European roots; still others, like Anasi the Spider (and his numerous progeny) or— more remarkably—Elephant (an animal whose memory is preserved by Saramakas at a remove of three centuries) are African to the core. The bulk of *kóntu-kôndè* characters are humans, more or less like Saramakas themselves, and familiar animals of their own South American rain forest—Bushfowl, Jaguar, Howler Monkey, Deer, Hummingbird, Cayman, Anaconda, and a host of others. And there are, in addition, frequent cameo appearances by special figures such as Death and Great God. One memorable character is the mysterious stranger whose impressive dancing inspires Anasi to run up to him and offer a congratulatory embrace; only after the damage is done does he, and the other spectators who smell his soiled body, realize that the stranger was Shit himself. The characters who inhabit folktale-land are familiar to all Saramakas, and their individual gifts and foibles are frequently alluded to, by way of comparison, in everyday discourse about the here and now.

The "scrawny little kid" (*makisá miíi*) is the Saramaka version of the Chiggerfoot (or Jiggerfoot) Boy of Anglophone West Indian tales, described by Abrahams as

> an almost invisible character . . . a "dark" figure: an "Old Witch Boy," a dirty and diseased misfit, a mysterious member of the [white] king's family. . . . He lives at the margins between the

family and the wilds, and can be seen as something of a con-
taminating anomaly, and . . . the upsetter of order. Described
variously as "dirty," "smelly," "covered with ashes" (like Cin-
derella), he is best known for his ugly foot, which is described
alternatively as diseased, constantly surrounded by fleas and
nits . . . or as a clubfoot. . . . [He is] contrasted with the king's
beautiful daughter, ostensibly his sister. (1985 : 22–23)

In certain ways the Saramaka kid resembles his West Indian counterpart. (In Saramaccan, *makisá* means crushed, mashed up, messed up,
weak, frail, and generally in a dilapidated state that could be regarded
as either pitiable or laughable, depending on the sympathies of the
observer; *mií* is the word for child, kid, or boy.) So physically they are
much alike. But there is an important difference. In Saramaka, this
ubiquitous character is the younger brother not of a white princess in
the family of a king but a member of a "normal" Saramaka family—
in Saramaka terms, one of "us," not one of "them." The difference is
crucial and points to an ideological contrast that helps us understand
how Saramaka tales—while in general very much a part of the Afro-
American tale-telling world—also stand alone in that comparative
context.

As Abrahams glosses a common West Indian plot involving the
Chiggerfoot Boy,

the daughter [the white princess] is courted by many of the
best men in the land, but she rejects them all until one man
comes riding by with whom she falls madly in love. Their
courtship and marriage is therefore quickly achieved, and her
new bridegroom carries her off with him to his home in the
bush. The boy, through snooping or using one of his witching
powers, is able to follow the couple and discover that his sister
has married an animal or bush spirit that has been able to
transform itself into human form. The boy also discovers how
the transformation is brought about—it is commonly a song—
and he persuades his father to accompany him to witness what
he has discovered. The boy sings the song, the bridegroom
is transformed, and the king then does what he must do.
(1985 : 22)

Here the West Indian audience is meant to empathize and identify,
at least to a point, with this rather bizarre royal family; it is the princess whose life is in danger and her brother who is the hero. But in
Saramaka, though white kings and princesses occasionally appear in

tales, they are consistently portrayed as part of an alien, foreign world. (Indeed, in the only truly developed depiction of a princess in the two evenings of tale-telling presented in this book, she appears as a proto-typical bitch—self-centered, fickle, spoiled, condescending, and nasty.) And the scrawny little kid, who in Saramaka as elsewhere in Afro-America saves his sister(s) from disaster, always saves *black*, "normal" sister(s), not a strange white one.

More generally, Saramaka tales contrast with those of other Afro-Americans in portraying the white world (with its kings and prin-cesses, palaces and cannons, horses and coaches, ships and their crews, as well as slave masters and wage-labor bosses) as completely "other," fully beyond the boundaries of Saramaka society. When Bajans or Nevisians or Alabamians depict those same characteristics, however, they are talking about a much more integral—if still in many ways distant—part of their own social universe. In this sense, then, the contrast in folktale conventions reflects social realities: those of the de-scendants of maroons versus those of slaves. And in this broader Afro-American context, the special ideological stance of Saramakas toward whitefolks renders unique the specific transformations that they have effected on African, other Afro-American, and European tales.

Abrahams has argued that "Afro-American 'In the beginning' stories underscore the value of accommodating yourself to the way things are (and always will be) . . . [and] underscore the fact that [one must accept that] life isn't usually very fair" (1985:39). But while the West Indian Chiggerfoot Boy, through his cleverness or witching powers, saves his sister or solves some other *domestic* problem, his Saramaka counterpart solves *communitywide* problems. Many Sara-maka tales describe the way a particular individual—often the scrawny little kid—refuses to accept a difficult, "unfair" status quo and sets out to alter it, changing some aspect of the world into the (better) way it now is. In various tales, often-unlikely heroes render a particular stretch of forest (or a path into the forest), which has been inhabited by devils or monsters, safe for humans; in others, through their cour-age and initiative, they introduce central aspects of life—drums, fire, polygyny, all-night dancing—into the Saramaka world. Slaves versus maroons/tales of playful antagonism within a world of social inequities versus genuine "hero tales." Because one ideologically central Sara-maka tale—not included in our two evenings—can serve as an em-blematic illustration of these contrasts, we cite it at length.

> There was a great hunter called Bási Kodjó. He had hunt-ing dogs that were killing off all the Bush Cows in the forest.

[The Bush Cow is a mythical animal resembling—but fiercer than—a tapir.] Finally the Bush Cows held a council meeting. They said, "What can we do to kill this man? Soon there will be none of us left." One of them, a female, spoke. "I'll go to him. I have a plan to lure him back here so we can kill him." And she changed herself into a beautiful woman in order to trick Bási Kodjó.

She arrived in his village with a basket on her head, saying that the man who could knock it to the ground would become her husband. She was really beautiful! No one could do it. Finally Bási Kodjó tried, and the basket fell. So this beautiful woman became his wife. Every night, when they were in their hammock, making love, she would ask Bási Kodjó what his secret was, how it was that he was able to kill so many Bush Cows without their ever hurting him. Each night she asked, and each night he told her a little more. She was so beautiful!

Often, during the night, the woman would go out behind the house to stare at the row of Bush Cow skulls that her husband had nailed against the rear wall as trophies. She would weep and weep, silently, for her dead relatives. When she had finished crying, she would return to the house, and Bási Kodjó would ask, "Where have you been?" "I went to urinate," she would say. But every few minutes she would go back out and just stare at those skulls and weep.

Every night she asked Bási Kodjó over and over, "Those animal skulls at the back of your house. How in the world did you kill those animals? They're fiercer than any animal alive!"

One night, Bási Kodjó finally told her: "Woman, those animals live in savannas. I go all the way to the middle of the savanna and fire my gun. When they come charging, I toss my gun aside and climb an awara [palm] tree. The animals circle round and furiously chew at the trunk to fell it. Meanwhile, my mother is back in the village, stirring the boiling pap that she feeds to my hunting dogs at the proper moment, to excite them. When I see that the palm tree is about to fall, I turn myself into a chameleon, sitting on the trunk, and I call out, '*fííí*,' and this makes the trunk grow even thicker than it was at first. I do this until I know that the dogs have had time to gobble up all the boiling pap, and really feel it. Then I let the tree fall. By then the Bush Cows have realized that I am the chameleon, so I turn into a spot of sand. When they try to eat that up, I use my final disguise and turn myself into a . . ."

Just then, Bási Kodjó's mother shrieked from her house, "Bási Kodjó. Bási Kodjó. Hurry. Snake. Snake!" [It was really the god in her head that was calling out.] Bási Kodjó jumped out of his hammock and ran to kill the snake. When he got to his mother's house she pulled him close and whispered, "There's no snake. But I must warn you. That beautiful woman is not really a woman! Don't tell her the last thing you know how to turn yourself into. Instead, tell her that you become a *nóuna*." Bási Kodjó returned to his wife. She said, "That thing you were about to tell me, the very last thing you turn yourself into, when the Bush Cows come charging at you, what is it?" He said, "I become a *nóuna* [a nonsense word, a word with no meaning]." At last she was satisfied. They slept.

In the middle of the night, the woman arose very quietly and went to her basket and took out a razor. She prepared to cut Bási Kodjó's throat. Bási Kodjó's gun said, "I will shoot her *kpóó!*" His machete said, "I will cut her *vélevélevélevéle!* His magic belt [*óbiatatái*] said, "I will tie her *kílikílikílikíli.*" All the posts of the house groaned loudly, "*hiiiiii.*" Bási Kodjó awoke with a start, saying, "What's going on?" She answered, "I have no idea. I was asleep." Not a single thing in the house slept during the rest of the night. At dawn the beautiful wife asked Bási Kodjó to go off to the forest with her to collect awara palm seeds. He told his mother to prepare the pap for the dogs, and they set off. The woman led them deeper and deeper into the forest until they finally reached the savanna. Bási Kodjó climbed the awara tree and began picking fruit. Suddenly the woman turned back into her natural form, a Bush Cow, and called out to her relatives. In a moment the savanna was black with Bush Cows, all coming to eat Bási Kodjó. Quickly he turned himself into a chameleon. She told them he was now the chameleon. So they began felling the tree. When it finally fell, they couldn't find the chameleon. She said, "Eat that spot of sand. *It* is Bási Kodjó." After a while they could not find the sand. Bási Kodjó had turned himself into a tiny awara palm thorn and hidden by sticking himself into a leaf. She said, "Destroy the *nóuna*. He's turned himself into a *nóuna*." The Bush Cows milled around in confusion. None of them knew what a *nóuna* was!

Meanwhile Bási Kodjó's hunting dogs, who by then had finished eating their boiling pap and had been untied, arrived on the scene, and ripped every last Bush Cow to shreds. Except for one. Bási Kodjó saw that this last Bush Cow was pregnant, and he called off the dogs. This Bush Cow was hiding in a cave near a stream. She called out, "Bási Kodjó, have mercy. You're about to kill your own offspring!" He grabbed her by one side, ripping off the whole leg, and then shoved her back into the cave.

Now you know the importance of *nóuna*.[14]

In the common West Indian plot (glossed by Abrahams, above) a white princess is seduced by an evil animal in disguise; the action unfolds on a purely domestic plane, involving personal dangers and triumphs, and the central characters are "empathetic" (if a bit strange) whitefolks. But in the *nóuna* tale (and others of the genre in Saramaka), two worlds are pitted in mortal battle—"our" world (that of Saramaka) and another (rhetorically that of "bush cows," historically and structurally that of "whitefolks"); the seduction is carried out in the service of the "bush cow" state, and the renunciation of the beautiful "woman" and her eventual destruction are carried out by the Saramaka hero on behalf of his people. The West Indian tale is largely entertainment, but the Saramaka story (in addition to its entertainment value) encodes perhaps their strongest ideological concern—community betrayal, treason vis-à-vis whitefolks, and the fear that "those times [the days of war and whitefolks' slavery] shall come again" (see R. Price 1983).[15]

In Saramaka, the strong tendency of scrawny-little-kid tales to privilege community-oriented altruism contrasts with the tendency of Anasi-the-Spider tales to privilege self-interest and cleverness for its own sake. Like the scrawny little kid, Anasi often changes the world for "the rest of us," but he almost always does so inadvertently, as an unforeseen consequence of his own greed, lust, or curiosity. Before Anasi's antics brought them, for example, sexual relations, death, fire, and sickness were not part of the Saramaka world.[16]

Anasi is at once man and spider. Like other animal characters, he participates in the social world of Saramakas, wearing a breechcloth, courting human women, hunting large animals with a gun, building canoes, and dancing at community funerals; but at the same time his spider attributes figure importantly in the stories about him, as he spins a web that other animals must walk on in a special ordeal, escapes to the rafters when chased by Death, or tries to take advantage of his unusually light weight.

Anasi is above all outrageous. As Abrahams notes for Afro-America more generally, we can see his "tremendous ingenuity in stirring things up and keeping them boiling; how he gets into a stew of his own making on many occasions, and how, as often as not, he uses his wits to get out of this trouble. . . . [His] unbridled egotism runs as high as his clever wit" (1985:180). He is admired for his creativity in meeting the boundless demands of his own ego and is much appreciated for the entertainment that his incorrigible naughtiness contributes to an evening of tale-telling. Even in tales about other sets of characters, Anasi often makes a cameo appearance, jumping briefly into the action to stake his claim when there are spoils to be had (a princess's hand in marriage, the prestige of having slain a monster, etc.). Win or lose, Anasi epitomizes the valued Saramaka (and Afro-American) strategy of trying things out, keeping multiple options open, and relying largely on one's wits to stay a step ahead of the competition.

In coastal Suriname (and elsewhere in the Afro-Caribbean world), Anasi frequently appears along with other members of his family. Indeed, although (like most men in those societies) he often enough runs after other women, he is depicted pretty much as a family man. Saramakas are familiar with these other members of Anasi's family—his wife (usually called Weno) and his multiple children (each of whom has a name and individualized characteristics)—but they have reshaped him into a much more independent fellow, reflecting Saramaka domestic realities (polygyny, residential independence of husbands and wives, and so forth) rather than those of the more Christianized, Westernized societies elsewhere in the region.

Together with the scrawny little kid and Anasi, the characters most frequently encountered in an evening of Saramaka tale-telling are the fearsome, giant, oafish but amusing "devils" (*didíbi*) who appear either singly or in bands of twelve (often under the care of an elderly female—mother or housekeeper). Employed as blacksmiths for Great God, they reside beyond the boundary of human habitation (sometimes across whole seas, but often just down a forest path from the village). In some ways devils are inversions of normal Saramakas. They eat through their assholes (swallowing pots and plates along with the food), cannot tolerate contact with water (which turns them into stones), catch fire and turn to ashes when they die, and speak Sranan (the language of coastal Suriname). They are supremely territorial, aggressively defending their land against human intruders—most commonly the scrawny little kid, who arrives in search of something for the betterment of Saramaka society (e.g., one or another kind of drum) or simply to liberate a stretch of forest or a particular path for Saramaka use. When threatened, devils become frantic, throwing things around, burning houses, running wildly in circles, and yelling out in characteristic excitable, repetitious speech. Devils have stereotypical tastes, strengths, and weaknesses. Their lechery knows no bounds, and like normal Saramaka men, they are especially fond of adolescent girls. Their gluttony is equally impressive, and they are connoisseurs of music and the original owners of drums, horns, and other musical instruments. Their ritual powers are prodigious: they dry up rivers or seas by throwing in a tooth or cast up mountains to block an enemy's escape with a magic charm. Their remarkable sensitivity to the smell of humans alerts them to the presence of intruders, but their susceptibility to the charms of music and dance generally brings their demise. Often a scrawny little kid succeeds in distracting a devil by playing a drum, finger piano, or horn; a beautiful nubile girl achieves the same end by singing or dancing; and either one of them may inspire a devil to sing or dance until he drops from exhaustion. Devils' names figure prominently in tale-telling. Like Saramakas, each devil has a set of personal names—appropriate for different social uses (boasting, being flattered, being insulted).[17] But the names themselves do not overlap with those of humans. In our two evenings, for example, one devil recites his own praise name, Ganganmuntúnbu; another one named Maanpáya is taunted with his "insulting name," Towêsinaagooo; and the insulting name of another devil—Tatá Asinalóónpu ku zaan zaan tíngi, Gangan fu Alakwáti (Father Asinalóónpu Who Stinks, Bigman from Alakwáti)—is used by a scrawny little kid (or in another version, a man) to incite him to come out and fight.

If Lion is king in much of Africa, it is Jaguar who reigns over the other animals in the rain forest of Suriname. Saramakas underscore his absolute authority in folktale-land by repeating the formulaic "all the animals called him tío" ("mother's brother," the ultimate authority in this matrilineal society). But though chief of all the animals and physically powerful, Jaguar often comes up short in the end, being tricked by smaller but smarter creatures such as Shrimp, Turtle, or Hummingbird. Normally referred to in folktales as Tatá ("Father" or "Old Man") Domó, he is—like devils—frequently goaded into a fight by an adversary's calling out one or another of his "insulting names," such as Mbónu ("My Bones"), Mi Lánga Húnya ("My Long Claws"), or Uncle Aladígwaha (untranslatable).

The plots of Saramaka tales—by turns dramatic, fabulous, riotous, and sentimental—combine the ordinary with the extraordinary. Many of their initial settings are familiar to Saramakas from everyday experience, and characters move the action forward on the basis of quite ordinary motives (such as greed, revenge, altruism, or fear). But though Saramaka parents, for example, must deal with the temporary loss of a daughter who marries out, it is only in tales that she goes off to the land of a husband who is an elephant, a cayman, or an eagle; though Saramaka men commonly call on magic charms to help them in hunting, it is only in tales that a feather plus a magic word allows them to kill without another weapon; and though Saramakas often argue about who has the right to raise a particular child, it is only in tales that they rip the child in two and each take half. Some tales depend on a character's raw cunning, as in the story of the boy who tricked a tough-skinned white boss into feeling pain or the tale of the young girl who escaped from the devil by a sexual distraction. In others the magical component is more central, as when characters are revived from the dead, usually by having special juices squeezed into their eyes, or when an ordeal determines the fate of those who have transgressed a taboo. Frequently an underdog hero benefits from the advice of a supernatural being or a character who possesses special ritual knowledge. Thus the Old Woman of the Forest whispers a magic word (*aditô*) to Goat, whose relatives are being killed off by Jaguar, enabling him to kill his enemy's entire clan, to the astonishment of both. In another tale, whose plot unfolds something along the lines of the Wizard of Oz, Great God himself lays out techniques by which a boy can solve a whole string of characters' dilemmas. Sometimes the ritual aid assumes a tangible form, such as a needle that can kill the devil or a magic bundle that turns an anus into a deadly weapon. Plots can also advance through the *rejection* of good advice. Stubborn children regularly get into trouble by disregarding the advice of their elders—for example, the two sisters whose mother has told them to take the more overgrown of two paths into the forest but who instead opt for the well-cleared one and meet up with a lecherous devil. Many tales center on a quest for the solution to a problem (for example, a boy's pilgrimage to the land of the devils explicitly to discover drums), but others bring about change inadvertently (as in the tale about how Anasi's interactions with Old Man Death ended in a fight in which Anasi sought refuge in his own village, bringing Death out of the forest and into human society, where he has been a part of life ever since). And the plots of many tales center on some kind of contest—a wrestling match to decide which of two men will get a woman, a life-and-death endurance contest between a dancing boy and a drumming devil, or a dance competition to determine whether Anasi will get to sleep with a beautiful young girl. Overall, the frequency of tales that in some way relate to funerals is striking—wrestling matches, all-night "plays," feigned death, and actual burials.

Many tales concern central structural tensions in Saramaka life; for example, those so common in a matrilineal society between consanguineal and affinal kin, those between men and women who are participating in a polygynous marriage system, the multiple ambiguities that characterize the relations between Saramakas and the animal world, or difficulties with outsiders (the coastal bosses Saramaka men must work for to earn wages, the Christians who attempt to introduce their religion, or the schoolteachers who hold the powerful key to literacy). Tale-telling sessions are a time when (as narrators sometimes remind their listeners) it is appropriate to celebrate publicly the ribald side of sexual relations; in our experience the most explicitly sexual encounters (of devils and nubile girls, of men taking on several women at a time, and so forth) are told very much from a male perspective, though women react to them with lively appreciation as well. There are also certain tales that highlight the more stressful aspects of sexual and conjugal relations, which tend to be recounted from a women's perspective; Kandámma offers a tragic tale about a woman who committed suicide out of anger at her husband's infidelity and another in which an already-married man defiantly went off in search of a second wife and met his death in the gut of a hungry anaconda. And it is primarily deeper structural concerns such as these, however much they may be masked dramatically, that provide episodes of genuine pathos. There are moments of melancholy when a character ponders the loss of relatives (as when the female Bush Cow in disguise contemplates the skulls nailed to Bási Kodjó's house, or when Elephant's human wife wonders whether his hunting kills might not include her own people), and there are emotionally charged "recognition scenes" (for example, between siblings who have never before met) that evoke in Saramakas sentimental reactions not unlike those intended in Voltairean tragedy.

The tales presented in this book were originally recorded in the 1960s as part of ethnographic fieldwork conducted in the region of Dángogó (see map), which was intended to provide broad coverage of Saramaka life. The entire corpus of recordings that we made during 1966–68 (which included other tales as well as riddles, religious and secular songs, drumming of many varieties, oracle sessions, prayers, council meetings, children's games, and speech in esoteric languages) was placed on deposit at the Archives of Traditional Music, the Folklore Institute, Indiana University, in 1974. We also placed on deposit at that time preliminary transcriptions of all verbal portions of the recordings, made by Adiante Franszoon, a young Saramaka man from the village of Dángogó who had returned to the United States with us in 1968. Access to that field collection, composed of 117 five-inch reels, 1,030 pages of typed transcriptions, and a brief introductory essay, is available to researchers upon request. Portions of the recordings, combined with materials collected in the same region during the 1970s, are also included on an Ethnic Folkways record, *Music from Saramaka,* which is available through the Office of Folklife Programs, Smithsonian Institution.

The translations of tales and conversation in this book are based on recordings of parts of two Saramaka performance events that we believe were little influenced by our presence or that of the recorder; telling tales explicitly for an investigator's tape recorder would have produced very different results.[18] Attending wakes was part of our general participation in the life of Dángogó and the surrounding villages; it was only later, after the recordings were made, that we began the active work of interpretation, going over the recordings with Saramakas (first in Dángogó, later elsewhere) to elucidate stylistic features, details of meaning, relationships between tales and tale nuggets, and so forth. In this book we attempt to capture the flavor of the initial experience for our readers by offering a text in which the men and women of Dángogó interact as individuals, producing tales that represent not so much a privileged or representative "folklore corpus" as two particular evenings of combined entertainment, joking, verbal and musical performance, and cultural/ritual instruction, in honor of specific personalities passing into the realm of the ancestors.

Prompted by the conviction that Saramaka tales make little sense outside the setting in which they are told, we present the two evenings of tale-telling relatively "intact." Rather than distilling tales into idealized story lines or grouping texts by analytical categories of one sort or another, we have attempted to present seriatim everything that fell within our tape recorder's range—from a mother reprimanding her child for knocking over a lantern and people arguing about the right way to chorus a particular song to the tale-teller excusing himself for some slip of the tongue or a listener announcing that she is sleepy and is going to stay for only one more story. We include (as post facto "stage directions" in our texts) nonverbal aspects of the recording, such as various kinds of laughter, clucks of moral disapproval, murmurs of condolence, exclamations of indignation, and so forth, as well as indications of the gestures and dances that contributed to the appreciation of the performance. It is our conviction that an understanding of what devices, routines, and incidents make *Saramakas* laugh, exclaim, feel sad, and so forth, is the main avenue leading to the understanding of meaning.

We do not reconstruct those pieces of the performance that are missing from our tapes, even when we have reason to believe they were part of the original performance; for example, if our microphone did not pick up the standard opening exchange (*Mató!*/*Tòngôni!*), it does not appear in our translation. And when collective laughter drowns out the conventional "responses" that punctuate a narrative segment, no such response appears in the text. The auditory experience of any individual present at such a session is imperfect in much the same way that a tape recording is, and one could argue that to reconstruct those elements we know "should" be present would create an artificial, hypercorrected text.

In introducing each of the two evenings, we try to give readers some sense of the larger social and ritual events to which the taletelling sessions contributed. In the tales themselves we cite speakers by name, as they offer tales, songs, questions, and comments. And we have included photographs of as many participants as we could. Because the speakers' personal styles shine through their contributions, we hope readers will come to know and appreciate these Saramakas as distinctive individuals.

In attempting to evoke complex bundles of speech, song, and gesture on the printed page, we have been aided and encouraged by the work of a number of folklorists who have, over the past decade or two, been developing textual strategies and notational devices to reflect voice, tone, timing, and other features of oral events. Like Basso (1987), Burns (1983), Cosentino (1982), Dauenhauer and Dauenhauer (1987), Seitel (1980), Tedlock (1972, 1983), and others, we do our best to help readers imagine an actual out-loud tale-telling session, with translations that pay careful attention to stylistic features such as rhythm, structure, and phrasing. Although we are indebted to these pioneers in folklore transcription, our mode of presentation is also molded by the specifics of Saramaka discourse. Rather than basing our phrasing on the relative or absolute duration of narrators' pauses (as in Seitel 1980 or Tedlock 1972, 1983) or on the literary analysis of versification (as in Hymes 1981), we segment our text at points when the speaker's narration was audibly "cut" by a conventional response, a listener's question, generalized laughter, or extraneous conversation that interrupted the story's continuity.[19] We discuss these textual conventions in greater detail below.

In addition (and in the spirit of Abrahams 1986), we have chosen a textual form that highlights the interactive nature of Saramaka taletelling. Partly because of this communal aspect (the collective participation in the unfolding of a story), Saramaka tale-telling encompasses both "composition" and "performance," both creation and enactment. Much of each narration is familiar to those who are listening: they may already know a song offered by one of the participants (or have heard one almost like it in some other context); they detect in a moment the motives of Anasi, Jaguar, the Scrawny Little Kid, the White King, and other stock characters when they appear on the scene (having witnessed their behavior in other tales); they can guess at the outcome of many situations on the basis of either generalized cultural knowledge or familiarity with a particular speaker's narrative style; and they, like people listening to jokes anywhere in the world, have the cultural knowledge necessary to anticipate the punch lines of many humorous remarks. At the same time each narration is new, in different ways for each person present. Depending on the experience of a particular listener, its originality may be at the level of specific detail, narrative style, side commentary, interruptions from others present, or even the entire story line. Some tales (or the briefer episodes out of which longer stories may be constructed) are more widely known than others, and some Saramakas have wider-ranging knowledge of tales than others. No Saramaka possesses a comprehensive command of the meaning of folktale songs, events, or esoteric expressions, but all Saramakas know a great deal about each of these. As we will see in the first of our two evenings, even the elderly Kandámma, generally acknowledged in the Dángogó region as the champion explicator of folktale esoterica, asked questions as she listened, for there is always something new to be learned. (Of course, some of Kandámma's questions were intended, rather, to keep such details alive for other, less well versed participants.) That our own notes and commentary include some puzzles that none of our field interviews could solve reflects a natural phenomenon of Saramaka knowledge: expressions, allusions, and other nuggets of tradition may be passed on and kept alive even without accompanying clarification of their meaning.

In presenting two evenings of Saramaka tale-telling in English translation, we have in fact been engaged in a *double* translation. To move a spoken utterance to a printed page (even without switching languages) is itself a significant act of translation (see Tedlock 1983; Jackson 1988). And to interpret Saramaka linguistic, cultural, and ecological realities to an English-speaking, Western-oriented audience is yet another. Aware that any distillation of voices on a page—whether transcription or translation, and no matter how exhaustively annotated—is partial and selective, only one of several evocations or representations of a lived event, we have made a set of choices intended to highlight social and cultural context. To give interested readers some notion of how our English texts relate to the Saramaccan originally spoken on those two evenings, we offer one long tale in interlinear transcription/translation (see Appendix). But we emphasize that the Appendix (like our texts more generally) remains but a pale evocation of what was a supremely multivocal speech event. Because of the participatory, interactional nature of Saramaka tale-telling, the linearization on the printed page of simultaneous, overlapping speech and other sounds represents a more radical act of interpretation (and simplification) than it would for tale-telling in many societies.

A few additional remarks on the nature of our translations may be helpful at this point. Throughout, we have attempted to retain Saramaccan phrasing, sentence structure, and even word order whenever there was a graceful English equivalent that retained both tone and meaning; but translation always involves difficult compromises in balancing these two kinds of fidelity to the original, and like all translators, we have sometimes had to sacrifice one for the other. When the respective advantages of two alternative translations have posed particularly acute dilemmas, we have sometimes inserted the original Saramaccan into the text in square brackets and sometimes discussed the problem in a note.

One recurrent translation problem stemmed from the fact that in Saramaccan the identification of an actor or speaker depends more heavily on context than in English. There is, for example, a single Saramaccan pronoun (*a*) that serves variously for English "he," "she," and "it." The following passage, for example, was communicated without ambiguity in Saramaccan through repeated use of *a* to designate both speakers, but it becomes more intelligible in English once "the boy" and "the snake" are specified. (The underlined terms in this example are all translations of the Saramaccan pronoun *a*.)

The boy said, "No, I couldn't kill you by myself." /íya/

The snake said, "*Máti*, the way things are here—" ("yes" he replied) "Well, my heartbeat isn't here on shore where I am. /íya/

My heart—" (the boy replied) "My heart is located far under the water. /íya/

It's down with Awó Mmá, [laughing] with the goddess of the river. That's where it is. /íya/

Well, could you get it? /íya/

Could you make it to there?" /íya/

The boy said, "No way. You couldn't get there. [Correcting a slip of the tongue:] I couldn't get there." /íya/

"That's right," the snake said. "And if you did get there, / . . . / my heart—" ("yes?" said the boy) /íya/

"It's inside an iron chest. /íya/

So if you could find the iron chest, would you be able to break it open?" /íya/

"No," he said. "You wouldn't be able to break it. And," the snake continued, "even if you managed to break the iron chest—" ("yes" said the boy) "My heart is a white bird. /íya/

And if the white bird flew out, there'd be no way you could catch it." /íya/

"Yes," said the boy, "it's true, Máti, you can't be killed." He said, "I really love you enough to become your máti." /íya/

(The snake replied.) [brief interruption]

The boy said, "Well, Máti, you and I will be máti." /íya/

He said, "Yes, well, wait just a minute, Máti." (the snake replied) "Let me go urinate. I'll be right back." /íya/

Moreover, we have sometimes not found it possible to retain the artfully elliptical turns of Saramaka speech. We write "Then he took a machete of his named Môsòmò" when what the narrator actually said was the equivalent of "Then he took a piece of iron of his named Môsòmò." This is because Saramakas understand that félu ("piece of iron")—which can also refer to a shotgun or a hoe—in this particular context is an intentionally elliptical substitute for the more direct "machete." We also sometimes find it useful to add intratextual precisions:

KÓDJI:
Finally Kentú got up to the long man.

A WOMAN:
Who's the long man?

KÓDJI:
The one at the edge of the water here [anaconda].

A second recurrent translation choice involved the "initial particles" that introduce many Saramaccan utterances and convey aspects of logical and temporal sequence (which in English are usually transmitted by tense and aspect, conjunctions and connectives, and other syntactic features).[20] Because in our judgment a consistent word-for-word correspondence between, say, English "well" and Saramaccan *wè* or English "now" and Saramaccan *nôò* would have lent a stylistic heaviness to the English text that is not present in the spoken Saramaccan, and because the "work" of these Saramaccan particles is spread among various other linguistic features in English, we have chosen to take some liberties both in conveying the frequency of these particles and in giving them consistent English glosses. A fragment from our Appendix may illustrate; the Saramaccan particles in question appear here as underlined words:

ADUÊNGI:
<u>Nôò hên</u> de dê dí dií dáka, <u>nôò hên</u> dí tatá dêdè. /íya/
Then three days went by and the old man died. /íya/

OTHERS:
[laughter and exclamations]

ADUÊNGI:
<u>Nôò</u> dí tatá dêdè,
The old man died,

SAKUÍMA [interrupting]:
Ná dêdè-dêdè a bi dê, nô?
Hadn't he been as good as dead already?

ADUÊNGI [simultaneous with Sakuíma's question]:
té a kabá dêdè kêê. /íya/
dead as could be. /íya/

<u>Nôò hên</u> dí sèmbè bi táa a bi ó kèê— /íya/
And the person who said he would cry— /íya/

<u>Nôò</u> a tá kèê té i kó dê <u>nôò</u> i tá fan seéi, de án tá yéi andí i tá táki. / . . . /
Well, he was crying so much that when you came there and tried to talk, nobody could hear what you were saying. / . . . /

OTHERS:
[laughter]

ADUÊNGI:

Nôò dí sèmbè dí bi táki táa wè a ó béi ên ku pèê— /íya/
And the person who said she would help by singing and
dancing— /íya/

Nôò a tá pèê téé.
Well, she's playing and playing.

OVERLAPPING VOICES:
[indistinct comments]

ADUÊNGI:

A tá kandá té tutú fèèn tapá búú, a píi uwíi,
She keeps singing until her throat gives out completely, and then
she prepares an herbal mixture,

A WOMAN [interjecting helpfully]:
bebé,
drinks it,

ADUÊNGI [without missing a beat]:
a dê a kandá. /íya/
and is right back in there singing. /íya/

Although some of the many onomatopoeic expressions that Saramakas use to embellish their speech suggest plausible English parallels
(such as "swish" or "plop" or "bang"), others (the anaconda who slithers
zalalalala toward the river, the cayman who limps *katja katja* along the
path, and so forth) seem best left in their original form. Saramaccan
exclamations do not always lend themselves to direct translation. We
sometimes write, for example, "[exclamation of astonishment]" or
"[exclamation of concern]" to stand for Saramaccan *Ké!* (whose meaning depends on intonation and context). We translate the common exclamation *Má[sa] nêngè!* variously as "My goodness!" or "My god!"
or "Good god!" depending on speaker and context. The choice of
whether to translate *bakáa* as "whites," "whitefolks," or "outsiders"—
always a delicate one, given the variability of its use by Saramakas—
has depended in each case on context and our understanding of
intent.

We capitalize the names of characters when they are used as proper
names in particular stories:

Elephant [who had adopted the form of a human] turned completely back into an elephant. Just the way an elephant is. Eagle
turned into an eagle, Cayman turned into a cayman.

The trickster spider is referred to by Saramakas as both "Anasi" (the name by which he is known in many African and Afro-American tale traditions) and "Adjáansi" (the normal Saramaccan word for spider); we acknowledge this stylistic variable by retaining the name Anasi in our translations and rendering Adjáansi as "Spider," but readers should not read major significance into this distinction, since the two are used largely interchangeably by Saramakas.

Whenever we transcribe a Saramaccan word or phrase rather than translating it into English, we print it in italics; our own intratextual clarifications and post facto "stage directions" are always enclosed in square brackets.

Much of the time, conventional English punctuation permits us to convey the rhythm of speech. For example, the Saramaccan words translated in the following passage were delivered by Aduêngi in one breath:

> He said, "My Boat Saayé, greetings," and it answered, "Greet-ings, Boy, where are you going?" and he said, "I'm going to where the devils live to look for Drum," and it said, "Boy, You'll never get there."

But those for the following example of text were spoken by Kandámma with full-stop intonation and pauses at the end of each sentence:

> He's not someone who just fools around with people. He kept right on coming until he got there. The devil said, "The thing you were doing there is incredibly sweet to my ears."

In general, when no full stop is intended we string sentences together with commas.

As we have seen, Saramaka tale-telling is also segmented by what could be described as a "compact" between narrator and responder. In our texts, we distinguish three kinds of interactions between these speakers: (1) when the narrator offers a "cue" (by pausing and using rising [or at end of sentence, falling] intonation) *and* the responder, picking up on it, supplies an *íya* or other conventional response; (2) when the narrator offers such a cue but the responder does not pick up on it; and (3) when the responder interjects a conventional response *in the absence of* a cue from the narrator. In our texts, the first case—by far the most common—takes the form of "/[response]/" fol-lowed by extra vertical spacing. Here the compact between narrator and responder, which drives the rhythm of tale-telling, is fully realized:

The boy walked off, and he went along until he came to another place. /íya/

He saw a woman /íya/

cutting wood. /íya/

She said, "Boy, where are you going?" and he said, "I'm going to ask Great God what we've done to deserve being left without wives." /that's right/

The second case, in which the narrator—in our judgment[21]—provides a cue but the responder does not pick up on it, appears in our texts as an intralinear "/ . . . /", as in:

They couldn't stop talking about it. / . . . / Finally, an old man went to sleep, along with a dog that he had, /íya/

The third (least frequent) case, in which the responder in effect intrudes upon the narration, appears in our texts as "/[response]/" with no special spacing, as in:

He said, "No way! Your husband can't kill me, /íya/ 'cause I'm [ritually] quicker than your husband. If he tries to fool with me, I'll kill him."

(Such "intrusions" sometimes occur shortly after a "missed cue," as a kind of delayed reaction by the responder.)

The actual implementation of the narrator/responder compact often becomes more complex, owing partly to the intervention of other participants in the tale-telling session. A responder who becomes inattentive to the narrator's cues (creating overlong, unbroken narrative segments) is often given a friendly reprimand, either by the narrator or by someone else, after which the responses usually pick up again:

KASINDÓ:
The devil says, "Boy, it's not true, not true, not true." The devil walked on. / . . . / He started out after the girls. / . . . / Then the others ran till all twelve were running. The boy's back there dealing with the other devils. /íya/

And what happened is—The first devil came up, and asked the boy, he said, "Boy—" (he replied) He said, "Aren't you the kid who cooled down my Môsòmò?" / . . . / He said, "Not at all, Father. Not at all." Then he played some music for the devil to dance to. / . . . / He played and the devil danced till it was enough, and he said [in response to the boy's playing, which sounded different from before:] "You're not the one, not the one, not the one. Go along."

OTHERS:
[laughter]

KASINDÓ:
Meanwhile, the girls were running and running and they got to the river. / . . . /

A MAN [to the responder]:
Hey man, don't forget about replies for the tale!

KASINDÓ:
And when the girls got to the river, /íya/

they came to a long straight place, /íya/

like from here all the way to Paramaribo. /íya/

They saw the devils coming. /íya/

In the same spirit, a responder whose voice is considered too soft may be chided or even replaced. And such interactions can involve several parties. For one tale told by Kandámma, Akóbo began as her responder in a less than forceful voice (see p. 60). Antonísi soon reprimanded her, but without effect. Several minutes later he repeated his complaint, at which point Kasólu broke into Kandámma's narrative with a loud emphatic "*ÍYA*," thus taking over the role of responder from Akóbo. Soon Akóbo volunteered a tale nugget for which Kasólu rather than Kandámma (as would have been expected) provided the responses. And at the conclusion of Akóbo's tale nugget it was Kasólu rather than Akóbo (as would have been expected) who signaled Kandámma, "Go ahead with your story." In this sequence Kasólu in effect took on responsibility for propelling ahead the tale-telling (which had been lagging in its interactional dynamic). Similarly, responders sometimes emit a loud "*ÍYA!*" to break an audible lull, in a sense giving a pulse that gets the rhythm of the session back in step (see, for example, p. 165).

Because a person takes on the role of responder for an entire tale (or tale nugget), we adopt the convention of identifying the responder only when there is a change. That is, the person who offers the first "/[response]/" of a tale is understood to continue in that role until a new responder is indicated.

Aside from *íya*, which we leave in Saramaccan, conventional Saramaccan responses are glossed here by a consistent, somewhat arbitrary set of English equivalents (often with ! for emphasis):

exactly	= *gbóló*
indeed	= *nôòmo*
no/certainly not/no way	= *nônô*
not at all	= *kwétikwéti/náseéi*
OK	= *aán sondí*
really	= *aái-o*
right	= *sôò*
that's how it is/was	= *a dê sô/sô a dê/naandê a dê*
that's right	= *léti sô*
that's the way it is	= *a tán sô*
that's true	= *tuú-tuú*
true	= *sôtu*
well	= *wèè*
yes	= *aái*

We also use the exclamations "hm!" and "ahh," the affirmative grunts "mm-hm" and "uh-huh," and the negative grunt "uh-uh" to correspond to equivalent Saramaccan expressions when they occur as responses. Note also that the response we transcribe as *íya* is occasionally—rarely—pronounced instead as *iyá* or *yá*.

When a Saramaka narrator reports direct discourse, the interactional nature of the conversation being reported is rigorously respected by means of what we might call "direct discourse responses." Because most of these perfunctory responses are delivered parenthetically (sotto voce, rapidly), we place them in parentheses and delete normal sentence capitalization and punctuation to indicate their nature as "asides":

> The daughters said, "Well, Mother—" (she answered) One of them said, "When that happens—" [extraneous noise]

> ("yes" she said) "Well, when people come to your funeral—" /*íya*/

> ("yes" she said) "As people arrive here—" /*íya*/

> (she replied) "I'll spread out a feast, cook things for them really well." ("yes" she said) /*íya*/

There are also cases, however, in which such direct discourse responses are spoken as full sentences, delivered at normal volume and pace, as part and parcel of the narration:

"What are you telling me?!!" she said. "Yes," he said. /íya/

"Quick! Quick! Quick! That's what he said!" She said, "No way!" The king turned and shouted back to her, "Quick! Give it to him quick! Give it to him quick! /íya/

Give it to him right away!" /íya/

She said, "OK, I hear you."

When a narrator shifts from Saramaccan to another language (most commonly Sranan, in direct discourse), we indicate the change in square brackets. The boundary between "Saramaccan" and "other languages" varies subtly from one speaker to another and even over the course of a particular speaker's life. When Kasólu, who had been raised in a village considerably downstream from Dángogó and had recently returned from several years of wage labor on the coast, began sentences with a rhetorical *Wel!* with the pronunciation that a Paramaribo resident would use for this Dutch word (rather than the Upper River Saramaka equivalent, *Wè!*), it constituted part of his habitual speech, at least in the months following his return, and in our texts we treat it as normal Saramaccan. But when Aduêngi, who normally spoke a relatively "pure" Upper River brand of Saramaccan, used words such as *fakánsi* (from the Dutch word, *vacantie* ["vacation"]) or *nafidjé* (from the French Guiana creole word for "navigate"), he was explicitly stepping outside his everyday speech patterns, playing with words and foreign concepts for effect. In our commentary we make note of "foreign expressions" only when they differ from the speaker's habitual mode of discourse as we knew it at the time.[22] In addition to pauses indicating full-stop sentence endings and those that serve as cues for the responder, there are others (usually longer) that in our judgment reflect dramatic intent (or sometimes merely "thinking time" for the narrator). We indicate such pauses in square brackets:

He turned and looked. He said, "Hey, Jaguar, look at me over here!" /íya/

He turned and looked [pause]: "*Aditô!*" /íya/

—as a doornail! /íya/

We use dashes to indicate the interruption of an utterance, either by narrators (who often cut off a sentence in midstream and begin a new one) or by their listeners (who may ask a question or offer a comment that cuts the continuity of the narration). When a portion of speech is particularly loud or emphatic, we print it in FULL CAPITALS.

The songs that punctuate some tales and most tale nuggets posed our most complex translating dilemmas. Composed mainly of expressions in a variety of esoteric languages, but often including some words or phrases in normal Saramaccan and sometimes a good dose of Sranan as well (for example, many of those sung by devils or by Anasi), they are understood to varying degrees by the participants in the wake, depending on their experience, especially in ritual matters. When Saramakas went over the recordings with us (in Suriname, in the Netherlands, and in French Guiana), they frequently could offer nothing more than educated guesses for the interpretation of songs—suggestions based on similar-sounding expressions or on the context of the tale. Even the identification of the language being spoken was shaky in many cases, though in others there was clear recognition of Komantí (warrior gods' language), Apúku (forest spirits' language), and so on. We have dealt with this situation by offering transcriptions of all songs, followed by a combined translation/commentary in which we lay out as much meaning as our Saramaka discussants were able to provide, indicating any uncertainties or differences of opinion that entered into their analysis. Song texts are indented farther than spoken portions, and those words or phrases that are sung by more than one person (either a chorused response to the soloist or voices joining in the singing) are underlined.

The musical transcriptions that precede many of the song texts were made by Kenneth Bilby. They are intended as indications for performance and not as technical documents. We hope these musical transcriptions will give English-language storytellers and other performers a sufficient idea of the songs and chants/shouts to permit a performance that captures something of the spirit of the Saramaka originals. One might think of these transcriptions as being "bracketed" within the more general flow of our two evenings of tale-telling; it is the *printed* text of each song performance that shows the precise number of repeats, the exact moment the chorus first chimed in, and other details of the particular performance transcribed in our book.

For songs transcribed in free rhythm, the durational value of notes is approximate. Some of the songs notated here in free rhythm may well have been performed (on other nights, which we did not happen to hear or record) with handclapping or other cues that would have permitted metrical notation. In all songs, pitch values have been transposed, that is, they are not absolute. There is considerable variation in Saramaka song performance—in embellishment, in pitch, and in rhythm. Indeed, in each of the many repeats that characterize the performance of most songs, there is notable variation. (For further information on Saramaka music, see Herskovits and Herskovits 1936; S. Price and R. Price 1980; and S. Price 1984; and for recorded examples of Saramaka song, R. Price and S. Price 1977.) Symbols employed in Bilby's transcriptions in this book include:

+   slightly higher than pitch as written
−   slightly lower than pitch as written
>   indefinite duration
(♩)   pitch uncertain
/   a glide (portamento)

Alternating solo and chorus sections of a song may overlap. An asterisk placed after the final note of a section indicates that the note's durational value has been shortened so as to allow transcription of both sections on a single staff.

FIRST EVENING

Sindóbóbi's Burial Wake

29 APRIL 1968, 10:00 P.M. We were already in our hammock when we heard Asabôsi's wails ring out, off in the part of Dángogó where her mother Sindóbóbi, paralyzed by a stroke several years earlier, had been in failing health.[23] Asabôsi's husband, Pomlá, who had been sleeping across the river in the neighborhood of his own matrilineage, shows up quickly and begins making the rounds of the houses, waking people and telling them that "the old woman isn't well." By the time we have put on some clothes and made our way to Sindóbóbi's house, eight neighbors have already gathered, and Pomlá has returned across the river to alert kinsmen and ritual specialists there. Inside the house Asabôsi is calling in a plaintive voice to her mother: "Woman, Sister-in-law, where have you gone? Don't you remember the garden we cleared and planted together in Mamá Creek? Talk to me, Sindóbóbi! Come back to me, Woman, talk to me." When she finally emerges from the house, it is in a frenzied dash for the bush at the edge of the village, and when the women drag her back into the clearing in front of the house, her body is lacerated by the thorns she had thrown herself into. As others assemble, including a number of village officials, she is held and soothed and tended to. Three men who have arrived from across the river—Basiá Takité, Basiá Apaasú, and Tioyé[24]—tie their waists with kerchiefs and carry Sindóbóbi feet-first from the house, in her hammock as she died, and place the hammock on three banana leaves in an open cooking shed that thus becomes the funeral house. They wrap the corpse tightly in the hammock, leaving only head and feet exposed, light a kerosene lamp at her head, and then go off to the river to wash the pollution of the corpse from their hands. Meanwhile Dosíli, whose first wife (dead in childbirth) had been Sindóbóbi's sister's daughter, runs home to get his shotgun, ties its trigger guard with a fiber charm, and next to the funeral house, fires three salutes to the west. Pomlá and Dosíli agree to set off at dawn to alert the village of the chief and its downstream neighbors, where people will have heard the shots and will surely fear that Naai, the chief's nonegenarian sister, has died. Sitting on low stools in front of the doorstep, those present are quick to find fault with the way particular people have responded: Basiá Kasindó (a village official and the illicit but acknowledged lover of Sindóbóbi's niece) should have come as soon as he heard the shots; Pánumáo (Sindóbóbi's twenty-seven-year-old son, a problem child who left for coastal Suriname seven years ago

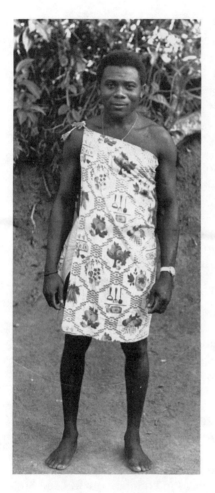 

Pomlá, Sindóbóbi's son-in-law, 1968 (left). Dosíli, another in-law, 1968 (right).

and has not yet returned) is surely not even going to cry when he hears the news. And where are all the women who should have showed up? Then come hunting stories, canoeing stories, discussion of recent divorces in the area, husbands who treat their wives badly, and the progress of particular rice gardens. An hour or two past midnight, people get tired and drift off to their hammocks, Asabôsi included.

Over the course of the next week, as people attended to the extensive repertoire of preparations for burial, we observed much that was familiar from other funerals as well as some things that were specially tailored to Sindóbóbi's personal reputation for involvement in malevolent ritual—she was widely considered to be a witch.[25] The most noticeable divergences, given Sindóbóbi's advanced age, were the relatively small attendance at each public event and the relatively brief time—eight days—the corpse was kept in the village before burial.[26] But in addition, the three sisters who lived near our house made plans to go off for several days to their gardens upstream, and Dosíli did not cancel a four-day trip to Paramaribo—neither of which would have been considered acceptable behavior for the death of a community member in good standing. On the other hand, the rhetoric of mourning was one we had heard many times before.

30 APRIL 1968. Pomlá's elderly grandmother Kandámma arrives early to address customary speeches on the doorstep of the funeral house. First to Asabôsi: "You must not kill yourself over this, Mamá. Alósa [Sindóbóbi's mother's father] died and Sindóbóbi lived on; Disên [Sindóbóbi's mother] died and Sindóbóbi lived on; now that Sindóbóbi has died, you must get on with life, forget your sorrow, do not kill yourself. You have Pomlá; he has no god in his head like Sindóbóbi, but he's there for you. Hold on to him and live. Even if everyone in the whole village died, it would be up to you to carry on, to tend to the ancestor shrine, to take care of the oracle. Stop crying for Sindóbóbi and start living for Agúba [another, ritually "heavier," name for Pomlá]." Then to Sindóbóbi: reminiscing about the days when they both had gardens along Mamá Creek, she admonishes her to release Asabôsi from her mourning, to allow her to cease her crying.

Meanwhile, Captain Faánsisónu lays protective leaves across the doorstep of Naai's house as well as Dángogó's various shrines. And then Faánsisónu, Basiá Apaasú, and Basiá Aduêngi walk down to the landing place to cut the bottom out of Sindóbóbi's old canoe—a piece some six feet by two feet, which will serve as proxy coffin at various points in the funeral rites. When they return, they lay the canoe bottom next to the corpse and go off to the ancestor shrine to alert the ancestors that there has been a death in the village and ask for their assistance in making the funeral a success. When the prayers are finished they are joined by Pomlá and four or five other men, who use their machetes to clean up the small area near the top of the river path where Dángogó's dead are washed, dig the trapezoidal hole in which the corpse will sit, and line its bottom with split banana trunks. Because no women volunteer for the job, the same group of men prepares a fire on banana-trunk "hearthstones" to heat the water for washing the corpse (though all will be reminded of the ideal of same-sex corpse washers the following week, when Apaasú falls sick and divination reveals his participation in the washing as cause). As Sindóbóbi's own black iron stewpot is placed on the fire (and as it is later removed), Basiá Takité and Basiá Apaasú perform a delicate ritual dance—part of funeral rites since the eighteenth century: each holds his side of the pot with one foot and the opposite hand, while his partner does the reverse. Then they switch and finally switch back once again (with the pot going on and off the fire three times at each end of the procedure). Takité and some other men go back to the funeral house to place Sindóbóbi's corpse, still wrapped in her hammock, on the canoe bottom, and then they return, two of them carrying their burden on banana leaf head pads, to commence the washing. A lively dispute breaks out about details of the ritual (Should they, for example, sing *papá* while they pour the water into the pot?), with different men arguing for one or another procedure. Washing the dead, like other parts of funeral rites, remains a privileged occasion for heated—and much appreciated—disputation about ritual details; "There are no burials without argument," approvingly runs the proverb.

Takité and Apaasú lift Sindóbóbi off the canoe bottom, seating her in the earthen hole, with Asópi—a former husband of Sindóbóbi's sister—holding her shoulders. Two young men hold a hammock sheet up as a screen to protect the privacy of the washing, but in fact all present watch and discuss the procedure. Apaasú fills two calabashes, one from a gourd of cold river water and the other from the boiling pot, and begins pouring cold water over Sindóbóbi's head as Faánsisónu prays, "Sindóbóbi, we give you cold water." They wash her thoroughly in both waters, using rags torn from a new white cloth, and then Takité takes a razor and shaves off a bit from her hairline, rubbing the shavings onto a cloth that will soon be attached to the canoe bottom, allowing Sindóbóbi's spirit to be consulted in divination. The wooden door of Sindóbóbi's house, which has been brought for the purpose, is laid over the washing hole, and her body is seated naked upon it for the dressing of the corpse. Apaasú and Takité begin with a new home-woven cotton waist string and a scanty breechcloth, but they dress her as well in seven or eight layers of skirts and capes, a similar number of beaded necklaces, and silver earrings, and take care to remove the protective charm she wore around her wrist. When a sudden rainstorm breaks, the corpse is summarily loaded onto the canoe bottom and carried back to the funeral house, where several men have constructed a crude wooden bed on which it is now laid out, with the canoe bottom returned empty to the washing area. Making the standard Saramaka association between a recent death and rain, people blame Sindóbóbi for the downpour.

During the storm a group of visitors—the sons of Kabuési (Sindóbóbi's mother's sister's daughter) and a couple of their lineage brothers—from the village of Gaánsééi have come ashore, bearing planks, saws, planes, and baskets filled with new cloths. Inside the funeral house a thick rectangle made from two hammocks and eight or ten hammock sheets, contributed by kinsfolk and neighbors, is now assembled and the corpse rolled tightly in it, mummy style, with feet and head exposed. Sindóbóbi's head is tied vertically and horizontally with two pieces of white cloth. Apaasú then prepares the *avò*—a ritually powerful cloth that he brushes down Sindóbóbi's body, head to feet, and whisks toward the west, the land of the dead. For the rest of the funeral rites, the *avò* will be left lying on the coffin at night and during periods of little activity (to keep the spirit quiet) and will be removed whenever Sindóbóbi is being consulted or prayed to and while the gravediggers are at work. All those who have touched the corpse or the utensils used in the rites thus far step forward as Apaasú pours rum over their hands, then passes around what is left in the bottle to drink. It is midafternoon, and the group disperses.

Naai (seated) with two grandchildren and two great-grandchildren, 1968.

At dusk eight men assemble in front of the funeral house and, facing west, fire some forty black-powder salutes into the air. That evening, though there should have been a "play," there is only a few minutes of halfhearted drumming with people sitting around chatting on stools before they return home to sleep.

1 MAY 1968. By midmorning about thirty men have gathered a few yards from the corpse-washing place at the edge of the village to begin constructing Sindóbóbi's coffin. Already leaning against a mango tree are ten rough-hewn planks, each a dozen feet long, that have been contributed by visitors and kinsmen; two were sent to Dángogó by the tribal chief himself. Asópi takes charge of the coffin's "large side," Basiá Aduêngi of the rest. Tasks are quickly divided: some men sharpen tools on whetstones, others begin sawing, others planing, still others go ashore to measure the corpse with a special reed (and after transferring the measurement to a long stick, quickly chop the reed to pieces and toss it into the bush). A small table is set up near what will be the head of the coffin, and a glass and a bottle of rum are placed on a tablecloth. Dosíli arrives with a tape recorder and begins playing popular *sêkêti* songs, recorded at an all-night play a few weeks before. (Had this been a funeral for a more honored elder, men would instead have sung some *papá,* the special music of death, accompanied by a hoe blade/knife blade gong, as the coffin making got under way.) After the end pieces of the coffin are set on the sides and bottom, Apaasú prays as a libation of rum is poured at the coffin's head. "Sindóbóbi, we give you rum. Not one of us wanted you to die! But now that you have gone, all of us want to bury you with celebration." And using a teakettle, the men pour a libation of Dutch cocoa onto some bits of cassava cake on the ground at the coffin's head. Then all present are served dry bread (imported from the city) and cocoa in fancy china cups.

Slowly, over many hours, the coffin takes shape, with its steep gables, complex angles, and decorative touches. Every step of its construction is surrounded with prescriptions and prohibitions. There is considerable banter while the men work, including discussion of a coffin so heavily loaded that it exploded when the corpse decomposed and swelled. By late afternoon the men have finished their task and set to cleaning up the area. Then the empty coffin is lifted onto the heads of Asópi and Aduêngi, and with Apaasú serving as interrogator, Sindóbóbi's spirit is asked what killed her. After some inconclusive answers, the bearers carry the coffin ashore to the funeral house, where

Sindóbóbi is informed that the coffin has been finished, and it is sprinkled with a mixture of kaolin and water, leaving white splotches all
over it. Inside the funeral house the bottom of the coffin is lined with a
number of new hammock sheets and hammocks, and the body is placed
on them. Then some thirty-odd skirt-length cloths are placed on top.
An extra pair of earrings is laid next to the ears and two pairs of
crocheted calfbands are put on top of the calves. Powder is sprinkled
liberally over the whole, the head is covered with a cloth, and Asabôsi
is summoned. As all present avert their eyes, she takes Sindóbóbi's
most intimate garment—her beaded "wrestling belt" (worn during
lovemaking)—and lays it on her waist, covering it with a cloth. Asópi
and Aduêngi carry the coffin back outdoors, and as a number of men
knock pieces of wood against the coffin to participate symbolically, the
top of the coffin is finally nailed shut. Then the coffin is "dressed" with
fabric—a large cloth is nailed on top, kerchiefs are attached to the
large end, and cloth straps are tied all around. Quickly the coffin is
raised, touched to the ground three times, and walked all around the
village, though special care is taken to avoid areas where anyone is
home sick. As it is placed back in the funeral house, Apaasú prays,
begging Sindóbóbi to leave her children and other kinsfolk unharmed
and not take them with her in death.

At dusk about fifteen salutes are fired—there would have been
more except there was a shortage of black powder. Asabôsi and Kabuési
lend their loud wails to the noise of the gunshots. We already smell the
sweetish odor coming from the coffin. The funeral house is filled with
baskets of cloth and sheaves of rice, contributed by various kinswomen
and neighbors of the deceased. That evening there is an enthusiastic play, with about fifty people. The young men from Gaánsééi—
Antonísi, Kasólu, and Sinêli—start things off with *sêkêti* singing accompanied by drums. Soon a line of Dángogó women are singing
their own *sêkêti* songs nearby, accompanied by handclapping. As more
people arrive the two groups join forces, and soon various men—
Basiá Takité, Basiá Aduêngi, Basiá Akudjunó, and the Gaánsééi con-
tingent—are taking turns singing solos and simultaneously jumping
into the center of the crowd to dance *tjêke*, head and torso immobile as
arms, legs, and feet move in flashes of brilliance. Asabôsi often *tjêke*s
along with the men, and other women hoot appreciatively and run up
to the male dancers to wipe the sweat from their faces with a cloth.
Kasólu starts one solo quietly, standing in place; then, as drums join in
and women begin clapping rhythmically, he very deliberately arranges
his cape and breechcloth and—still singing—begins to *tjêke*. As he

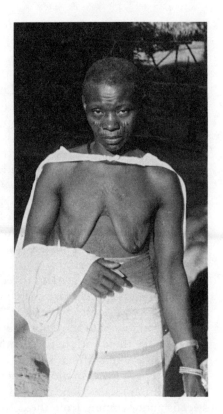

Kabuési, Sindóbóbi's mother's sister's daughter, 1968.

Facing page: Men dancing tjêke. *Top: Kasólu and Antonísi at Sindóbóbi's funeral, 1968. Bottom: Three men in the village of Gódo, about 1982.*

dances, he pulls from under his cape an oriental fan and slowly opens it wide; the women go wild. Aduêngi calls out supportively, "Not every Chinese store in the city sells those!" Women run up to embrace and congratulate Kasólu. The dancing continues. Before midnight people disperse, exhausted but exhilarated.

2 MAY 1968. Early in the morning a group of men gathers before the funeral house to discuss the progress of the rites. Apaasú makes a formal speech about how a death entails three major responsibilities: washing the corpse, making the coffin, and digging the grave. He has personally supervised the first two; now let the young men take over with the third. But of course he stands ready, once it's time to conduct the burial, to preside at the graveside as well. Apaasú then suggests they raise the canoe bottom in divination, and Asópi picks up the front and Aduêngi the rear as he speaks to Sindóbóbi, staring directly at the raised piece of wood with its cloth-and-hair attachment. After pleading that Sindóbóbi leave Asabôsi unharmed, Apaasú interrogates her,

inconclusively, about the cause of death. (Sindóbóbi's spirit moves the
canoe bottom, or the coffin, forward to indicate yes, slightly backward
to indicate no.) Then he asks Sindóbóbi whether the gravediggers can
safely begin their task today and whether there is anyone present who,

Asabôsi, Sindóbóbi's daughter, dancing tjêke, *1968.*

for one or another reason, should not go to the ritually dangerous cemetery. With Sindóbóbi's approval, the next stage of the funeral can commence.

Within an hour or two a dozen young men from Dángogó and neighboring villages have tied their heads with red kerchiefs, twisted to a point in front, fixed fiber charms around their waists, and begun gathering near the funeral house. These gravediggers (*baákuma*) will rule the village with an iron hand for the rest of the funeral rites. Soon the gravediggers set out to begin their dangerous job, carrying Sindóbóbi's paddle, a live black hen, and three cassava cakes, plus other food and cooking utensils and their gravedigging tools. As they stride through the village toward the landing place for the canoe trip to the cemetery, they blow wildly on a bugle (in the old days it would have been a wooden horn) and make much noise. Any canoe that has the misfortune to cross the gravediggers' path on the river must pay a fine—whatever the boisterous gravediggers wish to exact (a small bottle of rum, a chicken, the person's hat).

When they arrive at the cemetery, less than an hour away by paddle, the oldest among them pours a libation to announce to the ancestors why they have come and whom they are going to bury. After clearing a gravesite in the virgin forest they mark off the grave space, using a length of reed with which they have measured the coffin, and which they quickly destroy after use. Kabuési's thirteen-year-old son Lodí, participating for his first time as a gravedigger, kills the hen and prepares it, using the same calabashes and stewpot with which the corpse had been washed. They will all eat it with heavy doses of hot pepper—a strict taboo for the dead and therefore a reassuring protection that they are eating alone. The digging is strenuous, and teams of young men move in and out of the growing hole every few minutes, rubbing their bodies with earth to prevent sweating into the grave. In late afternoon, with their preliminary task complete, the gravediggers head toward the landing place without turning back, board their canoe, and paddle upstream to the village, many sporting a chicken feather in their hair to show what they feasted on. They signal their arrival at the Dángogó landing place by prolonged hooting.

At the funeral house the gravediggers raise the canoe bottom for divination, with Aduêngi carrying the front and Lodí the rear. Men address Sindóbóbi informally, asking if the site they have picked for her grave pleases her (yes) and telling her that all went well at the cemetery. They also ask her what is making Apaasú (who has come down with a fever) sick. Sindóbóbi's snake god? Her forest spirit? (Yes,

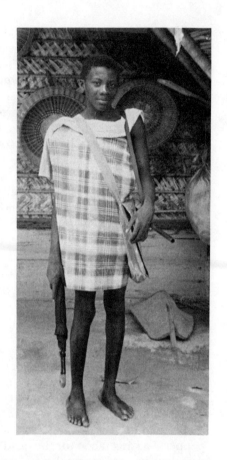

*Lodí, Kabuési's son, at the time of his
first gravedigging, 1968.*

the latter.) So word is sent across the river, where Apaasú lives, to tell
them to pray at the forest-spirit shrine there. The canoe bottom is
set down, and Aduêngi approaches the coffin, speaking directly to
Sindóbóbi and offering a libation of rum: "Sindóbóbi, we give you
rum. Don't be angry with us. Stop making people sick. Pray to the
kúnu [avenging spirit] on our behalf instead.[27] Help those of us who
are left to live." Later that evening the gravediggers light a fire in front
of the funeral house, which will be kept going for days. The visitors
from Gaánsééi play drums and sing *sêkêti*, local women clap their
hands and sing, and a dozen or so men sit around playing checkers.
Some of the gravediggers tie their hammocks in the funeral house,
above Sindóbóbi's coffin.

3 MAY 1968. Early in the morning the gravediggers stroll around the
village in small groups, blowing their bugle and pulling coconuts and

other fruit off people's trees. They raise the canoe bottom to report that they are going to the cemetery again and ask Sindóbóbi to see that they return safe and sound. They ask whether the rash of sickness in the village will pass soon and beg her to help the sick recover. The gravediggers cook and eat a meal, using food commandeered from villagers, before setting out for their canoe, hooting loudly and beating a drum. They again carry a live hen, but this time it is joined by a cock for their midday meal in the cemetery. In late afternoon they return to Dángogó, still hooting and blowing their bugle. After joking about the weight of the coffin, they instead raise the canoe bottom again for a brief report and interrogation. Aduêngi offers a rum libation at the head of the coffin. And in the evening there is a small play that never really gets off the ground. Several local youths challenge gravediggers from Gaánsééi at wrestling and are badly beaten, to the delight of most of the onlookers. Kabuési (whose sons are the victors) notes that Dángogó boys learn to wrestle on the sand by the river, but at Gaánsééi (which has no sandy landing place) boys learn to wrestle on the hard ground.

4 MAY 1968. Gravediggers "terrorize" the village with their licentious and outlandish behavior, to which everyone must submit without complaint. Some strap long wooden penises around their waists and go in search of teenage girls to startle; others appropriate fruit and cooked foods from people's houses without so much as asking; and still others catch villagers' chickens and bring them to the funeral house for later consumption. It is the final day of gravedigging, and before leaving the cemetery the men must "sweep their bodies," with their leader dusting them twice down and once up with handfuls of fowl feathers as they face east at the edge of the grave. "The evil must go to the ground, the good to the heavens." On their return to the village, the gravediggers discuss which two are strong enough to raise the coffin in divination. The large structure is quite a sight, propelling its bearers, Kokodó and Aduêngi, around the village. But Sindóbóbi refuses to "talk," and the coffin is lowered back into its place in the funeral house. They try again with the canoe bottom, and this time Sindóbóbi responds. Tioyé reports that they went to the cemetery and returned with no special problems; they finished their work, sang some *papá*, and ate a meal. Then he asks Sindóbóbi playfully if she's ready to go [to be buried], and she says yes. "Right now?" "Yes." "Let's go then!" he teases her. But Aduêngi interrupts the conversation and says, "We're not really ready yet. Let's wait till the proper day." Does Sindóbóbi have anything to tell them? She indicates that she does but that

she wants to do it in private, and she points to three men, who take the canoe bottom off to the side of the village, where she discusses how Asabôsi should "leave the evil things" they did together (witchcraft) and then she'll live. The carriers put the canoe bottom back in the funeral house. Asabôsi wails loudly throughout; Kabuési tells her to stop, but then she too breaks down and joins in. Comforting the mourners, other women comment that when the coffin is there it helps some, but that once it's taken away for burial, there's nothing but emptiness. The women discuss why the coffin and canoe bottom haven't been more communicative. Perhaps, they speculate, it's because Sindóbóbi had had a stroke. How could she be expected to talk to them now? Asipéi suggests there's a better reason: because she "lived so badly" (was a witch), Gaán Táta (a village god who protects against witchcraft) is keeping her mute as punishment. In the evening there are further gravedigger shenanigans and some desultory men's *sêkêti* singing.

5 May 1968. In the morning all who have had anything to do with the funeral to date "have their bellies tied"—a protection against the deceased's taking others with her. One of the men takes a new cloth from the baskets laden with gift cloths contributed by visitors and kin and wraps it around the person's belly, saying (to the person's *akáa* ["soul"]), "You see? I'm tying your belly. You must live!" In front of the funeral house, village women gather to pound rice in large mortars, hooting in unison when they feel enthusiastic; it is the whole community's responsibility to keep the gravediggers supplied with food.

In late morning the gravediggers raise the canoe bottom so that Sindóbóbi can distribute her material and spiritual belongings. She first indicates that Asabôsi should be left in the care of Captain Faánsisónu—he should see to her special needs now that her mother is no longer there. Asabôsi can continue to use their joint garden at Mamá Creek; Sindóbóbi does not see any evil lurking there. She leaves her "small things"—her pots and other utensils, her stools, her paddles, her clothes—to Asabôsi to distribute as she sees fit. She repeats that Kabuési had better leave off her "evil ways" or she'll find trouble. And she indicates that Aluntagô, another relative, will soon meet with troubles—but she won't tell what, or how to avoid them. When we walk by the funeral house, we notice that the large calabash that has been placed under the coffin is two-thirds full of body fluids, stained blue by the many layers of cloth they have passed through. In the afternoon there is a quarter of an hour interrogation of the canoe

Tioyé, Kasindó, and Aduêngi conducting a Dángogówide purificatory rite, 1968; in this photograph, Agumíí is being washed.

bottom, trying to persuade Sindóbóbi to talk about "people's problems"—sickness, social behavior, what the future may hold—but Sindóbóbi remains virtually unresponsive, even though Apaasú gives her a strongly worded dressing-down for not being more cooperative. In late afternoon a motor canoe filled with men arrives from Akísiamáu carrying a large dance drum, and Dángogó women rush down to the landing place, hooting in appreciation. Just after dark, gravediggers and other men gather before the funeral house and fire some seventy-five salutes, as Asabôsi and other women shriek out mourning wails. Later in the evening people gather for what should be an all-night play, with *papá* music between midnight and dawn, but heavy rains send the hundred or so participants scurrying for their hammocks after only an hour or two of singing, dancing, and drumming. And because of Sindóbóbi's "evil" reputation, it has been decided not to play *papá* formally at all.

6 MAY 1968. Burial day. In the late morning, four of the gravediggers visit the cemetery to see that that grave remains in good shape (that it has not caved in from rain and that there is no water in the grave itself). By early afternoon the gravediggers take the coffin out of the funeral house, touch it to the ground three times, and carry it around the village, stopping at each of the village ancestor shrines, before returning it to the house. Then it is taken out of the funeral house, put back in, and taken out—three times—and set down outside for the final rites of separation (*paatí*). As drums play, three men circle the coffin, sprinkling kaolin on the ground around it. Then two branches of *sangaáfu* plant, whitened with kaolin on one end, are held over the coffin and slashed in two with a machete. First a woman from Gaánsééi who has been washed in snake-god leaves holds one of the whitened ends and faces east, back to the coffin, as Faánsisónu says, "Sindóbóbi, we separate you from your snake god"; and as Apaasú slashes the branch in two, the woman hurries off with the whitened end. Then another woman does the same for Sindóbóbi's forest spirit. The canoe bottom, now filled with the detritus of death—sweepings from the funeral house floor, the two brimming calabashes of body drippings—is carried down the river path, preceding the head-borne coffin. Suddenly Asabôsi, who had been wailing on a stool in front of the funeral house, comes charging down the path, trying to grab at the coffin. Men pull her away, and Apaasú gives her a severe tongue-lashing, commanding her to remain with the living. Against her will, she is dragged ashore. The procession continues, but before reaching

the riverbank there is a final separation, from the village itself. Faán-siêti, a woman who happens to be standing close, is told to hold the whitened end of a *sangaáfu* branch, and once it is slashed she carries it quickly ashore. She cries as the final prayers of separation are spoken. When the coffin is loaded into a canoe, many women lament with wet eyes, "Mamá Creek is finished!" or "Sindóbóbi-éé!" A gun is fired in the air as parting salute, while about fifteen men in four canoes set out to accompany the coffin to the cemetery. The village is quiet and sad. People disperse, to gather again that evening in front of the now-empty funeral house and tell tales in honor of Sindóbóbi, who now lies in her final resting place.[28]

An hour or two after dark, when we arrived in front of the funeral house, there were already some forty people sitting around, men on folding chairs, women on low stools, with two kerosene pressure lamps illuminating the scene. The visitors from Gaánsééi—Kabuési's sons Antonísi, Sinêli, and Lodí, as well as their cousin Kasólu—sat near the center. Kabuési was near Asabôsi, with her four-year-old son on her lap; Kandámma, with a cloth spread over her knees for modesty, sat nearby, along with several younger people from across the river and a couple of small children. Sindóbóbi's neighbors—Konoi, Abátelí, Ayetimí, Akóbo and her sisters, and Asipéi (who made a practice of listening but never speaking at tale-telling sessions)—were there. Pomlá and Dosíli sat off to one side, and various village officials were also in attendance: Captain Faánsisónu and Basiá Kasindó from Sindóbóbi's part of Dángogó, and Basiás Takité, Aduêngi, and Apaasú from across the river. By the time we arrived riddling had already been completed, a couple of tales had been told, and people were chatting in a between-tales mode. We were struck by the general conviviality and lack of interpersonal tension of the sort that usually obtained between many of the participants. As we sat down, cradling our Uher tape recorder, Kabuési (who had adopted a playful joking relationship with RP) called out, "Husband, turn it on quick, [Kandá-]Mmá is beginning!"

The old woman—her considerable bulk settled on her finely carved round stool, walking stick lying next to her on the ground—begins her tale (pp. 60–74) about a path into the forest down which first a person and then a hunting dog disappeared, prompting the dog's owner to consult an *óbia*-man (ritual specialist). Kasólu interrupts her in midsentence to announce that he was there at that very moment and saw a man's wife going off to make love with a howler monkey (p. 62). When he finishes recounting what then happened and singing the song the husband used to entrap his simian rival, he tells Kandámma to go on with her story. She has just related the advice of the *óbia*-man—that a needle could kill the devil who had eaten the dog—and told how the man forged a horn in preparation for his encounter, when Akóbo breaks in (p. 66) to say that she was there and saw two children disobeying their mother by going off in search of Fire, and to sing the accompanying song—after which she tells Kandámma to pick up her tale again. Kandámma tells of the man's triumph over the devil using his magic horn and needle, ending by "explaining" her tale, almost macaronically, in relation to concepts of reincarnation.

Following several compliments on the tale's sweetness, and a few false start *Mató/Tòngôni* exchanges, Kasólu launches into a long tale about the marriage of Elephant, Eagle, and Cayman—disguised as handsome young suitors—to three human sisters and about their younger brother's quest to rescue them (pp. 74–110). The complex tale is broken into six times by tale nuggets: Antonísi's nugget centers on a song-dance mimicking Dog and Goat chasing after a beautiful woman (p. 76); Kandámma's first interruption centers on the familiar premise of Jaguar feigning death to entrap other animals (p. 78); Asabôsi contributes the song of the woman who never got tired of singing and dancing (p. 86); Kandámma's second tale nugget describes how a boy tricked the devil through song (p. 89); Asabôsi's next interruption tells how Anasi summoned the *tonê* god from the river (p. 97); and Akóbo's tale nugget recounts Anasi's efforts to keep his beloved's name in mind on his long journey to her village (p. 103). Kasólu's tale finally ends, after a cameo appearance by Anasi, with the boy slaying a twelve-headed monster and freeing the world from evil.

Kandámma then begins a tale about how a scrawny little kid sets out to confront a gluttonous devil who has been eating other small boys sent out to chase birds from gardens (pp. 111–22). Her telling is interrupted by Antonísi, with the story and song of how Hummingbird stole Jaguar's drum (p. 113), and by Kasólu, who sings the song of Shit dancing at an all-night play (p. 116). Kandámma concludes with a detailed account of how, by feeding the devil from magic plates until he drops, the kid makes it possible for all of us to have gardens without fear. As so often, her extensive knowledge of folktale esoterica lends special texture to the tale; she specifies, for example, which sounds were made by the devil's upper teeth and which by his lower teeth as he chomped on his fatal feast.

Antonísi, amid some hesitation and giggling, begins a tale he has heard on the coast about a horse named Bámbèl, but our tape reel gets tangled and we miss a few minutes (p. 123). When the machine picks up, Kandámma is in the middle of a lengthy and unusually pathos-filled tale nugget that explains why men present gifts to their wives (p. 123). Then we have more tape trouble while Antonísi continues, and it is only as he concludes that the tangles are straightened out.

The next tale, told by Kasólu, takes place on the plantation of a white king/wage-labor boss (pp. 126–38). It is interrupted twice with tale nuggets involving birds flying up to Great God, one by Antonísi in which two birds dance for the deity (p. 128), and another by Kandámma in which Hummingbird sets out to learn the name of a mysterious fruit (p. 132). Kasólu's tale, which holds deep moral significance regarding Saramakas' stance toward whitefolks' oppression, climaxes in a riotous scene in which a bold young boy manages to cuckold the white man who until then has never felt pain.

Kasólu, getting up a head of steam, interrupts the animated rehash of his just-completed tale by calling out *Mató!* once again, this time with a *kóntu* about the unlikely pair of Goat and Jaguar (pp. 138–53). Kandámma offers the only tale nugget, itself a complicated story about a boy who succeeds in bringing the *deindein* drum back from the land of the devils (p. 142). Kasólu's tale ends with defenseless Goat triumphing over powerful Jaguar by means of a magic charm given to him by Buzzard.

Kandámma continues the give-and-take with Kasólu by beginning another tale, with him as "responder," about a boy who sets off to ask Great God to solve problems—for him, his brothers, and various people he meets along the way (pp. 153–64). After repeated complaints that no one is relieving Kandámma's story with a tale nugget, Asabôsi finally breaks in with one about the man who rid the forest of a devil named Asinalóónpu (p. 162). Kandámma's story ends with an ungrateful brother being swallowed by a hungry anaconda.

As people begin to get restless and talk about going home to their hammocks, Kandámma protests that for her part she's ready to tell tales till the sun comes up, and Kasólu keeps the evening alive by starting one about the boy who goes off to the land of the devils to bring back the *apínti* (talking) drum for his mother's funeral (pp. 165–80). Interruptions are provided by Asabôsi, who sings the drum's song (p. 169), by Akóbo, who mimes Anasi singing about his courtship of a beautiful woman (p. 171), and by Kandámma, who tells and sings the story of Father Gídigídi Zaabwóngolo, the man who bore all the sicknesses of the world until Anasi inadvertently brought them back to where we all live (p. 174). The boy, after crossing three seas on the backs of three caymans, is almost eaten by a boisterous band of devils but manages in the end to escape, turn the devils into boulders in the river, and play the drum at the head of his mother's coffin.

As one man gets up to leave and others begin to follow, Kandámma and Kasólu reiterate their eagerness to continue—she says, "We could keep telling them for three whole days without ever repeating one," and he volunteers, "If people wanted to, I'd be happy to keep going till dawn." But the gathering breaks up and the evening of tale-telling is over.

Let's go back and listen to it.

KANDÁMMA: [29]

Well, there we were, and there was a village /AKÓBO: *íya*/

where there were more people than you can imagine. /*íya*/

The people who lived there went to sleep, and when they woke up in the morning, /*íya*/

one person was missing. /*íya*/

The person's house was empty. /*íya*/

They talked about it a lot: "Well, the person who used to sleep here isn't anywhere to be seen!" /*íya*/

They couldn't stop talking about it. / . . . / Finally, an old man went to sleep, along with a dog that he had, /*íya*/

and then morning came. Well, the thing is that the path—the mouth of the path was located right there. If you were to get up out of your hammock, you could walk right over to the path. /*íya*/

You could just go over and urinate *tjalala*, /*íya*/

till you were all finished, and go right back. But people didn't go past there. /*íya*/

So that morning the man woke up and let his dog out.

ANTONÍSI [to Akóbo, reprimanding]:
Hey, man, let's hear those replies!

KANDÁMMA:
It was his hunting dog. /*íya*/

So he let his dog out. The dog went off and didn't come back. He called and called the dog. /*íya*/

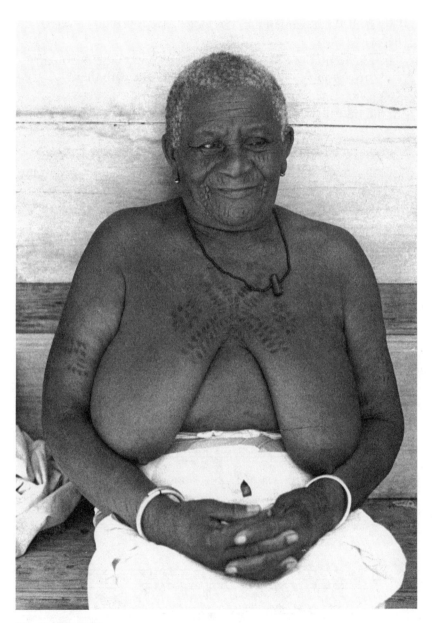

Kandámma, 1978.

"My god! What's gotten into that dog?!" He called till he was exhausted. /íya/

Then he went to the *óbia*-man. / . . . / He went to the *óbia*-man, and the *óbia*-man told him, "The mouth of the path there—"

KASÓLU:

At the time he was going to the *óbia*-man there— /KANDÁMMA: yes?/

At that time I was standing right there. /OK/

[starting to giggle:] It feels almost as if something doesn't want me to tell this story! [since he's laughing too hard to talk]

A MAN:

Go ahead and tell it.

KASÓLU:

At that time, a man took one of his wives off to work with him in the forest. But her idea was to make love to a howler monkey in the forest.

KANDÁMMA:

[an exclamation of shock]

KASÓLU:

She took the howler monkey, and eventually the man found out. / . . . / So he called the howler monkey by singing:

Hánse búka baabún, kiáyangòòò baabún, kiáyan[gòòò].
Gódo fútu baabún, kiáyangòòò baabún, kiáyangòòò.

Hánse búka baabún, <u>kiáyangòòò</u> baabún, <u>kiáyangòòò</u>.
Gódo fútu baabún, <u>kiáyangòòò</u> baabún, <u>kiáyangòòò</u>.

[This is the woman's love song to the howler monkey (*baa-bún*), praising his handsome mouth (*hánse búka*) and his gently curved legs (*gódo fútu*). (In the Saramaka ideal of physical beauty, being slightly bow-legged is considered attractive.) *Kiáyangòòò*, which is not a normal Saramaccan word, seems to be a term of praise. The cuckolded husband, spying on her, has overheard her calling her lover with this song, and now he sings it himself to entrap his simian rival. This song is full call-and-response between Kasólu and a chorus of others (represented by underlined text) and is accompanied by handclapping. Kasólu's "entrances" on the phrases *Gódo fútu* and *Hánse búka* are syncopated overlappings with the final *kiáyangòòò* of each line.[30]]

OTHERS:
[giggles]

KASÓLU [at a breathless pace, through the end of his story]:
Then the man jumped out and strode over and shot the howler monkey, *gwoo! húún! gwem!* He carried it back and threw it down, and said "Skin it, woman!" /*íya*/

She was speechless. She bent her head down limply. She wept torrents. He said, "Skin it!"

KANDÁMMA:
Was it her lover he had killed?

KASÓLU:
Her lover!! Go ahead with your story.

KANDÁMMA:
What a story!

OTHERS:
[laughter]

KASÓLU [recapitulating the story rapidly]:
The man took his wife off to work in the forest. When she saw the howler monkey there, she took him as a lover. And the man heard about it. Someone told him, and he hid and listened. He heard the song she sang to call the howler monkey to come to her. So the

man sang the song. And he shot it and it fell onto the ground, and he took it and brought it to her and said, "Skin it!"

AKÓBO:
Let her cook it 'cause that's meat they found to eat!

ASABÔSI:
It thought the woman was the one calling. That's why it came.

KASÓLU:
Continue your story.

OVERLAPPING VOICES:
[comments on Kasólu's tale nugget]

KANDÁMMA:
Well, he called the dog, just called and called. And when he went to the *óbia*-man, the *óbia*-man said, "That path there— /AKÓBO: yes/

People know not to walk on it. That path kills people."

ANTONÍSI [to Akóbo, talking over Kandámma's voice]:
You're just not answering the tale loud enough!

KANDÁMMA:
"There's a devil on that path," he said—

KASÓLU [loudly and emphatically]:
"*ÍYA!*" [signaling that he is taking over the role of responder from Akóbo]

KANDÁMMA:
—"and he eats people." /KASÓLU: that's right/

"OK, but what should I do /*íya*/

if I want to kill him?" He said, "You won't be able to kill him. The devil's got strong powers. /*íya*/

He's got protection against guns. / . . . / He's got protection against daggers. /*íya*/

He's got protection against swords. / . . . / There's nothing in the world that can kill him." /*íya*/

He asked, "Well, isn't there anything at all that can kill him?" He said, "Only Needle can kill him. /*íya*/

Needle is the only thing the devil doesn't have protection from." [long pause] ("I see") So the man went off and worked on a horn till he was completely finished. /*íya*/

Akóbo, 1968.

He had them forge a horn for him that was just right.

AKÓBO [breaking in]:
At the time they were making that horn, I was there.

KASÓLU:
Íya. What was happening there?[31]

AKÓBO:
There were some strong-earred children.[32] /KASÓLU: *íya*/

People would tell them not to do something, but they wouldn't listen. /*íya*/

Well, a woman was setting off to go somewhere and she left these children of hers in charge of keeping birds out of her rice field. /*íya*/

She warned them that they mustn't go take fire from places where they saw smoke. /*íya*/

When their matches were gone, they should just return to the village. /*íya*/

Well, there was a child who wanted to go get the fire.

KANDÁMMA:
[exclamations of indignation at the child's disobedience]

AKÓBO:
The other one told him not to go. He shouted, "Don't go!" but the first one said, "I WILL go!" /*íya*/

The two children went along till they got to a village. / . . . / They turned around, and there was a woman. /*íya*/

They called out to her. [pause] Oh, now I forget how it goes.

Ko ____ yéi, ____ Wee - duu. ____

We,m Ma-má We - duu, ___ mi ta lú-ku-ee ___ We - duu. ____

We,m Ma-má We-duu,— mi ta lú-ku-ee— We-duu.——

zi-na vi-ee——— ga-ní-a yo-loo, zi-na vi-oo.——

Ko yéi, Weeduu.
Ko yéi, /íya/ Weeduu.
We, m Mamá Weduu, mi ta lúku-ee Weeduu. /íya/
We, m Mamá Weduu, mi ta lúku-ee Weeduu.
Zina vi-ee ganía yoloo, zina vi-oo.

[This is the children's song of greeting to the old woman, Mamá Weeduu. It says, "Come listen, Weeduu. // Well, Mother Weeduu, I'm waiting. //" The final line, not in normal Saramaccan, was not intelligible to any of our Saramaka collaborators, nor were any of them familiar with the tale it alludes to. This song was sung in a very soft voice by Akóbo, without any chorusing.]

Go ahead with your story.

A WOMAN:
[appreciative laughter]

AKÓBO:
The woman was there sweeping the yard with her breasts.

KANDÁMMA [astonished]:
She was sweeping— with her breasts?!!

AKÓBO [laughing gently]:
Yes.

KASÓLU:
Íya. Go ahead with your story!

KANDÁMMA:
The person who'd been forging the horn had already finished. /íya/

He went up to the mouth of the path, and he blew the horn. He took the horn and put it to his mouth, and he blew:

Tandé nandé-ooo, teénza teénzaaa.
Tandé nandé-ooo, teénza teénzaaa.
Mamá táa nônô nônô, mbéi de tán, mbéi de tán.
Tatá táa nônô nônô, mbéi de tán, mbéi de tán.
Tatá Alekwéte-u-Makwébi-eee. I Tatá Asonugó-Sonukoóso-eee.
/íya/

Tandé nandé-ooo, teénza teénzaaa.
Tandé nandé-ooo, teénza teénzaaa.
Mamá táa nônô nônô, mbéi de tán, mbéi de tán.
Tatá táa nônô nônô, mbéi de tán, mbéi de tán.
Alekwéte-u-Makwébi-eee. I Tatá Asonugó-Sonukoóso-eee.

[In this song the horn is being played to call the devil, whose names are Tatá Alekwéte-u-Makwébi ("Father Alekwéte from Makwébi") and Tatá Asonugó-Sonukoóso ("Father Setting Sun–Rising Sun"). *Tandé nandé* was tentatively interpreted by several Saramakas as *Tidé da tidé* ("Today, it's today," meaning "Today we're going to meet"), but an alternative reading would be "Stay there, right there" (as in standard Saramaccan *Tán dê, naandê*), which would relate directly to the next lines. Lines 3–4 and 9–10, which are in standard Saramaccan, say that the "mothers" and the "fathers" all told the boy not to go after the devil but to leave the matter alone. The "chorus" here consists of a few voices, joining in very softly with Kandámma. This is not call-and-response.[33]]

OVERLAPPING VOICES:
[various remarks complimenting the song]

AKÓBO:
That's sweeter than anything could be.

KASÓLU:
It sure is sweet.

ANTONÍSI:
We weren't chorusing very well.

KANDÁMMA:
Well, the devil wasn't very far away.

KONOI:
He's killing everyone.

KANDÁMMA:
Right. He wasn't far away at all. As soon as the man[34] blew that horn—

ASABÔSI [anticipating]:
Djunkaán!

KANDÁMMA:
Djunkaán!

A WOMAN:
Ehh?! Danger!!

KANDÁMMA:
Who do you think was there? The devil. It was Father Alekwéte-u-Makwébi, /íya/

Father Asonugó-Asonukoóso.

KASÓLU [rehearsing the devil's name]:
—*kwéte*

KANDÁMMA:
He was the one the horn was calling. /*íya*/

The devil said, "Who? Who? Who? Who? Who?" The man said, "Me, Father!" The devil said, "OK, here I come!" The man said, "Well, come on then." / . . . /

KONOI:
Did he already have the thing? [Needle]

KANDÁMMA:
Yes. The devil's already on his way. /*íya*/

He's not someone who just fools around with people. He kept right on coming until he got there. The devil said, "The thing you were doing there is incredibly sweet to my ears. /*íya*/

Do it so I can hear it again."

OVERLAPPING VOICES:
[discussion of how the man is about to kill the devil]

KANDÁMMA:
He knew he was going to kill the man, so he asked him to play for him and then he'd kill him.

AKÓBO:
Yes!

KANDÁMMA:
Tandé nandé-ooo, teénza teénzaaa.
Tandé nandé-ooo, teénza teénzaaa.
Mamá táa nônô nônô, mbéi de tán, mbéi de tán.
Tatá táa nônô nônô, mbéi de tán, mbéi de tán.
Alekwéte-u-Makwébi-eee. I Tatá Asonugó-Sonukoóso-eee. /*íya*/

The devil walked up pretty close. The man said, "STAY BACK! You want me to play it for you, don't you?" ("yes" he said) "Then STAY BACK!" "OK," the devil said. "Blow it! Because there's nothing you can do today to keep me from killing you." /*íya*/

The man said, "You may be able to kill me, Father, but I know how to blow that horn for you."

AKÓBO:
The devil told him he would kill him? [She laughs.]

KANDÁMMA:

Yes. "There's no way I won't kill you." /íya/

The man said, "Well, Father, I know you're going to kill me, but first let me play the horn for you." /íya/

The man blew:

> *Tandé nandé-ooo, teénza teénzaa.*
> *Tandé nandé-ooo, teénza teénzaaa.*
> *Mamá táa nônô nônô, mbéi de tán, mbéi de tán.*
> *Tatá táa nônô nônô, mbéi de tán, mbéi de tán.*
> *Alekwéte-u-Makwébi-eee. I Tatá Asonugó-Sonukoóso-eee.* /íya/

The devil came rushing at the man. The man grabbed his spear. The spear disappeared.

OTHERS:

[exclamations of surprise]

KANDÁMMA:

He grabbed the dagger. The dagger melted.

OTHERS:

[more exclamations]

KANDÁMMA:

The man ran back. The devil came at him. The man took his gun. The gun vanished.

OTHERS:

[more exclamations]

KANDÁMMA:

The devil said [in a hushed voice, without pausing]: "I'm finished with you! I'm finished with you! I'm finished with you! I'm finished with you! /íya/

Blow your horn for me. Blow it for me, and I'll kill you. You'll see!"

OTHERS:

[laughter]

KANDÁMMA:

The man blew the horn some more and then he stopped. The devil jumped right at the man. The man remembered about the needle. /íya/

He took the needle, held it right up. The devil said [in an alarmed tone]: "Oh, Child— [pleading:] Please, please, please, please, please, please! /íya/

[in Sranan:] Don't kill! You mustn't kill! You mustn't kill!" / . . . / He said, "I shouldn't kill you?" "No!" said the devil. "Then spit up my dog for me!"

A WOMAN:
Ohhh!!

KANDÁMMA:
"Spit it up!" / . . . / The devil went *djukú!* [sound of spitting up], and he spit up a whole village, as big as Paramaribo. /*íya*/

It was the people he had eaten.

A WOMAN:
Right, the people who—

KANDÁMMA:
The man said, "Spit! Spit! Where's my dog? /*íya*/

That dog of mine. Avuun [the dog's name]. Where is it? Spit it up!" The devil went *djukú! djukú!* He spit up as many people as there are in Holland. /*íya*/

OTHERS:
[exclamations]

KANDÁMMA:
The man said, "Wake them up! Those people you spit up there, revive all of them!" /*íya*/

"I should revive them?" ("yes" he said) "WAKE THEM UP!" The devil went to gather leaves, came back and squeezed their juice onto all of those people and woke every single one of them up. /*íya*/

The man said, "Spit it up! Spit up the dog!" /*íya*/

[Kandámma makes a vomiting sound.] Ohh! he spit up a village as big as Guyába! [the second largest village in Saramaka] /*íya*/

So this kept going on and he kept spitting up more and more. The man said, "Well, how come I haven't seen my dog? It's that dog of mine I want! /*íya*/

If you don't spit it up—"

AKÓBO [talking over Kandámma]:
That's the one he'd lost.

KANDÁMMA:
"If you don't spit up the dog, I'll be sure to kill you with the

needle." The devil said, "Don't kill! My god, don't kill! I'll spit up the dog." /íya/

ASABÔSI:
He's that scared of the guy?

KANDÁMMA:
So he went on vomiting till he'd spit up a bunch of people. /íya/

He'd revive them all and set them out there. Then he'd spit up another bunch, revive them, and set them out. /íya/

He keeps setting them out and—

KONOI [breaking in and talking over the end of Kandámma's sentence]:
There must not be anyone left in his belly!

KANDÁMMA:
—spitting up more, over and over, until he's all finished. He was totally *dóvóó* [limp from exhaustion]. He went "*hôh! hôh!*" [vomiting noise] and spit out the dog onto the ground. /íya/

He said, "I've spit it up." ("yes" said the man) "Now make it strong! Wake it up!" /íya/

The devil went ahead and revived the dog. The man said, "My dog isn't looking spry enough. Get him so he's really standing up!" / . . . / The devil revived the dog some more. He squeezed leaves onto it. The dog stood up, and the man called the dog. The dog shook itself, *pákapákapákapáka*. /íya/

The man took the needle and stuck it *djá!* into the devil's fontanel.

AKÓBO:
He's done it!

OTHERS:
[laughter]

KANDÁMMA:
The devil cried out, "*Húúúú!*" and dashed off into the underbrush. The man cut off his head, *vélémm!!*

OVERLAPPING VOICES:
[exclamations and comments]

KANDÁMMA:
He really killed him. /íya/

So that's how it came to be that when you have someone who dies, he can come back again in a reincarnation.[35] The ones the devil spit up /that's right/

came back to life. When you're already dead, when he's already killed you, you come back in a reincarnation.

KONOI:
EHH!!

KASÓLU:
Your story was really sweet!

OTHERS:
[murmurs of assent]

ASABÔSI:
Well let's have some more!

KASÓLU:
Híliti! [36]

ANTONÍSI:
Mató, mató!

KANDÁMMA:
Mató!

KASÓLU:
[an embarrassed laugh]

ANTONÍSI:
Tòngôni!

KASÓLU:
Mató! [37]

ANTONÍSI:
Tòngôni!

KASÓLU:
So there they were. /ANTONÍSI: *íya*/

There was a woman who had three daughters. (This isn't a singing tale, y' hear? So you can cut into it with a song very nicely, and a little dance too!) A woman had three daughters /*íya*/

and those girls were more beautiful than you can imagine. / . . . /

ASABÔSI [to a child who's crying]:
My goodness, don't hang onto me like that!

Kasólu, 1987.   Abátelí, 1978.

KASÓLU:

So many men asked them to marry them that there weren't any men left in the whole world who hadn't.

ABÁTELÍ:

Except that I myself didn't ever get there. If I had been around, they certainly would have wanted me.

KANDÁMMA:

You're right. They would have.

KASÓLU:

Well, all the young men had already asked, but Elephant was still left. /íya/

Elephant set out vúúún— /íya/

He and Cayman, [long pause] as well as Eagle. /íya/

The three men set out along a path /íya/

and they went to propose marriage. They kept asking people for directions. /íya/

And finally they got there. /íya/

They turned themselves into sharp-looking young guys, really handsome. So they got there. That's all. / . . . / Once they got there, they went to propose marriage. Elephant asked for the oldest one. /íya/

Eagle asked for the middle one. /íya/

Cayman asked for the youngest one. /íya/

Well, once they all got there, nothing to it. Those women, well it was like something came over them. They all started pointing out which one they wanted.

ANTONÍSI [breaking in]:
At that time, I was standing there.

KASÓLU:
What was happening?

ANTONÍSI:
OK! Well, what's his name— [clears throat ostentatiously] Goat.
/KASÓLU: ÍYA!/

ANTONÍSI:
Goat and what's his name—Village Animal [Dog]— /right!/

They were going to run after a woman.

KASÓLU [chuckling]:
How were they going to run after her?

ANTONÍSI:
You want to know how they ran?

KASÓLU:
Yeah, how did they run?

ANTONÍSI [doing a little dance mimicking the funny way that Dog was running]:

Mbèè,___ mbèè Se-lí-na. Na f'i é-de mi e dê-dè

Mbèè, mbèè Se-lí-na. Se-lí-na, mbèè...

Antonísi, 1987.

Mbèè, mbèè Selína. Na f'i éde mi e dêdè
Mbèè, mbèè Selína. Selína, mbèè . . .

[*Mbèè, mbèè* is the bleating sound of Goat. Selína is the woman's name. *Na f'i éde mi e dêdè* means "I would die for you." A couple of voices join in the *mbèè, mbèè Selína*, but the song never really gets to a clear alternation of solo and chorus before being cut short by giggles. In 1987 Antonísi explained to us that the song alludes to a story in which Dog made love to the woman that Goat had lined up for himself. And that's why people always say that wherever Dog is absent, that's where Goat will go hunting. That is, Goat tries to avoid Dog, because Dog interferes, takes things away from him, and generally causes him grief.]

ANTONÍSI AND OTHERS:
  [hysterical laughter]

ANTONÍSI [still laughing]:
  Let's just forget it, guys. I can't go on talking. No, I really can't go on. It's too much for me.

A MAN:
Go on with the other story.

ANTONÍSI:
Go on with your story!

KASÓLU:
Well, as for the women themselves, /ANTONÍSI: right/

The oldest one points out the one she wants. /íya/

She points at Elephant, saying, OK, this is the husband she wants. /íya/

The other one said the same thing to Eagle. /íya/

The youngest one said it to Cayman. /íya/

Those guys! Even before they arrived, the women started wanting them. /íya/

They asked for wives, /íya/

beautiful wives. /íya/

The girls' mother didn't like it. /íya/

But the daughters said they wouldn't listen. /íya/

They went ahead and took husbands. /íya/

There they were with their husbands. The next day dawned. They went on like this for many days. Well, the way it is in folktale-land is just like, well, let's admit it, the things that happen in Saramaka don't happen there, 'cause in Saramaka, families lend out wives, /íya/

but in Western countries they give wives. /íya/

In folktale-land they give you a wife. /íya/

But Saramakas— Bush Negroes lend them. /íya/

So what they did there was they actually gave those men wives. /íya/

They really gave them, for them to take away, and even to bury them after they died.[38] /íya/

That's just how it was. /íya/

KANDÁMMA:
Well, at that very moment— /KASÓLU: íya/

Well, Jaguar's mother had died. /that's right/

They washed the body and laid it out. They did everything properly. Then Jaguar went to Howler Monkey to ask him to help
perform *papá*.[39] /*íya*/

OTHERS:
[laughter]

KANDÁMMA:
So Howler Monkey came. Howler Monkey came for the *papá*
play. /hm!/

He was there at the *papá* play for a little while. And then Howler
Monkey sang a song. Jaguar's mother was dead. /*íya*/

She was there with a club and a machete. /*íya*/

The mother, that dead-as-a-doornail person— They took a club
and put it on one side of her. They took a machete and put it on
the other side. /*íya*/

And Howler Monkey was supposed to come help perform the
papá. /that's right/

So Howler Monkey came and he sang:

KONOI:
Was it at the funeral house that they went to play *papá*?

KANDÁMMA:
It was at the funeral house that they went to play *papá*.

OTHERS:
[laughter]

KANDÁMMA:

A-héééé, ee a-héééé! A-hóóó, ee a-hééé! Am-bê yéi ká

Ta - tá Do- mó dê - dè wan tuú tuú dê - dè – oo,

ma a dê ku ahi - ti - góó ku a-gwam-toó -ku – ooo.

Ahééé, ee ahééé! Ahóóó, ee ahééé!
Ambê yéi ká Tatá Domó dêdè wan tuú tuú dêdè-oo,
ma a dê ku ahitigóó ku agwamtoóku-ooo. /íya/

Ahééé, ee ahóóó! Ahééé, ee ahééé!
Ambê si ká Domó dêdè wan tuú tuú dêdè-ooo,
ma a dê ku ahitigóó ku agwamtoóku-ooo.

[Line 1 is exclamations. Lines 2–3 mean, "Who'd ever believe that if Father Jaguar died for real, he'd have a club
and a machete with him there?" Although these two lines
are largely in Saramaccan, the terms for club (*ahitigóó*) and
machete (*agwamtoóku*) are Komantí words that are used in
papá singing.[40]]

Go ahead with your story.

KASÓLU:
OK! Well, once they had been given wives, they said, "OK, women,
no problem. We'll leave in the morning.

ASABÔSI:
[exclamation]

KASÓLU:
We'll go off together." (they agreed) They got everything together
until they were all ready, and then they set out on the path. / . . . /
They left. They continued on for a while, and then they said,
"Women, stay here." ("all right" they said)

ASABÔSI [complaining]:
This tale isn't being answered well.

KASÓLU:
Well, one of them had borrowed one limb. Let's say you'd borrowed an arm from some person. /ANTONÍSI: *íya*/

Now you go back, pull off the arm, and give it back. Then you
return and put on your animal limb. /*íya*/

The next one went off and came back and put on his cayman's
limb. /*íya*/

The last one went off and came back and took his wing. /*íya*/

A WOMAN:
Uh-oh, things are already getting really bad!

KASÓLU:
So back and forth they went, taking off limbs and putting others on, and then one of them turns around to ask, "Wife, are you afraid?" /íya/

AKÓBO [apprehensively]:
Uh-oh!

KASÓLU:
She says to her husband, "No, Husband, how could I be afraid? I loved you so much I married you." / . . . / Well, how could she answer otherwise?

OVERLAPPING WOMEN'S VOICES:
[discussion of the dilemma of how to act in such a situation]

KASÓLU:
Because if you said anything else, that'd be the end of your relatives. /íya/

KANDÁMMA:
That would really be the end!

KASÓLU:
Then they kept on going. /íya/

Elephant turned completely back into an elephant. /íya/

Just the way an elephant is. /íya/

Eagle turned into an eagle, /íya/

Cayman turned into a cayman. /íya/

KANDÁMMA:
With his bugging-out eyes!

KASÓLU:
Cayman starts limping along, *katja, katja.* /íya/

Eagle can't even walk. /íya/

He cried out, *hòòò!* His wings were really bothering him. /íya/

AKÓBO:
I bet he's going to fly.

KASÓLU:
As for Elephant, he's very uncomfortable too. /íya/

Finally he said, "Wife—" /íya/ ("yes" she said) "This business is bothering me, this walking. /íya/

It really is hindering us a little. If you could just jump onto my back, with your basket, and secure everything so it's not in your way, and then take hold of me, /íya/

we could head on out. We'd get to our village as quick as can be. Wouldn't even take half an hour." /íya/

He said, "Wife, that's all you have to do." / . . . / She climbed right on. /íya/

KONOI:
She's as good as dead already.

KASÓLU:
She got on and gave a kick, *gbem*, /íya/

gbem gidi, pííí, and off they went. / . . . / They went to their village. /íya/

AKÓBO:
Imagine a husband who carries you on his back!

OTHERS:
[laughter]

AKÓBO:
And with your basket on your head!

KASÓLU:
Eagle said, "Oh, Wife, the way we're walking along here, something's bothering me. /íya/

The way we're doing things, the way we're going along here— If you could just get under my wing, /íya/

along with your basket, and hold on to me, /íya/

it seems to me we could make it." /íya/

ASABÔSI:
Where's she going to put the basket?

KASÓLU:
"Mm," she said. "All right." She said, "I'm not afraid." /íya/

He flew off, /íya/

AKÓBO [speaking on top of Kasólu]:
How's she supposed to be afraid?! She's taken him as a husband!

KASÓLU:
and they left without a trace. /íya/

They went to their village. Cayman is walking along there and he says, "Wife, something's bothering me. /íya/

A WOMAN [speaking on top of Kasólu]:
Well, his teeth— They must be one of the things that are bothering him.

KASÓLU:
The way we're doing things, the way we're walking on the shore here, /íya/

it's difficult for me. /íya/

If you could take your basket and get on the back of my head, right on the point of my head here, holding on to your basket, we could make it. Hold on to me right here. /íya/

Quickly, quickly." He jumped into the water.

A WOMAN [speaking on top of Kasólu]:
The water's getting *tjen! tjen!* [filled with ripples]

KASÓLU:
She said, "No problem." Swoosh! In a moment, they're right there in their village. /íya/

They came out of the water. /íya/

AKÓBO:
Well, the woman there— Does she know underwater work?[41]

KASÓLU:
Mmm. They came out of the water. /íya/

Once they arrived there, they stayed there a VERY LONG TIME—for really quite a number of years! /íya/

Their mother and father never heard from them again. They said, "Uh-huh, we told them so. /íya/

We told them that those men there were not the sort of men they should marry. Here we are, and we don't hear a single word from them. They're finished." /íya/

They really didn't know what to do. All the [classificatory] mothers and fathers were back there. But the girls were off with their husbands. /íya/

So things went along like that, until one day a boy was born [back in their village]. /íya/

So there the boy was for a long time. Well! He eventually became familiar with ritual things, and after a while, an *óbia* talked to him and said, "The fact is that you have three sisters. /íya/

Your sisters are such and such, and they took husbands at such and such a time." /íya/

("I see" he said) Then after a while he came to ask his mother and father about it, and he said, "Mother—" (she replied) "When you gave birth to me, was I the only child you had in the world?" /íya/

They said, "Yes, son. You're the only child we have. We've never had any other children." /íya/

("I see" he said) Things went along for a long time. Then he asked them— He said, "Mother, the thing I asked you both about— You haven't really answered me. Am I the only child you've ever had?" /íya/

"Yes," she said. And then she said, "Son—" (he replied) She said, "You're not the only child we've had."[42] /íya/

We had three sisters before you were born. /íya/

But they took husbands in such and such a way. The fact is, they married trouble. /íya/

It's already been so many years since they left." He said, "Really?" ("yes" they said) He said, "I'm going to go find them." She said, "Well, all right." /íya/

He got everything ready, and when the time came he said he was going after them. His parents told him not to. And then the mother started crying. /íya/

She couldn't bear to hear such a thing. /íya/

He said, "I'm ready." He'd prepared [ritually] till he was as ready as he could be. /íya/

The boy— He said he would go. / . . . / He prepared [ritually] one of his hats. /íya/

He prepared a hunting sack. /íya/

And then he set out, *gwelei!* He said, "Let my 'hat'—"[43] He said for his hat to take care of him. /íya/

"Let my 'hat' take care of me." He set right out, and got to the path along Elephant's creek, /íya/ *tjálá!* He kept going on and on until he arrived. /íya/

Now when he got there, he saw the woman sweeping around her door, swish, swish, swish. He gave her a "Greetings, Aunt." She replied, "Greetings, Boy." /íya/

AKÓBO [surprised at the formal archaic greeting that has just been exchanged]:
Oh!! "Greetings, Boy"!!

KASÓLU:
He said, "How are you?" "Quite fine," she said. "Good," he said. "Say, Woman, please, I'd appreciate it if you'd give me a little water to drink." /íya/

She said, "Boy?" ("yes" he said) She said [and here Kasólu begins speaking in an exaggeratedly girlish voice:] "It's been so many years since I first came here." /íya/

("yes" he said) "Well, I never meet a soul anymore. Whatever brought you here? Look where you crossed the stream over there and came all the way here to ask me for a little water to drink. /íya/

Don't you know that my husband could show up here and kill you?" /íya/

"Woman," he said. (she replied) "Is that how mean you are? /íya/

IF YOUR BROTHER were the one who came here, would you be cruel to him like this?" They embraced each other over and over again. /íya/

They hugged and hugged. She said to him, "Boy, the way my husband is, /íya/

when he gets here, if he sees you, he'll certainly kill you." /íya/

He said, "No way! Your husband can't kill me, /íya/ 'cause I'm [ritually] quicker than your husband. If he tries to fool with me, I'll kill him."

OTHERS:
[exclamations of surprise]

KASÓLU:
He asked, "When your husband's coming, will you know it?" She said, "I'll know." /íya/

So that's all.

KANDÁMMA:
Was it his sister he met?

KASÓLU:
It was his sister, his oldest sister.

KANDÁMMA:
[an exclamation of sympathy]

AKÓBO:
The oldest sister is the one who married the big guy.

KASÓLU:
Yes. They were there for quite a while. /íya/

In the evening they cooked and ate. /íya/

Then, after a while, sure enough, there he comes, [gutteral rumbling sound]. The forest is breaking. /íya/

The ground is shaking. /íya/

She said, "Here he comes." The brother threw his hunting sack right down. He told her how to hide him. He hid himself in a certain place there, and you couldn't see him at all. /íya/

When the husband arrived, he saw that the wife looked all despondent. He called to her: "Woman, what's wrong?" "Nothing," she said. He tossed down— When he got there he tossed half of his hunting kill over there. He took the other half and tossed it down over here. /íya/

He said, "Woman, what's wrong?" "Nothing," she said. "It's nothing." "Mm?" he said. He came over and shook her shoulder gently. He said, "Woman, what's wrong? Ever since I came here, so many years ago, /íya/

I've never seen you like this. / . . . / The way you're acting today, there's got to be something wrong." "No," she said. /íya/

She said, "Husband, there is something that's bothering me." ("yes" he said) /íya/

"Since you and I arrived here— Since you arrived here— Well, I have a mother and a father, you know." /íya/

"Yes," he replied.

ASABÔSI [breaking in]:
At that time I was standing there.

KASÓLU:
Íya. And what did you—

ASABÔSI:
Well, there was a certain woman named Agangaai /KASÓLU: uh-huh/

who never got tired of singing and dancing. /that's right/

Even if the wind came up, really blowing up, she just kept on performing. /that's true/

Agangaai, i sá kíi m. M hmm.
Agangaai, i sá kíi m. M hmm.
Di hánse fa a du m te. M hmm.
A du m te mooi ta yáa sónu. M hmm.
Agangaai, i sá kíi m. M hmm.

["Agangaai, you could kill me, mm-hm // Your beauty really does something to me, mm-hm / It's enough to make the sun come up, mm-hm / Agangaai, you could kill me, mm-hm." Because Asabôsi has a noticeable speech defect, both we and the Saramakas who listened to the tape had great difficulty arriving at a transcription. The "chorus" is only two voices—Asabôsi and Akóbo.[44]]

A MAN:
No one's chorusing the song! [reprimanding:] The chorus is what makes a song really sweet.

A WOMAN:
It's not that no one's chorusing. It's that I'm the only one who's doing it.

ASABÔSI:
Continue your story. /íya/

ANTONÍSI:
Íya!

KASÓLU:

All right. Then she said [in a plaintive voice], "When you come back, /ANTONÍSI: íya/

you always toss half the meat over there and you bring the rest over here. /íya/

Well, I just feel as though it might be my own people. I don't know anything about the people you killed and set down there. /íya/

That's why I sat down [became dejected]." He said, "Mm. Wife, you can't play around with me like that!" /íya/

She said, "What if I feel as though, if a brother of mine, or some relative, came here, you would kill him?" He said [protesting indignantly in no-pause speech]: "If a relative of yours came here, you and I would sleep in separate hammocks,[45] if your brother came here, /íya/

the things I'm separating out over there, they're the ones that could kill me, the ones I kill and set over there are evil, /íya/

and the meat that I put over here— /íya/

If your brother came here," ("yes" she said) "you and I would sleep in separate hammocks." /íya/

Her brother jumped out: "Brother-in-law, greetings!" They hugged and hugged. The husband said, "Brother-in-law, jump on my back!" /íya/

Mm! He jumped on his back. He ran *bwelé, bwelé, bwelé*. He carried him around like— Well, it was almost like something in the city [they were riding all over]. /íya/

He took him all around to show him his various hunting places, one by one, and then brought him back home. /íya/

He said, "Brother-in-law, this is my home [you're always welcome]." ("yes" he replied) /íya/

The brother slept there with him three nights. /íya/

"Brother-in-law—" he said. (the other replied) He said, "I'm going to leave. /íya/

I'm going to visit my other sister, going to her village, going to see if I can find her and see how she's doing." /íya/

The husband said, "No problem, Brother-in-law." / . . . / He walked out to the path with him. /íya/

He pulled out one of the claws of his left hand,

OTHERS:
[exclamations of surprise]

KASÓLU:
and gave it to him. "Brother-in-law—" he said. (the other replied)

ABÓBO:
He pulled out his own claw for him!!

KASÓLU:
Yes. He said, "When you go off, /íya/

if you run into difficulties that you can't handle and your life is in real danger—" /íya/

"Yes," he said. "Go to the path /íya/

and gather some dry leaves. Strike your flint and light a fire [to heat the claw]. I'll come to you as if I were going to kill you. But you must be in serious need. If you're not," ("yes" he said) "then I will kill you, Brother-in-law. You mustn't call me for nothing. /íya/

I don't have anything else I can offer you." /íya/

Then he went away zéngee, téé djaláa. /íya/

KANDÁMMA:
Well, way back then, /KASÓLU: íya/

I was right there. /that's right/

And the devil was in the tree at the chief's doorway. /that's right/

He was killing people so much that they were all dying off. /that's how it was/

Well, the boy went to an óbia-man, who told him, "With the tree at the chief's doorway and people being finished off in the village— It must be that the devil is inside the tree." /well, that's right/

So he told the others in the village, "Today I'm going to do something here. Let everybody close the door to their houses. /íya/

No one should be outside." /íya/

They said, "Well, what about you?" He said, "No, I'm the one who's going to be doing all this. All the rest of you, close the doors to your houses."

A MAN [laughing]:
He was that ritually strong?!

KASÓLU:
   Íya.

KANDÁMMA:
   Then he went to the base of the tree. And he sang:

Asinailonpu-oo, Tatá Asinailonpu a tá tíngi-ee.
Asinailonpu-oo, Tatá Asinailonpu a tá tíngi-ee.
Un da mamá mi siná púu dadjá.
Un da tatá mi siná púu dadjá.
Tatá Gángama fu Alakwáti, Alakwáti tjóló tjóló tjóló tjóló tjóló
    tjóló tjóló tjóló. /íya/

[In this song the boy is taunting the devil, Father Asinailonpu, by saying that he stinks (lines 1–2) and by referring
to his mother and father (lines 3–4), inciting him to come
out and fight so he'll be able to kill him. And thanks to him,
there's no longer a devil that hides up in a tree next to the
door of the chief's house.[46]]

OTHERS:
   [gentle laughing]

KANDÁMMA:
> And once he had spoken, /íya/
>
> that devil just shook the tree *huyaa*. /íya/

OTHERS:
> [exclamations of apprehension]

KANDÁMMA:
> Here he comes!

A WOMAN:
> I'm trembling!

KANDÁMMA:
> It's that he had been in there killing people. /íya/
>
> But then the boy called him, "Tatá Asinailonpu a tá tíngi Gángama fu Alakwáti." That's the same as "Alakwáti tjóló tjóló." /íya/
>
> Go right ahead.

OTHERS:
> [murmurs of appreciation]

KASÓLU:
> Then he arrived at the path by Eagle's creek. /ANTONÍSI: *íya*/
>
> He walked along until he got to the young woman who was sweeping around her doorstep, swish, swish. /íya/

AKÓBO:
> He's got to Eagle's place.

KASÓLU:
> He walked up and said, "Greetings, young woman." "Greetings, Boy," she replied.

OTHERS:
> [laughter at the girl's disparaging term of address]

A WOMAN [sarcastically]:
> All the sisters answer the same way.

AKÓBO:
> Yeah. They're all equally gracious!

KASÓLU:
> He said, "Sister, I came to ask you if you'd be willing to give me a little water to drink." "Mm," she said. [Gently scolding:] "Listen, Boy, why did you come to me here? Look how you crossed the

creek there and came all the way here just to ask me for water. What makes you think Eagle won't come here and kill you? /íya/

I've been here so long and I've never seen anyone else." He said, "Woman, are you so unkind? /íya/

If a little brother of yours, born after you left, were to come to see you, is this how badly you'd treat him?" /íya/

They hugged over and over again. /íya/

OVERLAPPING VOICES:
[exclamations and comments]

KASÓLU:
They hugged and hugged. She said, "Boy—" (he replied) She said, "I took a husband here, as you see." ("yes" he said) "Well, he's not a husband. /íya/

Evil! / . . . / But there's no way out. We're already married." /íya/

("I see" he said) "If he were to come and see you here, he could kill you." "Mm," he said. "If he were coming, would you know it?" ("yes" she said) He said, "Your husband couldn't kill me by himself. /íya/

If he came to kill me—" ("yes" she said) "I would kill him." /íya/

She said, "All right." She cooked some food and they ate. So there they were until a certain point. /íya/

The wind came up like something else! No joke! She said, "Well, he's on his way. /íya/

At this very moment he's coming home." He came along till he was very close. The boy was already hidden, just as he had been before. /íya/

The husband arrived. He brought something to set down over there. /íya/

AKÓBO [talking over the end of Kasólu's sentence]:
My god, the woman who was their mother must be thinking that another one of her children is gone!

KASÓLU:
Another one's gone. The husband set something down over there. /íya/

He took half of it and set it down here. /íya/

He came up to his wife who was sitting there dejected. / . . . / He addressed her: "Wife, here I am." She greeted him. He said, "Why is it you're sitting there like that?" She said, "It's nothing." He said, "Well, the way you're sitting there— Since you and I came here—" ("yes" she said) "I've never seen you sitting like that. /íya/

There must be something going on /íya/

that makes you sit like that." /íya/

"No no," she said. She said, "Husband, there's nothing wrong. It's just that it's been so many years since you and I came here," ("yes" he said) "and every time you come here, you always set things over there, /íya/

and half of what you're carrying you set down over here. Well, I don't know. I have so many relatives. I never know if they're my relatives or what, and that's why I'm sitting here like this. /íya/

Those are the things I'm thinking about." He said, "No, Wife, don't play around like that. The things that I kill and throw down there are evil things that try to capture me to kill me, /íya/

that's what I kill and set down there. /íya/

And the [edible] meat is what I bring over here." /íya/

("I see" she said) "But if my brother—" He said, "If your brother came here—" ("yes" she said) He said, "You and I would sleep in separate hammocks." /íya/

The boy jumped right out and called, "Greetings, Brother-in-law!" "Brother-in-law, greetings!" he replied. They hugged over and over again. /íya/

They hugged. He said, "Brother-in-law, Brother-in-law, Brother-in-law! Come over here under my wing." /íya/

[Laughing:] He went *zuuu*, and held him tight. /íya/

They flew off and glided around. He showed him lots of places where he liked to hunt. /íya/

Then he brought him back and set him down. / . . . / The boy said, "Brother-in-law, I've come to visit you." ("yes" he said) They spent three whole days talking to each other. They slept there three nights. /íya/

Then the boy said, "Brother-in-law, I'm going to leave. /íya/

I'm going off to Cayman's village." /íya/

"All right," he said.

OVERLAPPING VOICES:
[indistinct comments]

KASÓLU:

He walked him to the path. When they got there, he pulled a claw out of his right foot. /íya/

The other one had pulled out of the left. This one pulled out of the right. /íya/

And he gave it to the boy. He said to him, "Brother-in-law, when you go, if you run into a problem that's too much for you, /íya/

if it's really about to kill you—" /íya/

("yes" he said) He said, "Just come out /íya/

and go to the path there, gather some dry leaves, strike your flint to light a fire. But, Brother-in-law, if you don't absolutely need help—" ("yes" he said) /íya/

"You and I will have a real problem. /íya/

I'll kill you." "That's all right," he said. /íya/

Then he set out and walked all the way /íya/

to the path by Cayman's creek. /íya/

He continued along until he got there. /íya/

When he looked around, he saw the young woman sweeping her doorstep. /íya/

He gave her a "Greetings, Aunt." She said, "Greetings, Boy." /íya/

AKÓBO:

It's that same "Boy" all over again. [She laughs.]

ASABÔSI:

Don't they have any other way to address him besides "Boy"?

KASOLU:

Yes, well, [chuckling:] it was the way things were done in the old days. He said, "Woman, I've come to ask if you'd be willing to give me a little water to drink." She said, "Look at how you've come down the path along the creek there." /íya/

("yes" he said) "What makes you think Cayman won't come and catch you here? Over by the creek is where you could've drunk water, but you didn't want to. /íya/

Just wait till he comes here. Let him rip off your kneecap and then you'll see!"[47] /íya/

He said, "Woman, is that how unkind you are? If a younger brother that was was born after you left came to see you, is that how badly you'd treat him?" /íya/

They hugged over and over again,

OVERLAPPING VOICES:
[various exclamations]

KASÓLU:
they hugged and hugged. /íya/

She said, "Boy—" (he replied) She said, "The guy I've married—He's a disaster. /íya/

The way you've come here—"

A WOMAN:
So why did she marry him then?

KASÓLU:
"Well, I'm not sure he wouldn't kill you." He said, "Woman, your husband couldn't kill me by himself. /íya/

When he's on his way, will you know it?" "Of course," she said. "As soon as he's on his way, I know it." "OK," he said. / . . . / So they visited with each other for a while. /íya/

They'd cook food and they'd eat, and they talked to each other the way sisters and brothers do. /íya/

They talked about family things. Then the time came. The water started to shake /íya/

and tremble. She said, "There! He's coming!" /íya/

("yes" he said) Then the water really started to shake violently. The boy hid himself. /íya/

His hunting sack is where he hid. He had a hunting sack with him. /íya/

KONOI:
When he hid, and when the man got there, didn't he notice the hunting sack?

KASÓLU:
No, he had hidden all his things. The way it was, the boy had gotten to be more dangerous than the other guy. The guy was on his way. The boy was really [ritually] quick.

KANDÁMMA:
Quickest kid in the world!

KASÓLU:
Mm-hm! So there he was. He was right there when the guy arrived. He tossed half the fish way over there. /íya/

Well, that guy— Fish is what he hunted. /íya/

He brought the other half and tossed it down in front of his wife. / . . . / There they were. The woman came over, completely silent. The animal came over, *katja, katja, katja, katja.*

He said, "Wife, what's wrong?"

AKÓBO:
My god, that husband's really baaad!

KASÓLU:
"Why are you so sullen? Since you and I came to this place, years ago, I haven't ever seen you so sullen. What's wrong with you today? /íya/

Is something the matter?" She said, "It's nothing, Husband. But do you know what's bothering me?" (he replied) "Ever since you and I came here—" ("yes" he said) "Whenever you kill something, you toss some away before you bring the other half of it and toss it down for me here." ("yes" he said) "I have a family out there. I have relatives out there. /íya/

I've got a father and a mother out there and I don't know how they are. Because you can't bring them here to visit." /íya/

"Yes," he said. He said, "Wife, I can't eat those things that I hunt and toss down over there, 'cause they're evil and they want to kill me. /íya/

Those I kill and throw over there. But if your [matrilineal] family were to come here—" ("yes" she said) "Like your brother—" ("yes" she said) "You and I would sleep in separate hammocks." /íya/

[laughing:] She's tricking him. The brother said, "Brother-in-law, greetings!" /íya/

The other answered, "Brother-in-law!" They hugged over and over again.

ASABÔSI:
How would he have hugged him?

KASÓLU [chuckling]:

They hugged and hugged. There they were, running all around, calling out to each other. The guy said, "Let's go over to the water's edge." /íya/

They went in the water. The boy jumped right onto the back of the guy's head. / . . . / They swam around. He took him to show him around for a long time. They came back again. /íya/

They stayed together. They were there for quite a while. /íya/

It was several days that he slept at his brother-in-law's. /íya/

Now there was another village just downstream. /íya/

A snake lived there. /íya/

He couldn't stand boys. /íya/

The boy said he would go visit the village nearby, just to visit. /íya/

That village was just downstream. /íya/

So he set out. So Cayman said that since he was going there to visit, he would be happy to walk him to the path. The boy said he was going to a village, the village just downstream there. /íya/

So he walked off with him. He pulled a claw out of his left hand /íya/

and gave it to him. /íya/

"Brother-in-law—" he said. He replied. "When you go—" ("yes" he said) "If you run into a difficulty you can't handle, and you think you might die—" /íya/

"Yes," he said. "Just go over to the path there /íya/

and gather some dry leaves, strike your flint, and light it up. /íya/

Then I'll come at you as if I were trying to catch you. /íya/

But if the problem isn't really big— If I get there and don't see the problem—" ("yes" he said) "I'll kill you." /íya/

"That's all right," he said. / . . / Then he left.

ASABÔSI [breaking in]:

At that moment I was standing right there. /KASÓLU: íya/

Now the cure for all problems used to be *tonê* leaves.[48] /that's right/

Well, Spider was the only one in the world who knew how to summon the *tonê* god from the water.

KASÓLU:

That's true; you can't tell a tale that doesn't include him!

ASABÔSI:

You really can't. When the time came he went to the river. /that's right/

Then he sang out, to summon the *tonê* god from the river: /that's right/

"Asúngúlú gwantan, asúngúlú gwantan, donkúlo."

Zu - ma weee,____ un bái__ zu - ma weee._____

Zu-ma weee, ____ e - a - lê - ke zu - ma weee. ____

Zuma weee, un bái zuma weee.
Zuma weee, e-alêke zuma weee.
Zuma weee, un bái zuma weee.
Zuma weee, e-alêke zuma weee.

[This is in fact a song used to call the *tonê* god from the river. It says, "*zuma weee,* you call out *zuma weee.*"[49]]

Continue your story. /íya/

A WOMAN:

That was Anasi bringing *tonê* out of the water.

KANDÁMMA:

You mean that even though he's a good-for-nothing, he's still sort of an OK guy?

KASÓLU:

He took his hat and headed off, continuing on till he got to the village there. /ANTONÍSI: *íya*/

He arrived right at the village /íya/

quick as could be. Well, the snake who lived there couldn't stand seeing boys. /íya/

He had twelve heads. /íya/

OVERLAPPING VOICES:
[exclamations of astonishment]

KASÓLU:
And he ate boys till there weren't any more left. /íya/

Then he went on to women.

AKÓBO:
In the village where the boy was going?

KASÓLU:
Yeah. Well, the women he ate there— The women would be catching lice for him. /íya/

And while they were catching lice for him— When a few of them were catching lice for him, he'd look them over and decide which one to eat next. /íya/

A WOMAN:
I would have left those lice right where they were!

KASÓLU:
Right. Now he's the one in charge in that village, so whatever he says goes. /íya/

He's got twelve heads.⁵⁰

AKÓBO:
And he's someone who never dies.

A MAN:
Twelve heads he's got?!

KASÓLU:
He's already eaten the men. /íya/

But there are still women around, so it's women he gets. /íya/

Well, he looked up and there was the boy coming toward him. /íya/

And he saw him. And the girls are still catching lice for him, because he hadn't fully noticed the man yet. /íya/

But now he's starting to push the women aside /íya/

because he's seen the man, and he wants to eat him instead. /íya/

He went over to him, walked right over till he reached him, and gave him a "Greetings, *Máti* [Friend]," and the snake replied, "Greetings, *Máti*." /íya/

SOMEONE:
The [twelve] heads are all over the place.

AKÓBO:
They're everywhere!

KASÓLU:
He said, "*Máti*—" (the boy replied) He said, "I like you so much that I'd like to become your *máti*." The boy said, "Me too. I'm fond of you too, *Máti*."[51] /*íya*/

KANDÁMMA:
You mean the boy liked the anaconda?!

OTHERS:
[laughter]

AKÓBO:
He saw the [snake's] body with all those heads and decided he liked him?!

KASÓLU:
Mm. The snake loved the boy. When the boy greeted the snake as "*Máti*," the snake replied the same way, said he loved the boy like a *máti*, and the boy replied by saying he had an affection EVEN GREATER than the affection you'd need to become *máti*. /*íya*/

The snake said that— Well, it was decided. They would be *máti*. He said, "*Máti*, the reason I love you enough to become your *máti*—" /*íya*/

(The snake's the one who's saying this.) He said, "*Máti*, it's because, the way things are—" He said, "Well, *Máti*, it's because you couldn't kill me by yourself."

A WOMAN:
Oh! The snake?

KASÓLU:
The snake. The boy said, "No, I couldn't kill you by myself." /*íya*/

The snake said, "*Máti*, the way things are here—" ("yes" he replied) "Well, my heartbeat isn't here on shore where I am. /*íya*/

My heart—" (the boy replied) "My heart is located far under the water. /*íya*/

It's down with Awó Mmá, [laughing:] with the goddess of the river. That's where it is. /*íya*/

Well, could you get it? /íya/

Could you make it to there?" /íya/

The boy said, "No way. You couldn't get there. [Correcting a slip of the tongue:] I couldn't get there." /íya/

"That's right," the snake said. "And if you did get there, / . . . / my heart—" ("yes?" said the boy) /íya/

"It's inside an iron chest. /íya/

So if you could find the iron chest, would you be able to break it open?" /íya/

"No," he said. "You wouldn't be able to break it. And," the snake continued, "even if you managed to break the iron chest—" ("yes" said the boy) "My heart is a white bird. /íya/

And if the white bird flew out, there'd be no way you could catch it." /íya/

"Yes," said the boy, "it's true, Máti, you can't be killed." He said, "I really love you enough to become your máti." /íya/

The snake replied.

AKÓBO [anticipating]:
"You and I will become máti."

KASÓLU:
The boy said, "Well, Máti, you and I will be máti." /íya/

He said, "Yes, well, wait just a minute, Máti." (the snake replied) "Let me go urinate. I'll be right back." /íya/

The boy left in a flash and zipped into the forest. /íya/

He pulled out Cayman's claw in an instant and quickly made the fire under it, and Cayman arrived in a flash. He said, "Look, my friend, what's up? What did you call me for? What's the big deal?

OTHERS:
[laughter]

KASÓLU:
You'll force me to kill you." He said, "Friend—" (he replied) He said, "It's nothing much that I called you for. Except that since I came here—" ("yes" he said) "There's this snake and there's this game we've been playing with each other," ("yes" he said) "and there's an iron chest down with the goddess of the underwater,"

("yes" he said) "and I called you so you could get it for me." He said [with surprise]: "Hm! I've just been hunting. /íya/

And when I was hunting this morning," he said, "it was right there on the crack of the iron chest that I sat down to rest! /íya/

OTHERS:
[laughter]

KASÓLU:
When I sat down on top of it, I really rested," he said. /íya/

"Let's stay here and talk a while." /íya/

The boy said, "Friend, don't play around with me like that. Let's not sit and talk. The snake will kill me. And if you let the snake kill me— If you let the snake kill me, I will kill you. /íya/

Go and get the chest for me!" /íya/

Splash! He plunged into the water. /íya/

After a while he came back with it séngéé, and he said, "Máti, I've done it already." /íya/

[Laughing:] The iron chest was there, but he didn't know what to do next. /uh-uh/

OTHERS:
[laughter]

KASÓLU:
Now at that moment— /íya/

AKÓBO:
The snake is there, all ready to eat him.

KASÓLU:
The snake was right there. /íya/

And he was beginning to feel tired in his heart. /íya/

OTHERS:
[exclamations]

A MAN:
He felt it coming already!

KASÓLU:
Well, the heart that had been underwater had been brought ashore. /íya/

ASABÔSI:
He's already getting tired.

KASÓLU:
His heart was beginning to be tired. /íya/

KABUÉSI:
They should make a fire and put the chest on it [to kill the bird].

KASÓLU:
And things were already starting to seem bad. He couldn't eat women anymore. /íya/

Before, when there were men around, he used to eat men. /íya/

And when the men were finished, he went on to the women who were delousing him. /íya/

And when he saw the boy approaching, he pushed the women away. /íya/

Well, what those girls did, when the guy went to bring back the chest— Well, the snake began to feel tired. /íya/

He said, "*Máti*, I'm done for." Then the cayman went back home. /íya/

The boy was there for a while. /íya/

And then he went out /íya/

and he took out the one that Elephant had given him. /íya/

Elephant came instantly. /íya/

Mmm! He came right up to him. /íya/

He said, "Friend—" /íya/

AKÓBO [breaking in]:
At the time when he arrived, I myself was there too.

KASÓLU:
Íya. What was it like?

AKÓBO:
At that time, Spider was asking for a wife. He was going off to look for a wife. [She giggles.] /KASÓLU: *íya*/

And people had told him the woman's name, and now he was walking along repeating the name so he wouldn't forget it. /íya/

He was singing [she laughs as she sings]:

Zegemôni-ee, tjèè tjèè tjèè.
Môni-ee, tjèè tjèè tjèè.
Môni-nò, tjèè tjèè tjèè.
Zegemôni-ee, tjèè tjèè tjèè.
Môni-ee, tjèè tjèè tjèè.
Môni-nò, tjèè tjèè tjèè.

[The woman's name was Zegemôni, or Môni for short. The chorus, *tjèè tjèè tjèè*, is simply vocables.]

Go on with your story.

KASÓLU:

OK! So he appeared instantly. /ANTONÍSI: *íya*/

He said, "Friend, why did you call me? What's the big problem?" /*íya*/

The boy said, "Friend, I've got this chest here, /*íya*/ this iron chest, and I'd like you to break it for me." /*íya*/

He said, "That iron chest there? /*íya*/

That's the one? /*íya*/

This thing here—" He touched it like this, squeezed it a bit. It was just like, you know, something very soft. /*íya*/

It was as if he had picked up a papaya, /*íya*/

a very ripe papaya. /*íya*/

[In a very relaxed tone:] "Let's sit and talk together, Friend. /*íya*/

That job's nothing." /*íya*/ The boy said, "I said to break the thing for me! /*íya*/

There's a guy who's playing around with me!" ("yes" he said) "And you're going to let him kill me! /*íya*/

That iron chest there, I want you to break it for me! I'm having an argument with this guy. /íya/

So just break it for me." /íya/

The other took hold of it *buwáá,* /íya/

smashed it open *pònyôn.* The iron chest's— [Correcting himself:] It flew off *vún vún vún* /íya/

vún.

A WOMAN:
From being broken?

KASÓLU:
No, it was the white bird [and not the chest] that was going like that. /íya/

He had already finished with the chest. /íya/

Elephant left. He said, "Friend, I've finished my part. /íya/

There's nothing more I can do for you." /íya/

And at that time /íya/

the snake's heart was really getting tired.

AKÓBO [anticipating]:
He started squirming.

KASÓLU:
He just didn't know what to do any more. He'd turn and squirm, just didn't know what to do.

AKÓBO:
He didn't know what to do, but did he know where the boy was?

KASÓLU:
The boy didn't go back to him. Once they had talked that time and they became *máti,* he told him to wait a minute, that he was going off to urinate. Well, if I were visiting you and I said, "Wait for me here. I'm going off to urinate," you couldn't stop me. Because I certainly wouldn't urinate there inside your house!

ASABÔSI:
That's true, I wouldn't urinate in your house.

KASÓLU:
Exactly. And once the boy went off—

AKÓBO:
He's gone off to urinate, and he hasn't returned yet.

KASÓLU:

—the snake's heart started feeling tired. And then the white bird escaped. /íya/

It flew out, and so the boy went on to Eagle's claw. /íya/

He struck the flint, he went to the edge of the forest just like before. /íya/

He lit it and put it there, and instantly Eagle arrived. He said, "Friend? Brother-in-law? What's up?" "Nothing," he said. /íya/

"Brother-in-law, did you see the bird flying off there?" ("yes" he said) "I want you to catch it and kill it for me. /íya/

I need to have its head cut off before it gets where it's going." /íya/

Eagle said, "Brother-in-law, sit down and let's talk a while." /íya/

OVERLAPPING VOICES:

[laughter and comments]

KONOI:

You mean they're letting the boy's bird escape?!

KASÓLU:

He said, "There's no place /íya/

where the bird can go that I can't get to it. /íya/

He's got to alight on a tree along the way, Brother-in-law." /íya/

"Yes," he said. "It's got to rest on a tree. /íya/

It's sure to. /íya/

So let's just sit and talk and when the time comes I'll go kill it." /íya/

"Brother-in-law," said the boy. (Eagle replied) He said, "Don't let the bird go. You'll make the snake kill me. /íya/

That white bird that's flying there— I want you to catch it and kill it." /íya/

Eagle said, "Come on, let's tell stories." /íya/

"Brother-in-law of mine, don't be like that!" Eagle flew off, vúún. He cut off the white bird's head gélém /íya/

gwaa gwíí. Night fell on the village. The snake was falling, and it was the dead of night. /íya/

AKÓBO:

The snake is dying.

KASÓLU:
He was ALREADY dead!

KANDÁMMA:
The chief of them all.

AKÓBO:
The chief of that place.

KASÓLU:
It was the dead of night. Everything was dark. For all the people who were there, all those people, it was completely dark.

AKÓBO:
The big man of that place that they used to catch lice for!

KASÓLU:
The boy left the place, just walked right out.

AKÓBO:
Was it because the snake's time to die had come that he told all about himself?

KASÓLU:
Well, if you're going to go ahead and do things like that— He just went too far. /íya/

The thing is that the snake had killed all the available men, and that's why he went on to the women. /íya/

Since they caught lice for him, they were really providing a service for him, but he still wanted to eat the ones who caught lice. /íya/

The boy rushed out, took his knife, and went up to the snake. /íya/

He pulled the snake's head on over, and he cut it *sóko sóko kélén* [sounds of sawing and then severing], /íya/

pulled it off and slipped it *zuu*, /íya/

into his sack. Then he went off to Cayman's place. It had already gotten light. After he cut off the head, it got light as could be again.

KANDÁMMA:
The head had made it dark.

OVERLAPPING VOICES:
[laughter and comments]

KASÓLU:
And he went off. /íya/

So that's how it was for a while, and then people wanted to investigate what had happened. /íya/

They said [in a tone of bewildered astonishment:] "Well, how is it that the snake here died? /íya/

Because, well, not a thing in the world had been able to kill that guy." /íya/

After a long time one of the girls told the whole story. One of the girls who had caught lice for the snake, one of those who caught lice for him, that he had wanted to eat— /íya/

Well, there she was until at one point she said, "You know what?" (others replied) "They sent a boat after them—" (Whoops! I got it wrong. /íya/

I got that part wrong.) /íya/

After they said those things, /íya/

night came and then it got to be dawn. He cut off the head and took it. /íya/

Then they asked who it was who had killed the snake. And Anasi said it was him! /íya/

KONOI:
But he hasn't got any of the snake's heads.

KASÓLU:
He went out and walked into the forest. /íya/

He killed snakes. / . . . / He killed snakes until he'd gotten twelve heads. /íya/

He was going to bring them back to stick them on. Anasi said he was the one. He kept on trying without success. /íya/

He'd put them together but they didn't fit. Well, when you bring back a snake's head /íya/

it must fit perfectly.

AKÓBO:
Right. All twelve of them.

KASÓLU:
Then you know who killed it. /íya/

He kept trying. He had cut twelve and brought them back, but some were bigger than others. He kept trying till he was exhausted.

AKÓBO:
He'd try them all out on each neck.

KASÓLU:
He couldn't get them to fit. /íya/

Then the girl, the one they had been asking about this, one of those girls said [with sudden enlightenment:] Oh, SHE knew! /íya/

A man had come there from Cayman's village. /íya/

And he and the guy had had some words. /íya/

And during the discussion, they talked a lot and at the end they decided to become *máti,* and they talked some more and the boy left. /íya/

Well, after he left, it wasn't even a half an hour before the snake's heart started feeling weak, and after a little longer, as it got dark, /íya/ the snake died. Well, since they didn't understand, that's why they paddled their canoe over to there. /íya/

They paddled their canoe over to where the boy was. The boy was still right there in Cayman's village. /íya/

They arrived and told him what had happened. He said, "Mm. Really?" /íya/

("yes" they said) "Well," he said, he would come have a look. /íya/

but it wasn't him, not him. /íya/

The boy set out and continued until he got there. /íya/

He reached into his hunting sack. /íya/

KONOI:
Well, if the snake was already put back together, wouldn't he come back to life?

KASÓLU:
The boy had already cut him apart. Even if he were put back together, he wouldn't be able to revive enough to do himself any good.

AKÓBO:
That guy was already dead!

KASÓLU:
So the boy reached right into his hunting sack, /íya/

and pulled out the head he had there. /íya/

He fitted it on *biingá babala baa* [sound of the snake starting to move again, proving that the boy was the one who had killed it]. Night fell immediately! /*íya*/

They screamed in fear. He pulled the head right off. /*íya*/

He put it on again: *biingá babababababa*. And took it off. /*íya*/

He put it on again: *Biingá ba*. And night fell. Then he pulled it off again. /*íya*/

He left. / . . . / Then the chief came along and split off one side of the place. /*íya*/

That made a village, let's say about the size of Paramaribo. /*íya*/

So the boy and his sisters and their relatives came there to live. And that's the part of the world we're living in here.

AKÓBO:
With the brothers-in-law?

KASÓLU:
Yes, with the brothers-in-law. It's the part of the earth the boy had, with his mother, where he brought his relatives. That's the part of the world we're in here.

A WOMAN:
Whatever happened to the snakes' heads that Anasi had?

AKÓBO [laughing]:
He just threw them away.

KASÓLU:
They just rotted.

AKÓBO:
It's that he wanted to be chief!

KASÓLU:
And that's the end of my story.

[In the midst of general conversation, Kandámma has apparently announced her intention to tell a tale.]

ANTONÍSI:
Well, I'll cut it for you.

VOICES:
[more background discussion, a child crying]

A Saramaka woman in her rice garden, 1968.

KANDÁMMA:
  Well, *Mató!*

ANTONÍSI:
  Tòngôni!

KANDÁMMA:
  Huh! There we were. /ANTONÍSI: *íya*/

  Children, the chief cleared a garden for himself /*íya*/

  till it was all ready, and he planted some rice. /*íya*/

  Birds kept eating the rice so much that the rice— /*íya*/

  well, he didn't know how to deal with it. /*íya*/

  In the morning the boy, the one who you'd wake up and tell to go
  chase birds away from the rice for you— /*íya*/

[At this point people are still settling in, finishing their own conversations, and not yet paying full attention to Kandámma.]

He got up and went off till he got there, /íya/

banged on a log *kwóó kwóó kwóó kwóó kwóó*, /íya/

made all the birds flap away, *buwaa*. /íya/

Then the devil appeared at the entrance to the garden! /íya/

OTHERS:
[exclamations of surprise]

AKÓBO [imagining the boy's reaction]:
"What will I do?"

KANDÁMMA:
He's walking along toward the boy. /íya/

Walking along toward him, /íya/

toward the person who went to take care of the birds there. /íya/

[chanting, in the devil's voice, loud and clear:]

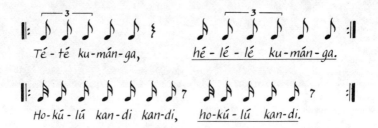

Tété kumánga, hélélé kumánga.
Tété kumánga, hélélé kumánga.
Tété kumánga, hélélé kumánga.
Hokúlú kandi kandi, hokúlú kandi.
Hokúlú kandi kandi, hokúlú kandi.

He came right up to him. /íya/

ASABÔSI:
Máa nêngè! [exclamation]

KANDÁMMA:
He said, "Boy, what do you think you're doing here?"

ASABÔSI:
Can't he see the boy's come to work in the garden?!

KANDÁMMA:

He said, "I've come to chase away birds." And as he was saying "I've come to chase away birds," /íya/

the devil finished him off.

A MAN:

He swallowed him that fast?

KANDÁMMA:

Swallowed that fast!

ANTONÍSI:

Keep track of your story. At that time, I was standing there.

SEVERAL VOICES:

[overlapping replies to Antonísi]

ANTONÍSI:

You know what happened with What's his name?

A MAN:

Well, what happened?

ANTONÍSI:

The jaguar went to Agouti and said they should cut off his [Agouti's] ear and make a drum with it right then and there.

THE MAN:

Then and there!

ANTONÍSI:

Then Hummingbird's going to come and take the drum.

ANOTHER MAN:

How did he take it?

ANTONÍSI:

*For an explanation, see p. 37.

Mbónu, Mbónu, tjèm tjèm tjè.
Agwolóófia, tjèm tjèm tjè.   [laughter]
Mi Lánga Húnyan, tjèm tjèm tjè.
Mbónu, Mbónu, tjèm tjèm tjè.
Mbónu, Mbónu, tjèm tjèm tjè.   [laughter]
Agwolóófia, tjèm tjèm tjè.
Mi Lánga Húnyan, tjèm tjèm tjè.
Agwolóófia, tjèm tjèm tjè.

[Antonísi and Kasólu do this song in call-and-response, Antonísi taking the "solo" part and Kasólu doing the "chorus." Mbónu ("My Bones") and Mi Lánga Húnyan ("My Long Claws") are insulting names for Jaguar; Agwolóófia appears to be a third. In 1987 Antonísi summarized for us the tale this fragment was taken from: All the animals got together to make a drum. Each cut off a piece of its ear to contribute to the drumhead. Jaguar declared that since more of his ear was cut off, the drum would belong to him. Agouti stole the drum from him and taunted him in song.[52] Jaguar charged after him and managed to get it back, but Hummingbird grabbed it away again. And that's why Hummingbird still hovers up and down, up and down. This song is what Hummingbird sings to tease and insult Jaguar, holding the drum just out of reach as Jaguar jumps at it in vain.]

Go ahead with your story.

OTHERS:
[lots of laughter]

A WOMAN:
My head's aching, I'm laughing so hard!

KANDÁMMA [chuckling]:
My goodness! What tale am I telling you here? I've forgotten the story.

KASÓLU:
The thing about the devil—

AKÓBO:
—and the "*tété kumánga.*"

KANDÁMMA [picking up the story again at the point when the devil arrives in the garden, repeating part of what she's already told]: The devil got to the garden *djaaa.* /*íya*/

As he approached, /*íya*/

he came:

> *Tété kumánga,* /*íya*/ *hélélé kumánga.*
> *Tété kumánga, hélélé kumánga.*
> *Hokúlú kandi kandi, hokúlú kandi.*
> *Hokúlú kandi kandi, hokúlú kandi.*

He got to the boy, /*íya*/

to the person who'd come to chase away birds. /*íya*/

He said, "What do you think you're doing here?" The boy said, "I came to chase away birds." /*íya*/

[The devil, partly to himself:] "This guy's going to chase away birds with his plate? Are you planning on taking your plate and your food with you when you get gobbled up?!"[53] /*íya*/

A MAN:
Good god!!

KANDÁMMA:
He gulped him down. The rest of the people are back there waiting forever for him to return. They gave up. /*íya*/

In the morning another one said, "I'm going." /*íya*/

He cooked the food to take along. As soon as he arrived: *kwóó, kwóó, kwóó, kwóó.* /*íya*/

The birds all flew off, flap, flap, flap, *buwaa.* /*íya*/

The devil's already coming:

> *Tété kumánga,* /*íya*/ *hélélé kumánga.*
> *Tété kumánga, hélélé kumánga.*
> *Tété kumánga, hélélé kumánga.*
> *Hokúlú kandi kandi, hokúlú kandi.*
> *Hokúlú kandi kandi, hokúlú kandi.*

He arrived. Well, with the "*tété kumánga, hélélé kumánga*" there, the people that he had been eating—/*íya*/

Well, that was their bones in his belly, just jostling around.

OTHERS:
[exclamations]

KANDÁMMA:

And the skin on his belly was going, "*Hokúlú kandi kandi, hokúlú kandi. Hokúlú kandi kandi, hokúlú kandi.*"

A WOMAN:

That was no ordinary belly!

A MAN:

That was no ordinary belly!

A WOMAN:

Some belly!

KANDÁMMA:

No ordinary belly: a place of suffering![54] Children, he was killing people till there was hardly anyone left in the village. /*íya*/

The birds were finishing off the chief's rice, so the chief said, "My goodness, don't let anyone else go, because we're losing everybody!" /*íya*/

But a scrawny little kid was there, and he said, "I'm going to go and have a look." /*íya*/

KASÓLU:

You know the moment when the scrawny little kid said he'd go and have a look? /KANDÁMMA: yes/

Well, at that moment, I was standing right there. /right/

In those days, Kaká [Shit]— That man, Kaká, used to come and dance in the village. /true/

OTHERS:

[laughter]

KASÓLU:

And no one knew who he was. /right/

[laughing:] You know how he came [to dance]? /no/

Zigbónu kwálá, sonú kwálá kpa.
Kwálá kwálá, sonú kwálá kpa.
Zigbónu kwálá, <u>sonú kwálá kpa.</u>
Kwálá kwálá, <u>sonú kwálá kpa.</u>
Azigbónu kwálá, <u>sonú kwálá kpa.</u>
Kwálá gwolo, <u>sonú kwálá kpa.</u>
Zigbónu kwálá, <u>sonú kwálá kpa.</u>

[This song, accompanied by lively laughter and handclapping, is done in syncopated call-and-response. In 1987
Kasólu told us the tale this nugget alludes to: It used to
be that a stranger would come and "play" in the village,
sweeter than anything, but at the end, when people ran up
to embrace him in congratulations, he would run off into
the forest and disappear. No one could figure out who
he was. One night Anasi succeeded in giving him a congratulatory embrace at the conclusion of his dance and discovered (by getting all dirty and smelly) who he was. Now
that people know who he is, Shit has to stay off in the forest, at the edge of the village.]

Go ahead with your story. As soon as Anasi saw him he knew this
was Kaká. Anasi went right up and hugged him!

KANDÁMMA:
He hugged him. He thought the dance and song were really sweet.

OTHERS:
[wild laughter]

KASÓLU:
Mm-hmm.

ASABÔSI:
You think Anasi could come back to the village?! [an allusion to
how foul smelling he would have become]

KANDÁMMA:
So the kid got himself all ready, /ANTONÍSI: *íya*/

prepared himself [ritually] till he was really ready. Then he said that they should make him an earthenware pot. /*íya*/

So they bought a pot for him. /*íya*/

Then he went to an *óbia* house, and he cooked some food in the pot till it was all ready. /*íya*/

Then he took the food and the pot /*íya*/

and he walked along till he got there. /*íya*/

The scrawny little kid. /*íya*/

He told them, "Now when I go off there, no one must follow me, y' hear?" /*íya*/

They said, "All right." And he set off, arrived, and *kwóó kwóó kwóó kwóó kwóó*. The birds all flew away, flap, flap, flap, *buwaa*.

ASABÔSI:
If it had been me, I wouldn't have knocked the stick *kwóó kwóó kwóó* anymore. I'd have just slipped in quietly.

KANDÁMMA:
He didn't even have to knock the tree.

AKÓBO:
If he knocks, the devil will come.

KANDÁMMA:
The devil was already on his way, coming into the garden:

> *Tété kumánga, hélélé kumánga.*
> *Tété kumánga, hélélé kumánga.*
> *Hokúlú kandi kandi, hokúlú kandi.*
> *Hokúlú kandi kandi, hokúlú kandi.*

The devil said, "Boy?" (he replied) /*íya*/

The devil said, "What do you think you're doing here?" / . . . / He said, "Father, I'm chasing away birds." ("yes" he said)

KABUÉSI [proposing a response the boy could have used to scare the devil]:
"I brought Dúnguláli."[55]

OTHERS:
[laughter]

KANDÁMMA:
"OK," the devil said. "What did you bring?"

AKÓBO [proposing a response]:
"I've brought food from the *óbia* house."

KANDÁMMA:
The kid said, "Father, look at some food I've got here. Come have some to eat before you kill me." / . . . / He said [in an eager voice:] "It's food?" ("yes" he said) "Hand it over!" The kid took an earthenware plate, and he dished out all the food. He put the side dishes in the little bowl. /*íya*/

Then he put the rice out and served it to the devil. /*íya*/

Then he scraped the pot. He ladled out the sauce. It looked delicious. The devil took it.

A nyán mi na gwa-laa, a sí mi na gwa-laa-o, yéi nôò mi

yéi-ee. Gwan-gu-lu gwan-gu-lu. A nyán mi na gwa-laa,

a sí mi na gwa-laa-o, yéi nôò mi yéi-ee. Gwan-gu-lu

gwan-gu-lu. A nyán mi na gwa-laa, a sí mi na gwa-laa-o,

yéi nôò mi yéi-ee. Gwan-gu-lu gwan-gu-lu.

A nyán mi na gwa-laa, a sí mi na gwa-laa-o,

yéi nôò mi yéi-ee. Gwan-gu-lu gwan-gu-lu.

A nyán mi na gwalaa, a sí mi na gwalaa-o, yéi nôò mi yéi-ee.
Gwangulu gwangulu.
A nyán mi na gwalaa, a sí mi na gwalaa-o, yéi nôò mi yéi-ee.
Gwangulu gwangulu.
A nyán mi na gwalaa, a sí mi na gwalaa-o, yéi nôò mi yéi-ee.
Gwangulu gwangulu.
A nyán mi na gwalaa, a sí mi na gwalaa-o, yéi nôò mi yéi-ee.
Gwangulu gwangulu.
A nyán mi na gwalaa, a sí mi na gwalaa-o, yéi nôò mi yéi-ee.
Gwangulu gwangulu.
A nyán mi na gwalaa, a sí mi na gwalaa-o, yéi nôò mi yéi-ee.
Gwangulu gwangulu.

[As Kandámma explained later on in her telling, this song represents the sounds of the devil's mouth chomping on his food: *gwangulu gwangulu* is the devil's mouth moving; *a sí mi na gwalaa* is the sound of his upper teeth; and *a nyán mi na gwalaa* is the sound of his lower teeth. In standard Saramaccan, *a nyán mi* and *a sí mi* mean, respectively, "he eats me" and "he sees me"; *yéi nôò mi yéi* means roughly "that's what I've heard." The Saramakas we discussed this song with speculated that the upper and lower teeth are talking, saying that they've seen and eaten, but that it's not enough.]

The food in the plate was finished. /íya/

"Boy?" (the kid answered) He said, "The food's all gone. /íya/

Dish some out for me. Boy?" (he replied) "Dish me out some more." /íya/

Now as the boy dished the food out of the pot there, /íya/

the place he took it from kept filling up with food again.

OTHERS:
[exclamations of astonishment]

KANDÁMMA:
He dished out some more into the plate and gave it to the devil.

A nyán mi na gwalaa, a sí mi na gwalaa-o, yéi nôò mi yéi-ee.
Gwangulu gwangulu.
A nyán mi na gwalaa, a sí mi na gwalaa-o, yéi nôò mi yéi-ee.
Gwangulu gwangulu.

Well, that was the devil's mouth moving! His mouth is working away: "*gwangulu gwangulu.*" /*íya*/

Now his upper teeth— They were going: "*a sí mi na gwalaa.*" The lower ones were going: "*a nyán mi na gwalaa.*" Those are the sounds his mouth makes. /*íya*/

ASABÔSI:
He realizes he's going to eat the boy.

KANDÁMMA:
He's going to eat the boy. /*íya*/

Children, the boy just keeps serving out more and more food into the earthenware dishes, giving it to the devil to eat, until the devil finally says, "But— Boy, /*íya*/

Boy—" (he replies) "Boy, should I keep on eating?" /*íya*/

The boy says, "Father, just go right ahead and eat. The food isn't gone yet. Just go ahead and eat." /*íya*/

YÉGI [to a child]:
Don't sit down on the bad side of the lantern.

KANDÁMMA:
The devil eats along for a while, and then he tells the boy to dish out some more. /*íya*/

"Boy! Boy!" (he replies) "Dish out some more," he says. /*íya*/

So the boy dishes out some more.

[very weak and tired:]

> *A nyán mi na gwalaa, a sí mi na gwalaa-o, yéi nôò mi yéi-ee.*
>   *Gwangulu gwangulu.*
> *A nyán mi na gwalaa, a sí mi na gwalaa-o, yéi nôò mi yéi-ee.*
>   *Gwangulu gwangulu.*
> *A nyán mi na gwalaa, a sí mi na gwalaa-o, yéi nôò mi yéi-ee.*
>   *Gwangulu gwangulu.*

"Boy?" "Yes, Father?" He says [exhausted], "Should I keep on eating?" He says, "Yes, Father, go right ahead."

AKÓBO:
"Just keep on eating."

KANDÁMMA:
"Just keep on eating." Children, the boy keeps dishing the food into the bowl, giving it to the devil. The devil keeps on eating.

He's working his mouth till it feels all limp. [Barely audible, totally exhausted:] "*Gwangulu* /*íya*/

gwanguluu gwangulu gwanguluu, gwangulu gwangulu." Finally, *gúdjaaa*— He collapses. /*íya*/

ASABÔSI:
When your belly gets that full, you can't take on any more food.

KANDÁMMA:
That whole pot of food— The little kid gave the devil the pot of food, and the devil finished it off. He keeled over, flat on the ground. /*íya*/

Dead as could be.

AKÓBO [anticipating]:
The world was freed.

KANDÁMMA:
The world was freed. The chief cleared his garden. They harvested the rice for him. So that's how things got to be the way they are. If the kid hadn't killed the devil, /*íya*/

you'd have planted your rice and it would have gotten ripe, but you wouldn't have been able to go chase the birds away from it. The devil was there on the path.

ASABÔSI:
"Boy, should I just keep on eating?" And the boy says, "Just go right ahead and eat. Your belly's not full yet."

OTHER VOICES:
[laughter, general conversation]

ANTONÍSI:
Well, we finished that one! [pause] We'll go on to another.

ASABÔSI:
That tale— I really liked it a lot!

KABUÉSI [to Akóbo]:
Well, I'm right here listening, Sister, so why don't you go ahead and tell one?

AKÓBO:
I don't have any tales I can tell.

KABUÉSI:
Antonísi, I think I've had about enough.

[At this point our tape recorder began having problems, and we do not have a coherent transcription of the next tale, which was told by Antonísi and involved a horse with the unlikely name of Bámbèl, a strange white princess whose skin was plagued by itches, a Bible, and other trappings of whitefolks' society such as "dumplings." However, twenty years later, Antonísi listened to our taped fragments and summarized for us the tale he had told: A boy heard that in a certain kingdom the king had promised his daughter in marriage to the man who could tell a riddle that no one could answer. But if the king's people could figure out the riddle, the suitor would be taken to an execution chamber and his head would be chopped off. The boy told his mother he was going to try his luck. She didn't want him to go and in anger cooked three dumplings, put poison in one of them, and gave them to her son. He set off with his horse, Bámbèl. On the way he ate one of the dumplings and found some water to drink that was neither rainwater nor dew nor river water. Then he fed his dog, Afiída, one of the dumplings. The dog died. Three ants fed on the corpse and died. Then seven vultures did likewise. When the boy arrived at the palace, he posed his riddle: "Afiída killed three; three killed seven." (Antonísi also referred in passing to a related riddle the boy posed about the water he had drunk, explaining that there been a fire in a church and that the charred Bible had exuded the water.) The king's people couldn't guess the answer(s), so the boy married the princess.[56]

   In the middle of Antonísi's tale, Kandámma offered a tale nugget that our tape recorder registered, except for the opening phrases, which described how men and women used to live in separate villages and how three brothers went off to seek women against their father's advice:]

KANDÁMMA:
   [They arrived] at the village on the shore. Then one of them—
   They gave them a place to sleep. One of them snuck off to meet a woman. Finally the people talked to him and told him there was no problem. /ANTONÍSI: íya/

   "We see that you've already made a woman pregnant here. /íya/

   So you should go back to your village and then return to take care of the pregnancy."[57] /íya/

   That's what the chief said. So he went back home /íya/

   intending to return so he could take care of the pregnancy. Well, the boys' father had buried a spear right there by the path. He said that if the boys went off to take women, when they returned, the spear would know. /íya/

So they got back. They called out, "Father, we're back!" ("yes" he said) "Wait a minute." He stood there. He said, "Jump across here, /íya/

for the ordeal." /íya/

One of them sang out:

A-yén - ge yén - ge yén - ge yén-ge maan yén - gee!____

A-yén - ge yén-ge yén-ge maan yén-gee, li-ba-ná baai-o,

yén - ge maan yén-gee.____ A-yén-ge yén - ge yén-ge

maan yén - gee.____ A-yén - ge yén - ge yén - ge maan

yén-gee,____ li-ba-ná baai-o, yén - ge maan yén-gee.____

Ayénge yénge yénge yénge maan yéngee! /íya/

Ayénge yénge yénge maan yéngee, libaná baai-o, yénge maan yéngee. /íya/

Ayénge yénge yénge maan yéngee.
Ayénge yénge yénge maan yéngee, libaná baai-o, yénge maan yéngee.[58] /íya/

He jumped right over and landed on the other side. /íya/

The other ones were left, the other two brothers. The father said, "Go ahead, cross over." /íya/

The second brother sang out:

Ayénge yénge yénge maan yéngee!
Ayénge yénge yénge maan yéngee, libaná baai-o, yénge maan
  yéngee.
Ayénge yénge yénge maan yéngee. /íya/

Ayénge yénge yénge maan yéngee, libaná baai-o, yénge maan
  yéngee.

Now there was only one left. The father said, "Go ahead, cross over." He started singing, and then began to cry. The father said, "Jump across!"

Ayénge yénge yénge maan yéngee!
Ayénge yénge yénge maan yéngee, libaná baai-o, yénge maan
  yéngee.
Ayénge yénge yénge maan yéngee.
Ayénge yénge yénge maan yéngee, libaná baai-o, yénge maan
  yéngee.

He leaped! He leaped up and fell down right onto the spear!

OTHERS:
[exclamations]

AKÓBO:
The kid wouldn't listen.

KANDÁMMA:
It pierced him right through and stuck there. /íya/

The father and the two brothers were right there. They cried out! They ran into their houses, there where they had lived. /íya/

OTHERS:
[laughter]

KANDÁMMA:
They untied their hammocks and pulled them down. They ran into the forest. /íya/

They left the third one stuck on the spear. /íya/

OTHERS:
[exclamations]

KANDÁMMA:
The woman he had made pregnant waited for him all day long. She didn't see him. /íya/

She set out on a path and followed it until she saw the man stuck on the spear. She pulled and pulled till she got him free /íya/

and she took him back to revive him. / . . . / She said, "Because of how I've saved you, you mustn't have any other women. /íya/

OTHERS:
[exclamations of surprise]

KANDÁMMA:
Don't you see how I've saved you from the spear and brought you back to life?" /íya/

("yes" he said) "If you have any other women, you'll see what happens!" /íya/

So they went on like that with the man living in the village for quite a while. /íya/

Then the man took another woman and got her pregnant. /íya/

People went and told his wife, /íya/

the one who had gone to help him [when he was in trouble]. /íya/

They told her how the man had got a woman pregnant. /íya/

Then the woman killed herself to get back at him. /yes/

OTHERS:
[exclamations of concern]

KANDÁMMA:
She killed herself because of him. So now, when a man takes a woman, / . . . / you make her a boat and set it in the water, you clear a garden for her. It's for the woman who killed herself because of the man who took a wife in Zabangáiginta behind her back. It's a payment that you men make to women.[59] /íya/

[When Kandámma's nugget ends, Antonísi resumes the tale about Bámbèl and continues only very briefly before our tape recorder again cuts out. Our recording picks up again just after Antonísi has concluded and Kasólu has launched into a new tale, with Antonísi as responder:]

KASÓLU:
OK, well at that time, there was plenty of work.[60] /ANTONÍSI: íya/

You'd go off to look for work in whitefolks' territory, and there would always be some job available. /íya/

There was one guy /íya/

and you'd just go ask him for work. /íya/

Well, if you set out to look for work with him— /íya/

This white man has his place there where he has the jobs, and you'd just go ask him for work. He was the one in charge of it. /íya/

Now when you went to ask him for work, /íya/

you'd say, "Well, Brother, I've come to ask you for a job." /íya/

He'd say, "OK." Then he'd say to you, "Well, look—"

A WOMAN [to Akóbo]:
Are you leaving?

AKÓBO:
No, I'm just going to light my lantern.

KASÓLU:
"I've got some—" [to Akóbo:] Come get your fire over here.

AKÓBO:
I don't want to bother anyone [by stepping over people's feet].

KASÓLU:
Here, let me give it to you. [Back to the tale:] He has a gigantic rice field. /íya/

He's got a cacao field. /íya/

He's got all kinds of fields spread out all around. / . . . / He's got pigs. He's got cows. /íya/ He's got chickens. He's got ducks. /íya/

So you just show up there, /íya/

and ask him for a job, and he says to you, "Well, Brother, what you could do is— Well, I've got some cacao over there. You could go gather the pods /íya/

and bring them back to me. I'll give you a bag. /íya/

So off you'd go. /íya/

But when you went to touch one of the cacao pods, all of them would break off, /íya/

and all the beans would fall down and run all over the place. The plant would be absolutely stripped. /íya/

All the beans fell down. /íya/

So you walk back to the king— /íya/

That's the white man who has the jobs. /*íya*/

But he's JUST like a king. /*íya*/

He'd talk to him and say, "Well, King—" (he'd reply) He'd say, "Here I am. /*íya*/

I went and touched one of the cacao plants to harvest it, /*íya*/

and all the beans fell on the ground."

ANTONÍSI:
Íya. Keep track of your story. /KASÓLU: *íya*/

Well, at that time, we were there.

KASÓLU:
Íya. Well, what was it like?

ANTONÍSI:
At one point, well, Parrot and Bushfowl were going to go sing and dance for Great God, and Parrot went and got Bushfowl so they could sing and dance. You know how they did it?

KASÓLU:
How did they perform?

ANTONÍSI:

Béin-ki ma-má, Kó-djo.   Béin - ki ma-má, Kó-djo ma-má.

Kódjo mamá, béinki mamá, Kódjo.
Béinki mamá, Kódjo-oo.
Béinki mamá, Kódjo.
Béinki mamá, Kódjo mamá.
Béinki mamá, Kódjo.
Béinki mamá, Kódjo.
Béinki mamá.

[This song is the call of Bushfowl in the morning. In 1987 the men in Kourou, including Antonísi, supplied a summary of the tale this tale nugget alludes to: Parrot always used to fly up to Great God to sing alone. But after a while his singing was no longer considered so sweet, so he asked Bushfowl to come with him. Because Bushfowl can't fly very well, Parrot carried him under his wing. Bushfowl's

singing was really sweet, but Parrot's had gotten so bad that
they hit him with a stick and told him his singing was no
good. He flew back to earth, leaving Bushfowl up there all
by himself. Bushfowl kept on singing for a long time. But
then he didn't know how to get back down. He said, "Well,
I'm going to go back anyway," and he flapped his way down
as best he could and landed splat in a mud puddle. That's
how he got the *tjubí óbia* (magic for being invisible). So that's
why, when we go hunting, he can be right there and we still
don't see him. (Bushfowl is a dark colored, speckled bird.)]

Go ahead with your story.

KASÓLU:
   OK! So he told him about how everything fell down to the ground.
   /ANTONÍSI: *íya*/

   The man said, "Really?" ("yes" he said) "Well, my boy, when the
   cacao fell like that, did it hurt you?" /*íya*/

   He said, "Yes, my king, it hurt me." He said, "OK, bring your butt
   over here." /*íya*/

   He sliced off a kilo of butt. One kilo of flesh that he just cut right
   off and took. /*íya*/

OTHERS:
   [laughter and exclamations]

KASÓLU:
   When the time came, you'd just go off to your house and die. /*íya*/

   Then the next person would come along /*íya*/

   asking for work. /*íya*/

   He'd say, "My king, I've come to ask you for a job. /*íya*/

   I've come to ask you." He'd say, "Well, no problem. /*íya*/

   In the morning, /*íya*/

   just go let out those cows that I've got over there, /*íya*/

   let them out of the pen and bring them outside." /*íya*/

   In the morning the man went and opened the pen right up. /*íya*/

   The cows fell down, *gulululu,* fell down, *gulululu,* all over the
   ground, /*íya*/

   dead. /*íya*/

"I see," he said. He went back and said, "My king—" /íya/

(he replied) He said, "I went like you said and opened the cows' pen over there. All of them fell down on the ground, dead." /íya/

He said, "My boy, did it hurt you?" /íya/

He said, "Yes, my king." The king said, "Bring your butt over here." /íya/

He turned his butt toward the king and went over. The king sliced off one kilo and took it. /íya/

The guy went off and died. /íya/

That's the way it went. He just kept killing people. /íya/ Well, you know what it's like not to have a job. /yes/

[You try even when] they're not playing by the rules.

ANTONÍSI:
Oh, I sure know what wage labor's like![61]

KASÓLU:
Everybody went, and he just kept on killing them, more and more. /íya/

You'd go and he'd say, "Well, I've got this rice field." /íya/

You'd go and he'd say, "Just go and cut the rice." /íya/

You'd touch one stem of rice, to cut it like this, and all of it would fall to the ground, spread out all over the place. /íya/

You'd go and you'd say, "My king, such and such a thing happened to me over there." /íya/

He'd say, "My boy, did it hurt?" You'd say, "Yes, it hurt me. /íya/

It hurt me." "Bring your butt over here." /íya/

But the name of the king— I should have mentioned that. /íya/

The king was "King Nothing Can Hurt Him." /íya/

"The One Nothing Hurts." /íya/

"King Nothing Hurts Him."/íya/

Because nothing hurts him. Not a single thing in the world hurts him at all.[62] /íya/

"Yes," he said. / . . . / Well then, the boy— A young guy was there and he decided to go ask for work. His family didn't want him to. /íya/

His mother didn't want him to. She said, "Child, don't go. The place where you're going to go ask for work— Well, not a single person has gone to ask for work there and returned. /íya/

If you go ask for work there, you're as good as dead and gone. /íya/

Don't go." He said he was determined to go. Then the boy left. /íya/

He arrived there. He said, "My king—" (he replied) / . . . / He said, "I've come to ask you for a job." /íya/

"All right," he said. / . . . / He said, "My boy, do you know who I am?" (he said "no") He said, "I am King Nothing Hurts Him." /íya/

"I see," he said.

AKÓBO:
Had the king told his name like that to all the other ones?

KASÓLU:
Yes. /íya/

He said, "OK, no problem." / . . . / And he went off to the work he had. /íya/

He went off to pick the cacao. /íya/

As he reached up to touch it, all the beans fell down and ran *gululúlu* all over the ground. /íya/

He went back to the king. He said, "King—" (the king replied) /íya/

He said, "Well, I went to touch the cacao over there to harvest it, and it fell off all over the ground. /íya/

It all broke off and fell down before I even touched it." /íya/

He said, "My boy, did it hurt?" /íya/

The boy said, "No. My king, it didn't hurt me." /íya/

He said, "OK." [long pause] He said [with exaggerated nonchalance:] "Well, no problem. /íya/

It's all right." He said, "Let's go to sleep for the night." In the morning he said, "Well, my boy?" (he replied) /íya/

"I'd like you to go harvest a field of rice I've got over there. /íya/

Just go on and cut the rice." /íya/

He went off, reached out to cut a stalk of rice, and they all fell and covered the whole area, *gulululu*. /*íya*/

He went back, and he said, "My king—" (he replied) "I went to cut the rice over there, /*íya*/

and all the stalks fell over, /*íya*/

to the ground." /*íya*/

He said, "My boy, didn't it hurt?" He said, "No. /*íya*/

How could it have hurt me?" /*íya*/

(he said "OK")

AKÓBO:
   It wasn't his rice, after all.

KASÓLU:
   So nothing happened. The next morning, he said, "I'd like you to let out some chickens I've got over there." /*íya*/

He went to let them out. /*íya*/

But as he opened the door, all the chickens fell down on the ground, /*íya*/

dead.

KANDÁMMA [breaking in]:
   Now, back at that time, I was right there. /KASÓLU: *íya*/

And at that time, a great famine was destroying the world. /*íya*/

So the birds were going off to Great God to ask about a certain fruit that was there, and whether they could eat it. /*íya*/

Not a single person knew its name, so they couldn't eat that fruit. /*íya*/

They kept going until there was no one left, and then Hummingbird said he would go too. /*íya*/

He'd go ask Great God what tree's fruit that was, and whether it was good to eat. /*íya*/

So off he went, and he said to the others, "Well, since I'm going off here—" (they replied) "There's a song I'm going to sing, /*íya*/

and you must all sing the chorus and keep on singing it, without stopping, until I get back to the ground." /*íya*/

Even with the hunger they were dying from. /*íya*/

So as he left he sang:

Alungwénu gánwe, tántan mayóo.
Alungwénu gánwe, tántan mayóo.
Alungwénu gánwe, tántan mayóo.
Alungwénu gánwe, tántan mayóo.
Alungwénu gánwe, tántan mayóo.
Alungwénu gánwe, tántan mayóo.
Alungwénu gánwe, tántan mayóo.
Alungwénu gánwe, tántan mayóo.
Alungwénu gánwe, tántan mayóo-ooo yoo, tántan mayóo.
Tántan mayóo-yoo, tántan mayóo, tántan mayóo,
Alungwénu gánwe, tántan mayóo.
Alungwénu gánwe, tántan mayóo.
Alungwénu gánwe, tántan mayóo.
Alungwénu gánwe, tántan mayóo.
Alungwénu gánwe, tántan mayóo.
Alungwénu gánwe, tántan mayóo-ooo yoo, tántan mayóoyóo.
Tántan mayóo, tántan mayóo, tántan mayóyóyóyóyó.
Tántan mayóo, tántan mayóo, tántan mayóo.
Alungwénu gánwe, tántan mayóo.

Alungwénu gánwe, tántan mayóo.
Alungwénu gánwe, tántan mayóo.
Alungwénu gánwe, tántan mayóo.
Alungwénu gánwe, tántan mayóo.
Alungwénu gánwe, tántan mayóo.
Alungwénu gánwe, tántan mayóo-ooo yoo, tántan mayóo.
Tántan mayóo, tántan mayóo, tántan mayóyóyóyóyó.

[Hummingbird sings *alungwénu gánwe* and the others chorus *tántan mayóo*. The song is accompanied by rhythmic clapping and the dance of Hummingbird—Kandámma's subtle bump and grind, with arms outstretched to the sides and fingers flapping. Each of the other birds had tried out a name (asking Great God if it was correct), but none had guessed correctly. Hummingbird's attempt, which he sang all the way up and all the way back, turned out to be right.]

And Hummingbird was dancing. The way he was dancing there was "*alungwénu gánwe.*"

OTHERS:
[laughter]

KASÓLU:
OK, well, nothing to it. Now where were we? OK, I remember the story now. Here's where we were. /ANTONÍSI: *íya*/

[rapid-fire:] As things fell, he would take something and just kill them right off. It didn't bother him if things fell. This was a kid who wasn't hurt by anything. /*íya*/

He'd just cut things down.

AKÓBO:
Nothing hurt him— just like the king.

KASÓLU [still speaking rapidly]:
Nope! He'd just cut it down and kill it. The king said, "Well, man— My boy—" (he replied) He said, "In the morning you'll go and open a cow pen I've got over there." /*íya*/

He opened it— [Correcting himself:] No, he'd already let the cows out, and this time he was letting the chickens out. /*íya*/

The king said, "OK, let out some ducks." /*íya*/

He went to let them out. /*íya*/

Whoosh!! Flap! They just kept on coming out and falling down. That finished every one of them off, just cut them up, dead! /íya/

He went back and said, "My king, those ducks I went to let out, well, such and such a thing happened." He said, "Well, my boy, did it hurt you?" and the boy said, "My king, it didn't hurt me."

A WOMAN:
He's run into someone just like himself.

KASÓLU:
"Oh," he said. Well, this kept going on and one until there was nothing left in that place. I don't need to list all that was gone. There was absolutely nothing left. /íya/

He'd killed everything. /íya/

All that was left was some pigs he had. /íya/

So he said, "Well, my boy—" They slept until they woke up the next morning. He said, "My boy—" (he replied) He said, "Go open up the pigpen over there." /íya/

So he went to let out the pigs. The pigs all fell down. /íya/

So he jumped out and he clubbed them all to death. /íya/

Cut them all up. Cut off their tails and took them. /íya/

Then he buried those tails, and took the rest of the pigs' bodies and hid them off in the underbrush. /íya/

He just buried those tails till all that was left aboveground was a teeny-tiny bit. /íya/

He buried those tails. You know how pigs' tails are. He took the rest of them off into the forest. And he buried them so the tips were barely sticking up. /íya/

AKÓBO:
The boy did?

KASÓLU:
Mm-hmm.

AKÓBO:
Did he intend to eat them?

KASÓLU:
What did you say?

AKÓBO:
Wasn't he going to eat them?

KASÓLU:

He just did it to make a problem with the king. / . . . / He killed absolutely all of them. /íya/

Then he came out and he ran to him. He went straight to his king. [Feigning concern and urgency:] "My king, my king!" he said. (he replied) He said, "I went to go let out the pigs—" (he replied) "And all of them burrowed down under the ground! /íya/

So I ran back to tell you!" /íya/

OTHERS:

[laughter]

KASÓLU:

The king said [very agitated]: "Where?" He said, "Over there!" The king said, "Let's go!" /íya/

[Kasólu adopts a hurried, jerky style, which lasts through his next ten "segments."] He ran off, and when he arrived he looked around. Now, the way they were buried, the pigs' tails went deep into the ground, and only a little piece was sticking up so you couldn't grab it to pull it out.

AKÓBO:

No way!

KASÓLU:

They grabbed them as tight as they could. The king said, "This won't work. You know what we'll do?" "What?" said the boy. "Run back to my wife, in the house over there.

OTHERS:

[laughter]

KASÓLU:

Go have her give you a shovel. /íya/

OTHERS:

[more laughter]

KASÓLU:

Quick! Bring it back." /íya/

The boy— The kid ran back there. /íya/

He really ran fast to get there, and he said, "Quick! Hurry up, as fast as you can. My king says to!" ("all right" she said) So then he told her— He said, "My king says to tell you— Well, what he says is that I should 'live' with you."

OTHERS:

[exclamations and laughter]

KASÓLU:

"What are you telling me?!!" she said. "Yes," he said. /íya/

"Quick! Quick! Quick! That's what he said!" She said, "No way!" The king turned and shouted back to her, "Quick! Give it to him quick! Give it to him quick! /íya/

Give it to him right away!" /íya/

She said, "OK, I hear you." The king shouted [in Sranan]: "Give it to him! Give it to him! Give it to him! Fast! Fast!" /íya/

OTHERS:

[hysterical laughter]

KASÓLU:

That's what he said. [in rapid-fire Sranan]: "Give him! Give him! Give him! Give him! Give him!" /íya/

[Slowing down to a more normal pace:] The boy had already taken the wife and thrown her down on the bed. And then he went to work. Well, that shovel that the king sent the boy back for, in a rush, so they could dig up the pigs— Well, the boy didn't bring it back so quickly. He was gone for quite a while, and finally the king said, "Something's wrong." He ran *gaagaa,* back to the house, looked in, and the boy was on top of his lady.

OTHERS:

[exclamations]

KASÓLU:

He said— He fell over backward and just lay there. The boy said, "My king, did this hurt you?" He said, "Yes, this hurt me." The boy said, "Bring your butt over here!"

OTHERS:

[wild laughter]

KASÓLU:

The king turned his butt toward the boy and backed on over. He brought his butt over. The boy lopped off a kilo. The king died. And that's why things are the way they are for us. Otherwise, it would have been that whenever you asked for work from a white man, a king, he'd kill you. [pause] The boy took care of all that for us.

AKÓBO:
What hasn't changed is that they still lop off your ass at Kourou.

KASÓLU:
That's as far as my story goes. Because that was one thing that did hurt. He had claimed nothing hurt him. But that in fact did. There's where my story ends.

[There follows a several-minute period of overlapping voices, laughing, and rehashing the story, after which Kasólu apparently says *"Mató!"*]

A MAN:
Tòngôni![63]

KASÓLU [speaking at a fairly sleepy, plodding pace for the first several minutes of this tale, gradually accelerating until, around his mention of the magic word, he is back at his normal speech]:
So, well, there they were. /THE MAN: *íya*/

Well, that is— Well, Goat was going to look for a garden site. /*íya*/

OTHER VOICES:
[background conversation, as people settle in, not yet having turned their full attention to the tale]

KASÓLU:
So Goat went to choose a site in the forest /*íya*/

and he set up a palm-leaf structure for divination.[64] /*íya*/

He got it all ready. /*íya*/

Then he went away and the next morning /*íya*/

he came back again. He came back at dawn, came back to spend time there, /*íya*/

to start cutting the underbrush. As he worked, he looked up, /*íya*/

and he saw the big man himself: Claw-fist [Jaguar]. /*íya*/

He'd gone to find a garden site too, /*íya*/

right next to where Goat had. /*íya*/

They cleared their gardens. Mmm, cleared the gardens. That fellow Goat cleared his garden, cleared his garden, cleared his garden. The other man is also clearing his. After a while: "Friend, how are you?" He said, "I'm fine, Brother." /*íya*/

("yes" he said) They kept clearing the sites, ohh, just kept right on working. /*íya*/

Goat cleared his garden site and burned it. /íya/

The big man himself cleared his garden site and burned it. /that's right/

They made a camp to live in. They became friends. /íya/

Because when you live right next door to a person, you become friends.

THE MAN:

You become allies.

KASÓLU:

So there they were, and one day the big man went off hunting, /íya/

and later he returned. They were already settled in. /íya/

The big man went off hunting and then he returned. /íya/

He went over here, and he shot some meat. /íya/

He made a nice palm-leaf wrapper to bring the meat back. [long pause] He made it. He brought the meat back and set it down. Now what meat do you think he killed there?

THE MAN:

Tell us, what meat did he kill?

KASÓLU:

Goat meat. /íya/

He picked off one of the other goats, and he brought it back in the palm-leaf wrapper and set it down right there. He said [in a studiedly offhand tone], "Friend! Friend, I went hunting, Brother. /íya/

Didn't get much. /íya/

But here's a little meat. You can go cut it up." /íya/

(he said "yes") Goat went. /íya/

Hm! He went to look. /íya/

He went, "hmmm" and came back to the house. /íya/

Well, OK, so he opened up the palm-leaf wrapper and he butchered the meat. /íya/

He cut up the meat till it was all done. /íya/

He said, "Here. Take it to the children. Take it and give it to your children." /íya/

Abátelí butchering a hunting kill, 1968.

(he said "yes") And then he took it. Brother, what's he supposed to do? The guy's too much for him. /íya/

That's just the way it was, things kept on like that. After a while the guy went hunting again. At dawn, /íya/

he went hunting and returned. He killed some meat, /íya/

and brought it back. /íya/

A MAN:
Were goats the only game in the forest?

KASÓLU:
He killed a goat. /íya/

He said [in a casual voice], "My friend, I've been hunting, Brother. Didn't get much. /íya/

There's some meat over there. You can cut it up. /íya/

Goat went over. He said, "Mmmm." His children called him over. They said [in a hushed voice], "Father, it's our people, only ours, that Jaguar— that Jaguar's killing." /íya/

He said, "Yes." /íya/

They went on like this for some time, and then Jaguar said, "Well, you know what?" /íya/

He said, "Yes." /íya/

AKÓBO:
When they take the meat, do they cook it and eat it?

KASÓLU:
Well, what else could you do? They put it aside. They put it aside. They both eat it and put it aside. /íya/

AKÓBO:
Their very own people!

KASÓLU:
Jaguar said, "Well, you know what? I've been hunting, Friend. I've been off hunting. /íya/

It's been many days— two days or three days already. Here we are working together. /íya/

[in a studiedly offhand manner:] Well, it's time for you to do some hunting too." /íya/

He said, "Really?" He said, "Yes." /íya/

Hm! And what's happening is that the other ones, the children of Jaguar, are laughing [gleefully] "héééi. There's meat in the house!" /íya/

They're teasing Goat. Well, Goat knows very well that they've been killing goats. Goat is sitting there in the house right next to the old man. /íya/

There's meat in the house indeed! /íya/

AKÓBO:
There's meat in the house, and as for Goat— If they want to, they'll just kill him.

KASÓLU:
Right. /íya/

Goat didn't know what to do. Goat entered the forest. He went off to hunt. He walked along and cried a lot. He didn't know what to do. /íya/

Well, if he didn't kill some meat, Jaguar would— If they ran out of meat, he and his children would be eaten. Mm!

KANDÁMMA:
Why couldn't he just leave that place?

KASÓLU:
Well, the way he went to choose a garden site and the guy followed him like that, and cleared a site right next to him— What could you do? /íya/

AYETIMÍ:
Yeah, 'cause while you were sleeping, I'd come slit your throat.

KASÓLU:
So he's walking along and walking along and finally he got to a savanna. He lay down and went to sleep. /íya/

He just didn't know what to do anymore. /íya/

After a while he turned around and saw something. /íya/

It was the chief of the forest, the bird.[65] /íya/

He'd come there. /íya/

He said, "What's wrong? Why do you look so worried?" Goat's crying so much he doesn't know what's happening. He said, "Look here." (he said "yes") He said, "Brother, I went off to find myself a garden site to clear, /íya/

and to make a place to live next to it. The animal came to live there with me. /íya/

KANDÁMMA [trying to break in]:
At that moment I was right there.

KASÓLU [not hearing her]:
Every time he goes hunting, when he comes back he's killed a goat. /íya/

The way things are, the guy just goes off hunting and comes back."

AKÓBO [to Kasólu]:
'Mmá says she was right there.

KASÓLU [to Kandámma]:
You were there?

KANDÁMMA:
Yes. I was right there.

KASÓLU:
And what was it like, 'Mmá?

KANDÁMMA:

Well, the little drum didn't exist at that time.[66]

KASÓLU:

Not at all!

KANDÁMMA:

It was off in the forest where the devil lived. /KASÓLU: that's right/

And then a boy went to take it. /well, that's right/

They told him— They said, "There isn't any little drum here. But it does exist in a certain devil's village. /well, that's right/

The boy said he could go get it. /íya/

Then he set off and went along till he got to where the devil lived. The devil had gone fish drugging, /that's right/

he'd gone off to drug a stream. The boy took the little drum and set it down. He played it, *Timm. Timm. Timm, timm.*

kô-ni an - go - lééé. Mba-mu-tjaan-ga a-kí tjó-ló-lóó,

kô-ni an - go - lééé.

Zan zan zan kilómbo-éé!
Tim, tim, zan zan zan kilómbo.
Oléle mbamuma ta lóntu búsi, oléle mbamutjanga akí tjólólóó.
Kôni angolééé, mbamutjaanga akí tjólólóó, kôni angolééé.
Mbamutjaanga akí tjólólóó, kôni angolééé.
Mbamutjaanga akí tjólólóó, kôni angolééé.
Mbamutjaanga akí tjólólóó, kôni angolééé. /íya/

Kôni angolééé, mbamutjaanga akí tjólólóó, kôni angolééé.
Mbamutjaanga akí tjólólóó, kôni angolééé.
Mbamutjaanga akí tjólólóó, kôni angolééé.

[This song is accompanied by clapping and weak chorusing. Some Saramakas suggested that when the boy sings *"zan zan kilómbo"* he is calling out the devil's name and that *"kôni angolééé"* is his own praise name ("Cunning Angoléé"), but the appearance of almost identical (nonnormal Saramaccan) words in a completely different song/tale nugget (p. 327) casts considerable doubt on the usefulness of word-by-word interpretations of this kind. At the same time such comparison suggests the possibility that African-language phrases have been "retained" wholesale, though they are no longer amenable to semantic analysis by Saramakas. As Kandámma's tale nugget unfolds, the boy's drumming serves as magic to make the devil's groundnuts spill so he has to pick them up, giving the boy time to escape. The tale purports to explain the way both the little drum and groundnuts came to Saramaka.]

The devil jumped out, *vúúú!* /íya/

He said, "Whoever's fooling with that drum of mine, it's me and him today!!" /íya/

The boy grabbed the drum and got out of there in a hurry. /íya/

He ran till he got to the path and set it down. He played it: *Timm. Timm. Timm.*

ASABÔSI [talking over Kandámma's voice]:
I would have snuck quietly off with it. I wouldn't have played it anymore.

KANDÁMMA:
He came back with it. He brought it back to the village. /íya/

Timm, timm.

> *Zan zan zan kilómbo-éé!*
> *Tim. Tim. Zan zan zan kilómbo.*
> *Oléle mbamuma ta lóntu búsi, oléle mbamutjanga akí tjólólóó.*
> *Kôni angolééé, mbamutjaanga akí tjólólóó, kôni angolééé.*

The boy brought it all the way back to his village. /íya/

The devil himself [who had been off in the forest] set out. /íya/

He's running after the drum and he got to— He got to his own village. He went into his two-story house. /íya/

He went and took a gourd groundnut container.[67] /íya/

He's running and running and he's getting very worked up. He banged the groundnut gourd, *gwoo!* and broke it [by mistake]. /íya/

OTHERS:
[laughter]

KANDÁMMA:
He picked up the groundnuts. /íya/

[The devil, chanting:] "*Watjí koónpana, koónpana. Watjí koónpana, koónpana.*" He mended the gourd. He filled it up again.

AKÓBO:
He's closing it up tight.

KANDÁMMA:
Finally the boy arrived in his village with the little drum. /íya/

They took the little drum and carried it inside, went and put it in a house. /íya/

The devil arrived.

KONOI:
He's going to get himself killed.

KANDÁMMA:

He said, "I've come for my drum." /íya/

The people said, "Well, come sit down." /íya/

By that time they'd dug out a hole as big as a sugarcane cauldron there [and built a seat on top, as a trap]. /íya/

He came and sat down on it, *gwuu gwongo hólonmm* [the sound of his falling down into the hole]. /íya/

They took the groundnut gourd and set it down there. They took the little drum. When you see someone who's got lots of ground-nuts, /íya/

that's who got that gourd. /íya/

OVERLAPPING VOICES:

[laughter and exclamations of appreciation]

KASÓLU:

OK, well, what happened— /KASÓLU'S RESPONDER: *íya*/

Well, Goat— The way the old man [Jaguar] was killing things, /íya/

he killed the guy. He went and killed the guy's uncle and brought him back. /íya/

He killed the guy's brother and brought him back. /íya/

The guy's mother he killed and brought back. The animal was doing all this. /íya/

Well, there the guy is. He doesn't know what to do. /íya/

So he went off. He lay down and went to sleep. Then the man [bird] came up to him. /íya/

Of all the birds that fly around here, he was the chief. /íya/

Goat lay down in the savanna and rested for a while, and then the bird turned and went up to him. He got there and said, "What's the matter? What's on your mind that you're crying like that? What in the world could be so terrible?" It was just as if Great God himself had sent the bird there. /íya/

He came up to him just like that. Because everyone in the world was under his care. /íya/

He just came up and asked him what the matter was. /íya/

He explained how such and such had happened, and how the guy had been causing problems for him. /íya/

That the guy had killed so many people in his family and brought them back. That when he arrived, he'd make him butcher them. /íya/

He'd killed the meat and brought it back. When Goat took a look, he saw his uncle. /íya/

He came and he saw his brother. /íya/

He saw his mother. /íya/

And all this was very hard on him. He didn't know what to do anymore. So he was just walking around crying. Jaguar had sent him off and said he should go hunting too. /íya/

He said, "Really?" (he said "yes") /íya/

He pulled one feather from his left wing, /íya/

and gave it to him. /íya/

He said to him, "Well, look here. /íya/

When you go— /íya/

When you go off here, don't go very far. /íya/

Take a quick walk over there. There's a big savanna. It's a jaguar savanna. /íya/

Now take this feather, and once you get there, call out to the jaguar there: 'Hey, Jaguar! Turn and look at me here. /íya/

Just turn and look at me.' Then say, '*Aditô*.'"

KANDÁMMA:
What was that he was supposed to say?

KASÓLU:
Aditô.

KANDÁMMA:
Aditô?

OTHERS:
[laughter]

RESPONDER:
ÍYA!

KASÓLU:
So that's all!

AKÓBO:
I wish things were like that everywhere in the world.

A MAN:
Are you so afraid of things?

A WOMAN:
Yes.

AKÓBO:
I wish it were like that everywhere in the world, so if you called out like that, the thing would just die, dead.

KASÓLU:
So he turned and entered the forest. He went along till, ohh, he got to the savanna. Mmm, it was chock-full of jaguars! /íya/

All over the place! He turned and looked. He said, "Hey, Jaguar, look at me over here!" /íya/

He turned and looked [pause]: "*Aditô!*" /íya/

—as a doornail! /íya/

He went on and made a good palm wrapper, picked it up and put it there. Then Goat really trembled. He brought it and threw it right down on the ground. /íya/

He said, "Uncle—" (he replied) "Well, Brother, I went hunting. /íya/

[imitating the exaggeratedly offhand tone that Jaguar had used with him earlier:] Didn't get much. /íya/

Just got that little bit of meat. /íya/

There it is. You can cut it up." /íya/

ASABÔSI:
Ohh! He brought it to him to butcher!

KASÓLU:
He went. He went to cut it up. /íya/

Then he came back. He went to cut it up and then he came back. He said to his children, "Oh no! Wife! [whispering:] Goat— This thing is really amazing to me! Goat has no gun. He doesn't have anything at all. /íya/

He killed a jaguar and brought it back. It's one of our own people. Ehh!" /íya/

OTHERS:
[laughter]

KASÓLU:

He went and butchered it. Stayed there till the next morning. /íya/

Goat got up and took his hunting sack. It was cock's crow, not even light yet. Goat didn't care what time it was. He went running off into the forest. /íya/

He got to the savanna. There they were, *gwadigwadi* [lots of them]. He said, "Hey, you animal there, turn and look at me here!" He said, [pause] "*Aditô!*"

OTHERS:

[laughter]

KASÓLU:

Finished him off! He made a big palm wrapper, set it on his head, and brought it back. /íya/

Ohhh, he came back, came back with the guy's uncle. He'd already brought back his brother. This time he brought back his uncle, stiff as a board. /íya/

There was Jaguar. He turned and stared at the dead jaguar on the ground there. He said, "Mmm. Unbelievable! /íya/

This is more than I can handle." /íya/

Goat said, "Well, Uncle, I brought back some meat. You can go cut it up." /íya/

He stared at it for a long time and then went into the house. He said to his children, "Something terrible's happening. Things are really falling apart. /íya/

The way Goat is killing things here— I just don't know how to deal with it." /íya/

He butchered. Time passed. In the morning, /íya/

Goat went running back into the forest. / . . . / He went and brought back another one. He brought back the guy's father. /íya/

AKÓBO:

His father? Just like that?

KASÓLU:

He got back. He got back and said, "Well, Uncle, I've brought— I've brought some meat back." /íya/

Well, the jaguars— The jaguars the guy is killing and bringing back— Jaguar didn't know what he used to kill them. It was the most baffling thing in the world to him. Because Goat didn't have a single weapon. /íya/

Jaguar said, "Ohh, How am I going to deal with this situation? Wife! Wife! Wife! Wife, I've brought you to a place where all of us, even our children, will die. As I see it—" /íya/

AKÓBO:
Well, when you clear a garden with someone and then start killing off his people—

KASÓLU:
"As I see it, I've brought you all here to die! Well, because Goat— Well, I've always considered myself a real man. /íya/

But my uncles, my father, my brother— They're even more so. But Goat's cutting them down one after another. The way things are, I can't deal with it. I don't know what to do. I don't have any 'back door.'"[68] /íya/

OTHERS:
[lots of laughter at idea that Jaguar is admitting impotence]

KASÓLU [talking more and more excitedly]:
Now at that moment— Before, the goats had been depressed. But now Goat and his wives and children were really laughing, next to the house there: "titter titter." Now it was their children who were calling out, "There's meat in the house!"

AKÓBO [sarcastically]:
Oh yeah, "There's meat in the house!" That's just what the other ones had said!

KASÓLU:
So then Jaguar arrived. The guy can't handle things and he's not feeling so great. Goat got ready for another day of hunting, /íya/

[adopting a hushed, suspense-filled voice:] and then Jaguar hid [to spy on him]. Goat entered the forest and walked along. He went along. He got to the edge of the savanna. He said, "Aditô!" Quick as could be, he'd killed. He came back home. Oh! He brought his brother— [correcting himself:] his mother, and put her down there. /íya/

He'd already brought back the father and brothers. Now he brought the mother and threw her down there, plunk. /íya/

He brought her and threw her down. /íya/

When that happened, Jaguar said, "Mmmm." Now the jaguar on the ground there was no small specimen! How Goat had managed to carry her back, /íya/

only Great God knew. Jaguar came into the house. He said, "Wife—" (she replied) "I just don't know what to think anymore. Here we are." As soon as he got there— /íya/

(He'd come back first.) /íya/

He said to her there— He said, "The way things are for us, whether we run away or whether we stay here, we've got a real problem with Goat. We're going to run away."

OTHERS:
[laughter at Jaguar's helplessness]

KASÓLU:
(she said "yes") "But if anyone turns around to look back, /íya/

I won't be able to help you. /íya/

OTHERS:
[laughter]

KASÓLU:
The way things are here, Goat is out to get us."

AKÓBO:
He's really getting scared!

KASÓLU:
Goat said, "Uncle—" (he replied) He said, "Well, there's the meat on the ground. I brought some meat back and put it there. You can go ahead and cut it up." /íya/

Jaguar said, "Yes, Brother. OK, I'll go sharpen my machete." He went into the house, going to get his machete. Then Jaguar sharpened his machete. /íya/

Goat said, "Uncle—" (he replied) He said, "What are you doing? / . . . / Aren't you going to come cut up the meat? Come and cut the meat!" /íya/

Jaguar said, "Mmmm. I'm coming."

AKÓBO [with a guffaw]:
Looks like he doesn't want to butcher his mother.

KASÓLU:

Then he kept sharpening the machete. He sharpened the machete, got it very sharp. He said— Well, Goat was getting restless. He glanced over at Jaguar. He said, "Uncle, what's up? Aren't you going to cut the meat? / . . . / Come cut the meat!" Now Goat was just waiting for him to come outside.

AKÓBO:

And now the old man's getting scared. He realizes that Goat's going to kill him.

KASÓLU [laughing]:

The old man was sharpening his machete. He came running out of the house. His wives and children came charging out. They scattered all over.

AKÓBO:

They're going to run away!

KASÓLU:

Ohh, Goat leaped into action. Goat grabbed his hunting sack. /íya/

[Talking excitedly over lots of laughing, as well perhaps as some replies, which we cannot hear because of all the noise:] Goat set out after them. They're running and running for a long time. Then Goat said, "Hey kid, turn around and look at me over here!" The jaguar child turned toward him. He said, "Aditô!" Keeled over. Goat went over and kicked him in the belly with his hoof. It went right through. He went on. After a while he said [to another one], "Hey kid, turn and look at me over here!" The jaguar child turned and looked back— Keeled over. Well, if you had gotten tired, what would you have done? You turn around: "Aditô!" Gone in a flash!

KANDÁMMA:

Is he killing all those animals?

AKÓBO:

He's killing them.

KASÓLU:

He kept on killing them till they were completely wiped out. The wife turned back. He finished them all off. That's why they say that if a person sets himself up somewhere—

AKÓBO [breaking in]:

What about Jaguar himself?

KASÓLU [talking over a lot of laughter and rehashing of the story]:
You shouldn't go bother him. If you think you're better than the
other guy— Well, Great God made all of us. You shouldn't feel as
though you're more of a man than the next guy. Even if you're
stronger than another person, if that person doesn't mess with
you, you shouldn't cause problems, or else Great God will see that
you end up the same way. It would end up like the thing between
Jaguar and Goat. Goat had nothing. But Great God arranged
things so he could kill them. When Goat got home, he called Jaguar to come and butcher the meat. The animal didn't dare come
outside!

AKÓBO:
He called him to butcher his own mother.

KASÓLU:
Jaguar didn't dare come outside! [pause] That's where my story
ends.

[There follows several more minutes of quiet laughing and rehashing
the story, everyone talking at once.]

[Kandámma begins to speak in a soft voice, and its only when she's a
sentence or two into the tale that people quiet down and our tape recorder begins to pick up her tale.]

KANDÁMMA:
—at a certain time, a woman

KASÓLU [calling out over the jumble of voices]:
Íya! Hey, let's listen to the tale, pay attention to the tale!

KANDÁMMA:
had three daughters. /KASÓLU: *íya*/

And there was another woman /*íya*/

who had three sons. /*íya*/

So there they were. And eventually the three daughters grew up,
but without finding husbands, *gbólo! /íya/*

The three sons grew up, but without finding wives, *gbólo! /íya/*

Both the boys' mother /*íya*/

and their father were dead. / . . . / Children, those boys had to
cook for themselves, and it was getting so that just couldn't cope
any more. /*íya*/

The girls didn't have any meat or fish to serve with their rice. /íya/

Well, they had no husbands. /íya/

Well, they went along like this until one day they sat down and called a meeting. /íya/

The three boys said they should go to Great God to ask him what they had done wrong, /íya/

that they had grown up till they were this big, old enough to be married, but they couldn't find wives. /íya/

All they ever did was cook their own food. /íya/

If they planted rice, they were the ones who had to harvest and pound it. /íya/

So what was wrong and how could they fix things? /íya/

That's why they called a meeting. /íya/

Then the middle one /íya/

of those boys /íya/

addressed the oldest one and said, "Well, Older Brother—" (he answered) "You should go. /íya/

Go to Great God." /íya/

The older brother said, "No, man, I can't go." /íya/

The middle one said, "Man, I can't go," but the little one, the mother's last-born child, said, "Well I can go." /íya/

So he set out on the path /íya/

and he just kept going.

AKÓBO [breaking in]:
Great God existed at the time they were doing all this?

KANDÁMMA:
Yes, Great God was there at the time this was happening. /íya/

A MAN:
It's the three brothers who are doing all this?

KANDÁMMA:
Yes, so he went along until he arrived at a village. /íya/

And there he saw a young girl / . . . / hoeing her yard clean. /íya/

He watched her for a long time. [In a voice of gentle, polite concern:] "Young girl there, I see you're really cleaning your yard." /íya/

("yes" she said) "Why is it that you're cleaning the yard?" She said, "Because ever since Great God created me /íya/

and put me here, all I ever do is hoe the yard clean. /íya/

[After pausing:] And where are you going?" He said, "I'm one of three brothers, and not one of us has a wife. We've been dying of neglect, /íya/

so I'm going to see Great God, /íya/

to go ask him what to do." /íya/

She said, "When you go, /íya/

ask him something for me too. /íya/

Tell him that we're three sisters and not a single one of us has a husband. /íya/

Ask him what we've done to deserve this fate." /íya/

AKÓBO [in a deprecating tone]:
Couldn't they just have gotten together on all this?!

KANDÁMMA:
The boy walked off, and he went along until he came to another place. /íya/

He saw a woman /íya/

cutting wood. /íya/

she said, "Boy, where are you going?" and he said, "I'm going to ask Great God what we've done to deserve being left without wives." /that's right/

She said, "Boy, when you go, ask Great God for me what it is I've done wrong /íya/

that I'm stuck here just cutting wood and cutting wood until I could die."

AKÓBO:
That's all she ever does?!!

AYETIMÍ:
If all you ever do is the same work over and over again— You call that living?!

KANDÁMMA:
He went along some more until he arrived. /íya/

He arrived at a citrus tree. /íya/

The citrus tree asked him, "Boy, where are you going?" and he said, "I'm one of three brothers, /íya/

and not one of us has a wife. We've been dying of neglect. /íya/

So I'm going to Great God to ask him what we've done to deserve this fate." /íya/

He said, "Well, when you go, /íya/

ask him something for me too. Tell him I keep making tremendous numbers of blossoms, /íya/

and then I keep dropping them. I can't seem to hold on to the fruit. /íya/

So what have I done wrong that I can't hold on to the fruit?" /íya/

("yes" he said) People keep giving him more and more messages. Then he came to a woman. /íya/

The woman said, "Boy, where are you going?" and he said, "I'm going to Great God," /íya/ and she said, "Oh yes, /íya/

when you go, ask Great God something for me. Ever since I was born, I've done nothing but clean yards and the hoe is just about killing me and I can't even throw it down. /íya/

So what have I done to deserve being stuck with this hoe in my hand?" /íya/

He got to an old man. /íya/

The man had an ax in his hand, and he said, "When you go, ask for me why it is that the ax here is stuck in my hand." /íya/

ASABÔSI:
He can't just drop it on the ground?!

A FEW VOICES:
[laughter]

KANDÁMMA:
Isn't the boy carrying an awful lot of messages?

KASÓLU:
They're really a lot!

KANDÁMMA:
Well, anyway, he continued along, and he continued on his way to Great God. /íya/

He arrived at a big pond.[69] /íya/

There was an anaconda in the pond, and it was in charge of carrying people across the water there. /íya/

So it slithered on over, *zalalalala*. /íya/

It said, "Where are you going?" and the boy said, "I'm going to Great God" and it said, "OK, come on and I'll take you across the water. /íya/

Where are you going?" The boy said, "I'm going to consult Great God, to tell him that we're three brothers and not one of us has a wife. /íya/

So I'm going to ask him what we've done wrong that we're stuck without wives." /íya/

(the anaconda replied) It said, "Child, when you go, /íya/

ask him something for me too. Tell him this is where I've always been. /íya/

Ever since he made me, I've always been here in this pond, till this very day. /íya/

There's no way for me to leave this place, and I'm dying of hunger 'cause there's nothing here for me to eat. /íya/

Ask him what I should do so I can walk around and look for something to eat. /íya/

Will you take the message for me?" ("yes" he said) Then he left. /íya/

He continued on until he arrived /íya/

and consulted Great God. /íya/

Great God said, "Hmm, is that what you came about?" (he said "yes") "Well, when you go—" /íya/

("yes" he said) "You see those three girls without husbands?" /íya/

("yes?" he said) "Those are the wives that I made for you three brothers. /íya/

When you go—" ("yes" said the boy) "You should take those three girls as wives. /íya/

When you go, you'll give them to your brothers. One person takes one, another takes the second, and you have one too." /íya/

("OK" he said) "And when you get there, tell the anaconda something. /íya/

Tell it that it should find a person to swallow. /íya/

And when it has finished swallowing the person, the stretching out that it will do will stretch it out all the way to the river /íya/

and there it will find something to eat." /íya/

ASABÔSI:
If it were me, I wouldn't give that message.

KANDÁMMA:
"And when you go back—" /íya/

("yes" said the boy) "Well, the hoe that you saw there in the woman's hand— You just take it from her and throw it to the ground. /íya/

Then take that woman along. That's your own mother. /íya/

And the man you saw with the ax— Just pull the ax out of his hand /íya/

and throw it to the ground, and take him along with you. He's your father." /íya/

("yes" said the boy) "Then take those three girls. /íya/

Just take them. They're wives for the three of you. /íya/

And you should tell the citrus tree, /íya/

tell it that there are three barrels of money in the ground at its base." /íya/

AKÓBO:
Ehh!

KANDÁMMA:
"It should ask someone to dig out those three barrels of money /íya/

for it. Then, when it bears more fruit, it will hold on to it." /íya/

AYETIMÍ:
I myself would be happy to do the digging.

ASABÔSI:
You'd do that, wouldn't you!

KANDÁMMA:
(the boy agreed) Then he set out. /íya/

KASÓLU:
Isn't someone going to cut this tale?

ASABÓSI:

Man, my throat isn't in shape for singing at all, man.

KANDÁMMA:

"I'm back!" /íya/

"You're back, Boy?" It was the anaconda. /íya/

"Yes," said the boy. "Father?" (the anaconda replied) He said, "Take me across. Once you get me across the water, /íya/

I'll be able to give you the message." /íya/

KASÓLU:

Isn't there anybody who can cut this tale for us?

ASABÓSI:

My throat isn't up to singing.

KANDÁMMA:

It took the boy across. /íya/

It carried him across the water, on and on until /íya/

they hit shore. It said, "Give me the message, quick as you can! /íya/

You did bring a reply for me, didn't you?" "Yes, I brought it. But Father, wait a minute." /íya/

Then the boy climbed up till he was far from the edge of the water. /íya/

And he said [calling out in a loud voice, since he was very far away], "Great God said—" /íya/

("yes" said the snake) "He said you should find a person /íya/

to catch and swallow up. /íya/

Then, once you've swallowed him, the stretching that person will make you do, that stretching will help get you to the river and you'll find things to eat. /íya/

When you get to the river, you'll be all set to wander around eating." /íya/

It said [in a loud voice, drawing out the syllables], "C-O-M-E, B-O-Y, L-E-T M-E S-W-A-L-L-O-W Y-O-U.

OTHERS:

[laughter]

KANDÁMMA:
C-O-M-E, L-E-T M-E S-W-A-L-L-O-W Y-O-U." "OK, Father, I'm going off but I'll be right back." /íya/

Swish! He was off and on his way. /íya/

He pulled the ax from the old man's hand and threw it down. Then the boy, /íya/

as it happened, came upon a horse.

AKÓBO:
He found a horse and was already on its back?

KANDÁMMA:
He found a horse and was on its back. /íya/

He pulled the ax from the old man's hand and threw it to the ground. /íya/

He put the old man on the horse. /íya/

He got to the old woman, pulled the hoe from her hand, threw it on the ground, took the woman, and put her on the horse. /íya/

He went on to the three girls. He took the three girls. He put them on the horse. /íya/

He got to the citrus tree. He gave it the message. The citrus tree said, "Boy, don't go. Do the digging for me." /íya/

The boy dug at the base of the citrus tree till he got the three barrels of money and loaded them on the horse's back. /íya/

Then he went on.

AKÓBO:
He was giving it its fruit.

KANDÁMMA:
Right, its fruit.

ASABÔSI:
Hey, kids, someone should cut this tale. I can't sing the songs.

KASÓLU:
Íya.

KANDÁMMA:
He continued along and along.

AKÓBO:
My god, can't some man help out here?! [by cutting the tale]

KANDÁMMA:

When he arrived, they said, "Hey, man, you're back?" (he answered) /íya/

"Older Brother?" (the brother replied) "I'm back! /íya/

Older Brother—" (he replied) "You know the oldest one of the three girls there?" ("yes" he said) "Great God says she's for you." /íya/

[To the second brother:] "Man—" (he replied) "The other one, the middle one—" ("yes" he said) "Great God said she's for you." ("OK" he said) "And the youngest one— /íya/

Since I'm the youngest, she's for me." /íya/

("yes" the others said) Then the boy went and took one barrel of the money /íya/

and gave it to the oldest brother, and he took the second barrel. /íya/

He gave it to the middle brother. /íya/

He took the last barrel for himself. /íya/

He took the old woman and the old man. He set them up in a house. /íya/

AKÓBO:

Was that their mother?

KANDÁMMA:

Yes. /íya/

They went along for a while like that. /íya/

Then one of the brothers said that the wife his brother brought him wasn't the one he wanted. /íya/

It was the oldest brother: "I don't want her. /íya/

That woman you brought back to me here. Man, I don't want her. I'm older than you. Who do you think you are to go find a wife for me?! /íya/

I don't like this one. I'm going to go look for one myself." /íya/

OTHERS:

[clucks of disapproval]

KANDÁMMA:

"Older brother?" (he answered) "See those women Great God gave me to bring back here?" /íya/

("yes" he said) "Don't go off! Don't go off to look for another wife! Great God already gave us wives." /íya/ The oldest brother said, "I'm not going to change my mind."

ASABÓSI:

Won't somebody cut this tale, my god?!

AKÓBO:

You men should cut it. Those machetes you carry around with you, what about using them?

KASÓLU:

All I could do would be to make something up.

AKÓBO:

Well, make it up then, and let's hear it!

KASÓLU:

I always forget the songs when I sing, and it ends up being a half-assed thing.

[There is silence for about ten seconds, while people wait for someone to cut the tale.]

ASABÓSI:

'Mmá, at that time, I was already there. /KANDÁMMA: Aah./

Well, at a certain time in the history of the world, people weren't able to go off into the forest to go hunting. /not at all!/

There was a devil in the forest. Whenever he saw a person come along, he'd eat you up. Then one man took a stick and fashioned it, until it was just the way he wanted. /true/

And then he stood there. He sang:

A-sí-na-lóón - pu, Ta-tá A-sí-na-lóón-pu, ku zaan-zaan

tín-gi-ee.   A-sí-na-lóón - pu, Ta-tá A-sí-na-lóón-pu,

ku zaan-zaan tín-gi-ee. A púu di ma-má, ma-má si-na.

Gan-gan fu A-la-kwá-ti. Ahai-pá-ki tjó-ló-lóó. ___

Asínalóónpu, Tatá Asínalóónpu, ku zaanzaan tíngi-ee.
Asínalóónpu, Tatá Asínalóónpu, ku zaanzaan tíngi-ee.
A púu di mamá, mamá sina.
Gangan fu Alakwáti.
Ahaipáki tjólólóó.

[In the tale to which this tale nugget alludes, the man rids the forest of the devil by calling him names, "Father Asínalóónpu Who Stinks" and "Bigman from Alakwáti" (lines 1–2, 4–5) and insulting his mother (line 3), inciting him to come out and fight so he can be killed. Asabôsi's speech defect renders lines 3–5 of our transcription tentative.[70]]

Continue your story.

KANDÁMMA:
Children, the older brother said he wouldn't have that wife. He'd go look for one himself. /KASÓLU: *íya*/

So he set off. /*íya*/

The youngest brother said, "Older brother?" (he replied) He said, "Don't go off looking for a wife!" /*íya*/

AKÓBO:
"Don't go get killed. We've already found wives."

KANDÁMMA:
"Let's just take the ones we've got." The older brother said, "I don't want the wife you gave me. I'm going to look for one on my own." /*íya*/

And he set off, and continued till he got /*íya*/

to the pond. /*íya*/

He saw the anaconda. /*íya*/

It slithered on over to him. /íya/

It said: [long pause] /íya/

"Boy, where are you going?" He said, "I'm going to see Great God." It said, "Come and I'll take you across." /íya/

("OK" he said) It stuck out its head, gwákáá. By the time the boy had come up to climb onto its head, /íya/

it snapped its mouth onto him, gbá! It grabbed him gbá! gulululu, and pulled him into the water. /íya/

It entwined itself around him.

ASABÔSI:
He's already in the river!

KANDÁMMA:
And then it starts swallowing him. It swallowed him all the way. Then it stretched until it finished stretching. /íya/

and it slid on over to the river. And as you see, it's been in the river ever since.

AKÓBO:
The boy did this to himself. Or maybe it was the anaconda's "soul" [akáa] that got the boy to come there.

KANDÁMMA:
That's right. It swallowed him up completely, and that's how it came to live in the river.

The wife that had been given to the brother /íya/

remained there. The two brothers took care of her as a sister-in-law, /íya/

since she didn't have a husband anymore. /íya/

Her husband went off and got himself killed. That's why, if one of your relatives treats you well, once you see the good that the person's brought you, /íya/

you should accept what you've been given. You should appreciate what you have.

KASÓLU:
Want to hear some more?

A WOMAN:
Sure do!

KASÓLU:
You want to hear one I've got? It's long!

KANDÁMMA [with enthusiasm]:
Yes, tell it!

KASÓLU:
All right. *Mató!* [71]

A MAN [in the midst of lots of competing conversation all around]:
Tòngôni!

KASÓLU [after waiting for things to quiet down a little]:
There they were.

[More general shuffling around and talking. A few adults tell children where to sit or lie down if they're getting sleepy. Kandámma says that as far as she's concerned, the reason she's sitting there is to hear tales, and even if they last till the sun comes up, that's what she's going to do.]

THE MAN:
Íya!

KASÓLU:
One woman,

KANDÁMMA:
Yes!

KASÓLU:
well, she had three sons. /THE MAN: *íya*/

And she had three daughters. /*íya*/

Well, now, she asked them—

AKÓBO [calling out to Kabuési]:
Woman, let's just listen to this one and then we'll leave.

KABUÉSI:
No, Momma! I'm not feeling well. Just as sure as you see me sitting here, my belly's killing me!

KASÓLU [simultaneous with Kabuési's remark]:
Well I asked them if they already knew this one or if they wanted to stay and hear it. It's long. /right!/

Because if not, I could have made it real short, but that's not possible now since I've already begun it. I'll just have to go on.

AYETIMÍ:
> Just go ahead with the story.

AKÓBO:
> Tell it anyway. Tell the story and we'll just do our best to sit
> through it.

KASÓLU [playfully]:
> You should stay here and listen to the thing. It's one you've never
> heard before. What're you bitching about?

AKÓBO:
> Let's just listen to this one and then we'll go home.

A MAN:
> Tell it. Tell it just to me. I'd like to hear it.

AKÓBO:
> Go ahead and tell it, kid.

KASÓLU:
> OK, so she had three daughters and she had three sons. /íya/

AKÓBO:
> Just go ahead and tell it, however it's supposed to be. Hey guys,
> you should be giving replies for the tale!

THE RESPONDER:
> *Íya!*

KASÓLU:
> So then she said to them, "Well, here we are together. /íya/
>
> Yes, well, you're all here with me now, but the time will come /íya/
>
> for me to die, so how are you planning to honor me at my funeral?"

AKÓBO:
> [guffaw]

KASÓLU:
> The daughters said, "Well, Mother—" (she answered) One of
> them said, "When that happens—"

[At this point, people are still shuffling around, talking to each other,
not yet giving full attention to the tale.]

> ("yes" she said) "Well, when people come to your funeral—" /íya/
>
> ("yes" she said) "As people arrive here—" /íya/

(she replied) "I'll spread out a feast, cook things for them really well." ("yes" she said) /íya/

One said, "When they arrive here, no one /íya/

will go hungry." The other one was gong to take care of all the washing. /íya/

They'd do all the things that women officials [basiá mujêè] do. /íya/

One said that absolutely no one would go hungry /íya/

for the whole time the funeral rites were going on. /íya/

And the other one was going to take care of the washing. The mother said, "You'll be giving me a proper burial indeed." /íya/

She said to one of them, "Woman, you'll really be burying me well." /íya/

The last one said, "Every young man who comes here—" /íya/

("yes" she said) "I'll tie his belly [with a cloth, as a ritual protection and sign of gratitude].[72] /íya/

As soon as he gets here, I'll help him out of his canoe as quick as a flash."

THE RESPONDER:
Íya. Your story's really going!

KASÓLU:
"What a good way to help bury me!" /íya/

The mother said, "And boys, what will you do?" /íya/

One of the brothers said, /íya/

"Mother—" (she answered) "No one's neck will be strong enough to carry your coffin. /íya/

The goods— the goods that I'll load into it will really be something to see!" /íya/

Another one spoke up and said, "Mother—" (she replied) He said, "Those people—" ("yes" she said) "Rice with plain water is one food they won't be eating [because he'll do a lot of hunting], /íya/

from the moment you die until the end of your funeral." /íya/

She said, "Children, that would be a fine funeral indeed!" /íya/

Well, it wasn't more than three days later— / . . . / [Backtracking to mention something he'd forgotten to include:] The other brother— After the two brothers had spoken, the other one of the brothers said, "Mother—" (she replied) (There was no such thing as a drum.) /íya/

He said, "Well, no matter. /íya/

When you die—" ("yes" she said) "Well, people say that 'Drum' is out there where the devil lives. /íya/

Well, I'll go and get Drum, and at the head of your grave—" ("yes" she said) "I'll be sure to play the drum /íya/

for your funeral. I'll go take the drum and bring it back to play at your funeral, even if they've gotten up to the burial itself—" (she replied) "I'll be sure to bring it back and bury you /íya/

with the drum." "Yes," she said, /íya/

"That's fine. That's a good way to bury me, children." Well, less than three days went by. The mother was gone. /íya/

She died. /íya/

OTHERS:
[exclamations of concern]

KASÓLU:
Well, that was that. You just couldn't find words to describe the mother's funeral. Mm! There was plenty of meat and fish. /íya/

There was rice. They put so many goods in the coffin! It was so heavy it could hardly be lifted. /íya/

The daughter— The men couldn't arrive without being taken care of. /íya/

As soon as another one came, she'd take care of you, /íya/

another one would arrive. She'd take care of you. /íya/

Another one would come. The funeral got really big. The men were coming from all over, word spread to all the villages around.

AKÓBO [breaking in]:
The word went out that cloths were being given out.

KASÓLU:
Cloths were being tied on bellies right and left! /íya/

The other son was out hunting like something else! Everyone who came was treated really well. The other child was washing things for people, really taking care of everyone. The last child set out right away, fast as could be. /íya/

He started out. /íya/

He went along, and he arrived at a pond. /íya/

It was a big pond, almost like a sea. /íya/

And there he saw a cayman. He'd brought a parrot feather /íya/

and a ball of kaolin and a cowrie shell. /íya/

And he saw a cayman. /íya/

Well, the devils— That was the devils' boat there. /íya/

And the drum that they had was over on the other side of the water. /íya/

So the boy got there and called the cayman and asked it to take him across. And as they were crossing—

ASABÔSI [breaking in]:
Hey there, man! /KASÓLU: íya/

The drum that they went to get— /íya/

Do you know how he played it as he brought it back?

KASÓLU:
How did he play it?

ASABÔSI:

Kaa-díí, kaa-díí, ki-tóó - le-ya —oo.

Ki-sa-má-oo ki-sa-má, ki-sa-má-oo ki-sa-má,

ki-sa-má-oo ki-sa-má. Kaa-díí, ki-tóó - le-ya - ooo. ___

Kaadíí, kaadíí, kitóóleya-oo.
Kaadíí, kaadíí, kitóóleya-oo.
Kisamá-oo kisamá, kisamá-oo kisamá, kisamá-oo kisamá.
Kaadíí, kitóóleya-ooo.

[Note that this tale nugget alludes, in fragment form, to the very tale it is interrupting and that the song is a variant of the one Kasólu uses later in the tale. Saramakas could not provide a translation of these esoteric words.]

KASÓLU:
Íya. Well, so then he— /KASÓLU'S RESPONDER: íya/

So he got there and he took the cowrie shell and the parrot feather and the ball of kaolin, and he paid for the boat ride. One cayman /íya/

could carry twelve men [devils], but it couldn't carry more than that. /íya/

AKÓBO:
So he would pay to be taken across?

KASÓLU:
Right. The cayman's head served as their boat, and it could carry twelve men. It couldn't carry more than that. /íya/

AKÓBO:
That's some boat!

KASÓLU:
So he paid the cayman. /íya/

And once he'd paid, it crossed over the water. /íya/

It crossed over the water zaaaaa and dropped him on the opposite shore. /íya/

So the boy continued on some more. /íya/

And he saw the old woman. /íya/

The twelve men were asleep. /íya/

Now the drum itself— You couldn't just pick it up without its playing. /íya/

If you picked up the drum, it was sure to start playing. /hm!/

So there they were. He came along and he saw the woman. The woman asked him, she said [in a high, anxious voice], "Boy, what have you come to do here? What brought you here?" He said, /íya/

[in a hushed, conspiratorial whisper:] "Well, here I am." /íya/

He explained to her that he had come because he needed something. /íya/

She replied [in the same hushed tone:] "But," she said, "you're wrong. You won't find what you want. You'll be killed. /íya/

This place you've come to—" He said, "Oh, no." /íya/

She said, "They'll kill you. These children of mine here can't get along with anyone." /íya/

She said, "You're in trouble. But I'll hide you." /íya/

So there they were until the time came. /íya/

Over and over, the woman had to keep making twelve earthenware plates /íya/

and cooking food /íya/

and putting it in those twelve plates. /íya/

AKÓBO:
At that time, I was right there.

KASÓLU:
Well, how was it?

AKÓBO:
Spider was on his way to a village to marry a woman named Kwasiba, /KASÓLU: íya/

and as he walked, he sang [in Sranan]:

Tu-wa-lu-fu pa-da mi e ko a yu a Kwa-si-ba, _____

ko-ee mi e ko a yu-oo, a Kwa-si-ba-ee

"Mi mei mi boto mi e ko a yu
a Kwasiba, ko-ee mi e ko a yu-oo, a Kwasiba-ee.
Tuwalufu pada mi e ko a yu
a Kwasiba, ko-ee mi e ko a yu-oo, a Kwasiba-ee.
Aiti pada mi e ko a yu
a Kwasiba, ko-ee mi e ko a yu-oo, a Kwasiba-ee."

["I've made a boat and I'm coming to you / Kwasiba, I'm coming to you, Kwasiba. / I'm coming with twelve paddles for you / Kwasiba, I'm coming to you, Kwasiba. / I'm coming with eight paddles for you / Kwasiba, I'm coming to you, Kwasiba."[73]]

Go on with your story.

KASÓLU:
OK! Well, at a certain point the woman said, "They're coming," the woman said, "Well, they're on their way." /KASÓLU'S RESPONDER: *íya*/

The boy turned into a needle and inserted himself into a crack in the palm-leaf wall. /*íya*/

Then they arrived. /*íya*/

Those guys arrived there *vuuuuuuu*. They called out [in Sranan]: "Someone stinks here, someone stinks here, someone stinks here." /*íya*/

They said, "Mmmm." [Speaking rapidly:] They picked up the woman and they threw her from one person to another, and the next one would catch her and then the next and then the next. /*íya*/

[Still rapidly:] She said, "Children!" They put her down. They said, "Mother, where is he? Someone stinks here." They picked up their house, carried it to one side, and set it down. /*íya*/

She said [deliberately:] "Children, what's going on? Me— I'm someone. I must be the one who stinks. /*íya*/

I got here in the morning, and I've been here in the sun making these things."

AKÓBO [breaking in]:
Don't they say that a human mother is the one who gives birth to devil children?

KASÓLU:
"Since morning I've been here in the sun making earthenware plates. I have to make twelve of them." /*íya*/

("yes" they said) Now there were twelve drums. /*íya*/

Twelve men, twelve drums. Every man had his own /*íya*/

drum that he played. /*íya*/

She said, "I must be the one who stinks. /*íya*/

Because I'm the one who's been here cooking and putting the food in the twelve earthenware plates so you'd have something to eat." /íya/

("yes" they said) "Mmm! But not so fast, Mother! That's not what's going on. /íya/

We didn't just start living with you here today! /íya/

Someone has come here, someone has come here." They started running all around, heading off into the forest *gulululu,* coming back into their clearing again. /íya/

They said, "No, no!" / . . . / Now the way they were used to doing things, each man would take his earthenware plate— /íya/

What they'd do is, they wouldn't just eat and then give their plates back. /íya/

Every man would gobble down his own earthenware plate *hólom!* /íya/

Each man with his own. Every day the woman had the same task. /íya/

They'd toss the whole thing down their throats *hólom, hólom, hó-lom!* /íya/

The boy saw this. So, there they were. But they felt that something was wrong. /íya/

Finally they went off to their hammocks, pulled on their covers, and went to sleep. /íya/

Then the boy moved a little. They started snoring.

AKÓBO:
They're going to pretend to be asleep.

KASÓLU:
Right. [Nasal snoring sound:] "*Hn. Hn, Hn. Hn. Hn, Hn.* /íya/

Hn. Hn, hn, hn." [Almost whispering:] The boy squirmed a little. But the woman said, "Don't do that." She tapped him and said, "They're not asleep yet." /íya/

(After a while the devils started telling tales, but I don't know their tales well enough to tell them.) /íya/

[Laughing:] I forget all their tales. /íya/

AKÓBO:
You just don't want to tell them.

KASÓLU:

> They told the tales on and on until they'd finished, and then they fell asleep like that, or pretended to sleep, as quiet as could be.

AKÓBO:

> You could go ahead and tell us the tales, because we're not getting sleepy yet.

KASÓLU:

> I just don't know the tales. I've forgotten them. /*íya*/

AKÓBO:

> You just don't want to tell them.

KASÓLU:

> They're like that for a while and finally they fall asleep for real: /*íya*/
>
> "*a tiá gbéngbelen*—

KANDÁMMA:

> Back when that happened, I was right there!

KASÓLU:

> *a tiá gbéngbelen, a tiá*— [to Kandámma:] *Íya!*

KANDÁMMA:

> Well, they say that all illnesses in the whole world were carried by a single person. /KASÓLU: that's right/

OTHERS:

> [laughter]

KANDÁMMA:

> Headache, stomachache, toothache— /*íya*/
>
> Every single problem that you'd call a "sickness"— /*íya*/
>
> one solitary individual bore them all: /*íya*/
>
> the old man called Gídigídi Zaabwóngolo. /*íya*/
>
> Well, Spider went off hunting and he came to a hill and there at the foot of the hill he listened, /*íya*/ and he heard: /*íya*/

Di   Di   Gí - di - gí - di   Zaa-bwón-go - lo - éé

*Di. Di. Gídigídi Zaabwóngolo-éé, Zaabwóngolo-éé, zagi a
    maamá mmm.*
*Di. Di. Gídigídi Zaabwóngolo-éé, Zaabwóngolo-éé, zagi a
    maamá mmm.*
*Gídigídi Zaabwóngolo-óó, Zaabwóngolo-éé, zagi a maamá mmm,
    óó-ii.*
*Gídigídi Zaabwóngolo-éé, Zaabwóngolo-éé, zagi a maamá mmm,
    éé.*
*Gídigídi Zaabwóngolo-óó, Zaabwóngolo-éé, zagi a maamá-éé
    mmm.*

[The song evokes the shaking of Gídigídi Zaabwóngolo's
body, under the weight of all the sicknesses he bore. In the
longer version of the tale Anasi, driven by curiosity, goes
off and discovers the person who bore all sicknesses, and
when he comes back he brings them all back with him,
which is why they're spread out among all people today.]

Go ahead. [She chuckles.]

KASÓLU [excitedly]:
Right! Well, while all this was going on, the people [back in the
boy's village] were busy with the funeral. And the dead person, the
one we were talking about, was almost ready for burial—

AKÓBO:
Right, they must be burying already.

KASÓLU:
They had been working on it. The women had really been screw-

ing the men who showed up, making the funeral a great success. /KASÓLU'S RESPONDER: *íya*/

The boy was hot after the drum. He swore he'd succeed. /*íya*/

Then came the sound: "*a tiá gbéngbelen, a tiá gbéngbelen, a tiá gbéngbelen, a tiá gbéngbelen.*"

AKÓBO [talking on top of Kasólu's voice]:
Were they asleep?

KASÓLU:
They were sound asleep.

AKÓBO:
When they did that, did it mean they were asleep?

KASÓLU:
They were really sleeping. /*íya*/

A MAN:
"*A tiá gbéngbelen, a tiá gbéngbelen.*"

KASÓLU:
Well, nothing to it. The boy got up. When they pretended to be asleep, they'd go [in a high, innocent, childlike voice]: "*píí páá, píí páá.*"

AKÓBO:
Was one of them pretending?

KASÓLU:
That was when they were pretending to be asleep. That was what they did for pretending to be asleep. But when they were going "*gbéngbelen,*" that meant they were really sleeping.

AKÓBO:
Their snoring—

KASÓLU:
Hm.

AKÓBO:
was what made the "*a tiá gbéngbelen?*"

KASÓLU:
So that's all. The boy got up quickly.

AKÓBO:
But how was he planning to get the drums?

KASÓLU:

No, he's only going to take one. /íya/

At the moment when he grabbed the drum, well, once you'd touched it, there was no way it wouldn't start playing. /íya/

As he touched it to pick it up, it tapped out, "*kpim!*" / . . . / They jumped up! The boy dashed into the forest and ran lickety-split. They grabbed up their drums, every single one. /íya/

AKÓBO:

There must have been one person left.

KASÓLU:

One of them was left empty-handed. And then they ran. /íya/

They ran and ran, till they were worn out, and the boy slammed down an *atígo*.[74] *Gbem!* /íya/

The place turned into a sea. They slammed down an *atígo. Gbem!* It turned into a vast expanse of dry land. /íya/

Then he put the drum down on the ground and he played:

Tim ki tim, ki tim, ki tim, ki-tóó - li-aa.

Ma mi bó-to, mi bó-to Zaa-li-é, mi bó-to-oo, po-ti mi na á-ba-ooo.

Tim ki tim, ki tim, ki tim, kitóóliaa.
Tim ki tim, ki tim, kitóóliaa.
Ma mi bóto mi bóto Zaalié, mi bóto-oo, poti mi na ába-ooo.

[The first two lines are the sound of the drum. The next two say, "My boat, Zaalié, my boat, carry me to the other shore."[75]]

Ohh! Then they ran! /íya/

They ran till they were exhausted. /íya/

And the boy— When they caught sight of the boy, /íya/

he slammed down an *atígo. Gbem!* And the path split into twelve parts. /íya/

The other guys got there. /íya/

They slammed down an *atígo*. *Gbem!*

AKÓBO [anticipating]:
—and the paths became one.

KASÓLU:
And the paths became one again. /íya/

Then they ran. /íya/

KANDÁMMA:
Was it the devil boys who were doing all this?

KASÓLU:
Yes, it was the devils. /íya/

They ran till they were exhausted. The guy put down the drum and played:

> *Tim ki tim, ki tim, kitóóliaa.*
> *Tim ki tim, ki tim, kitóóliaa.*
> *Ma mi bóto, mi bóto Zaalié, mi bóto-oo, poti mi na ába-oo.* /íya/

As he was singing, and calling there, he was singing to call the boat—

AKÓBO [talking on top of Kasólu's voice]:
So it'd come fast.

KASÓLU:
—to make it come there so it would be ready and waiting. /íya/

They ran /íya/

till they were exhausted. The boy jumped right up, he slammed down an *atígo*. *Gbem!* And the path was completely blocked off by hills. /íya/

[pause] Uh-oh. I think I'm getting the tale wrong here.

KANDÁMMA [prompting]:
The boy knows how to use his *atígo*.

KASÓLU:
He was slamming down *atígo*s. Every time he did it, those guys would have three *atígo*s of their own to counter his. And when those were used up, they'd go off to their village and get another one and slam down that one. /íya/

The boy ran and ran until he was exhausted. /íya/

The boy put down the drum and he played:

Tim ki tim, ki tim, kitóóliaa.
Tim ki tim, ki tim, kitóóliaa.
Ma mi bóto mi bóto Zaalié, mi bóto-oo, poti mi na ába-oo.

They keep on running and running. The boy is running and the guys are there. He slams down his *atígo*. They do theirs. He does his. He used one to turn land into water. The boy changed every imaginable thing. Until finally he arrived, and the cayman was right there at the dock. /*íya*/

He leaped right on. /*íya*/

They crossed over quickly and smoothly and hit the other side. /*íya*/

He put down the drum and played it:

Tim ki tim ki tim, kitóóliaa.
Tim ki tim ki tim, kitóóliaa.
Ma mi bóto mi bóto Zaalié, mi bóto-oo, poti mi na ába-oo.

[Akóbo joins softly in the song as the only "choruser."]

He'd already gotten across, so it was OK. /*íya*/

Those kids, those devils ran out. They called, "My boat! My boat! My boat! My boat! [in Sranan:] Come put me on the other shore!" The cayman turned around and glided over. The boats in that place could carry twelve men and no more. /*íya*/

It glided on over to them. /*íya*/

They got on, and they started across. The boy was there on the other shore watching. /*íya*/

They got on and started on over. /*íya*/

He called out to the cayman, and said [in Sranan:] "My boat! Sink!" / . . . / The devils said, "My boat, don't sink!"

OTHERS:
[laughter]

AKÓBO:
Those guys are the ones who had the boat, but the boy's going to outwit them.

KASÓLU:
He said [in Sranan], "My boat, sink!" They said, "My boat, don't sink." /*íya*/

He said, "My boat, sink." They said, "My boat, don't sink." /íya/

He said, "My boat—"

KANDÁMMA:

Who's telling it to sink? The boy?

KASÓLU:

The boy. He said, "My boat, since I paid you one parrot feather, one cowrie shell, /íya/

and one ball of kaolin—" ("yes" it replied) "You have to sink." So it sank right down, *guvuuu*.[76]

OTHERS:

[laughter]

KASÓLU:

The devils turned into rocks. That's why, when you walk until you get to a certain place at the river, you see rocks all over. They're the devils. The boy carried the drum along till he got to the head of his mother's grave. He played it and played it till he was finished. So you see, the drum has been around ever since. Otherwise we wouldn't have it.

KANDÁMMA:

We wouldn't have it.

KASÓLU:

But the boy is the one who brought it.

KANDÁMMA:

How come devils are so involved in things having to do with drumming?

KASÓLU [in Sranan]:

That's as far as my story goes.

AKÓBO:

Didn't you say it was going to be long?

KASÓLU:

Well it IS a long one. Well, you know? If you want to tell it so it's really sweet /AKÓBO: hm?/

you start talking and every so often, every little while, a man's canoe arrives [from the coast]. /mm-hm!/

You hear shouts of joy. The young woman runs out to greet him. The man has gone away to work and returned. /uh-huh!/

River rocks, dry season, Dángogó, 1968.

If you tell a tale that way [with lots of interruptions], it ends up being long. /mm-hm!/

A MAN:
Excuse me, everybody. I'm just going to take this stool of mine and head off.

AKÓBO:
Are people leaving?

KASÓLU:
They're leaving. So, we'll just stop there.

KANDÁMMA:
Right.

KASÓLU:
I hadn't been planning to tell any more tales, but if people wanted to, I'd be happy to keep going until dawn.

KANDÁMMA [enthusiastically]:
You're not the only one. We could keep telling them for three whole days more without ever repeating one.

Second Evening

In Memorium: Alébidóu and Bèkióo

5 March 1968, Paramaribo. Having come to the capital for a few days to buy supplies and do museum work, we hear that Alébidóu (the son of Apênti, an elderly Dángogó man), who had been working as a housepainter in the city, had fallen off a building and died. A few days later, a week after his burial, we attend a gathering at his house, where a feast is laid out for the ancestors. About thirty Saramaka friends and relatives who happen to be in the city have assembled for the wake. In the mud yard partially roofed with corrugated iron, folding chairs and card tables have been set up, and some of the men play dominoes or cards. Most people wear wear city clothes—only one woman is bare breasted. Javanese and East Indian neighbors peer out their windows from nearby houses. Lots of talk, some rum and soft drinks passed out by close relatives, and—once night falls—some tale-telling.

Back in Saramaka, Alébidóu's death is handled with special ritual precautions, like any *ógi dêdè* ("evil death," a category that also includes death by drowning, in childbirth, or in a forest accident). Had this particular kind of "evil death" occurred in Saramaka territory, specialists from the Nasí clan in the village of Páda would have been called in to administer esoteric rituals before the corpse could be specially disposed. In Alébidóu's case even the hair-and-nail relics (which would otherwise have been brought back to his matrilineal village for burial) are considered too dangerous to transport to Saramaka. Nevertheless his matrilineal village on the Gaánlío honors his memory three weeks after the death with an all-night drumming/dancing/singing "play," followed by a feast for the ancestors, with tales told later that night. (*Papá* playing, considered too "heavy" for a man of such relative youth, is not part of these festivities.) From Dángogó, Alébidóu's father, his father's brother, and a few other relatives journey to the Gaánlío to take part.

9 April 1968, Dángogó. Basiá Akudjunó arrives in the heat of the afternoon with a message from the tribal chief that Bèkióo (who left Dángogó, his maternal grandfather's village, as a young man in the 1930s and had since been living in French Guiana) has died on his way back from the coast. Konoi, the dead man's mother's sister, breaks into mourning shrieks, calling out, "It hurts, it really hurts. Bèkióo-eee! Bèkióo-eee!" Asipéi, the dead man's mother's sister's son (and hence

185

his "brother") sits on a stool in Konoi's cooking shed, wiping tears from his eyes with a rag. Neighbors arrive and persuade Konoi to stop her wailing, but every five minutes or so she begins anew. A few houses away we overhear Akóbo and her two sisters remark that "if you've never known someone, wailing for him doesn't come easily," but Akóbo says she'll go up and wail a bit with Konoi anyway. An older woman from across the river, standing near them, says, "There's no way I'm going to wail. I've hardly ever heard of the guy. And besides, as far as I know he never sent a single thing back here [from the coast]."

That morning Konoi's son Kôndèmása—who had been charged with bringing the seriously ill man back to Saramaka—had arrived with several kinsmen in Akísiamáu, Bèkióo's matrilineal village just downstream from Dángogó, bringing news of the death, and carrying the hair-and-nail relics in a little metal chest.[77] During the previous week, as their canoe had passed each village along the river on its way upstream, Kôndèmása and his companions had fired salutes and, at villages where Bèkióo's friends or kinsmen answered, had gone ashore

Akudjunó and his father, Asipéi, both 1978.

for a spontaneous "play" in his honor. When Kôndèmása finally arrived in Akísiamáu, three gunshots rang out, women began wailing, and village elders poured water and rum on the earth to apprise the ancestors of the news. Soon a "play" broke out, with drumming, singing, and dancing, and later in the day a simple miniature coffin was constructed for the hair-and-nail relics.

Over the following days, Bèkióo's Dángogó relatives spend most of their time in Akísiamáu, attending to their funeral responsibilities. Because he died on the coast, Bèkióo's funeral is unusual in several ways—burial of his minicoffin takes place after only a week, in a shallow grave, and libations are poured in front of a house in his matrilineal compound rather than at the ancestor shrine and from a bottle instead of a clay jug. But the hair-and-nail coffin is raised in divination on several successive days, and many other standard funeral procedures are followed: the final sequence of libations, *papá* playing the night before burial, the feast for the ancestors, and the tale-telling on the night of the burial. Within a week and a half of first hearing the news of Bèkióo's death, his matrilineage in Akísiamáu, assisted by its Dángogó offshoot, has fulfilled its obligations to bury its kinsman "with celebration."

In mid-May, only a week or so after Sindóbóbi's funeral wake, the elders of Dángogó begin to discuss the possibility of holding joint ceremonies to honor Alébidóu and Bèkióo. With the primary funeral rites for these men already carried out in their respective matrilineal villages, it seems the proper time for their "fathers' village," Dángogó, to pay its respects as well.

MONDAY, 20 MAY 1968. Basiá Apaasú visits Asipéi to suggest that it's time to hold a feast for Bèkióo. He'd like to pour libations next Monday and have the feast Tuesday. Asipéi agrees but makes the rhetorical point that they are in no way trying to upstage Bèkióo's matrilineal village; it's only that since he had lived in Dángogó before leaving for French Guiana his relatives and neighbors would now like to give him a little celebration. Asipéi walks down toward our house, telling each person of these plans so they will be sure to come back from their gardens in time. Meanwhile Apênti's brother, Captain Faánsisónu, mobilizes his own kinsfolk in the same way: "That death," he remarks, speaking of his young nephew Alébidóu, "really hits you hard!" During the next few days, men from both kin groups go hunting upriver, and women drug streams for fish.

MONDAY, 27 MAY 1968. An open-sided community-owned shed has been set up as "funeral house" (*dêdè ósu*), with two identical sets of water bottles, china bowls, calabashes, and round stools that have been brought to Dángogó from each of the dead men's villages, where they had served in the funerals. As twilight falls, some fifteen men and four women drift over, stools in hand, and sit down before the house. Each man offers a tiny bottle of rum to Captain Faánsisónu for use in the ceremony, and eight of them have brought shotguns and three shells loaded with black powder for the salutes to follow. Captain Faánsisónu begins praying as Basiá Aduêngi and Basiá Kasindó tilt the bottles, dribbling water intermittently onto the ground. Because he is the older of the two, Bèkióo's bottle is tilted first.[78]

A libation at the Bongóótupáu shrine, where ancestors are addressed when a funeral is not in progress, 1968 (left). Head Captain Faánsisónu, 1978 (right).

Well, Ancestors, we give you water. Grandfather Bongóótu, we give you water *gwóló!* [79] Well, what's the water for? Our son, the one called Sedjí—that's Bèkióo—has died. We give you water. Chief Djankusó, Chief Atudéndu, we give you water. Kónuwómi, we give you water. My "wife" Wabé, we give you water. Mother Daída, we give you water. Bukêtimmá, we give you water. Máti Makoyá, we give you water. Máti Agáduánsu, Captain Bitjé, we give you water. Basiá Akamí, we give you water. My grandfather Dooín, we give you water. You, the important men from downstream to upstream. Grandfather Díki, Grandfather Kólo, we give you water. Djangasó, we give you water.

Bèkióo has died on the coast. Well, no one has ever eaten the cassava of a stay-on-the-coast man. [80] No way. With food, when there's nothing in your house, you go off in search of a little "salt" [coastal imports] to take care of the problem [and then you return]. So he went off [to French Guiana] until Death caught him there and killed him *gwóló*, Ancestors. When Death killed him there, we didn't lick our fingers and say it tasted sweet to us. We didn't [merely] call out as if a dog had died either. It truly made us sad! Well, because the way it was: when we saw that something was crushing him, that it was knocking him *gwoo, gwoo*—if it had been a living person we would have pulled that person right off of him. But the one thing that's stronger than any of us is Death. Well, when we heard about what had happened, we could hardly just stay here [without doing anything] until his thing was over, without holding an all-night "play" for him, and without inviting you ancestors to come share a bit of cassava with us.

So we've come to you, the chiefs of the river, along with the captains and *basiás* and elders to ask you to pray to the great *kúnu* for us.[81] We're going to invite the child to come eat some cassava. We're no longer talking to the great *kúnu*. Well, because it [the *kúnu*] has already killed him [Bèkióo]. Well, since he's already been killed, we should offer him a bit of cassava. Ancestors, there's nothing that can come back [from the dead]. That's why we've come before you. Captain Gónima, we give you water. Father Guusé, we give you water. Captain Fáya, we give you water. We give you water for your son. He's the one who fell down dead. Gónima, we give you water, we give you water, you're a captain of Akísiamáu and Dángogó. Well, those villages never separated.[82] Saayé, we give you water. Potjí, Captain Amútu, Grandfather Afaadjé, we give you water. Captain Bitjé, Kwabátatái, Apeéli, we give you water. For the son of yours who died. Because he died, we have come to call you, you the ancestors, for you to take him onto your laps, for you to give him a bit of cassava. Great Thanks! So, *gwóló!*

[Others present chorus "Great Thanks," accompanied by slow, rhythmic handclapping. Captain Faánsisónu continues:]

Well, Sedjí. We give you water, Bro. Well it's really sad, Man. You went off with the idea of returning. No one's ever eaten a stay-on-the-coast man's cassava. But something happened to you, Man. Well, because when you went off to live there, we never heard anything about your having stolen and getting caught and being put in jail or that you were like someone who someday would turn up at Pont Djòbê[?] where people would come to stare and say, "My God, look at that Saramaka man who drank himself to death in the middle of the street." Certainly not! You never lost your good judgment. And then, on a day like today, Death killed you. Well, your mothers and fathers heard. And they brought you to pour libations of water in your grandfather's village and in your mother's village. They'll come eat a bit of cassava tomorrow afternoon. Well, today people will sit down outside in your honor. When they sit down like that, each one will have his own avenging spirits lurking around ready to kill him during the all-night "play." Brother, we don't want it that way. Go back to your Chief Atudéndu. Tell him, "Older Brother, well, look what's happened to me. Well, you should be the one to pray on my behalf." In the afternoon tomorrow, they're going to come eat a bit of cassava. So we're coming to pray to you *gwóló*, to say Great Thanks. That's what the community says.

[Others chorus, as before, "Great Thanks." Then Dooté says, "We've finished tilting that bottle (for Bèkióo). Start the next one, Captain." Faánsisónu continues:]

Well, Chief Djankusó, we give you water. Well, that child there [Alébidóu]—you're the one who ritually conceived him.[83] We give you water, *gwóló!* Chief Tudéndu, we give you water. My father Mánpana, my grandfather Síkeei, my grandfather Waisó, it's your offspring we're talking about. We give you water. Captain Abemazóo, Basiá Yetí, Basiá Toou, Basiá Pólu, we give you water. Grandfather Mandéa, Grandfather Kwênkwên, Grandfather Bongóótu. Máti Amánabentá, the person we're talking about is someone who wrestled at your own burial rites, with the other young guys. Because he was a gravedigger [for you]. Today you've lost him. Another one of our own has fallen. We can't call on him anymore to help bury others. Well, now. Death killed Alébidóu in whitefolks' territory. He died in a ritually dangerous way. We couldn't even get his body [here]. But in any case, when a person dies Father Monkey says, "When a person dies, there's nothing to do but bury him." Those are the words of the Big Monkey himself, the forest animal. It's a person who needs to be buried, so they bury him. We do whatever has to be done. We've gone to Lángu [Alébidóu's matrilineal village region]. We've gone to the city and returned. The mothers [matrilineage] held a feast for the ancestors there [in Lángu]. Well, we're the village of his father and grandfather. So we want to call the boy to offer him a bit of cassava. But we have no power on our own, and so we are calling on you, the chiefs, and you the captains, and you the elders. The evil things that killed the boy there—they're not the ones we're calling. Not at all. The way things are, Dángogó is falling apart. People might be ready to say, "Right. Alébidóu's dead and they're holding an all-night 'play,' and someone else has fallen dead there." Ancestors, that's not what we want. Or

else another person might die in the matrilineage of Grandfather Makambí in Lángu [Alébidóu's lineage]. Ancestors, that's
not what we want. So we've come to pray to you, to tell you that
tomorrow afternoon we're going to call the boy and give him a
bit of cassava, so that you—his elders—make sure that no evil
spoils his feast. Great Thanks. So, *gwóló!*

[Others chorus "Great Thanks!" Faánsisónu turns to Dooté
and suggests he pray as well. Dooté demurs, saying "Captain, go
ahead." Faánsisónu continues:]

Well, Alébidóu, Man, we give you water. Well, the reason
we're giving you water, Bro, it's that you've died. We're giving it
to you with great sadness. But there's no help for it, Man. When
Death came, I went to Lángu to the all-night "play." Your older
brother sent word from the city that I should come. We got involved with your money things [life insurance] and went round
and round with it. Well, the way you made out that paper, that's
the way it stuck. You acted as if your only relatives were your
own children [instead of your lineage] and said they should get
your death money. The city people refused our request, they
wouldn't change a word. And that's the way it's stayed till today.[84]
So we came back to Saramaka, Man. Well, the death you died
there, we have no way of knowing what killed you. When Chicken
eats something on the garbage heap and then goes off to die
inside its house, who in the world can know what killed it? We
don't even want to know [what killed you]. Because if you don't
know a certain village—Father says to Mother's Brother, "If you
don't really know a certain village, you'd better not accuse someone there of wrongdoing." We would never say that we wanted
to know what's really going on in the land of the ancestors. But
Child, don't you see, Death has killed you. We threw a feast for
you in your mother's village. Now we've turned around and called
you to your father's village, invited you to eat a bit of cassava.
Just like before you go off to the coast, you go pour libations
over there [mother's village] and then you come do the same
here. Well, we're not giving this [feast] for the Death that killed
you. We're not giving this for the great *kúnu*. But we're praying
to your ancestors, the mothers and the fathers, to give you a bit
of cassava tomorrow afternoon. That's what we're asking you
gwóló, Man. Tomorrow afternoon, you come eat, you hear?

[Others chorus "Great Thanks." There's a several-minute
pause in the ceremony. Dooté then asks, "Shouldn't we pour

the rum?" Someone says yes, and Faánsisónu picks up again, as Bèkióo's jigger of rum is tilted:]

All right, you the old ones we're calling on here, we give you rum. Chief Tudéndu, they say that the person who smokes open a canoe is the one whose nostrils get blackened. Well, the canoe that you have to take care of, it's in the lineage of Father Kónuwómi and my "wife" Wabé. We didn't treat you as if you only had a father here. You were the child of a mother and a father. All the children, if a person came here, he wouldn't know which were which [matrilineal children of the village or others].[85] And then on a day like today, Death killed Bèkióo in whitefolks' territory, *Máti*. So we've come to you once again. Máti Makoyá, Máti Agáduánsu, a sister's son of yours has fallen over dead. And so we're holding an all-night "play" in his honor right here before your very eyes. We didn't take it to Akísiamáu. This is where he set off from [for French Guiana]. And he went off and met Death. Well, evil things are finishing off the lineage. Ancestors, those are not what we're inviting to come sit down and eat with us here. No way. But that little child of yours. We are calling out our sorrow about him. Well, when you call out your sorrow like that, you should give him a bit of cassava. Just as if he had come back from whitefolks' territory, we would have boiled up some cocoa and drunk it in celebration. Well, but now Death has killed him. So let's drink a little rum, *Máti*. Great Thanks. So *gwóló!* Brother Sedjí, we give you rum.

[Others chorus "Great Thanks." Faánsisónu continues:]

Well, my father, we give you rum. Chief Djánku[só], we give you rum for the child of yours [Alébidóu] who has fallen down dead. Well, don't you see? We summon him to his mother's village and his father's village. Well, because the lineage never really separated. Well, don't you see? We must see to it that the great *kúnu* does not pull food out of the child's mouth any more. It's such a sad thing, Ancestors! If a person comes to the all-night "play" for Alébidóu and meets up with misfortune, let it be one that can be cured, so that the person doesn't die, so that he lives. That's what we're asking of you. Alébidóu, take a little glass of rum, Bro. Great Thanks, drink it up, *gwóló!*

[Chorus: "Great Thanks." Faánsisónu continues:]

In the afternoon [tomorrow], we'll gather outside in your honor. Even if there's rain, we'll pour water for you. And tomorrow afternoon you'll come and eat cassava. Great Thanks.

[Chorus: "Great Thanks." Faánsisónu continues:]

My father Mánpana, take some rum. My grandfather Síkeei, my grandfather Waisó, take some rum. Father Abemazóo, take some rum and care for us. Mother's Brother Alébidóu [the man the deceased was named after], Father Djúa, Potjí, Saayé, Gidé, Kositán, we give you all rum. Amánabentá, Asápampía, you the elders. Máti Agáduánsu, take some rum and have a meeting and bear us along on the side of Good. So be it, *gwóló!*

As Faánsisónu begins passing around what is left of the rum, the gunmen form a ragged line facing west and fire into the air, lighting up the nighttime sky with their blasts. Mourning wails from the women join the noise. The wails die out soon after the last gunshot, and people sit around talking for a few minutes. A heated discussion erupts among Dooté, Faánsisónu, and some other elders: How many libations are "correct" for an ancestral feast at a funeral? Asópi claims that a new method has been adopted in Akísiamáu that involves a sequence of five—in the morning and again in the evening preceding the all-night "play," on the next morning (the "hunting libation," to pray for meat/fish for the coming feast), and then at the feast itself that afternoon, and then, finally, on the following morning. Tremendous commotion as everyone talks at once, arguing for one or another variation. Faánsisónu says that Lángu people use the same sequence Asópi has described except that they eliminate the first libation—and that's the way he's going to carry out the rites at hand. Soon people disperse to their houses, women carrying tin kerosene lamps, men with flashlights or lanterns. Within the hour young boys have started beating the drums off to one side of the funeral house, and before long scores of people—many who have paddled to Dángogó from villages downstream—are gathering near the libation site for the all-night "play."

We leave that night's festivities early because we are tired, and we listen from our hammock to women's *sêkêti* singing and handclapping, some men's *sêkêti* with drums, and a bit of the Ndjuka "play" *awasá* by a couple of men who have recently returned from visiting that tribe in eastern Suriname. It is not as large or enthusiastic as most of the all-night "plays" we have seen in Dángogó.

TUESDAY, 28 MAY 1968. Just after dawn, a somewhat smaller group than that of the night before assembles before the funeral house. This time it is Basiá Apaasú from across the river who leads the prayer. Again, water is poured first for Bèkióo, then for Alébidóu, followed by

Asópi and his son Katayé, 1968.

rum in the same order. Though the ancestors invoked are largely the same ones as on the previous day, the rhetoric now focuses on a request for meat and fish for the feast that afternoon (even though large quantities of food are already on hand and being cooked by the women). Apaasú warns the ancestors that if they don't send game and fish, the feast will simply be "all-white [ungarnished] rice." Once the libations are finished, Asipéi designates his "brother" Amáka as "re-

Dooté, 1978.

sponder" and makes a formal speech of thanks to Apaasú for having contributed game for the feast. Apaasú replies, also using Amáka as responder, with equal formality.

Captain Faánsisónu then opens a wide-ranging, animated debate by playfully asking, with mock innocence, "Is there any fish that isn't supposed to be used for an ancestral feast? I," he claims, "use them all!" The elderly Dooté expresses shock.

"There are *lots* of fish that are prohibited: piranha, eel, *pèndêfísi*, *dèêma*. And as for game, you can't use deer, iguana, anteater, porcupine, 'animals of the above' [monkeys, etc], agouti, or *kapasí* and *kámba* [two kinds of armadillo], though turtle is OK. The hawk family—the whole bunch— is out. But toucans, bushfowls, and curassows are fine. The trumpeter is OK, except if the deceased was a forest-spirit medium." People interrupt Dooté to ask why the armadillos are prohibited while a turtle, which also has a shell, is all right. "We don't know why," he smiles. "That's just the way it is." Amáka volunteers that iguana is neither a bird nor a fish nor an animal. He isn't sure what it is, but to him it seems most like a bird. Others argue. Dooté points out that it's important for birds not to outnumber animals in a feast. After a half-hour of this, people pick up their stools and begin strolling about the village, offering morning greetings to others in their doorways.

In late afternoon, some forty or fifty people carry their stools over to the funeral house for the feast in honor of Bèkióo and Alébidóu—relatives and neighbors from Dángogó, but a few kinsfolk who have paddled up from Akísiamáu and Lángu as well. All day long, in a cooking shed nearby, women have been preparing the festive meal, stirring gigantic pots filled with rice, fish, fowl, and game. Now they have set this out on the clean-swept earth in a couple of dozen enamel or ceramic bowls in front of the house, and women stand before a massive pot calling children, and anyone else who wishes, to come "burn their hands"—to dip their hands quickly in a calabash of cool water and then receive a steaming double handful of peanut rice to gobble up before the official ceremony begins. After some light banter between Faánsisónu, Dooté, and Apaasú, Faánsisónu begins washing his hands in a carved calabash and pouring water on a banana leaf, inviting the ancestors to do the same and to come join the living for the feast. He then offers them some water from a separate carved calabash to drink. "You old people, don't you see? We've prepared a bit of cassava for you today. Come join us!" The invocations parallel those of the previous day—important village ancestors, his own ancestors, and then Bèkióo's and Alébidóu's own dead kinsfolk. The two dead men are also addressed personally, with reminiscences about times they all passed together in Dángogó. And as the captain prays, periodically interrupting his conversation with Bèkióo and Alébidóu to call on other ancestors, he slowly loads up the two large wooden rice-winnowing trays (one for each of the deceased), placed on the banana leaf, with bits of food, carefully including some of each delicacy laid out in the women's bowls. When the trays are fully heaped, and as he continues to speak quietly to the ancestors, Faánsisónu takes a bit of each kind of food from the trays—a piece of cassava cake that he has dipped in broth, some white rice, peanut rice, meat, and fish from each—and with his cupped hands tosses it onto the banana leaf for the ancestors to eat. Then, rising, he and Basiá Aduêngi (who has been assisting him throughout the ceremony) take double handfuls of peanut rice and distribute them into the waiting hands of Konoi, Asipéi, Amáka, Kódji, Kôndèmása, and the other close relatives of Bèkióo, and to Apênti, Apaasú, Agumiíi, Sakuíma, Tíanên, Kasindó and others related to Alébidóu, to be eaten on the spot. Portions are set aside for several distinguished kinsfolk and villagers, like Kandámma, who were unable to attend because of sickness. Faánsisónu then calls out to the village children to take their turn: in a mad melee, they rush for the still-heaped trays, scrambling to grab as much as they can in their hands. Agumiíi pours some palm oil into the remaining rice on the tray and rubs the mixture onto the bodies of four youngsters and two adults who share the tutelary spirit (nêséki) of one or the other of the deceased.[86] Repeating the opening gestures of the feast, Faánsisónu—after washing his own hands—offers the ancestors first hand-washing water from a calabash and then water to rinse their mouths. He then takes a calabash of Parbo beer and a bottle of a French aperitif (favored drinks of the deceased) and pours libations, followed by rum, asking them and the other ancestors to accept what has been offered and to protect them in the future. Each of the trays is turned over on the banana leaf, and two young men standing nearby fire three shotgun salutes each into the air. (Adults avert their eyes and rush children from the scene as the trays are inverted, since this is the dangerous moment when the ancestors are thought to be physically present.) Then Faánsisónu taps the bottom of each tray three times with a stick (alerting the ancestors that it is time to leave) and rights the trays once more. The food offering is over—but people sit around chatting for a few minutes more and, before departing, remind one another they will meet again later that night to tell kóntu.[87]

Dángogó women preparing a communal feast, 1968.

While we were setting up the tape recorder in our house, getting ready for the evening's tale-telling, a few ten- and twelve-year-olds stopped by and said they wanted to sing and tell riddles for the machine. We got wrapped up in this session, lost track of time, and arrived at the funeral house well into the evening of *kóntu*-telling—as people were already beginning to talk about breaking up for the night. We settled in, nevertheless, amid a group of fifty or so people—Apênti's kin (Basiá Kasindó, the three sisters Agumiíi, Tíanên, and Sakuíma, Captain Faánsisónu and his wives, and a dozen or so others, including five or six children), Bèkióo's relatives from Dángogó and Akísiamáu (Asipéi and his "brothers" Kódji and Amáka, Kôndèmása and his wife and children, and a number of others), and about twenty Dángogó neighbors, including Basiá Aduêngi, Akóbo and her two sisters, Abátelí, the tribal chief's aged sister Naai, and Asabôsi. We heard Agumiíi volunteer that she had a tale to tell that wasn't very long so people should stay, but it was actually Kasindó who determined the further course of the evening by launching into a brief tale about Jaguar feigning death in order to get food (pp. 203–8).

Amáka follows quickly with a tale about a problem child whose father abandoned him in the forest, where he was adopted by some wildcats (pp. 208–18). It is cut into twice—by Aduêngi, who tells and sings the story of a boy who bested a devil by playing his finger piano (p. 211), and by Agumiíi, who tells of a boy's visit to the old woman who had all the gods in the world in her head (p. 215). Amáka's story ends as the boy, having frightened the wildcats with a magic charm, returns to his village in triumph.

Aduêngi then begins a long tale with a familiar theme—how a boy goes off to the land of the devils to discover Drum (pp. 218–43). There are six tale nuggets, all with songs: Amáka tells of Mouse's triumph over Squirrel in wrestling (p. 223); Kasindó tells how Anasi, by hiding a little songbird inside his breechcloth, created a sensation at an all-night play (p. 224); Agumiíi, following directly on Kasindó's nugget—without a return to Aduêngi's tale—tells of a confrontation between a boy and a devil (p. 226); Tíanên adds a cryptic song allusion to a tale about monkeys (p. 228) and follows a few minutes later with the song of a cayman that Aduêngi has been describing in the main tale (p. 231); Kódji contributes the final tale nugget about a fish dragging a mother and child, who had been drugging a stream, down into a deep (p. 239). Aduêngi's tale concludes with the triumphant return of the boy, who plays the *apínti* drum at the head of his father's coffin.

Kasindó picks up immediately, drawing on his much-appreciated repertoire of stories featuring innocent nubile girls, to tell of two sisters who set off into the forest to have cicatrizations cut but met up with a lecherous devil (pp. 243–61). The tale is interrupted by four nuggets—first by Aduêngi, who sings Anasi's song of triumph in fulfilling the chief's challenge to buy a ship with a corncob (p. 244); then by Kódji, who tells how a couple tricked an old man who was hoarding all the world's cassava (p. 249); then by Aduêngi, who tells a version of Kandámma's tale from our first evening about the scrawny little kid and the gluttonous devil (p. 253); and finally by Agumiíi, who describes, in song, how Housefly volunteered to "salt" the meat that Toad had hunted (p. 257). Kasindó's tale describes how the girls were saved from the devil by their scrawny little brother, who magically cooled down the devil's machete and then revived his sisters from death.

As soon as Kasindó has finished, Amáka calls out "*Mató!*" and begins the story of a woman who was starving because her three sons ate all her food (pp. 261–67). A man (whose identity we were unable to reconstruct) interrupts with a song, in Sranan (the language of coastal Suriname), about a shameless woman who lured a man into the forest to make love under a tree (p. 265). Amáka concludes his tale by describing how the mother's best friend almost succeeded in killing the sons but one of them outwitted her in the end.

Amáka's brother Kódji quickly begins a contest tale about a man who was repeatedly challenged to wrestling matches by other men who coveted his wife (pp. 267–79). Aduêngi interrupts with a long tale nugget in which a nubile girl distracted a lecherous devil by fully displaying her charms (p. 268). Agumiíi later cuts into Kódji's tale with an account of how Anasi, too clever by half, inadvertently killed his wife while trying to persuade her to utter his name (p. 274). And Aduêngi then offers another nugget with a song—sung in a different version as a tale nugget by Akóbo toward the end of our first evening—about Anasi's courtship of a beautiful woman (p. 276). Kódji's tale concludes with Anaconda—the final challenger for the wife—being bested by the hero.

Without pause, Kasindó launches into a ribald tale about how Anasi introduced sex and procreation to the world (pp. 279–95). Two tale nuggets break into the narrative: Amáka describes the wrestling triumph of Turtle over Jaguar (p. 281); and Aduêngi—in the most riotous moments of either of our two evenings—mimes the way a man named Sòkôtiláma accepted the chief's challenge to screw four women at one time and laid the foundations for polygyny (p. 287).

Amáka, again without pause, begins a tale about how Rabbit (an animal Saramakas know only through folktales from French Guiana) tricked first Deer and then Jaguar into letting him keep all the fish they jointly caught (pp. 296–307). Aduêngi offers two tale nuggets, one about the woman who, by besting a devil, made it possible to hold all-night plays (p. 298) and another about three sisters who caught enormous amounts of fish with the help of a devil (p. 302). Kasindó contributes the third interruptive nugget alluding to a tale about a dance contest in which a troop of look-alike monkeys outlast a devil (p. 305).

Kasindó contributes a relatively brief tale that is unbroken by tale nuggets, telling how Anasi gave his daughter in marriage to Death, who killed and ate her, how Anasi tried to burn Death, and how Death chased him back to his village and has been with us ever since (pp. 307–14).

A number of people talk about calling it quits. Sakuíma remarks,

"We've really put in a night's worth." but Aduêngi breaks in with a new "*Mató!*" warning people that it's a long one but boasting that it's "pure gold." And Kasindó, rising to the challenge, announces that he's got one too and he wants to tell it tonight! Aduêngi's tale is the most complex story of our two evenings, combining a core heard in French Guiana with an imaginative apparatus of his own invention; it ranges over such diverse topics as Christianity, literacy, paternity, and Western technology, and it features a bitchy white princess and her cruel father/king, a boy who has been literally ripped in two by his mother and godmother, and a supporting cast of ships, horses, cannons, and other whitefolks' paraphernalia (pp. 314–46). There are six tale nuggets, three of them by Kasindó, two by Kódji, and one by Aduêngi himself, who appends an interruption of his own to the last one told by Kódji. The tale nuggets involve a disobedient girl who drugged a stream for fish (p. 315); a fetus that asked its mother to walk more gently (p. 317); a dispute between Piká-bird and Jaguar over rights to a garden (p. 320); Anasi's intervention while the two sides of the split boy were wrestling with each other (p. 323); how humans discovered the identity of some mystery dancers (howler monkeys) at their plays (p. 325); and how the identity of another mystery performer (Trumpet-bird) was unveiled (p. 327).

Kasindó follows Aduêngi's conclusion by making a formal speech about the evening's progress and asking everyone's indulgence to stay for just one last tale—which he promises won't be too long. Others respond supportively, and Aduêngi announces that besides serving as Kasindó's responder he's going to be cutting in with nuggets of his own. Kasindó's tale (pp. 347–56) begins with Anasi and two animal friends going off to clear gardens together. Aduêngi cuts in twice: first with the story of how Anasi tried to take credit in a log-hauling ordeal to win the chief's daughter (p. 348), and then with one about how Shrimp tried to trick Jaguar while fishing with him (p. 349). Kasindó's tale unfolds with Anasi, driven by greed, trying to trick his friends by setting up an ordeal. But he ultimately gets caught at his own game and, realizing he is about to die, sings a sentimental song of farewell to his wives, fathers- and mothers-in-law, and children (with active participation in chorusing from all those present)—which serves as an appropriate envoi for a rich and satisfying evening of *kóntu*.

But let's begin at the beginning.

AGUMÍÍ:
The one I've got isn't very long.

OVERLAPPING VOICES:
[General discussion of whether to tell more tales or to call it an evening and disperse.]

ADUÊNGI:
Well, let's tell just one more before we go.

KASINDÓ:
There's nobody here who could say you don't know what an Anasi story is.

SOMEONE:
No, there really isn't

ADUÊNGI:
The women don't want to tell Anasi stories. But they're the ones who really know the things. [pause] Women's Anasi stories are really sweet!

[Here the tape was switched off for a moment; Kasindó must have said "*Mató!*"]

A MAN:
Tòngôni!

KASINDÓ:
Hey, Man! Are you going to do the responses?

THE MAN:
Íya!

KASINDÓ:
Well, so there they were. /THE MAN: *íya*/

And the old man of the deep forest was there. /*íya*/

All the various kinds of animals were there in the forest. /*íya*/

(Hey, Man, are you doing the responses?!)

THE MAN:
Yes!

KASINDÓ:
Yes, well, all the various animals were already in the forest then. /*íya*/

And they all called the old man *tío* [mother's brother]. /*íya*/

They called him *tío*. /*íya*/

Kasindó, 1968.

The old man, that mother's brother, /íya/

well, his name was Domó. /íya/

But the other animals called him Uncle. /íya/

Well, one day the old man died. /íya/

[Laughing:] He wanted to eat those children who called him
Uncle. /íya/

And so he just "died." /íya/

The old man died, /íya/

and everyone went to look at the old man's body, lifeless on the
ground there. /íya/

A WOMAN:
[laughter]

KASINDÓ:
But listen to something strange. The old man's eye was trembling,
gigigigi, even though he was supposedly dead. /íya/

A WOMAN:
The old man's dead, but his eyes are still moving!

KASINDÓ:
Ohhh! They all got together for a meeting /íya/

since they were going to wash their uncle's body. /íya/

The whole community came together. /íya/

They had to wash the great uncle, so they sat down and discussed
it all. /íya/

They all sat in a big circle. /íya/

Then Brother Brocket [a small deer] sat with his back to one
side. /íya/

So they washed the uncle, /íya/

and when they finished, they laid him out. /íya/

They were ready to dress the body. /íya/

Brocket, who was off to one side, said, "Well, when someone dies
in a sly way, we should bury him in a sly way." /íya/

Everyone turned to listen to what he was saying. [Adopting a tone
of mock concern:] "Brother, the death of our uncle really tears me
apart." /íya/

OTHERS:
  [laughter]

KASINDÓ:
  "It really grieves me." They keep on dressing the body till it's all set. /íya/

TÍANÊN:
  But he's not really dead.

KASINDÓ:
  Now every single animal considered him an uncle, /íya/

  and every one of them was present. /íya/

  They really dressed the body elaborately. Brother Brocket said [again with mock concern]: "Well, my goodness. /íya/

  My very own uncle has died, /íya/

  and I have nothing suitable to contribute to the funeral. /íya/

  But there's nothing to do about it. /íya/

  It wouldn't be right to steal something to contribute to my uncle's funeral. /íya/

  This is really terrible. /íya/

  I feel so awful about it. /íya/

  I really have nothing. /íya/

  But [brightening up:] look at this brand new needle here! /íya/

  It's the only thing I have in the world to give for my uncle's funeral. /íya/

  Just dress him till he's all ready, /íya/

  and then slip it in right at the base of my uncle's claw for me." /íya/

OTHERS:
  [lots of laughter]

KASINDÓ:
  They dressed the body till it was all set. [To the responder:] Are you answering this tale, Man?! /íya!/

  So they dressed the body till it was all set. /íya/

  And they were all ready to take the needle, /íya/

  and place it at the base of the uncle's claw there. /íya/

  Then Brocket said— /íya/

TÍANÊN:

That will really get him hopping!!

KASINDÓ:

He said, [indistinct on tape]. They just slipped it right in, and a scream rang out. All the grave goods the body had been dressed in fell off, /íya/

and flew all over the place. /íya/

OTHERS:

[laughter]

KASINDÓ:

The uncle sat right up, /íya/

the [classificatory] nieces and nephews /íya/

all ran off into the forest. This one— He gets grabbed up [by Jaguar]. /íya/

Agouti— Jaguar grabbed him too. [Agouti cried out:] *"tío tío tío TÍO TÍO TÍO TÍO TÍO."* /íya/

OTHERS:

[laughter]

KASINDÓ:

He carried him back and set him down. /íya/

Brocket was already very far away. /íya/

He said, "Well, didn't I tell all of you, /íya/

that if a person dies in a sly way, you've got to be sly when you bury him?" /íya/

Brocket went off. /íya/

That's why today you always hear Agouti in the forest calling *"tío! tío!"* / . . . / He's calling his uncle. /íya/

So. That's as far as my story goes.

SAKUÍMA:

Jaguar finished him off by eating him?

KASINDÓ:

He finished him off by eating him.

SAKUÍMA:

His own sister's son!

KASINDÓ:

He got him to come pay his respects, and then he ate him right up.

SAKUÍMA:
[laughter]

KASINDÓ:
That's how it was.

AMÁKA:
Mató![88]

OVERLAPPING VOICES:
[indistinct]

SAKUÍMA [to one of the men, after there's no reply to Amáka]:
Hey, Man. He said "*Mató!*"

AYETIMÍ:
Tòngôni!

AMÁKA:
Well, there we were. /AYETIMÍ: *íya*/

SAKUÍMA:
My goodness, someone better cut into this tale!

AMÁKA:
And a certain man had himself a child there. /*íya*/

There was no mischief that he didn't get into. /*íya*/

SAKUÍMA [to a child]:
Watch out for my lamp. If you're tired I'll take you back home
and let you go to sleep.

AMÁKA:
They yelled at him, but it did no good. /*íya*/

They beat him again and again. /*íya*/

He just kept on being bad. /*íya*/

Well, the boy and his father went hunting. /*íya*/

They went way into the forest. /*íya*/

They took a path that went way deep into the forest. The virgin
forest. /*íya*/

And then the father abandoned him there in the forest. /*íya*/

He said, "Man, wait here. /*íya*/

I'm going off to shit. I'll be right back." /*íya*/

So he went off. /*íya*/

[The boy thought:] "Ah! The world is full of wonders! Ah! The world is full of wonders! Ah! The world is full of wonders!"[89] /íya/

Complete stillness. He didn't see his father anymore. /íya/

He called and called. /íya/

He walked off in the direction his father had gone. /íya/

He walked around and around the forest /íya/

without finding anything. /íya/

He went along until he noticed a cleared path. /íya/

"Mmm," he said, "that's the way I'll get back to our village." /íya/

He went along it till he got to the end. /íya/

He got there and all he saw was lots of black wildcats [*baáka tjáti,* probably black jaguars], everywhere he looked /íya/

in the village. /íya/

Well, when he arrived at the edge of the forest there, /íya/

he saw one of the wildcats coming back with a chicken. /íya/

"Mmm! That chicken is one of my own chickens! /íya/

Mm, mm. Ah! The world is full of wonders! /íya/

Ah! The world is full of wonders!" /íya/

So he walked on over. /íya/

And they started talking, and they continued. The wildcat said [casually]: "Well, Brother, when you got to this village— Well, you happened upon some real hospitable folks. /íya/

You can just live here!" /íya/

So they went on like that. /íya/

This person would bring back some meat to eat, and that one would bring meat, and the next one would bring meat. /íya/

They all contributed. They would cut the meat up nicely, skin it, cook it, and eat it. /íya/

Those wildcats were delighted to have another person living there.

OTHERS:
[laughter]

SAKUÍMA:
Well, the person who took him off to the forest— Did he just abandon him forever?

AMÁKA:
> He didn't know what had happened to him. He just went right back to his village. /*íya*/

> He had no patience for teaching the boy things about the world. /*íya*/

> So the boy lived with the wildcats until one day they called him. /*íya*/

> "Man—" (he replied) "Well, nothing much," they said. "It's just that we're all living together here, /*íya*/

> but you don't have a gun. /*íya*/

> You don't have a machete. /*íya*/

> Well, how are you going to hunt anything for us to eat?" /*íya*/

> "I don't know," he said. "Well, tomorrow you should go off hunting too." /*íya*/

> ("all right" he said) "I understand." /*íya*/

> Well, he stayed there for a while and then he got up and went off to the creek. /*íya*/

> Awó Mamá ["Old Mother"] called him over right away. /*íya*/

> (he replied) Awó Mamá said, "Find such and such a thing and bring it here." /*íya*/

> He looked for all the things he was told and he brought them there. /*íya*/

> Awó Mamá said, "Boy—" (he replied) Awó Mamá said, "Do you realize what village you've come to here?" /*íya*/

> ("no" he said) Awó Mamá said, "Well, the fact is that you are as good as dead. /*íya*/

> The wildcats are sure to kill you. /*íya*/

> You see how they sent you off to go hunting? /*íya*/

> Well, you'll go off hunting without anything at all to hunt with. Did you bring anything when you came here?" /*íya*/

OTHERS:
> [laughter]

AMÁKA:
> "No," he said. "You see?" said Awó Mamá. /*íya*/

"They've as much as killed you. Because if you go hunting and don't get anything, they'll kill you and cook you for dinner."

ADUÊNGI [breaking in]:

Well, at that time I was there. /AMÁKA: right/

And there was a devil right there in the forest.[90] /OK/

You couldn't go hunting overnight. /certainly not/

If you went hunting overnight, he was sure to kill you. /well/

Well, there was a boy and an old man who went into the forest, very deep. /right/

So of course the devil was all set to kill them both. /true/

He was getting ready to kill the boy. The man had let the boy go off hunting and the devil was coming to kill him. /well/

Now, he was coming to kill him, but the boy had a finger piano. /right/

So he's playing the finger piano, and the old man [the devil] is coming to kill him, and the boy said [in a very calm, reasonable voice], "Well, Father, are you going to kill me now?" "Yes," he said. "Well, I'd like to play my finger piano for you so you can dance before you kill me," and he said [politely]: "Well, Boy, that sounds fine to me. /right/

A Dángogó youth posing with his finger piano, 1968.

Play your finger piano for me to dance to and then I'll swallow you." Well, nothing to it. The boy started playing his finger piano: *tíngíníngínín tíngíníngínín tíngínín. Tín tín tín tín.*

Bò-kôô-zi-na, Bò-kôô-zi-na, un djén djén kó-ti djéin.

Bò-kôô-zi-na, Bò-kôô-zi-na, un djén djén kó-ti djéin.

Bòkôôzina, Bòkôôzina, un djén djén kóti djéin.
Bòkôôzina, Bòkôôzina, un djén djén kóti djéin.
Bòkôôzina, Bòkôôzina, un djén djén kóti djéin.
Bòkôôzina, Bòkôôzina, un djén djén kóti djéin.

[The finger piano's "*tíngíníngínín*" plays on a single note. Bòkôôzina appears to be the devil's name.[91]]

Go ahead with your story.

OTHERS:
[laughter]

AMÁKA:
Well, nothing much else. /*íya*/

She said, "Boy—" (he replied) She said, "They're going to kill you." "Yes," said the boy.

AGUMIÍI:
Now they won't be able to kill him.

AMÁKA:
"But I'll teach you something."

AGUMIÍI:
[a satisfied laugh]

AMÁKA:
"OK," said the boy. "When you go hunting, / . . . / I'll give you some magic." /*íya*/

She showed him the magic very completely, /*íya*/

and he pushed it up his ass. /*íya*/

OTHERS:
[laughter]

AMÁKA:
The boy went back to the village.

SAKUÍMA:
He couldn't have just put it in his hunting sack?!

AMÁKA:
He was there until morning. /íya/

They said, "OK, Man. Well, Brother— Well, we've all slept the night and now it's your turn to go hunting for the rest of us." /íya/

He got up, /íya/

without a machete, /íya/

without a gun. /íya/

He went along until he saw a bush rat. /íya/

He called out, "Brother Bush Rat!" (it replied) He said, "Brother, look at this *atanganí!*"[92] / . . . / The bush rat veered around. The boy opened up his ass toward it. /íya/

The bush rat keeled right over.

OTHERS:
[loud laughter]

AMÁKA:
The boy went to take the bush rat. /íya/

He went back to the village. /íya/

When he got there, they celebrated because he had hunted something. /íya/

They cooked it up and ate it. /íya/

In the morning they said, "Well, Brother, when you went hunting you killed a bush rat, so you should go off again." /íya/

So he went. /íya/

He went along until he saw an *akúsu* [a small agouti]. /íya/

"My friend *Akúsu!*" (it replied) "Brother," he said, "look over here." / . . . / He turned to look. The boy bent over and let go.

OTHERS:
[laughter]

Agumíí and her husband, Dooté, 1968.

AMÁKA:

So the boy kept killing food for them to eat. /*íya*/

Whenever he went out, he'd get something, and this went along until one day— He went out and returned. /*íya*/

He had killed a tapir. /*íya*/

Well, that's all. / . . . /

AGUMIÍI:
At the time when he killed the tapir, I was standing right there.

AMÁKA:
Íya. So what did you see?

AGUMIÍI:
Well, the old woman was right there in the village. /AMÁKA: right/

Now she was the only one— *Komantí,*[93] other gods, every single god in the world— /well/

Well, she was the only medium for all of them. /right/

If, for example, there was an avenging spirit that was troubling your family— As long as you didn't go to her, you'd wouldn't be able to appease it. /hm!/

So, well, there was another woman who scratched her kneecap, *gwè, gwè,* and then she gave birth to a child.[94] And he asked her, "Well, Mother, I'd like to know where our avenging spirit is kept." /right/

She said, "Boy, you can't go to the place where our avenging spirit is." "I'm going to go, Mother," he said. / . . . / "I'm going to get it and bring it back." She said, "No, you can't go." /no/

Well, the boy turned right around and dashed off into the forest. /right/

A MAN:
Was he going to look for the avenging spirit?

AGUMIÍI:
Yes, he hunted little birds along the way and finally came to the old woman's village. / . . . / The only person in that village was the old woman. She was there alone, with her gods' house /indeed/

and another house to live in. /right/

She'd gone off to her garden. /hm!/

The child saw her drum. So he pulled the drum on over, /hm/

and he tapped out: *Tím, tím, tím.*

(♩ = ca. 160)

Kí-ni-mám-zu, ki-ni-zé. Zen zen zen ké-len-za.

Ma-má tá-ki zaan zaan zaan kí-oo kí-oo mu-téé kwá-mi-na.

Kínimámzu, kinizé. Zen zen zen kélenza.
Kínimámzu, kinizé. Zen zen zen kélenza.
Mamá táki zaan zaan zaan kíoo kíoo mutéé kwámina.

[Although we cannot translate this song, the point of the story is clear: through the boy's altruistic intervention, humans gained access to their various gods and avenging spirits so that henceforth they could summon them, and appease them, through their mediums.]

Go ahead.

ADUÊNGI [to the much older Agumiíi, using a playful term of address]:
Is that how it was, Gal?

AGUMIÍI:
That's how it was, Poppa! That's as much as we know about it.

ADUÊNGI:
Wéndje, e i bulí mi akí— ógi! [Roughly: "My sweet, If you keep pushing me, things'll get really baad!"—i.e., I might just go on telling tales till daybreak.]

OTHERS:
[laughter]

SAKUÍMA:
That tapir would hardly have been something to eat. 'Cause he killed it with his asshole hair, so how could they possibly eat it?!

A WOMAN:
OK, let's be quiet!

AMÁKA:
They went and brought back the tapir, brought it back and threw it right down. This person said, "I won't butcher it."

AGUMIÍI:
That tapir isn't fit to eat.

AMÁKA:

That one said, "I won't butcher." /AYETIMÍ: íya/

This one said, "I won't butcher." The other one said, "I won't butcher." This one said, "I won't butcher." And on and on until every single wildcat had refused. /íya/

No one would butcher the tapir. /íya/

Only the boy was willing to butcher the tapir. /íya/

SAKUÍMA:

The thing is that the boy had no machete. Now he's really in trouble!

AMÁKA:

He had no machete. He had no gun. / . . . / He went to take one of their machetes. He went over to one of them and bent down [to pick up the machete]. [In an alarmed tone:] "No, no! Don't bend over near me!" [pause] He went off to the other side. "No, no! Don't bend over near me!"

AKÓBO:

Well, couldn't they all have sat over to one side?

AMÁKA:

Not at all. They couldn't sit to one side. What they had done is they had sent someone off to watch how the guy was hunting in the forest.

AKÓBO:

You mean how he killed things?

AMÁKA:

Mmm. So, they saw him and they were scared.

AKÓBO:

They tipped off their friends about him.

AMÁKA:

Right. They were scared he'd bend over near them. If you looked at his asshole, you'd die.

OVERLAPPING VOICES:

[lots of simultaneous comments]

AMÁKA:

The boy said, "Hey, guys, what's with all of you?" This person ran off *báábolou*. That one ran off. The boy grabbed the one who had first stolen his chicken, and said, "You aren't leaving! / . . . / You're going to take me to the place where you found the chicken. Otherwise I'll kill you!" He said, "Well, look, Brother, don't kill." He led the way and they went along, carrying the chicken, /íya/

and they kept on going till the wildcat said—

AGUMIÍI [talking over Amáka's voice]:
Isn't the wildcat going to eat the chicken?!

AMÁKA:
"You see that clearing there?" /íya/

("yes" he said) "Well, that's where your village is." He said, "Oh no, I can't go in yet. Take me all the way to where you got the chicken, and then you can go back." /íya/

So they went along till they got to the garbage pile where he had stood and caught the chicken. /íya/

He said, "Brother, do you see where I'm standing here? Throw the chicken down right here!" He threw the chicken right down, and the chicken ran lickety-split back to the village. /íya/

So that was all. The boy went too. /íya/

Oh, did people celebrate! / . . . / All the [classificatory] mothers and fathers ran to hug the boy. /íya/

"Child, how did you find your way back?!" /íya/

So that's how they got back together. /íya/

And that's why, if you have a child, and if you are too hard on it, it'll end up like the child in the folktale.

SAKUÍMA:
It'll go off to the wildcats.

A WOMAN:
To the devils.

SAKUÍMA:
"Sondí dê a múndu!" ["The world is full of wonders!"]

OVERLAPPING VOICES:
[a minute or so of discussion, continuing to rehash the tale]

ADUÊNGI:
Mató! [95]

A MAN:
Tòngôni!

ADUÊNGI:
Well, there we were. /THE MAN: *íya*/

We were there once upon a time. /*íya*/

And, well— There was a man. /*íya*/

And he had some children. /*íya*/

He had three daughters. /*íya*/

And he had three sons. /*íya*/

Now the old man called Anáni from Akísiamáu— /*íya*/

Well, he has something he likes to say when tales are being told. /*íya*/

He says that in the old days, they would say that a father called Donú /*íya*/

had a son called Aduêngi. /*íya*/

OTHERS:
[quiet laughter]

ADUÊNGI:
That's the way they told tales in the old days. /*íya*/

You'd give the name of the father who had the child. /*íya*/

But today all that sort of thing is getting lost. /*íya*/

We don't know the people's names anymore. /*íya*/

So you just say that there was a father who had a child. /*íya*/

OK, so there we were, and there was a man who had three daughters, /*íya*/

and he had three sons. /*íya*/

SAKUÍMA:
Who's singing? [meaning: "Who's going to cut into this tale with a nugget?" No one responds.]

KASINDÓ:
That's like: "There was a woman who had a child."

A MAN:
That makes six.

ADUÊNGI:
Correct. /*íya*/

Well, so there we were until the time came, and it came time for the old man to die. /*íya*/

So he called them, /*íya*/

got them together, and said, "Children—" (they replied) He said, "Well, I am going to die. /*íya*/

Well now, since I'm going to die— Well, I've called you here to ask you— /*íya*/

When I die, what do you plan to do for my funeral? /*íya*/

I want to know." /*íya*/

("yes" they said) The oldest one said, "Well—" The oldest boy /*íya*/

said, "Well, Father—" /*íya*/

(he replied) He said, "Well, when you die—" /*íya*/

("yes" he said) He said, "There's only one thing that I'll be doing. /*íya*/

Nothing but crying. /*íya*/

I'll keep on crying, just wailing and wailing, until they bury you." /*íya*/

OTHERS:
  [laughter]

ADUÊNGI:
  ("yes" he said) /*íya*/

  The oldest daughter said, "Well, Father—" /*íya*/

  (he replied) She said, "When you die now—" /*íya*/

  She said, "The one thing I'm going to do is sing and dance, without stopping, /*íya*/

  for your funeral." /*íya*/

  The middle brother /*íya*/

  said, "Well, Father—" (he replied) He said, "When you die now—" ("yes" he said) "Well, I'll bury you with grave goods. /*íya*/

  And I'll make your coffin /*íya*/

  so it's really nice, and supply goods for your funeral, /*íya*/

  just as many goods as you may need, /*íya*/

  so that when you're dead, not a single person will come to your funeral / . . . / without receiving at least a length of cloth from me." /íya/

SAKUÍMA:
He'll tie their bellies, *puaan.*

ADUÊNGI:
"That's how well I'll bury you." /íya/

The middle daughter said, "Well, Father—" (he answered) She said, "When you are dead and still as can be here—" ("yes" he said) "I will help bury you. /íya/

I will help bury you with food. /íya/

Talk about food— Not a single person who comes here will leave hungry. /íya/

Every child— Every person, once they step ashore here, will have plenty to eat." /íya/

He said, "Yes, Child, you're really helping to bury me." The very youngest daughter said, "Well, Father—" (he replied) She said, "When you die now—" ("yes" he said) "Every single man who slips into this village—" /íya/

OTHERS [who know what's coming next]:
[laughter]

ADUÊNGI:
("yes" he said) She said, "I'll be sure to screw him!"

OTHERS:
[exclamations and laughter]

TÍANÊN:
That person is really contributing well to the funeral!!

KASINDÓ:
She'll give it all she's got!

TÍANÊN:
Those people who helped out with goods didn't bury him all that well. But this one did it just right.

OVERLAPPING VOICES:
[wild laughter and animated discussion]

KASINDÓ:
That kind of contribution is really fine!

ADUÊNGI:

"Child—" (she answered) He said, "Yes, you're really helping to bury me well." /íya/

The very youngest brother /íya/

said, "Well, Father—" (he replied) He said, "When you die now—" ("yes" he said) "Well the thing known as Drum— /íya/

I keep hearing its name, /íya/

but, well, I don't know it firsthand. /íya/

But wherever Drum may be, /íya/

I'm going to go get it and bring it back to play at your funeral, play the *apínti* drum at the head of your coffin, even if it's not till the day they bury you, even if it's the seventh day of your funeral, I will absolutely play it at the head of your grave. /íya/

Because, well, the thing that's called *apínti*, I hear people saying that it's, well, that it's a really important thing in Bush Negro land. /íya/

So wherever *apínti* may be, I'll go find it and be SURE to play it at your head." /íya/

("yes" he said) "That's the way I'll help with your funeral." /íya/

"The very day you die—" ("yes" he said) "I'll leave the preparations for your burial, /íya/

and I'll go off in search of the *apínti* until they're ready to bury you, and even if you've already been buried, I'll still play it at the head of your grave." /íya/

He said, "Yes, Son, you will really have contributed to my funeral, because, well, *apínti* is an important thing for us Bush Negroes." /íya/

Then three days went by and the old man died. /íya/

OTHERS:

[laughter and exclamations]

ADUÊNGI:

The old man died,

SAKUÍMA [interrupting]:

Hadn't he been as good as dead already?

ADUÊNGI [simultaneous with Sakuíma's question]:

dead as could be. /íya/

And the person who said he would cry— /íya/

Well, he was crying so much that when you came there and tried to talk, nobody could hear what you were saying. / . . . /

OTHERS:
[laughter]

ADUÊNGI:
And the person who said she would help by singing and dancing— /íya/

Well, she's playing and playing.

OVERLAPPING VOICES:
[indistinct comments]

ADUÊNGI:
She keeps singing until her throat gives out completely, and then she prepares an herbal mixture,

A WOMAN [interjecting helpfully]:
drinks it,

ADUÊNGI [without missing a beat]:
and is right back in there singing. /íya/

AMÁKA [speaking very deliberately, in contrast to Aduêngi's excited delivery]:
Well, Squirrel and Mouse were wrestling.

ADUÊNGI:
Right. How was it they were wrestling?

AMÁKA:
You know how they were wrestling?

ADUÊNGI:
No.

AMÁKA [singing]:

Djeen-djé   ku A-du-má-kaa,   Djeen-djé wo-li.

Djeen-djé   ku A-du-má-kaa,   Djeen-djé wo-li.

Djeendjé ku Adumákaa, Djeendjé woli.
Djeendjé ku Adumákaa, Djeendjé woli.
Djeendjé ku Adumákaa, Djeendjé woli.

[Roughly, "Squirrel versus Mouse, Squirrel tries to keep his balance." *Adumákaa* (used in the song) and *Mafendjé* (used elsewhere in the nugget) are synonyms meaning Mouse; *woli* was explained to us as a defensive maneuver used in wrestling. For Saramakas, the point of the story is that smaller Mouse wins over bigger Squirrel.]

Mouse threw him in the air. Squirrel landed with a thud. Mouse pinned him. Squirrel grabbed Mouse. He threw him in the air. He landed right on his feet, *tjálá!* / . . . /

A YOUNG WOMAN [laughing]:
Even though Squirrel's so quick!

SAKUÍMA:
Mouse beat Squirrel.

AMÁKA:
Right. Go ahead with your story.

ADUÊNGI:
So that's all. /*íya*/

The performing one is performing like nothing else. /*íya*/

The one who said she'd help by providing food— /*íya*/

Ohh, the day they came to wash the corpse there, every person in the village, every single one, ate so much they couldn't take another bite. /*íya*/

KASINDÓ:
And while they were "playing" there, /ADUÊNGI: *íya*/

Father Anasi was his son-in-law. /*íya*/

It was his father-in-law who'd died there. /*íya*/

He said, "Well, the most important thing to do to help at a father-in-law's funeral is to sing and dance," so he went to perform at his father-in-law's funeral. /that's right/

Well, he decided to make a private arrangement with someone who was off on the side there. / . . . / Well, there was a certain bird there, and he decided to catch it and perform with it under his breechcloth. /*íya*/

Mm! The singing and dancing had been going on for quite a while there.

A MAN:
What kind of bird was it?

KASINDÓ:
Well, let's just say it was a *pítawóyo* [a songbird].

THE MAN:
Mm-hm.

KASINDÓ:
He just took it and slipped it discreetly into the inside of his breechcloth.

SEVERAL WOMEN:
[laughter]

KASINDÓ:
The singing and dancing went on for a while, and then it got to be Anasi's turn to dance. / . . . / So he leaped into the center. / . . . / That's all, the little bird was right there inside his breechcloth:

OTHERS:
[laughter]

KASINDÓ:

Nôò, tjéin tjéin tjééin kí-na-ee.   Tjéin tjéin tjééin kí-na-oo.

Nôò, tjéin tjéin tjééin kína-ee.
Tjéin tjéin tjééin kína-oo.
Tjéin tjéin tjééin kína.
Tjéin tjéin tjééin kína-ee.
Tjéin tjéin tjééin kína-oo.
Tjéin tjéin tjééin.

[While singing the bird's song—which is not translatable—Kasindó mimed Anasi's dance.]

Then people fell all over Anasi to congratulate him.

WOMEN:
[Wild laughter, in the midst of which someone seems to have asked where the bird was.]

KASINDÓ:

The bird? It'd already flown away.

A MAN:

And when he dances the next time, will the bird come back?

KASINDÓ:

Oh! What makes you think he could ever find it again?!

OTHERS:

[laughter]

AGUMIÍI:

Hey, Bási! [Kasindó]

KASINDÓ:

What?

AGUMIÍI:

Just when that, when that thing was singing inside Spider's breech-cloth, /KASINDÓ: *íya*/

well, the devil was right there, /mm-hm/

thinking about eating the child. /*íya*/

He came right up. /mm-hm/

He called out:

Maanpáya-ee, Maanpáya-eee, m'Towêsinaagooo.
Maanpáya-ee, Maanpáya-eee, m'Towêsinaagooo.
M'zaukúnde-oo, gwôyòtòò. M'zaukúnde-oo, gwôyòtòò.
Madjaáfo m'péneni-ee.
Mi dánsi-oo m'péneni-ee.

[The first two lines are what the boy sings (or plays on a horn) to taunt the devil, calling out his name, Maanpáya, as well as his insulting name, Towêsinaagooo. The last three lines are not in normal Saramaccan—they seem to be partly Papá, partly Komantí—and we have not been able to translate them.]

He called out, "*Zánguna m'kolóbi, zángana m'koló.* Now I can claim my victory, Kid." He took his foot and stamped out the fire. / . . . / Go right ahead.[96]

OTHERS:
[hooting, noise]

ADUÊNGI:
So that's all.

KASINDÓ:
You see?

ADUÊNGI [excitedly—a tone that continues into the tale itself]:
Yes, it's the women— I told you, they're the ones who know these things! /ADUÊNGI'S RESPONDER: *íya*/

So, nothing much. At that point, the one— the one in charge of the goods— /*íya*/

well, all the people who came for the washing of the corpse—

SAKUÍMA [anticipating]:
He tied a cloth onto every belly.

ADUÊNGI:
He tied a cloth onto every one. /*íya*/

And he provided a hundred cloth sheets and a hundred hammocks. /*íya*/

The smaller cloths he gave were too numerous to count. /*íya*/

He made the coffin with— with cedarwood and brownheart mixed with canela, more beautiful than you can imagine. /*íya*/

A WOMAN:
And inserted some purpleheart too.

ADUÊNGI:
Right. [He pauses a moment while others finish talking in the background.] OK! And at the same time, the person who said she would be screwing— /íya/

Well, her house was jam-packed. /íya/

All the men who came there were given a little pussy to enjoy (please excuse me, folks, but this is tale-telling that we're doing here).

MANY VOICES:
[laughter, comments]

ADUÊNGI:
A whorehouse if ever there was one! / . . . / So that's all. /íya/

Now the one— the one who said he'd— that he'd go off to find Drum —/íya/

Well, once they'd washed the corpse, he was already out of sight. /íya/

He'd already gone. /íya/

So they were going ahead with the funeral. /íya/

They're going ahead with the funeral, on and on, and he was gone. /íya/

He went along for a while and then he took a parrot— [correcting himself:] three parrot feathers, /íya/

three cowrie shells, /íya/

and three balls of kaolin. /íya/

And he set out with them. /íya/

Then he went along until he came to a river. /íya/

Now when he got to the river, he sees an endless expanse of water, and there's no way for him to get across.

TÍANÊN [breaking in]:
You know when he saw the endless expanse there? /ADUÊNGI: íya/

Well, he met up with Monkey. /that's right/

And Monkey called out, /true/

Tíanên spinning cotton, 1968.

and said, "Well, we see people here who are good to eat, /that's right/

but we're not going to eat them." /certainly not/

He sang:

Kizáán mi na kasúle záán-oo.
Kizáán mi na kasúle záán-oo.
Kizáán kó lúku a máwè.
Kizáán kizáán-ee.[97]

[The transcription of this song is somewhat problematic. The Saramakas we discussed this nugget with in 1986 and 1987 could not elucidate.]

Go right ahead.

ADUÊNGI:
Eh! My turtle foot is really short![98]

A WOMAN:
Yes, it's short!

ADUÊNGI:
Well, so that's all. /ADUÊNGI'S RESPONDER: *íya*/

As he was gazing out at the void, he turned and looked. /*íya*/

He noticed something surfacing out there in the middle of the water. It came swimming, *dalala,* toward him and arrived at the sho— at the— at the mouth of the path, and it set its head out right there, and he saw that it was an enormous cayman. /*íya*/

It was as big as this house here. /*íya*/

The boy— The boy walks over till he comes right up to it. / . . . / He went: "My Boat Saayé, greetings." (it answered "greetings, Boy") /íya/ It said, "Boy, where are you going?" He said, "My Boat Saayé, take me across." /íya/

It said, "Where are you going?" He said, "I'm going to where the devils live to look for Drum." /íya/

It said, "Boy, you'll never get there." /íya/

He said, "Father, I can get there. /íya/

Take me across." /íya/

It said, "Yes, well, Boy—" (he replied) It said, "If I take you across, you must pay me." /íya/

He said, "What will I pay you?" /íya/

It said, "Whatever you happen to have. /íya/

No matter how shoddy it may be— But you must pay me something. /íya/

I mean, you've got to give me some kind of a payment." /íya/

("yes" he said) He took one ball of kaolin, one parrot feather, and one cowrie shell, /íya/

and he gave them to it. /íya/

SAKUÍMA:
Uh-oh! So it would ferry him over to the village.

ADUÊNGI [interrupting the end of Sakuíma's remark]:
So that's all. The boy climbed right onto the middle of the cayman's head, *gwébòò*, and said, "My Boat Saayé, cross me over." /íya/

It cut right through the water, *zalalalalalalalala*, and up onto the shore on the other side.

TÍANÊN [breaking in]:
At the very time it was cutting through the water, /ADUÊNGI: *íya*/

I was standing right there.

ADUÊNGI:
What did you see?

TÍANÊN:
It sang:

A-fún-gu-ya-ni-ee,___ a-fún-gu-ya-ni-ee, a-fún-gu-ya-ni

Afúnguyani-ee, afúnguyani-ee, afúnguyani afuumá-ee.
Afúnguyani-ee, afúnguyani-ee, afúnguyani afuumá.
Eé-afuumá, ma di ya yéi-oo anáki kítoonya.
Toonya kíi wanapú-éé, kíyoonya-éé.

[The Saramakas who listened to our recording of this tale nugget were unable to elucidate at all, though Tíanên seems to be contributing a song sung by Cayman to Aduêngi's tale.]

It set him down at the landing, *zalala*. Go right on.

ADUÊNGI:
Oh! This thing is getting really sweet!

A MAN:
It's as sweet as—

ADUÊNGI:
OK! /ADUÊNGI'S RESPONDER: *íya*/

It carried him, *zalala*, right up onto the bank, *gbabáu*. / . . . / He said, "My boat Saayé—" (it replied) He said, "The very day I get back, when I return back to this place, you've got to be here." /*íya*/

It said, "Child, don't panic, 'cause I've already taken your payment, so don't even bother to worry about it." /*íya*/

A WOMAN:
"I'll be there."

ADUÊNGI:
He went on. / . . . /

A MAN [anticipating]:
Because he'll be running when he comes back to the river!

ADUÊNGI:
Yes.

OTHERS:
[laughter]

ADUÊNGI:
He kept on going for a long time.

OTHER VOICES:
[more remarks on how fast he'll be running]

ADUÊNGI:
Really. He went on until he got to a really enormous river. /íya/

Another cayman was there, just waiting. [Aduêngi pauses and then rattles off the rest of this segment in one breath.] He said, "My Boat Saayé, greetings," and it answered, "Greetings, Boy, where are you going?" and he said, "I'm going to where the devils live to look for Drum," and it said, "Boy, You'll never get there." /íya/

He said, "My Boat Saayé, take me across," and it said, "If I take you across, you'll have to pay me." /íya/

He said, "What will I pay you?" and it said. "You'll pay me whatever you happen to have, that's what you'll give me, even if it's something very shoddy, you'll still give it to me."

SAKUÍMA:
Aren't the others busy with the funeral by now?

ADUÊNGI:
Back at the funeral there things are really heating up. / . . . / All those things that we mentioned before, they're all in full swing.

SAKUÍMA:
Mm-hmm.

ADUÊNGI:
All those things—

SAKUÍMA [interrupting]:
All the different ones—

ADUÊNGI:
But you know about all that.

SAKUÍMA:
Sure do!

ADUÊNGI:
All of them are back there, doing things.

SAKUÍMA [interrupting]:
Right! There's really a lot to do! [99]

ADUÊNGI:
[a phrase drowned out by Sakuíma's comment, then:] That's
all. /íya/

It took him across, *zaa,* and set him down, *gbagbaa.* / . . . / He said,
"My Boat Saayé—" (it replied) He said, "You've accepted a payment from me." /íya/

("yes" it said) "So the very day I get back here you must be ready
to take me across, there can't be anything so important that it
prevents you from taking me across," and it said, "Boy, don't
panic." /íya/

He went on. / . . . / He continued on and on until he got to a really
enormous sea /íya/

that stretched as far as the eye could see. /íya/

He looked out and saw the same thing again. It came up, *gbagbuu.*
He greeted it. (it answered) It said, "Where are you going?" He
said, "I'm going to where the devils live." It said, "Well, Boy—"
(he replied) It said, "When you go to the devils' village—" ("yes"
he said) "You'll arrive there and you'll see an enormous open-
sided shed. /íya/

And the thing known as Drum— /íya/

Well, that whole place is crammed with them! /íya/

You'll see long drums. /íya/

You'll see *mamá* drums, you'll see *apínti*s, you'll see *agidá*s, you'll
see every kind of drum there is. [100] /íya/

[In rapid, run-on speech:] Now some will be calling, 'Don't touch
me! Don't touch me! Don't touch me!' And other ones will be calling, 'Come grab me! Come grab me!' The one over here: 'Come
take me! Come take me!' The one over there: 'Don't take me!' [He
draws a quick breath.] Now the one that's calling out, 'Don't touch
me!'— that's the one you must be sure to take. /íya/

But the ones that are calling out, telling you to take them— If you take them, Boy, there'll be nothing I can do for you. / . . . / But the one who's saying you mustn't take it, that you mustn't even touch it— that's the one you must be sure to take."

OVERLAPPING VOICES:
[laughter and comments]

ADUÊNGI:
"OK," he said, "No problem." / . . . / He said, "Well, no problem." He took the parrot feather and the cowrie shell, / . . . / and he put them on the cayman's head, gave them to it. /íya/

It carried him right across, *zalalalala,* and set him down.

SAKUÍMA:
The things he had were all used up.

ADUÊNGI:
Ohh! There was nothing at all left in his hands. [Very rapidly:] He said, "Well, my Boat Saayé—" (it replied) He said, "I've paid you, and you've accepted my payment." ("yes" it said) "When I come back, you've got to be here." It said, "Don't even bother to worry, Boy." /íya/

(he said OK) That boy there— Then the boy went up— He went up the hill to the top, and he got to Bongóótu-písi, *djaláa.*[101]

SAKUÍMA:
Right! He must have looked up and seen the open-sided shed up there.

ADUÊNGI [continuing over Sakuíma's last several words and still rushing his speech:]:
Right. And then he got there. And when he got there, he saw the drums all over the place. Some of them are calling out, "Come grab me! Come take me! Come take me!" Others are calling, "Don't take me! Don't take me! Don't—" Others are saying, "Come take me! Come take me! Come—" Ohhh! They're all talking at once in that place.

SAKUÍMA:
In that village, you couldn't tell what was what.

ADUÊNGI:
Not at all. The boy got there. He came up till he was very close, and he stood there completely still. They're calling out to him. They're calling out to him to tell him what to do. / . . . / He goes up and

one of them calls out, "Don't take me!" and when he reaches out
to touch it, its shouting is so fierce that the boy gets scared. / . . . /
He said [reflectively]: "But my Boat Saayé told me that's the one I
should be sure to take, and I'm going to take it." So he went over,
took it and untied it. Then the ones that had been saying "Come
take me"— Well, scorpions! stinging ants! venomous lizards! poi-
sonous snakes! and every imaginable dangerous thing was crawling all over them.

KASINDÓ [volunteering helpfully]:
And wasps.

ADUÊNGI:
Right. / . . . / So that's all. He went and took the *apínti,* untied it,
and set it on the ground. / . . . / [In the voice of the boy, marveling
at what he's found]: "Ah! The thing they call a—"

TÍANÊN:
And where were the people who lived in that village?

ADUÊNGI:
The people who lived in that village— Not a single one was there.
They'd gone off. Because they used to go off and do blacksmiths'
work for Great God until evening and then they'd come back. And
then they'd play the drums. / . . . / So, that's all. The boy untied the
drum and set it down there. He took a stool and sat down. / . . . /
He looked at the drum there, he turned it all around to look at it,
and said, "Yes, this thing is certainly beautiful!" Then he played it:
"tim! tim! tim! tim!" He heard:

Kaadím, kaadím, mitóóliaa.
Kaadím, kaadím, mitóóliaa.
Sibámalé, sibámalé.
Kaadím, kaadím, mitóóliaa.[102]

The devils were out there and they said, "Help! We're dead! Someone has come to our village. Whoever's there, you've had it!"

OTHERS:
[exclamations]

ADUÊNGI:
The boy picked up the drum and ran. He ran till he was almost at the river, and then he set it down again.

SAKUÍMA:
That boy's really baaad!

ADUÊNGI:
He said, "This thing is just too sweet to resist. I'm going to play it just a little more." / . . . / He played: "*tim, tim,*"

> *Kaadím, kaadím, mitóóliaa.*
> *Kaadím, kaadím, mitóóliaa.*
> *Sibámalé, sibámalé.*
> *Kaadím, kaadím, mitóóliaa.*

Oh! The devils were charging through the trees, falling all over themselves. / . . . / Then when the boy got there, he said, "My Boat Saayé, here I am." It said, "Boy, I'm all ready." Nothing to it.

SAKUÍMA:
Ahh. He knows that once he gets across, he'll be OK.

ADUÊNGI:
So he said, "Well, Boy, since you're here, play a little for me to hear, because I keep hearing about Drum, and I'd like to hear what it sounds like too."

SAKUÍMA:
My god! This is getting to be too much for me!

OTHERS:
[laughter]

ADUÊNGI:
He said, "My Boat Saayé, take me across." It said, "No, no, play the drum for me."

OTHERS:
[clucks of concern]

ADUÊNGI:
No problem. So he played for it. It really sang and then it stopped. The cayman said, "OK, Boy, climb on." Now by that time, the

devils weren't any farther than that landing just over there. / . . . /
Ohhh! The wind was coming up! It slipped into the water. /*íya*/

A MAN:
Hey! What's happened to the responses?!

THE RESPONDER [emphatically]:
ÍYA!

OTHERS:
[laughter]

AGUMIÍI:
He'd really gone to sleep!

OVERLAPPING VOICES:
[more comments]

ADUÊNGI:
It had set out into the water till it was right out in the middle, and
there it was, bobbing gently in the water. /*íya*/

KASINDÓ:
Was it waiting for the devils?

ADUÊNGI:
Ohh! They all swarmed up. /*íya*/

They called out, "My Boat Saayé, sink!" The boy said, "My Boat
Saayé, don't sink, 'cause you've accepted a payment from me!
Who can tell you to sink?" The devils said, "Sink!" /*íya*/

One of them pulled out a tooth and flung it through the air. /*íya*/

It dried up all the water. My Boat Saayé said, "No, no, you can't
stop me." /*íya*/

OTHERS:
[laughter and comments]

AGUMIÍI:
That's the tooth known as "*Azángana mi kolóbi*"!

ADUÊNGI:
What did you call it?

AGUMIÍI:
The tooth he's pulling out is *Azángana mi kolóbi, azángana mi koló*.[103]

[The exchange between Agumiíi and Asabôsi goes on simultaneously
with that part of Kódji's tale nugget that precedes his song:]

KÓDJI:

Well, at the moment when it was saying "No, no," /ADUÉNGI: *íya*/

well, I was there.

SOMEONE:

What did you see?

KÓDJI:

At that moment a woman had gone off with her child to do some
fish drugging, and she had caught herself a fish. /*íya*/

So there they were, and the fish pulled the boat and it dragged
them down to the bottom. /*íya*/

Mi físi, mi físi, a vènuvèè asidáiloo.
Mi físi, mi físi, a vènuvèè asidáiloo.
Éé mi físi, a vènuvèè asidáiloo.
Dáiloo dáiloo.
Éé mi físi, a vènuvèè asidáiloo.

[This is the song of the woman calling out to the fish, "My
fish, my fish," but we have no further explication.]

Go on with your story.

SAKUÍMA:

Your leg is as short as a turtle's! [104]

ADUÊNGI:

OK. /ADUÉNGI'S RESPONDER: *íya*/

That's all. Well, My Boat Saayé is taking the boy over to the other shore, *badaa*. The devils are there on the bank, and they just don't know what to do, and they're doing all kinds of things, but all in vain. Breaking up their houses, burning the whole place down. /*íya*/

There's nothing left there.

KÓDJI:
Couldn't they jump in the water?

ANOTHER MAN:
That wouldn't help.

THIRD MAN:
They're stuck there.

ADUÊNGI:
Well, as this was happening, my Boat Saayé really wanted to sink! /*íya*/

Well, whatever the devils would tell it to do— Since they lived together there— Whatever they would tell it to do, it would do. /*íya*/

But it had accepted a payment from the boy.

TÍANÊN:
It had accepted his payment because they had made an agreement.

ADUÊNGI:
Yeah. He says to it, "My Boat Saayé, you accepted my payment, so you can't sink." /*íya*/

OTHERS:
[laughter]

ADUÊNGI:
Ohh! Nothing to it, so the cayman came up on the other shore, and it said, "Boy, play for me." He played for it:

> *Kaadím, kaadím, mitóóliaa.*
> *Kaadím, kaadím, mitóóliaa.*
> *Sibámalé, sibámalé.*
> *Kaadím, kaadím, mitóóliaa.*

It said, "Yes, Boy, it's sweet. Go along." /*íya*/

Ohh! He went along till he got right up to another one. /*íya*/

He said, "My Boat Saayé, here I am," and it said, "Yes, well, play for me." He played for it, /íya/

and when he was done he went on. /íya/

It carried him smoothly and set him down on the shore. /íya/

AGUMIÍI:
Well, he said he was going to play the drum at the head of the grave. And he's on his way to play that drum.

TÍANÊN:
The head of the coffin thing is what he'd gone looking for.

[Agumiíi and Tíanên's remarks here overlap with Aduêngi's next few phrases.]

ADUÊNGI:
Finally he got to the other one. He played for it, till he was done and he went on. /íya/

He continued along. He kept on going and going until— the very moment when they were taking the coffin outside, / . . . / performing the ritual separations, sprinkling the kaolin for the separations. So that's all. The boy arrived. / . . . / He said, "Everyone, I'm back." They said, "OK, well, we're just going off for the burial." /íya/

He said, "Yes, well, let's do what we have to do. But listen to me." /íya/

He pulled the drum over and set it right at the head of the coffin, and then he played it. /íya/

> Kaadím, kaadím, mitóóliaa.
> Kaadím, kaadím, mitóóliaa.
> Sibámalé, sibámalé.
> Kaadím, kaadím, mitóóliaa.

They lifted the coffin up onto the bearers' heads. And so you see that the *apínti* came to stay, and every kind of drum in the world, 'cause the drum that the boy went to get, well, it became the drum for the whole world. /yes/

As a result, *apínti* for us Bush Negroes— If you play it, people hear the *apínti*, and you say, "Yes, such and such a thing is what it's saying." It was taken from the land of the devils, and if it hadn't been, we never would have had drums.

Saramaka apínti, *collected 1928–29 by Melville and Frances Herskovits.*

SAKUÍMA:
Right, let's all give thanks to the boy!

ADUÊNGI:
That's as far as my story goes.

KASINDÓ:
Mató! [105]

A MAN:
Tòngôni!

KASINDÓ:
There we were. /*íya*/

And after a while a certain woman had a daughter. /*íya*/

OVERLAPPING VOICES:
[discussion of the possibility of leaving]

KASINDÓ:
We're not breaking up yet.

SAKUÍMA:
Don't go to sleep yet. Your job is to do the replies.

KASINDÓ [talking over all the competing conversation]:
So a woman had a daughter. A woman had a daughter. /*íya*/

Mm. Well, Man, she raised that daughter till she was grown
up. /*íya*/

Now in that region, all the women were very beautiful. /*íya*/

So that's why all the women would get asked for in marriage. /*íya*/

But there was just one who wouldn't hear of it. /*íya*/

So they went along like that until the day came /*íya*/

when they gave the girl her skirts of adulthood. /*íya*/

Well, over there in folktale-land, /*íya*/

they had a really large village where people went to have their
bodies incised.[106] /*íya*/

So the woman decided to send her daughter /*íya*/

to go there and have designs cut. /*íya*/

Well, Brother, so they settled on a day. They decided on a
day. /*íya*/

When that day came, they would go. /*íya*/

Well, the woman herself /*íya*/

had a rather small son, just a scrawny little one. /íya/

So the girl was ready to leave. /íya/

The boy got up too and said, "Older sister?" (she replied) He said, "I'll come along with you." /íya/

She said, "No, don't come. /íya/

You're such a scrawny little thing. How do you think I could manage to carry you on my back?"

ADUÊNGI [breaking in]:
  Well, when she was saying that to him, /KASINDÓ: íya/

  I was there pleading with her, saying, "Let the kid come along." /hm/

OTHERS:
  [soft laughter]

ADUÊNGI:
  Well, that's all. At that time, there was no such thing as a ship. /that's how it was/

  So Old Man Anasi decided to go get Ship and bring it back for the chief. [107] /íya/

  So he addressed the chief and said, "Well, Chief, I'd like you to give me a corncob /íya/

  so I can go buy Ship for you." /íya/

  So the chief said, "Yes. But Anasi, you think you can buy Ship with one corncob?!" ("yes" he said) /íya/

  So Anasi jumped right up— (I'm not going to tell the long version.) And he took the corncob. Then he waited until the time came for the ship to arrive, and he said:

Anasi mi kôni, o yaa.
Báa Anasi mi kôni, O Yaa.
Anasi mi kôni, O Yaa.
Mi téki wán kálu páu, O Yaa,
mi bái wán kakafóu, O Yaa.
Mi téki wán kakafóu, O Yaa,
mi bái wán hágu fu mi, O Yaa.
Mi téki wán hágu fu mi, O Yaa,
mi bái wán dêdè pikín, O Yaa.
Mi téki wán dêdè pikín, O Yaa,
mi bái wán sípi fu mi, O Yaa.
Báa Anasi mi kôni, O Yaa.
Báa Anasi mi kôni, O Yaa.

[This song is mainly in Saramaccan, but some of the words are Sranan; for example: *kakafóu* (instead of Saramaccan *ganía*) for "chicken," and *pikín* (instead of Saramaccan *miíi*) for "child." It translates as: "Anasi, I'm clever, oh yes. / Brother Anasi, I'm clever, Oh Yes. / Anasi, I'm clever, Oh Yes. / I take a corncob, Oh Yes, / and buy a chicken, Oh Yes. / I take a chicken, Oh Yes, / and buy myself a pig, Oh Yes. / I take that pig of mine, Oh Yes, / and buy a little dead child, Oh Yes. / I take that little dead child, Oh Yes, / and buy myself a ship, Oh Yes. / Brother Anasi, I'm clever, Oh Yes. / Brother Anasi, I'm clever, Oh Yes.]

He got on the ship. Well, right away he was there at the helm.

SAKUÍMA:
Yes, he's already steering it.

ADUÊNGI:
He had already taken over the ship. He had already bought the ship with those things.

SAKUÍMA:
He's strutting his stuff.

ADUÊNGI:
And he steered the ship right up to the chief's pier. Go ahead with your story.

KASINDÓ:
Íya. So the girl is all ready to set off. / KASINDÓ'S RESPONDER: *íya*/

They were setting out and the mother pointed out the way. / . . . /
She said, "Child, the way you'll go— /*íya*/

Well, after a while you'll get to a fork in the path. /*íya*/

[Explaining very conscientiously:] You'll see one path that's all
overgrown, /*íya*/

and one that's nicely cleared. /*íya*/

Please, my dear, when you see the cleared one, /*íya*/

don't take it. /*íya*/

Take the overgrown one." /*íya*/

(she said "all right") So on they went. /*íya*/

And after a while, the path split in two. /*íya*/

They arrived at that place. /*íya*/

Ohh, I made a mistake. /*íya*/

There were really TWO daughters. /*íya*/

So the two sisters /*íya*/

plus the brother made three. /*íya*/

So they continued along until they got to the fork in the path. /*íya*/

And they stood there. /*íya*/

The two sisters wanted to discuss it. /*íya*/

[Here it starts to rain, and people move into a large open-sided shed.
Various people talk about what pots, glasses, lanterns, and so on, need
to be brought in out of the rain. The tape recorder is turned off while
we move inside. Then the tale picks up again as the rain becomes a
downpour.]

The two sisters /*íya*/

had come up to the fork in the path. /*íya*/

So they were standing there. /*íya*/

And when they'd go around a turn in the path /*íya*/

the scrawny little kid /*íya*/

would hurry up and follow the same way. /*íya*/

But the sisters didn't see him. /*íya*/

Adolescent girls and a younger brother, 1968.

Mm. They got up to that fork in the path and the two sisters stood there discussing it. /íya/

They stood there and they said [in a voice of girlish innocence]: "Well, Sister—" /íya/

(the other one replied) She said, "Well, look at the fork we've come to here. /íya/

The path is so overgrown here! /íya/

And even with the morning moisture that's all over it, this is the one we're supposed to take. /íya/

Well, no, I really wouldn't like to go that way." /íya/

"Really, Sister?" ("that's right" she said) /íya/

She said, "Well, Sister, just as you say, I too would rather take the cleared one." /íya/

She said, "Come on then, let's take the cleared one. /íya/

The other path's too overgrown for us to get there by this morning." /íya/

("OK" she said) So they took the cleared path. /íya/

So they went along and went along, and sure enough, [dramatic pause] they got to the devil's village. /íya/

Oh!! The devil called to them: "*Pikí pikí pikí pikí pikí pikí pikí.*"[108] /íya/

They replied, "Yes, Father?" /íya/

He said [fiercely, in a rapid-fire nasal voice]: "Why'd you come? why'd you come? why'd you come? why'd you come?" They said, "Oh, Father, we've come here to have designs cut." /íya/

"I see," he said. /íya/

[altering his voice for sweet talk:] "Well, that's exactly what I do here! I'm just the one who cuts designs!" /íya/

OTHERS:
[laughter]

KASINDÓ:
("yes" they said) "Well, children, first you'll sleep. /íya/

In the morning, I'll cut designs for you both, and then you'll go back." /íya/

The girls said, "All right." /íya/

As they were talking there, /íya/

the scrawny little brother of theirs /íya/

was right there at the side of the house. /íya/

AGUMIÍI:
He'd never abandoned them. He was following them all along.

KASINDÓ:
Yes, but they didn't see him. / . . . / Mm! They slept, /íya/

very soundly. Later on, when they drifted off to sleep, /íya/

well, the devil /íya/

was going to come to them. /íya/

KÓDJI:
At the time when he was coming along there, /KASINDÓ: íya/

well, there was a terrible famine. /mm-hm/

People were so hungry!! Brother, it was really something! /íya/

Well, there was a man who had a cassava garden. /íya/

And the people wanted to ask for some cassava. /mm-hm/

But when they went, he would never share the cassava. Wouldn't break off even a little for anyone else. /right/

Well, a certain young woman called her elders, and they took her off behind the house to prepare her ritually. /that's how it was/

And they prepared her very well. /indeed/

Then she called her husband. She said, "Come on, let's go look for cassava too." /that's how it was/

So off they went. /mm-hm/

They continued on, and as they were just getting up to the garden's entrance, on the path, at the landing, /indeed/

the man went to go dig up the cassava, and the woman went to the other man in his garden house there. /mm-hm/

WOMEN [anticipating her plan of action]:
[laughter]

AGUMIÍI:
Their plan's working out!

KÓDJI:
Well, that's all. / . . . / She continued on till she got to the entrance there. /íya/

She'd dropped her old man off at the upstream landing— her husband. /íya/

Well, he was going to dig up the cassava. That's all. / . . . / When she got to the entrance posts, she dropped her skirt and tossed it right up onto the posts.

Awínsi awínsi pélenga, pélenga na mi seéi.
A pasá m'báta pélenga, pélenga na mi seéi.
A pasá m'báta pélenga, pélenga na mi seéi.
A pasá m'báta pélenga, pélenga na mi seéi.
A pasá m'báta pélenga.

[In the tale from which this nugget is drawn, the woman sings this song while dancing *bandámmba*—a sinuous bump-and-grind—for the man, as he dances around and around her. Her song makes fun of Father Awínsi (either a devil or Death himself), who owns the cassava.]

[Recapitulating the story rapidly, and talking over general laughter:] The old guy was right there in the garden shed, stripping reeds to make a basket. He bolted! He said, "Who's being so rude? Who's playing with me?!" He flung his breechcloth right up onto the center beam of the shed. He was rubbing his hand all over the girl. Then she went back to the canoe. They went and got cassava and took it back to their village. And that's why, Brother, when there's a big famine, if you have a little cassava to sell, even if you've never sold cassava, still, when someone comes along, you break off a piece and give it to them.

AGUMIÍI:
Also, don't send your wife off alone to get cassava!

KÓDJI:
Don't pretend you don't have any. Go on with your story. Go on with your story, Brother.

OTHERS:
[lots of laughter]

KASINDÓ:
OK, well, that's all. The girls were sleeping.

OTHERS:
[continued laughter and hooting about Kódji's tale nugget]

KASINDÓ:
And up came the devil. He made the girls faint, /KASINDÓ's
RESPONDER: íya/

did that till he was all done. /íya/

Then he pulled out their eyes, /íya/

and put them in a calabash salt container. "Heh! Heh!" The old
devil. /right/

Well, then, later on the devil put together a big cooking fire in the
house, there where the girls were. / . . . / He arranged the fire so
that it got very big. /íya/

Then he took a machete of his named Môsòmò. /íya/

A MAN:
Môsòmò.

KASINDÓ:
Môsòmò. /íya/

And he was going to use it on the girls' asses. /íya/

SOMEONE:
That was his design-cutting knife [instead of a razor]?

KASINDÓ:
Yes. /íya/

OTHERS:
[laughter]

KASINDÓ:
He put it in the fire till it was red hot. /íya/

Then he pulled his Môsòmò out quickly and took it over to one of
the girls' asses. /íya/

The boy heard [chanting]:

Gan-gan-mun-tún-bu tá bu-tá Mô-sò-mò.   U-léé-lee.

Ganganmuntúnbu tá butá Môsòmò.
Uléélee.
Ganganmuntúnbu tá butá Môsòmò.
Uléélee.

[In lines 1 and 3, the devil is announcing: "Ganganmuntúnbu (his own name) is using Môsòmò (his machete's name)." The chorus represents the boy immediately responding from his hiding place with the magic word "*uléélee*," which turns the machete cold again.]

Môsòmò cooled instantly! "Ohh!" [the devil's cry of alarm]

A MAN:
   Who said that "*uléélee*"?

SAKUÍMA:
   It was the scrawny little kid.

THE MAN:
   He was the one?

OTHERS:
   [laughter]

KASINDÓ:
   The devil ran outside! / . . . / He ran and got a broom. Then he came back and swept all around the house very thoroughly [to get rid of whatever had cooled Môsòmò]. He swept the ceiling. He brought the sweepings together and put them in the fire. / . . . / Then he put Môsòmò back in. / . . . / Whatever it was that was playing tricks on him, it hadn't been able to kill him. / . . . / Yes, it was the thing hiding in the palm-leaf wall that was doing this to him. /*íya*/

   Well, it was the little kid. He was the one.

ADUÊNGI:
   So he was doing it! You mean he followed them there?

KASINDÓ:
   He had followed them there. He was right there in the palm-leaf wall. /*íya*/

SAKUÍMA:
   Next to the house?

KASINDÓ:
   Right. /*íya*/

Well, that's all. The devil built up the fire, till Môsòmò was really hot. /íya/

He pulled it out and brought it over to the girl's ass. He heard:

> *Ganganmuntúnbu tá butá Môsòmò.*
> *Uléélee.*
> *Ganganmuntúnbu tá butá Môsòmò.*
> *Uléélee.*

OTHERS:
[laughter]

KASINDÓ:
Môsòmò went stone cold. / . . . / Mmm, the devil jumped up and rushed outside. /íya/

He took his twig broom and went up on top of the house with it.

ADUÊNGI [breaking in]:
When he went outside, /KASINDÓ: íya/

I was the one he called on to help him with the sweeping. /mm-hm/

I was trying to tell him that I didn't know how to sweep. /íya/

So that's all. Well, the devil child— The devil— The girl— The woman with the child— Well, she sent the boy off to go chase birds away from the rice in her garden. /exactly!/

It was time to harvest the January rice. /right/

So the kid set off and eventually got to the entrance to the garden. /íya/

Then he passed through the palm frond right into the middle of the garden and knocked the tree trunks, *kwóó kwóó kwóó*. /hm!/

He heard: "*Sama toofia nyaka sóóndi!*" ["Who is here chasing things?"] [109] He answered, "*Oyáá.*" / . . . / That's all. The old man [i.e., the devil] walked right up to him. "Boy?" (he replied) He said [chanting]: "*Sôkò na mí. É yá sôkò na mí, nô sôkò na mí!*" [In "devils' language," roughly: "Give me something to eat. If you don't feed me, I'm going eat you."]

OTHERS:
[laughter]

ADUÊNGI:
The boy said, "Yes, Father." The devil bent his head quickly to the ground, threw his ass up in the air, and the boy tossed those things, *hólon hólon hólon*, right into the devil. [Chanting:]

(♩ = ca.140)

Hó-lo bi-gó-do, tjaau tjaau. Hó-lo gwë-ge-de, tjaau tjaau.

Hólo bigódo, tjaau tjaau.
Hólo gwégede, tjaau tjaau.
Hólo bigódo, tjaau tjaau.
Hólo gwégede, tjaau tjaau.

[cascading pitch:] *Gúdu gwulúu, gudúu, gwúgwulu gwulúu, gudúu.*

[*Hólo bigódo* and *Hólo gwégede* are the sounds made by the things being thrown into the devil's asshole. *Tjaau tjaau* is the devil's "chomp, chomp." The last line is the devil expiring.[110]]

OTHERS:
[laughter]

ADUÊNGI:
Continue your story.

KASINDÓ:
OK! So he swept the top of the house, /KASINDÓ'S RESPONDER: *íya*/

swish, swish, over the whole area, /*íya*/

and then climbed down. /*íya*/

Then he swept the ground all around the house. /*íya*/

Then he took the sweepings and tossed them in the fire. /*íya*/

He lit them. /*íya*/

Now at the time that he went to sweep the house like that, /*íya*/

well, the boy was right there. He had come out from the palm-leaf wall and gone inside the house. /*íya*/

So he went and took the girl's eye from the salt container there, just one of them, /*íya*/

and he rinsed it off very quickly, /*íya*/

and he put it back in its socket. /*íya*/

Then he tapped her on the left foot. /*íya*/

The girl yawned. /*íya*/

Mm! He tapped her on the right foot. /*íya*/

The girl stood up and stretched and said, "Ohh— I slept SO-O soundly!" / . . . / He said, "No you didn't. You weren't asleep. You died a long time ago." /íya/

She said, "Really?" He said, "That's right." She said, "No, I was just asleep. /íya/

All I did was go to sleep. What a ridiculous idea that I died! I was asleep, Brother." "I see," he said. "You were just sleeping?" "Yes!" she said. "Well, then look at your sister on the floor there." She turned to look and saw her eye sockets all empty. She said, "Help!! DON'T SHOW ME THAT!"

OTHERS:
[wild laughter]

KASINDÓ:
"Well, you weren't asleep. You were exactly like that! / . . . / You were exactly like that!" "Really?" she said. "That's right," he said. "Mm." "Well listen." /íya/

("yes" she said) The girl whose eyes he had put back in place, well, he took her outside while the devil was away. He said, "Take this path and just keep going. / . . . / If the old man sees you here, you're dead!"

A WOMAN:
Is he going to leave the other one there?

KASINDÓ:
The other one was still there. / . . . / Mm. After a while the devil came back. He got the fire together. /íya/

He put things in the fire, just so. He got the fire together and heated up Môsòmò. /íya/

He pulled it out and took it over to the girl's ass. He heard:

Ganganmuntúnbu tá butá Môsòmò.
<u>*Uléélee.*</u>
Ganganmuntúnbu tá butá Môsòmò.
<u>*Uléélee.*</u>

OTHERS:
[laughter]

KASINDÓ:
Môsòmò went stone cold. Ahh. / . . . / This was really something!! Ho!

SAKUÍMA:
   He was getting really hungry.

KASINDÓ:
   You're not kidding! The devil jumped up. /íya/

   He left the house quickly. /íya/

   Then he went off to the village of some other devils, /íya/

   calling them to help, saying that things had gotten out of hand at his place. /íya/

   Some people came to him that were good to eat, and he just couldn't manage to eat them! / . . . / So he got twelve devils and brought them back with him. /íya/

   Counting him there were thirteen. /íya/

   Now while he was going to the twelve devils' village, /íya/

   the girl who was on the ground, the second one— /íya/

   Well, the boy went and opened the calabash salt container. He took out the eyes and rinsed them off very thoroughly. /íya/

   He tapped her on the left foot. /íya/

   She stirred. / . . . / Tapped the right foot, and she stood up and yawned and said, "Ohh, how deeply I slept!" and he said, "No you didn't, you weren't asleep. /íya/

   You died a long time ago."

A WOMAN:
   "The devil ate you."

KASINDÓ:
   "So listen. Take the path you see there, /íya/

   and stay on it all the way to the river. /íya/

   Just keep going, no matter what you hear."

A MAN [breaking in]:
   Was he sending them back to where they came from?

KASINDÓ:
   To where they came from, to their village. /íya/

   "All right," she said. Ohh! As she was leaving, /íya/

   the other sister—

AGUMIÍI [breaking in]:
At the time when they were going along there, /KASINDÓ: *íya*/

well, Toad and Housefly had gone hunting. /mm-hm/

So, well—

A MAN:
Who were the two who went?

AGUMIÍI:
Toad, along with Housefly. So Housefly said he would salt the meat he got. /hm!/

And Toad said he would smoke his. /mm-hm/

Then Housefly said, "No, let's salt all our meat," but Toad said, "No, I'm going to smoke mine," and Housefly said, "Once I've salted mine, I'll salt yours too."

OTHERS:
[laughter, since Housefly will eat the meat, leaving it with white eggs, which make it look as though it's been salted]

AGUMIÍI:
Toad put his over the fire. /mm-hm/

Housefly salted his. [Chanting:]

A *tòn tôn-kí tôn-kí toón toón tòn. Tòn tôn-kí bá-si-a u-me toón tòn.*

A tòn tônkí tônkí toón toón tòn.
Tòn tônkí básia ume toón tòn.
A tòn tônkí tônkí toón toón tòn.
Tòn tônkí básia ume toón tòn.
A tòn tônkí tônkí toón toón tòn.
Tòn tônkí básia ume toón tòn.
A tòn tônkí tônkí toón toón tòn.
Tòn tônkí básia ume toón tòn.

[This is the song of Fly dancing all over the meat and spoiling it, getting back at Toad for taking the bigger portion. It's done as call-and-response.]

OTHERS:
[laughter]

AGUMÍÍ:

He finished salting his. He jumped up and worked on Toad's. / . . . / He salted it thoroughly. Then he ran off and slipped into a hole. / . . . / He'd finished salting it.

A MAN:

Go ahead with your story.

OTHERS:

[laughter]

KASINDÓ:

OK! The devil set out from the twelve devils' village, /KASINDÓ'S RESPONDER: *íya*/

and when he got back, /*íya*/

the girls were gone. /*íya*/

The devil opened the door. Nothing there. /*íya*/

He said, "What?!"

A WOMAN:

Was the boy there?

A MAN:

What boy do you mean?

A WOMAN:

You couldn't see him.

KASINDÓ:

The scrawny little kid— The scrawny little kid— /*íya*/

He was right there. So after a while the twelve devils got there, all twelve. / . . . / They arrived, and they saw the boy /*íya*/

in the village. /*íya*/

Oh! So the devil called to him: "*pikí pikí pikí pikí pikí pikí.*" /*íya*/

He replied, "What is it, Father?" /*íya*/

The devil said, "Who's this little person who's in my bed?" The boy said, "Father, I'm Témba." /*íya*/

[The boy sings:]

O-lé-le u-lé,   Tém-baa ku-ma Lém-baa, Tém-baa.

Oléle ulé, Témbaa kuma Lémbaa, Témbaa.
Oléle ulé, Témbaa kuma Lémbaa, Témbaa.
Oléle ulé, Témbaa kuma Lémbaa, Témbaa.
Oléle ulé, Témbaa kuma Lémbaa, Témbaa.

[The boy seems to be singing his praise name, which includes his special magic word, *oléle* (elsewhere *uléélee*) and the claim that "Témba is as strong as Lémba."[111] Listeners clearly knew this song, since they chorused it on the very first line.]

The devil says, "Boy, it's not true, not true, not true." The devil walked on. / . . . / He started out after the girls. / . . . / Then the others ran till all twelve were running. The boy's back there dealing with the other devils. /*íya*/

And what happened is— The first devil came up, and asked the boy, he said, "Boy—" (he replied) He said, "Aren't you the kid who cooled down my Môsòmò?" / . . . / He said, "Not at all, Father. Not at all." Then he played some music for the devil to dance to. / . . . / He played and the devil danced till it was enough, and he said [in response to the boy's playing, which sounded different now]: "You're not the one, not the one, not the one. Go along."

OTHERS:
[laughter]

KASINDÓ:
Meanwhile the girls were running and running, and they got to the river. . . .

A MAN:
Hey man, don't forget about replies for the tale!

KASINDÓ:
And when the girls got to the river, /*íya*/

they came to a long straight place, /*íya*/

like from here all the way to Paramaribo. /*íya*/

They saw the devils coming. /*íya*/

They were really coming. /*íya*/

The wind was blowing up. /*íya*/

The girls didn't know what to do anymore. /*íya*/

They kept seeing those things coming. /*íya*/

They were coming after them. /íya/

Well, Brother, those men who had wanted to marry those women /íya/

were coming along in their canoes and passing right by. /íya/

"My god, man. Please! Be so kind as to take me away." /íya/

One said, "Woman, when I asked you to marry me, you didn't want me. /íya/

I can't come take you." / . . . / And he went on. /íya/

Mm! The bird known as Fishcatcher [kwátá-kwátá] had come to try his luck, /íya/

again and again. /íya/

They never wanted him. /íya/

The devils were coming up REALLY CLOSE, /íya/

all ready to grab the girls, /íya/

and just then Fishcatcher appeared at the bend in the river there. /íya/

[Chanting:]

Sikeím gbò, sikeím gbò gbò.
Sikeím gbò, sikeím gbò gbò.
Sikeím gbò.
Ta seezanki daagoo dimbemsi gòndôô.

[This is the chant of Fishcatcher as he paddles along toward the girls. Saramakas explained that the reason Fishcatcher had originally been refused as a suitor was that he stank from the fish he caught. Here, when the women say they want him, he replies that he still smells because he's still a

fisherman. He paddles on to the end of the long stretch before, on hearing their continued pleading, he decides to
come back and take them. The transcription of the final
line is uncertain.[112]]

Fishcatcher came across, toward the girls who were right there on
the shore. /íya/

He came gliding by the girls, *liyoo*. Their screams were ringing
out. /íya/

Oh! Then he turned his boat toward them. He paddled so the
front of his canoe came right up where the girls could jump
in. /íya/

He paddled smoothly off to the next bend in the river. /íya/

The girls said, "Really, young man, the favor you've done for us
here— We just don't know how to thank you enough." Then they
took out a white kerchief and they draped it around his shoulders.
And it's still there.[113] /íya/

The devils came rushing out and plunged into the water, and they
became the stones that are in the rapids.

A MAN:
What about the little kid?

KASINDÓ:
The little kid?

THE MAN:
Mmm.

KASINDÓ:
He just went off. The girls said he wouldn't see them again. / . . . /
Because they hadn't wanted him to follow them, so he went back
to their village. The girls didn't want to see him again. /well!/

AMÁKA:
Mató![114]

A MAN:
Tòngôni!

ANOTHER MAN:
Íya.

AMÁKA:
Well, there we were. /ONE OF THE MEN: *íya*/

There was a woman who had three sons. Well, she gave birth to these three sons. So that's all. She'd cook for them. She'd cook till the food was ready and serve it /*íya*/

for them to eat. /*íya*/

So they'd eat. They'd eat the food till it was all gone. /*íya*/

They'd eat it all up. /*íya*/

They'd eat the mother's food too. /*íya*/

The mother never ate at all anymore. /*íya*/

So one day the boys went off hunting and caught themselves a fish. /*íya*/

The mother cooked it up in a cassava sauce that was really something. /*íya*/

[From "*Mató!*" up to this point, people have been moving around and having extraneous conversations.]

She dished some out for the boys. /*íya*/

They ate up everything she served them, /*íya*/

and then they went on to the mother's portion and ate that too. /*íya*/

"Ahh, children! What's happening between you and me? Don't you want me to have even a little bit to eat? /*íya*/

Well, let me kill you all and have some peace." /*íya*/

She picked up a club, *valam!* The boys ran. They really took off! /*íya*/

They ran and kept going till they passed through another village, *valáu!* Mmm! / . . . / The mother got there, /*íya*/

to the village. /*íya*/

Someone called to her: "*Síbi!*" ("*Síbi*" she answered) "What's going on?" "Well, nothing, *Síbi*.[115] /*íya*/

Those children I gave birth to are so cruel to me. /*íya*/

As for eating— I can't even get a single thing to eat. From the moment they were born till today, I haven't eaten at all. /*íya*/

I'm going to kill them so I can have some peace." /*íya*/

AGUMÍÍI:
She hadn't heard that when you have children, you don't eat?!

AMÁKA:
"*Síbi*," the other one said, "you know what? Go sit down and rest. /*íya*/

Go cook something to eat and let me go kill them for you." /*íya*/

Then she picked up a drum she had, /*íya*/

and she picked up a club. /*íya*/

And she ran off. /*íya*/

The mother turned right around, quick as could be, /*íya*/

and put her pot on the fire. She cooked her food till it was done just right. She ate till her belly was full, /*íya*/

and then she went to bathe in the river. /*íya*/

She said, "I'm free of them." /*íya*/

Mm. The boys ran and ran and got to a *mamádósu* [a tree with brown, thorny fruit]. /*íya*/

They climbed right up and were very still. /*íya*/

The woman ran right by them. /*íya*/

She turned around /*íya*/

and said, "Those boys are here!" /*íya*/

She sat down on the ground right there. /*íya*/

She rested till she was all rested. She took her drum, /*íya*/

and she tapped it: "*Tím!* [in Sranan:] Child to the ground!" /*íya*/

The oldest boy dropped down, *zalala gbíí!* /*íya*/

She clubbed him, *gwôô*, and dragged him over to the side. /*íya*/

AGUMIÍI:
I thought she was fooling the other woman when she said she'd kill the children!

AMÁKA:
Then she tapped the drum again: "*Tím!* Child to the ground!" /*íya*/

The middle one dropped, *fíín, gbíí!* /*íya*/

She clubbed him, *gwôô!* /*íya*/

OTHERS:
[exclamations]

AMÁKA:

Then she tapped the drum again: "*Tím!* Child to the ground!" /*íya*/

The boy in the tree called out [in Sranan]: "Mother up here!"

OTHERS:

[exclamations]

AMÁKA:

"Mmm, what's that?"[116]

She tapped the drum: "*Tím!* Child to the ground!" He said, "Mother up here!" /*íya*/

She tapped it: "*Tím!* Child to the ground!" He said, "Mother up here!" She put the drum down. /*íya*/

She climbed up a tree /*íya*/

and sat down on a branch. The boy climbed down from his tree and went on over. [He tapped the drum] "*Tím!* "Mother to the ground!" Down she fell. /*íya*/

OTHERS:

[loud laughter]

AMÁKA:

He clubbed her, and he dragged her over there. /*íya*/

Then he went to pick ritual leaves. /*íya*/

He did it carefully. /*íya*/

AGUMÍÍ:

That woman took death in the other woman's place.

AMÁKA:

Then he came back and crushed them up just right. Then he squeezed the juice from the leaves into his brothers' eyes. /*íya*/

ADUÊNGI [to people who are engaging in extraneous conversations]:

Hey, listen to the Anasi story! Quit bullshitting!

AMÁKA:

Now when the woman had killed those two brothers, /*íya*/

ants had gotten into their eyes and were eating them. /*íya*/

But when the other brother squeezed the leaves into his brothers' eyes, /*íya*/

the liquid fell right onto the ants. The brothers were fully revived. /*íya*/

Then they ran off. /íya/

They kept on running and running. The ants came out again back there, and they went into the woman's eye. They were going to eat her eye.

AGUMIÍI:
Eh!!

AMÁKA:
The moisture from the ants' bodies got carried into the woman's eye. Right away, she woke up.

OVERLAPPING VOICES:
[comments and discussion]

ADUÊNGI:
They left the drum.

AMÁKA:
They left the drum there. /íya/

Oh! The woman grabbed the drum, she picked up the club—

A MAN [breaking in with an uncommon opening for a tale nugget]:
Bullshit! That's not true.

AMÁKA:
—and she ran off after them. [To the man:] Well, what did YOU see, then?

THE MAN [singing in a raspy voice]:

We so wan moi moi moi pi-ki u-man___ na a-bi

sen-ee___ tja a man go na on-do buun.___

Mi go fu go ba-ka, mi go si en. A-dai-soo___
[fe-si,]

kai-na a-fan-ti ku-na-ni-ee u-tee na-nai-ee.___

So wan moi moi moi moi piki uman na abi sen-ee tja a man
go na ondo buun.
We so wan moi moi moi piki uman na abi sen-ee tja a man
go na ondo buun.
Mi go fu go baka, mi go si en.
Mi go fu go fesi, mi go si en.
Adaisoo kaina afanti kunani-ee utee nanai-ee.

["Such a pretty, pretty, pretty, pretty little woman who had no shame brought a man under the tree. / Well, such a pretty, pretty, pretty little woman who had no shame brought a man under the tree. / I started back, and there I saw him. / I started forward, and there I saw him. / (untranslatable line)." The gist of the song, which is in Sranan except for the final line, is that a shameless woman persuaded a man to make love in the forest. The Saramakas who listened to the tape had great difficulty discerning the words of the final line, and none could provide an interpretation; this transcription is their collective best guess. Several remarked that it sounded like Papá.]

Go on with your story.

AMÁKA:
Ohh! The ants came and entered the woman's eye, and she regained consciousness. The boys really took off. /íya/

They kept going till they got to a great big— They got to a great big creek, about as big as Mamákiíki [a large creek upstream from Dángogó]. /íya/

The third brother knocked his two brothers' heads together. /íya/

They turned into little stones.

OTHERS:
[exclamations of surprise]

AMÁKA:
Then he crossed the creek. /íya/

A MAN:
He could cross over?

AMÁKA:
Yes, he crossed over. /íya/

He went over to the other side. The woman was running, just kept on coming. She got to the bank, all tired out, and sat down to rest. She called across to him, "Akêkènyánso!" He answered, "Mother!" /íya/

She said, "You ran off." He said, "Yes, Mother. I did." "Yes," she said, "well, what do I have to do to catch you?" He said, "You want to know what to do?" ("yes" she said) "OK, you see those two little stones there? /íya/

Pick them up. Throw them right at the middle of my forehead here, and you'll get me."

AGUMIÍI:
So he's going to get his brothers back?

AMÁKA:
She took one stone and threw it hard, *vúún, gwii!* She took the other one and threw it, *vúún, gwii!* They hit him right on the head. The two brothers stood right up. /íya/

She said, "Akêkènyánso!" (he replied) /íya/ She said, "You got away." He said, "Right, Mother, I did." She fell right into the water, splash! And she turned into an underwater thicket [*gánkutu*] in the creek. Whenever you get to such a place, you see the thicket and the *nyumáa* [a large carnivorous fish] are right below there.[117]

OTHERS:
[laughter]

[A few seconds of discussion, within which there's an indistinct "*Mató!*" and "*Tòngôni!*"]

KÓDJI:
There we were, and there was a woman who had a child. /A
MAN: íya/

So many men asked to marry the girl that— Let's just say that not a village was left out. /íya/

They came to ask until there was no one who hadn't tried. /íya/

AGUMIÍI [to the others, who are still talking among themselves]:
Hey, listen!

KÓDJI:
And the man called Kentú went to ask too. /íya/

Now as he was on his way there, well, what happened was that she said, "Ah, that man who's on his way over there, he's the one who'll be my husband!" /íya/

He got himself all ready to go and take his wife. /íya/

So he stayed with her there until the time was up. /íya/

He went back home for a while and then returned to her place. /íya/

Then, when he was ready to go back home again, he told her, "Wife, we're going to go to your in-laws' village together." /íya/

That's all. The woman got herself ready till she was all set. /íya/

She loaded up her basket with everything she needed.

ADUÊNGI [breaking in]:
Well, while she was loading her basket, /KÓDJI: true/

I was right there, helping her load the basket.

KÓDJI:
You were?

ADUÊNGI:
Mm! I was going to walk with them to the beginning of the path and then say goodbye. /true/

Well, in folktale-land, you couldn't go off to your horticultural camp on Tuesdays, you couldn't enter your garden.

KÓDJI:
It's true, you couldn't.

ADUÊNGI:
That was the big sabbath for the forest.[118] /true/

If you went there, something bad would happen to you for sure. / . . . / Well, there was a girl who grew and developed very nicely until she got to be really ripe in her little pubic apron. /well/

She was already quite fulsome by this time. /really!/

Well, she asked her mother— She said, "Mother?" (she replied) and she said, "Why is it that people don't go into the forest on Tuesday?" /hm!/

She said, "Child, I don't know about that. But you mustn't try to find out. If you go into the forest, you'll surely die. That's all I know to tell you." /hm/

She said, "Right. Well, I'm going to have a look."

Two Dángogó "apron girls," 1978.

OTHERS:

[exclamations of surprise]

ADUÊNGI:

She quickly put together some things. She took her sewing basket and put it on her head, wearing her little apron. /right/

Then she set out on the path, /well/

and went along until she got to the garden. As soon as she got there, she walked right up, and bent an okra plant toward her to take the pods. She heard: "Whoosh!" [sound of the devil arriving] /hm/

He said, "Child—" (she replied) He said, "I'm going to eat you," and she said, "Yes, Father, you're indeed going to eat me. / . . . / But Father—" (he replied) She said, "Wouldn't you like me to sing?" /hm/

He said, "Go ahead and sing, because I'll eat you anyway." Ohh! The girl was really fulsome! / . . . / The girl took off her apron and— (Please excuse me, but since what we're doing here is tale-telling, let's just tell it the way tales are told!)

OTHERS:

[raucous laughter and murmurs of agreement]

ADUÊNGI:

Well, that's all. The girl dropped her apron right off. /hm/

There she was, just the way she was when her mother and father gave birth to her. /that's how it was/

So that's all. Nothing more.

OTHERS:

[laughter]

ADUÊNGI:

So she said— She leaped up in the air, and then she fell down, *kwalaa*. And when she fell down, she landed just like this! [He mimes her spread-eagle position.]

AGUMIÍI:

Right, with her legs spread wide open!

OTHERS:

[wild laughter and hooting]

ADUÊNGI:

Then the devil shouted out:

He! He! He! Ha! Ha! Ha!

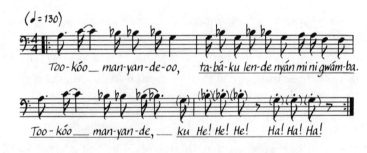

Tookóo manyande-oo, tabáku lende nyán mi ni gwámba.
Tookóo manyande, ku He! He! He! Ha! Ha! Ha!
Tookóo manyande-oo, tabáku lende nyán mi ni gwámba.
Tookóo manyande, He! He! He! Ha! Ha! Ha!
Tookóo manyande-oo, tabáku lende nyán mi ni gwámba.
Tookóo manyande.

[*He! He! He! Ha! Ha! Ha!* is chanted; the rest is sung. Our interpretation, based on discussion with Saramakas, glosses *tookóo* as a cry of joy: *manyande* as "What have we here?" (Saramaccan *Ma andí dí-dê?*), and *tabáku* (tobacco) and *gwámba* (meat) as the girl's pubic hair and ripe flesh. Whether or not this interpretation is accurate on a literal level, the song is clearly the devil's expression of delicious anticipation.]

[Excitedly:] Right then, the girl— While the devil was starting his song, she set out running, and she kept right on going all the way home. She led him back to get killed. That is, when she fell spread-eagle there, well, the devil wanted to dance around her before enjoying his treat. The thing he saw there was unlike anything he'd ever seen!

OTHERS:
[laughter]

ADUÊNGI:
So that's all. While he was dancing, the girl got up and she was already on the run. The devil stayed right behind her.

OTHERS:
[laughter]

ADUÊNGI:
Go on with your story. Go ahead.

A WOMAN:
So they got back to the village?

ADUÊNGI:
They got all the way to the village, where they killed the devil. She led the devil back to be killed.

KÓDJI:
They got everything all ready. They cooked food till it was all done, loaded up a basket till it was just so. /KÓDJI'S RESPONDER: *íya*/

That's all. They set out. /*íya*/

Kentú was in front, /*íya*/

with his gun and his hunting sack. /*íya*/

[All in one breath:] They went on till they arrived where a certain man was and he said, "Brother Kentú, where are you going with this woman? She's my wife," and Kentú said, "This woman isn't your wife, she's MY wife," and the other man said, "Put your things on the ground." /íya/

Kentú put his gun and hunting sack down right there. The woman took off her basket and set it down. /íya/

The man said, "Brother, we're going to wrestle before you pass by me." / . . . / The woman sang:

Di hánse mánu fu mi dê na míndi goómbe.
Kentú báa dê na míndi goómbe.
Kentú báa dê na míndi goómbe.
Kentú báa dê na míndi goómbe.

["The handsome husband of mine *dê na míndi goómbe.* / Brother Kentú *dê na míndi goómbe. ///*" Kalusé, in contrast to the other Saramakas who listened to the tape with us, heard the second phrase as *dê na míndi goón-dê* ("He's there on the ground").]

He threw him to the ground.

AGUMIÍI:
From now on I'm just going to be quiet when I don't know the chorus to a song.

KÓDJI:
He picked up his gun and his sack. The woman put her basket on her head. And off they went.

ADUÊNGI:
Was it Kentú who pinned the other man?

KÓDJI:
Kentú pinned the man.

Saramaka youths wrestling, 1968.

ADUÊNGI:
  OK.

KÓDJI:
  They went on till they got to the next man there. He said, "Brother
  Kentú, where are you going with this woman? She's my wife, not
  yours."

AKÓBO:
  Where does he get the idea she was his wife?

KÓDJI:

[In one breath:] Kentú said, "What?! This woman's not your wife, she's my wife," and the other said, "OK, put your things down on the ground, 'cause we're going to wrestle."

AGUMIÍI [to Kódji]:

Oh Brother-in-law, you know when they were wrestling like that?

KÓDJI:

Right.

A MAN:

What did you see there?

AGUMIÍI:

Well, Spider had a wife, /KÓDJI: right/

and the wife had never uttered his name. So he was going to a pond on the other side of the river to make himself a canoe. /true/

Well, he went and told the pond— He said, "The woman I married doesn't ever say my name. /uh-uh/

Now when she comes over here, as long as she doesn't say my name, don't let her go by."

A MAN:

A-MAZ-ing

AGUMIÍI:

Well, the girl got everything all ready. She was going to bring some food over to where he was making the canoe.

KÓDJI:

He's over there dying of hunger.

OTHERS:

[laughter]

AGUMIÍI:

Right. So she got to the pond. She went right up to the pond, and as she was stepping into the pond water, the pond rose up around her. / . . . / Then she called out:

Ma-yo-ee ___ Ma-yo-ee, ___ sa-ni e ___ gu-li mi-oo

Mayo-ee Mayo-ee, sani e guli mi-oo Mayo-ee.
Mayo-ee Mayo-ee, sani e guli mi-oo Mayo-ee.
Mini mini nai naan Anasi-oo.
Mini mini nai naan Anasi-oo.
M'manu Boonsi Ankama Anasi-oo.

[This is Anasi's wife's song of distress. Lines 1–2: "Mayo (the name of a parent or spirit she is invoking), what is it that's swallowing me?" Lines 3–4: we cannot provide a translation. Line 5: "My husband Boonsi Ankama Anasi (Anasi's full name)."]

She said his name!

A WOMAN:
She called her old man's name!

AGUMIÍI:
Spider cried out, he stuck up his head, he ran wildly all around,

AKÓBO [talking over Agumiíi's voice]:
She called his name.

AGUMIÍI:
he threw down his ax. His wife had said his name! He ran up to where she was, he grabbed at her, but all he managed to get was her fontanel place.

OVERLAPPING VOICES:
[exclamations and discussion]

AGUMIÍI:
And that's how it came to be that people like to play with babies' fontanels.

OTHERS:
[exclamations of distress and sympathy]

AKÓBO:
He killed her?

AGUMIÍI:
He killed her. Go right on.

A WOMAN:
Your legs are as short as a turtle's.

KÓDJI:
He said, "OK, put your things down on the ground. We're going to wrestle before I let you by me." /KÓDJI'S RESPONDER: íya/

So Kentú took his gun and his hunting sack and put them down there. The woman took off her basket and set it down.

> Di hánse mánu fu mi dê na míndi goómbe.
> Kentú báa dê na míndi goómbe.
> Kentú báa dê na míndi goómbe.
> Kentú báa dê na míndi goómbe.
> Kentú báa dê na míndi goómbe.
> Kentú báa dê na míndi goómbe.

Kentú finished him off quickly. The woman took her basket and put it on her head. He picked up his gun and his sack, and off they went.

ADUÊNGI [trying to break in]:
Yes, well, at the time they were walking along there—

KÓDJI [continuing to talk, not hearing Aduêngi]:
They went along until they got to a certain place. "Hey, man—" the next one said. "Brother Kentú!" (he replied) He said, "Where do you think you're going with my wife?" Kentú said, "The woman isn't your wife, Brother. She's MY wife." The other said, "Take off your gun and hunting sack and set them on the ground."

ADUÊNGI:
Well, as he was putting his things down there, /KÓDJI: hm/

he and I were the ones who were wrestling. He nearly killed me.

KÓDJI:
Well, how were you wrestling?

ADUÊNGI:
Well, there was a certain woman there in folktale-land who refused every man who asked to marry her. /true/

So Anasi went and tricked her into taking him. /mm-hm/

And once he tricked her into sleeping with him, he was ready to
sing his song to her. He made seven paddles, he made seven canoes, he bought seven hunting sacks, he bought seven guns. /hm!/

Every kind of thing that men have— He had seven of each.

AGUMÍÍ:
Seven machetes and seven axes.

ADUÊNGI:
Right. So he went to the downstream landing /íya/

to the *sumésédu* tree there [at Dángogó], and he got into his canoe,
along with his brand-new paddle, /well/

and off he went:

Kwa-si-ba, ko-li mi ee ko-li yu-oo Kwa-si-ba.

Sei-bi bo-to mi me-ki. Kwa - si - ba,

ko-li mi ee ko-li yu-oo kwa- si - ba.

Kwasiba, koli mi ee koli yu-oo Kwasiba.
Seibi boto mi meki.
Kwasiba, koli mi ee koli yu-oo Kwasiba.
Seibi pali mi meki.
Kwasiba, koli mi ee koli yu-oo Kwasiba.
Seibi pangi mi nai.
Kwasiba, koli mi ee koli yu-oo Kwasiba.

[(In Sranan:) "Kwasiba (the woman), I'm tricking you (with flattery), Kwasiba. / I've made seven canoes. / (chorus) / I've made seven paddles. / (chorus) / I've sewn seven skirts. / (chorus)." Note that the humor of this story inheres in the way Anasi, a good-for-nothing, is able to "snow" the unsuspecting Kwasiba with an excess of presents. Compare this with Akóbo's version, p. 171.]

He really took her. Anasi took her.

A MAN:
Your leg is short!

ADUÊNGI:
Right. I don't know— I don't— That's as far as I got with it.

OTHERS:
[laughter]

ADUÊNGI:
Go on with your story.

KÓDJI:
Kentú took his gun and his hunting sack and put them down. The woman took off her basket and set it there. They locked limbs.
/KÓDJI'S RESPONDER: íya/

The woman sang:

> Di hánse mánu fu mi dê na míndi goómbe.
> Kentú báa dê na míndi goómbe.
> Kentú báa dê na míndi goómbe.
> Kentú báa dê na míndi goómbe.
> Kentú báa dê na míndi goómbe.
> Kentú báa dê na míndi goómbe.

Kentú whipped him easily. He took up his gun and his sack. The woman took up her basket. Mm, Brother, they just kept going on like that. Every man— If it was a human being that you'd label by the word "man," then he was involved in this thing. Finally Kentú got up to the long man.

A WOMAN:
Who's the long man?

KÓDJI:
The one at the edge of the water here [anaconda].

AKÓBO:

It's as if the woman's avenging spirit didn't want her to have a husband!

KÓDJI:

Now, so he's the— He's the very last one. / . . . / That's where they were going to meet. That's where they were going to settle this thing. So that's all. He slithered right on over. Then he addressed him and he said, "Brother Kentú, where do you think you're going with my wife?" and Kentú said, "Well, Sir, this wife of yours is really MY wife," and he said, "If you want to see how much she's NOT your wife, /íya/

just take off your hunting sack and set it on the ground." /íya/

But the woman didn't put down her basket this time. And the man didn't put down his gun and his sack this time. So that's all. The two of them began wrestling right away. The woman sang out:

> Kentú fu mi, *a dê na míndi goómbe.*
> Kentú báa, *a dê na míndi goómbe.*

The snake threw him up in the air and gulped him right down. Kentú quickly thrust his hand into his hunting sack and took out the razor knife he had there, and split the snake clean open. He finished him off, *kálen kálen kálen kálen.* That's why, when you see Parrot go up to the top of a tree, singing and dancing, he'll turn around and look at his tail. Well, that's his wife that turned into his tail.[119]

SAKUÍMA:

He took what belonged to him? [his wife]

KÓDJI:

He carried his thing off with him.

OTHERS:

[exclamations]

A MAN:

Mató!

KASINDÓ:

Mató! [120]

AMÁKA:

Tòngôni!

OTHERS:
[laughter at anticipation of hearing one of Kasindó's tales]

KASINDÓ:
I've been asleep a long time! So now listen to me. /AMÁKA: yes/

Well, there we were. /íya/

[to the man who had first said *Mató:*] Oh, Mother's Brother, excuse me. /íya/

THE MAN:
No problem.

AGUMIÍI [to Kasindó]:
Did you elbow in in front of him?

TÍANÊN:
Yeah, he elbowed in.

KASINDÓ:
Yes. So there we were until, at a certain time— Well, Old Man Anasi— /íya/

Well, let's just say that, / . . . / if you really told it like it was, /íya/

Well, the ladies— / . . . / Exclusively ladies—

TÍANÊN:
There's going to be some dancing in this one.

KASINDÓ:
—were there by themselves in their own village. [To Amáka:] Hey, Man! /íya/

Are you doing the replies?!

AMÁKA:
Yes.

KASINDÓ:
Mm?!

AMÁKA:
Well, look, I'm very far away from where you are!

KASINDÓ:
No, we're not too far apart!

OTHERS:
[laughter and discussion]

KASINDÓ:
The ladies were all off by themselves. /yes/

The men were off by themselves. /íya/

Men had their own village. /íya/

And women had their village. /íya/

That's how we used to be. /íya/

So they went along like that for some time, and the women— /íya/

Mm, well, Brother— If you were a man and you went to where they lived all by yourself, /íya/

and they saw you there— /íya/

Man, I wouldn't envy you. /íya/

You think you'd ever get back alive? /íya/

No way! Well, anyway, there they were, and one day Anasi said /íya/

he'd heard it said that if you went off to the women-only place, /íya/

you wouldn't return.

AMÁKA [breaking in]:
At that time, I was there. /KASINDÓ: íya/

The turtle was wrestling with Jaguar.

KASINDÓ:
How did they wrestle?

AMÁKA:
Well, the fruit that's known as "turtle fruit"—

OTHERS:
[laughter at idea of a turtle and a jaguar wrestling]

AMÁKA:
It was originally Jaguar's fruit. /íya/

So that's all. /íya/

The fruit falls from the tree. Turtle comes to eat it, and Jaguar comes to eat it too. /íya/

OTHERS:
[laughter]

AGUMIÍI [talking over Amáka's voice]:
Those two will be the death of the place!

AMÁKA:

So he got there, Jaguar got right there, /íya/

and he didn't see any fruit on the ground. /íya/

So he shouted:

Húléé húléé! Ambê nyán mi aladáfala-oo? Húléé!
Húléé húléé! Ambê nyán mi aladáfala-oo? Húléé!

["(Roar) Who's eaten my *aladáfala*? (Roar)."]

Turtle answered. He said, "Me under the Shell."

Mi kòô-oo, húléé!
Mi nyán dí aladáfala-oo, húlééé!

["I'm the one (roar)! I ate the *aladáfala* (roar)!"]

Turtle set out and came right up to him. /íya/

Jaguar grabbed him, *gwou*, flung him up, *vúúún*, knocked him into the sky, *gwuu*. /íya/

AKÓBO:

Turtle's really something!

AMÁKA:

Turtle came back down to the ground, landing on his two— On his four feet, *djala!*

AGUMÍÍ:

Jaguar didn't get him.

AMÁKA:

Turtle grabbed Jaguar, *gbaa*, and tossed him up, *vúúún*, so he crashed, *gwuu* onto the ground. He doubled over in pain.

AKÓBO:

Turtle's really something!

AMÁKA:

He said, "Turtle?" (he replied) He said, "You threw me like that?!" "I sure did," he said. Jaguar said, "I'm leaving the fruit for you to eat as long as I live." /íya/

So that's why it belongs to Turtle, and you hear people calling it "turtle fruit." It's because they wrestled over who would own it. /íya/

Go on with your story.[121]

AKÓBO:

Well, Turtle won it!

SAKUÍMA:

My goodness, Turtle's quite a guy!

A MAN:

Íya.

KASINDÓ:

Well, Old Man Anasi— Old Man Anasi set out. /AMÁKA: íya/

He said, well, he swore by his father / . . . / that he'd go have a look at how it was that women were killing men in that place. /íya/

Right, so Anasi took a path and was going along, /íya/

till he got very close to the women's village. /íya/

And he saw a big tree /íya/

that had fallen right across the path to the village. /íya/

It was the path where women went to get water. /íya/

(Mmm, well, pardon me for what I'm saying here. / . . . / We're going to be talking about clitorises. /íya/

And how they rubbed over the tree trunk.)

AGUMIÍI:

Clitorises that were as big as cassava cakes.

KASINDÓ:

Exactly!

OTHERS:

[laughter]

KASINDÓ:
Now this had eaten away at the tree till it had gotten almost completely worn through.

OTHERS:
[more laughter]

KASINDÓ:
The tree was thick, so the women couldn't just step over it. /íya/

They had to rub their asses over it.

OTHERS:
[laughter]

SOMEONE:
They could barely get their asses over it.

KASINDÓ:
Right! /íya/

So this ate away the tree till it got very worn down, as if they had sawed it. /íya/

Well, so Old Man Anasi went to get himself all ready. /íya/

He hollowed out the tree—

SAKUÍMA:
He's going to get inside the log!

KASINDÓ:
—the inside of the tree. /íya/

He scraped away at it till there was a big open hole. /íya/

Then he looked to see exactly where those things had worn down the tree, /íya/

and he bored into it, *kwii kwii kwii, búlún!* /íya/

till he got to the center. /íya/

The Old Man Anasi slipped neatly into the inside of the trunk. /íya/

Then he lay down on his back and he got his little man growing— (My excuses to the public!) /íya/

Then he got his thing growing till it came up outside. /íya/

AGUMÍÍ:
Ahh, it was so long that it grew all the way out?!

KASINDÓ:
Mm-hmm! So he guided it right on out through the hole. /íya/

Then he stayed there, very still, lying on his back. /íya/

Ah! Well, it wasn't even going to be one hour— Not even an hour before the women would pass by on their way to the river. /íya/

Oh! They were already on their way! /íya/

Now one of the women was out in front, and she came— She came to pass over.

MANY DIFFERENT VOICES:
[loud talking and laughing]

KASINDÓ:
I want you all to listen to me!!

TWO VOICES [in quick succession]:
Íya!

SOMEONE:
Go on.

KASINDÓ:
Well, the woman who was in front stepped up to pass over. /íya/

She started over. She took quite a while. /íya/

Then, mmm! Her ass— Her ass started wiggling a little there: "Aahhhhhh."

OTHERS:
[laughter at Kasindó pantomiming the young lady lingering in ecstasy as she straddles the log]

KASINDÓ:
She didn't get over quite as quickly as she usually did. /íya/

She sort of stuck there a little bit. /íya/

A WOMAN:
[uncontrollable giggling]

KASINDÓ:
That is, well, she noticed that crossing over the log— Mm mm! /íya/

A MAN:
The wood slowed her down.

KASINDÓ:
Mm, mm! The wood was doing something there. /íya/ The wood had gotten awfully sweet.

OTHERS:
[laughter]

KASINDÓ:

Right. /íya/

Well, she stayed there for a while. Then she said, "Sister, oh, Sister! Something's happening to me here. /íya/

I'm really confused. The tree that we've always crossed over here, /íya/

well, there's something going on with it that keeps me from getting across." /íya/

AGUMIÍI:

You mean that people just walked around naked then?!

KASINDÓ:

"But, but, how is it— What's going on to make the log so very delicious?"

ADUÊNGI [to Agumiíi]:

Well, they wouldn't have clothes covering the place where they sit down.

AGUMIÍI:

You mean they'd lift up their skirts to step over the log?

KASINDÓ:

Now at that point, she turned around. She turned around and she began to sing: /íya/

Ún údu súti sô? Boontána!
Ún údu na údu? Boontána!
Ún údu súti sô? Boontána!

(YOU'RE SUPPOSED TO BE CLAPPING YOUR HANDS!)

Boontána!
Ún údu súti sô? Boontána!
Ún údu súti sô? Boontána!
Ún údu súti sô? Boontána!
Ún údu súti sô? Boontána!

Ún údu súti sô? Boontána!
Ún údu súti sô? Boontána!
Ún údu súti sô? Boontána!
Ún údu súti sô? Boontána!
Ún údu súti sô? Boontána!
Ún údu súti sô? Boontána!

[The girl sings, "What is this wood that is so sweet?" and Anasi, using a neologism whose anatomical meaning is clear to the listeners from the context, calls out "*Boontána!*" Kasindó's song is accompanied by rhythmic handclapping (once he reminds people to supply it), and by Kasindó's dance (which mimes Anasi's activities). It ends amid wild laughter, deafening hooting, and clapping.]

So at that point, /*íya*/

well, the other one said, "Come on, Sister. Get off so I can have a turn. [As wild laughter continues:] Whatever it is that the wood's doing to you, /*íya*/

give me a turn at it too." /*íya*/

The other one got off. But only because she had to. / . . . / She didn't want to get off. The other one finally pulled her away. /*íya*/

Mm. The second one got on. Ohh! Really something! /*íya*/

OTHERS:
[more laughter, as Kasindó pantomimes]

KASINDÓ:
Ohh! The wood was working away like mad. /*íya*/

And she said, "Well, Sister, this thing here— What is it that makes this wood so delicious?"

ADUÊNGI [breaking in]:
Well, at that time, /KASINDÓ: *íya*/

I was there.[122] /mm-hm!/

So at that time, when we were over there in folktale-land, a man wasn't allowed to have four wives. /right/

You could have one wife. /that's how it was/

But if you took four wives, the chief would summon you and shame you publicly. /indeed/

Gaamá *Agbagó (Abóikóni), chief of the Saramakas (1951–89), 1978.*

Well, there was a man named Sòkôtiláma, /mm-hm!/

and he had four wives. /íya/

So the day came when the chief called him to a public hearing. /íya/

(Well, when you're doing tale-telling like this, there are certain things you say, so everybody please excuse me. /mm-hm!/

If fathers-in-law are present— /right!/ If mothers-in-law are present, we're not doing that kind of talking. Today is for Anasi stories, / that's the way it is!/

not for father-in-law or mother-in-law matters! /uh-uh/

We mustn't take offense.) /uh-uh/

So that's all. Well, Sòkôtiláma— Well, the chief called him to answer the charges. /mm-hm/

And he said they should bring in the four wives as well. /mm-hm/

[To someone who's talking in the background:] (Be quiet, Man, don't bullshit me.) /íya/

They brought the four wives in and had them stand there for him to "tôtò." /íya/

All at once. You already know, I think, what Dutch people mean when they use the word tôtò [stoten (which in slang means "to screw")].

SEVERAL VOICES:
Sure do!

ADUÊNGI:
OK, well, they brought in the four wives and set them up. /íya/

Then they had Sòkôtiláma stand right there. /uh-huh/

OTHERS:
[laughter]

ADUÊNGI [pantomiming the placement of the women in a circle around him]:
They put one of the women right here, /íya/

and they put one right here. /íya/

They put one here, /íya/

and they put one there. /íya/

Then the chief said, "Well, Sòkôtiláma, we warned you not to take four wives, /íya/

but you went ahead and took four wives. /íya/

Screw all four of them together so we can see! /íya/

Then we'll leave you alone. But if you can't, we'll kill you. /íya/

Eh! Yes! Eh! My goodness!

[As he begins the song, Aduêngi mimes Sòkôtiláma, using a long stick held straight out from his crotch. At each emphatically sung "*pína*" ("punish"), he thrusts toward one of the imaginary women, rotating ninety degrees after each verse.]

Sòkôtiláma, de gó PÍNA i tidé, de gó PÍNA i tidé.
Sòkôtiláma, de gó PÍNA i tidé, de gó PÍNA i tidé, de gó PÍNA
*   i tidé.*
Sòkôtiláma, de gó PÍNA i tidé, de gó PÍNA i tidé, de gó PÍNA
*   i tidé.*
Sòkôtiláma, de gó PÍNA i tidé, de gó PÍNA i tidé, de gó PÍNA
*   i tidé.*
Sòkôtiláma, de gó PÍNA i tidé, de gó PÍNA i tidé.
Sòkôtiláma, de gó PÍNA i tidé, de gó PÍNA i tidé, de gó PÍNA
*   i tidé.*
Sòkôtiláma, de gó PÍNA i tidé, de gó PÍNA i tidé.
Sòkôtiláma, de gó PÍNA i tidé, de gó PÍNA i tidé, de gó PÍNA
*   i tidé.*

["Sòkôtiláma, they're gonna PUNISH you today, they're gonna PUNISH you today." Wild laughter, hooting and rhythmic clapping, all during and well beyond the song and dance.]

And that's how people came to have four wives, or three wives. Sòkôtiláma got rid of the prohibition. Go on with your story. /íya/

KASINDÓ:

OK, so there they were. /AMÁKA: íya/

And Anasi was working on the women, /íya/

until he had had every last one of them. /íya/

That whole village of women— /íya/

Anasi finished them off. /íya/

So things went along until, one day, the first woman who had taken on the work, /íya/

she got to a certain point where she said, "Oh, Sister! Something's happening in my belly! /íya/

I don't know what it is. /íya/

I just don't know what's going on with my belly." She said, "Really?" She said, "Yes." So they went along until, mm! the woman starts spitting up. /íya/

Her body isn't well. /íya/

AGUMIÍI:

Is a pregnancy going to be involved in this thing?

KASINDÓ:

The pregnancy's already there! /íya/

After a while, the other one called out and said, "Oh, Sister, the problem that you were having— /íya/

I've got it too!" /íya/

Ohhh! After a while, the bellies got really big. /íya/

So they went along like that. Then they said, "My goodness! Something's going on. [In a bewildered voice:] Sister, what's happening here? What kind of illness is this?!" /íya/

The other one said, "Well, we just don't know. /íya/

What should we do? We're really in a bad way!" / . . . / "Ohh! Well, could it be because of that tree that did that thing to us over there?"

A MAN:

Is Spider still in the same place now?

KASINDÓ:

Oh no, he already left. /yes/

Once he'd finished with them, he took off.

TÍANÊN:

Well, will all of them get in the same fix?

KASINDÓ:

Mm, Brother— /íya/

So they went along for another while, their bellies heavy. /íya/

It got to be three women. /íya/

Then it was four. /íya/

Mm-hmm! /íya/

Big bellies all over the place!

A MAN:

One right after the other.

KASINDÓ:

One right after the other. /íya/

When the time came, the first one began to give birth. /íya/

She gave birth. /íya/

She said [in an excited whisper:] "Sister, come look! I gave birth to this thing here!"

OTHERS:

[laughter]

KASINDÓ:

She said, "What did you give birth to, Child?!" / . . . / She said, "Just come and look." /íya/

[Astonished:] "Well, I never saw anything like— Well, the thing is— It looks to me as though it's just like you and me! It's made just the way you are!"

OTHERS:

[laughter]

ADUÊNGI:

Well, at that time giving birth hadn't yet gotten to folktale-land?

KASINDÓ:

Not at all! They didn't know about men and they didn't know about having babies. /íya/

[Whispering:] "Mm. Sister, dear Sister, I'm going to kill it!" The other one said, "No, don't kill it. Let's leave it alone and see what becomes of it." /íya/

She agreed. After a while, sure enough, /íya/

the other woman— /íya/

[looping back on the story:] That first one— /íya/

It was a boy she gave birth to. /íya/

She had a boy. /íya/

"Well, the thing that's there on the baby's bottom there— /íya/

Well, the thing— This thing here— Well, we've never seen such a thing. /íya/

Sister, I'm going to kill this thing here."

ADUÊNGI:
He had a *boontána!*

KASINDÓ:
They didn't know that it was a child. /íya/

They thought it might be something else. / . . . / So she decided to kill the thing. /íya/

The other said, "No, Sister, don't kill it."

A MAN:
In other words, she thought it was a "sickness" she had in her belly?

KASINDÓ:
RIGHT!! /íya/

So she was going to kill it. /íya/

But the thing moved around, it had all its parts, and all of them were made the same way. But that thing it had between its legs there—

A MAN:
Right, they'd never seen such a thing.

KASINDÓ:
Exactly. They'd never seen such a thing. /íya/

So she wanted to kill it. /íya/

The other one said, "No, Child, don't kill it. /íya/

Leave it alone. Let's see what becomes of it." /íya/

("all right" she said) Then, after a while, the other woman /íya/ started giving birth. /íya/

She gave birth and she noticed that the way she was made— Well, the thing was made the same way. /íya/

"Mm! Sister, look at something I gave birth to here. I've done it too. I don't know what it is." /íya/

They didn't know about giving birth, that it was something people did.

WOMEN:
[laughter]

KASINDÓ:
"Well, Sister, this thing you've done, /íya/

It looks to me as though you've made something just like yourself. /íya/

It looks to me as though the thing resembles both of us." ("yes" she said) Things went along like that. /íya/

Anasi fathered boys all through the village. /íya/

So that's all. /íya/

A MAN:
From now on, they'll eat meat [because they'll have men to go hunting].

KASINDÓ:
There got to be men.

A MAN:
Not a single one had a [known] father?

KASINDÓ:
Not a single one had a known father. /íya/

Anasi had done them all. /íya/

He fathered those children without the women knowing, and he left. /íya/

He just took off. /íya/

So they lived there with the children until they got to be grown up. /íya/

Ohh! Ahhhh. /íya/

So the one they were wondering about killing— /íya/

Well, he'd been carrying around his thing for a while, not knowing what it was for. /íya/

The time came, but he'd never learned. /no/

OTHERS:
[laughter]

KASINDÓ:
He said— Well the girl and he got together, /íya/

and his heart began to notice her. /íya/

Exactly how he did it with her, we don't know. /íya/

OTHERS:
[laughter]

KASINDÓ:
But the thing that happened was something special. /íya/

Well, there's really nothing more to tell. /íya/

That sort of work became the rage. /íya/

Old Man Anasi said, "There! I've taken care of you all. /íya/

What a ridiculous idea for women to be off in a village where men couldn't come!" /íya/

They had been right next to each other, like here and across the river [referring to the fact that Dángogó lies on both sides of the river]. /íya/

And if you crossed the water to go to the women-only village over there, /íya/

you'd never return. /íya/

The one thing they were sure to do with you was that they would take you and kill you. / . . . / They didn't know anything about that particular line of work, so if you went off there by yourself, /íya/

you really got yourself into trouble. /yes/

They'd do their thing, and then they'd leave you lying there.

A MAN:
That sort of thing still goes on when you go to the city.

KASINDÓ:
So that's how that particular kind of work and this way of life came to exist. /íya/

That's as far as my story goes. /íya/

AMÁKA:
　　Mató! [123]

A MAN:
　　Tòngôni!

AMÁKA [in plodding speech]:
　　So we came to be there. /THE MAN: *íya*/

　　And one day, well, nothing much. Old Man Rabbit /*íya*/

　　and Deer were going to drag a pond for fish. /*íya*/

　　Deer went to Rabbit's place. The pond was right there next to where Rabbit lived. /*íya*/

　　So, well, Deer showed up. /*íya*/

　　So he said, "Well, Friend, I've come to you. /*íya*/

　　You know that we're dying from lack of meat and fish, and the creek you've got here is full of fish. /*íya*/

　　Well, I think you and I should drag it." /*íya*/

　　He said, "Yes, Brother. Well, no problem, let's drag it." /*íya*/

　　So then they did the thing. /*íya*/

　　They did the dragging. /*íya*/

　　They prepared the palm fronds and got everything all ready. /*íya*/

　　They dragged it right then, and piled the catch up on the bank. /*íya*/

　　They kept pulling in more and more fish till they'd finished. /*íya*/

　　They found a basketful. /*íya*/

ADUÊNGI:
　　There's fish in that pond!

AMÁKA:
　　Rabbit said to Deer, "Well, that's all. /*íya*/

　　Well, Uncle [Mother's Brother]—" (he replied) "Well, look. We've caught a basketful. /*íya*/

　　Why don't you take this basketful here. /*íya*/

　　And when we come back tomorrow, /*íya*/

　　and catch two basketfuls, /*íya*/

　　I'll take those two. /*íya*/

　　This one basketful is for you."/*íya*/

A MAN:

Who owned that place?

AMÁKA:

Rabbit. /íya/

It was right next to where he lived. /íya/

"Well, Nephew, you know what? /íya/

Take the two basketfuls. /íya/

[Correcting himself:] Take the one basketful. /íya/

And tomorrow when we catch more, /íya/

I'll take the two basketfuls." /íya/

AKÓBO:

I bet they won't catch any more.

AMÁKA:

Rabbit said, "OK, but you could claim /íya/

the first catch since you're the uncle. /íya/

You could be the one to take the first basketful." /íya/

AGUMIÍI:

Which one called the other uncle?

AMÁKA:

Rabbit called Deer uncle.

AGUMIÍI:

Ah.

AMÁKA:

Ohh! Rabbit took the one basketful, /íya/

and off he went. /íya/

Deer went off. /íya/

In the morning they returned. /íya/

They fished again, /íya/

and they caught their two basketfuls. /íya/

Rabbit said to him, "Well, Uncle, you see how we've caught two basketfuls? /íya/

Well, yesterday I got one basketful, /íya/

so now why don't you take the two we've got here. /íya/

And then tomorrow, when we go fishing again, and catch three basketfuls, /íya/

I'll be the one to take the three baskets." /íya/

AGUMÍÍI:
Well, are they eating them? [Someone answers in background—indistinct.]

AMÁKA:
He said, "Oh no, well, Nephew, the way it should be— /íya/

You go ahead and take the two basketfuls. /íya/

Then when we come back tomorrow, I'll take the three basketfuls." /íya/

OVERLAPPING VOICES:
[discussion of how greedy Deer is]

AMÁKA:
The two of them kept going like that, and Rabbit ended up taking the two basketfuls as well. /íya/

He took the fish back to his wife. /íya/

AGUMÍÍI [anticipating]:
They salted it.

AMÁKA:
They salted it. They smoked it. They slept till morning.

ADUÊNGI:
Well, at that time, I was there. /AMÁKA: well/

And the woman named Asíminti who was such a great singer and dancer— /right/

In those days people weren't able to sing and dance all the way till dawn. /no/

Well, she went to a village where someone had died, and she decided to sing and dance the whole night through. /true/

She sang and danced till four in the morning, and that's when the devil comes to join in with the people in the village, and so he showed up there,

OVERLAPPING VOICES:
[indistinct comments]

ADUÊNGI:

jumped right into the center of the "play," and the woman sang out:

A- gan - gai, i sá nyán mi, *mm hmm!*

Mi hán-se té mi sá dê - dè, *mm hmm!*

Agangai, i sá nyán mi, mm hmm!
Agangai, i sá kíi mi, mm hmm!
Mi hánse té mi sá dêdè, mm hmm!
Mi hánse té mi yò a sónu, mm hmm!
Agangai, i sá nyán mi, mm hmm!
Mi hánse té mi litólia, mm hmm!
Agangai, i sá kíi mi, mm hmm!

[The woman sings, taunting the devil (who replies to each phrase with "mm-hmm"): "Agangai, you might eat me. / Agangai, you might kill me. / I'm so beautiful I might die. / I'm so beautiful I melt in the sun. / Agangai, you might eat me. / I'm so beautiful, I'm *litólia*. / Agangai, you might kill me." [124]]

Go on with your story.

AMÁKA:

Now when they caught the two basketfuls, and the uncle said to go ahead, Rabbit took them home.

A WOMAN [talking over Amáka's voice]:

Why weren't people doing the chorus better?!

ANOTHER WOMAN [answering the first woman, as Amáka continues]:

I'm too tired.

AMÁKA:

They left. In the morning they returned. They fished some more and caught their three basketfuls. /AMÁKA'S RESPONDER: *íya*/

Rabbit said, "Well, Uncle, you know how yesterday we caught two basketfuls? And how the day before we caught one? /íya/

And I took them? /íya/

Yesterday we came back and we caught two basketfuls. / . . . / So now go ahead and take these three basketfuls. /íya/

And then tomorrow, when we catch four basketfuls, I'll take those four." / . . . / Deer said, "Yes, well, Nephew, the way it is— /íya/

You go ahead and take the three basketfuls here.

ADUÊNGI [talking over Amáka's voice]:
Well, is Deer ever going to get his part?

AKÓBO [answering, as Amáka continues]:
Deer is so greedy that he'll never get anything to eat.

AMÁKA:
And when we return, I'll take the four baskets." Brother, well, we don't need to belabor the thing. They kept on dragging the creek like that till they got up to nine basketfuls.

ADUÊNGI:
Deer didn't have a single one in his house.

AMÁKA:
Not a single one in his house. Rabbit's whole village reeked. Fish all over the place!

AGUMÍÍI:
Couldn't they have taken a day off to fix up the fish and dry them?

AMÁKA:
They slept until morning and then came back. They dragged again, *suu*— Nothing at all! They didn't catch any more. /íya/

Rabbit waited there a while and then he turned and said, "Uncle—" (he replied) "You know that place where there are lots of bubbles over there? Well, I really need to shit, so I'm going off to shit. My belly's really killing me." /íya/

"All right," he said. Meanwhile Deer goes over to try to see the fish feeding on the bottom [making the bubbles]. /íya/

Rabbit runs off, *wiliwiliwili píí*. /íya/

Deer stayed there and waited for him a very long time. Then he finally left. /íya/

He made his way to Rabbit's village. Not a soul in sight. He didn't see Rabbit. /íya/

He kept on looking for Rabbit, but never found him. /íya/

By that time, well, the old man had gotten pretty thin. /íya/

He hadn't had anything to eat for quite some time. /íya/

Deer got to a certain place and just keeled over. /íya/

He was dead. /íya/

So there was Rabbit. /íya/

In a little while, Jaguar came along. /íya/

He said, "Nephew!" (he replied) He said, "I'm dying from lack of meat and fish. /íya/

I hear you've got a dry-season pool here, /íya/

that's good for dragging. /íya/

So, since you've got the dry-season pool for dragging, /íya/

I'd like to drag it with you." Rabbit said, "Yes, well, Uncle, no problem. Let's drag it. /íya/

Just a while back, Deer and I dragged it together."

AGUMIÍI:
Wouldn't Rabbit have thought of telling Jaguar that he was too sick? [no reply]

AMÁKA:
(he said "OK") Ohh! So they really dragged it. /íya/

They dragged it and they caught a whole basketful. /íya/

Rabbit said, "Well, Uncle—" (he replied) He said, "You see how we caught one basketful today? /íya/

Why don't you take the one basketful."

A MAN [anticipating]:
"And then when we divide it next time—"

AMÁKA:
"And then tomorrow, when we come back again and catch two basketfuls, /íya/

I'll take those two baskets."

AKÓBO [talking over Amáka's voice]:
Couldn't they have just taken their fish and divided them up?

ADUÊNGI [also talking over Amáka's voice]:
Rabbit was getting at those others by using *politíki* ["cheating, deception"—from Dutch *politiek* ("politics")].

AMÁKA:

He said, "Nephew, if that's the way it is, why don't you just go ahead and take this one basketful." /*íya*/

AGUMIÍI:

Rabbit is amazingly greedy!

OTHERS:

[laughter]

AMÁKA:

"Then tomorrow, I'll take the two basketfuls." Then they caught some fish. /*íya*/

They kept on catching till they had caught as many as before.

ADUÊNGI [breaking in]:

Well, at the time when they were catching fish, on that day, on the first day they were doing it, /AMÁKA: well/

I was right there with them, /right/ I was right there warning them about what they were doing. And Rabbit was telling me to watch out for myself because Jaguar wasn't someone to mess around with. /well/

So, well, there were a bunch of girls there, the three daughters that woman had, three of them, and they were going to drag the dry-season pool. /OK/

So they went off to the dry-season pool and dragged it until they got up to a place where there were so many fish it was no joke. /really a lot/

Then they didn't know what to do, 'cause the water was too high for them to bail out. /well/

Then they turned around and listened: "Whoosh!!" They saw an enormous old man come up, a devil. /true/

He came to them and said, "Children—" (they replied) "Where are you going?" They said, "Father, well, we've come to drag the pool." /right/

He said, "Let me help you drag the pool. /mm/

But once I've dragged it for you, if you tell anyone that I've dragged it for you, I'll kill you all. /right/

But if you don't tell anyone about it, then any day you like, just come and I'll drag it for you." / . . . / They said, "Mm, Father, we won't tell." [One said:] "Woman, will you tell?" She said, "Oh no, Woman, I won't tell."

A MAN [anticipating]:
Oh, they've as good as told already.

ADUÊNGI:
The devil pulled his ear off, the ear on one side, he pulled it off and started bailing out the pond with it:

A haa_a-ku-taa, ka-pêè-ma. Ka-pêè-ma a-fi-á-ma go-yáá-yaa.

A haa akutaa, kapêèma. Kapêèma afiáma goyááyaa.
A haa akutaa, kapêèma. Kapêèma afiáma goyááyaa.
A haa akutaa, kapêèma. Kapêèma afiáma goyááyaa.
A haa akutaa, kapêèma.

[The tale this tale nugget alludes to explains why people nowadays must drag dry-season pools without the help of the devil—ever since the three sisters broke their promise not to tell how they caught all those fish. The song seems to be the devil's work song, as he bails out the pool with his ear. Based on similar songs in other tales, we suspect that Kapêèma is the name of the devil's ear and Akuta the name of the pool; if so, the first line might translate as "Kapêèma drags Akuta. Kapêèma throws the water over there."]

It went bone dry, an enormous river like this one. They got twelve basketfuls of large fish. Go ahead with your story.

AGUMIÍI:
For them to eat?

SAKUÍMA:
Well, what else would they do with them?!

AGUMIÍI:
Twelve BASKETS full! [not just twelve fish]

AMÁKA:
Then Rabbit pulled in more and more fish with Jaguar, until they'd gotten just as much as when he'd done it with Deer. /AMÁKA'S RESPONDER: *íya*/

Then they kept on going. /*íya*/

Just pulling them in and piling them up. They'd go back and get more, pile them up. /*íya*/

Rabbit said, "OK, well, Uncle—" (he replied) He said, "My belly's killing me. /*íya*/

My belly's really killing me, so I'm going to have to 'go to the savanna' again. I'll be right back." /*íya*/

SAKUÍMA:
That guy's belly sure is giving him trouble!

OTHERS:
[laughter]

AMÁKA:
"You just keep an eye on the place where the fish are feeding." /*íya*/

"OK," he said. Ohh! He dashed off and disappeared. Jaguar stayed there, but nothing happened. He got very angry, and he ran lickety-split over to where Rabbit lived. /*íya*/

No one there. /*íya*/

SOMEONE:
Didn't see him!

AMÁKA:
Didn't see him. Rabbit ran off /*íya*/

to the place where Deer had keeled over and died. /*íya*/

When he got there, he saw Deer's hide. /*íya*/

So he grabbed it and slipped it right over his own body. /*íya*/

Then he lay down next to the path, lay right down. /*íya*/

He stayed there, very still. /*íya*/

SOMEONE:
He went to hide.

AMÁKA:
He's hiding. /*íya*/

Jaguar was coming along, *gudja gudja gudja*, as angry as could be and got up to there. Rabbit called [in a falsetto voice:] "Father, oh, Father!" Ohh! Jaguar wasn't interested in being distracted from watching for Rabbit. Not at all!

AGUMIÍI:
Where's he going in such a hurry that he can't hear it?

OTHERS:
[laughter]

AMÁKA:
He's going after Rabbit, looking for Rabbit.

TÍANÊN:
And when Rabbit called out like that, Jaguar wasn't going to answer?

AMÁKA:
He didn't want to answer. He was too furious. Rabbit said, "Wait a minute! You shouldn't refuse to talk to me! / . . . / The problem you're having just happened to me too! So you could ask me about it and we could discuss it." He said, "Nephew, what are you saying there?" He said, "Where are you going?" /íya/

KASINDÓ [breaking in]:
Well, now, at the time he was saying, "What are you saying there"—

ADUÊNGI:
Yes, what was it that you saw?

KASINDÓ:
OK, the old man was right there in the forest /AMÁKA: well/

saying, "Child, while you all were dragging the pool here, I watched you for a long time. /right/

I'm going to play the drum for you, and if you don't dance, you won't take your fish back home." /not at all/

AMÁKA:
Not at all.

KASINDÓ:
Then the old man pulled his drum over and set it between his legs.

A WOMAN:
You mean Jaguar?

KASINDÓ:
Just an old man who happened to be there. / . . . / Then he went ahead and played his drum:

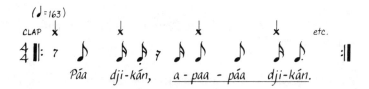

Páa djikán, apaapáa djikán.
Páa djikán, apaapáa djikán.
Páa djikán, apaapáa djikán.
Páa djikán, apaapáa djikán.
Páa djikán, apaapáa djikán.
Páa djikán, apaapáa djikán.
Páa djikán, apaapáa djikán.
Páa djikán, apaapáa djikán.
Páa djikán, apaapáa djikán.
Páa djikán, apaapáa djikán.
Páa djikán, apaapáa djikán.
Páa djikán, apaapáa djikán.
Páa djikán, apaapáa djikán.
Páa djikán, apaapáa djikán.
Páa djikán, apaapáa djikán.

[The tale this tale nugget is abstracted from is told frequently by Kasindó: It used to be that you couldn't go hunting. There was an old man, a devil, who would play his drum and make you dance till you dropped from exhaustion, at which point he'd kill you and eat you. A troop of small black monkeys sewed little black suits for themselves that covered their whole bodies (including their hands and faces) so that they all looked exactly alike. When the dance ordeal began, one of the monkeys jumped out and began dancing; once he got tired, another took his place, and so on—fooling the devil into thinking they were all the same dancer. As the drum kept playing "*páa djikán,*" the rhythm got slower and slower until the devil, exhausted, finally expired. And that's why, ever since, it's been safe to go hunting.

Kasindó's call-and-response song is accompanied by syncopated handclapping from all present as he imitates the monkeys' dance, even while verbally encouraging everyone to join in. Kasindó imaginatively linked his tale nugget to Amáka's tale by incorporating Rabbit, Jaguar, and the dry-season pool and having the monkeys' role be played by an unspecified "Child," though everyone present, having at one time or another heard his more customary rendition, was aware of the devil and monkeys story line.]

AMÁKA:

"Father—" (he replied) He said, "Is Rabbit the one you're chasing?" (then he said "yes") "You see how I've started rotting?" (he said "yes") "Well, Rabbit and I dragged the pool till we were all done. He tricked me and ate every last fish himself. Then when I came to talk to him, he coughed up some phlegm that got onto my skin, and that's what's rotting me away like this." "Really, Child?" (he said "yes") Jaguar said, "Well, Man. I knew what you looked like before, Deer, but the state you've ended up in here— Well, it would be even worse in my case. I think I'll just go home and forget it."

OTHERS:

[laughter]

AMÁKA:

And that's why they say that if you and another person do something together, and you get a little something out of it, be sure that he takes some and you take some. Otherwise you'll end up like Rabbit and Jaguar and Deer.

[Here there are a few moments of conversation, rehashing Amáka's tale.]

KASINDÓ:

Mató! [125]

TWO MEN [simultaneously]:

Tòngôni!

ADUÈNGI:

Rabbit is baaad!

KASINDÓ:

Well, then, we came there. / . . . / They came there, /*íya*/

and at one point, well, Old Man Anasi— /*íya*/

That is, there was an old man known as Adjáansipái ["Spider's son-in-law"].[126] /OK/

He had a place where he lived over there. /well/

Mm. So Old Man Anasi went along till he arrived and saw Adjáan-sipái there where he lived. /well, true/

He went to see /well/ the old man in his village. /right/

He went up to him. / . . . / The old man was there with his— ([Reprimanding people who are conversing among themselves:] Will you listen to me?!) The old man was there with his head bent down, /true/

scraping reeds, *sèè, sèè, sèè.* / . . . / Anasi said [in his nasal voice]: "Old man!" The old man just stayed there, /right/

scraping the reeds. Anasi said [nasal]: "Mm! My goodness! This son-in-law of mine here— I'd like to give him a wife.

WOMEN:
[laughter]

KASINDÓ:
Mm! I'd like to give this son-in-law of mine a wife!"

SAKUÍMA:
Does the old man really want Anasi to give him a wife?!

KASINDÓ:
As quick as a flash, Anasi found the old man a wife. /OK/

A little time passed. / . . . / He said, "Hmm!" He went off and came back the next morning. [Nasal:] "Mm! Greetings, my son-in-law!" /íya/

The old man sat there, scraping away at his reeds. /that's how it was/

He waited a bit and then [nasal]: "Well, Son-in-law, what do we have here to eat?"

A MAN:
Had he already given him the wife?

KASINDÓ:
He'd promised him the wife and was already addressing him as his son-in-law. The old man hadn't seen the woman yet. / . . . / Mm! The time arrived /right/

and Old Man Anasi went off and came back. He'd brought the girl back /true/

to present to the old man. /true/

Captain Kála, splitting reeds for a house under construction (our own), 1967.

[Nasal:] "Mm, Son-in-law, we've brought this woman!" The old man sat there scraping his reeds. "OK," he said. [Nasal:] "OK, ahh, uhh, Girl, the man says you should go right on into the house there." /well, true/

OTHERS:
[laughter]

AGUMÍÍ:
My god, Anasi's going to get her killed!

KASINDÓ:
Oh! The girl went right into the house. /well, true/

She stood inside the house and looked all around. She said [alarmed]: "Oh! The house that my father has set me up in here—! Well, what in the world has this person been hunting?! [That is, she sees human remains and is suspicious.] Hmm! This thing really troubles me!" /well/

So there she was for a while. Then Anasi said [nasal:] "Well, Son-in-law, well, now that I've brought you the woman here, I'll just be going." The old man sat there scraping away at the reeds. /yes/

Anasi went off, planning to return in the morning. As soon as he had turned his back, /eh/

the old man jumped up, *vaaa!* He grabbed his club! Mm! He clobbered the girl. / . . . / He dragged her on over. Then he prepared her and put her in the pot. / . . . / Then he did his cooking. / . . . / Time passed. In the morning Anasi arrived. / . . . / [Nasal:] "Son-in-law, greetings!"

OVERLAPPING VOICES:
[laughter and comments]

KASINDÓ:
"Well, what do you have for us to eat?" The old man just kept scraping his reeds. [Nasal:] "Ah, well, that is— Son-in-law, I mean, should I go have a look in the pot over there?" /right/

Mm! Anasi got up to go over to the pot. He took the pot off the fire and set it down. /right/

He opened the pot and was serving out the meat till at one point— [With surprise]: "Hm?! Mm!" /hm/

He noticed the metal anklets that had belonged to the girl, that had been on the girl's legs. He saw them clear as could be at the bottom of the pot, there in the broth. /right/

He said [stuttering, nasal]: "B— b— b— b— but, Old Man!"

AGUMIÍI:

Well, he was so involved in fixing something to eat that he didn't even think about taking out the anklets.

KASINDÓ [nasal]:

"You may not want to talk, but today you're going to talk!

OVERLAPPING VOICES:

[laughter and comments]

KASINDÓ:

The child of mine that I brought to give you— You killed her! You killed and cooked her. Today you're going to talk, whether you're used to talking or not. Today you'll talk!"

OVERLAPPING VOICES:

[laughter and comments]

KASINDÓ:

Old Man Anasi was at his wits' end. /eh/

Once he'd said that, Old Man Anasi went to cut some banana leaves,

OTHERS:

[laughter]

KASINDÓ:

and got them all ready.

OVERLAPPING VOICES:

[more comments]

KASINDÓ:

He said— He said [nasal]: "Today I'm going to show you! You're as good as dead! /right/

You pretend you're not able to speak. I even went to get a wife for you, and then you killed my girl and cooked her! Today I'll show you, whether you can talk or not!" / . . . / Then he went and wrapped Death in banana leaves. The old man was still sitting there working away on his reeds. / . . . / Anasi wraps him in banana leaves till he's all done. / . . . / Then he set him on fire! /right/

[Talking against a background of comments and laughter that prevents us from hearing the responder:] Ohh! *Woló!!* It's all over! / . . . / The old man threw his reed work to the ground, *gwilili si,* and he and Anasi went at each other. The old man was chasing

Anasi, opening and then closing the gap. They were really having it out. They kept going, and Anasi shouted out to his children [nasal]: "Children, go to the granary! Go to the granary!" Mmm! Anasi's running back home. Death is right behind him, with his club. He's running toward home. When he got very close, he shouted out [nasal:], "Children, everyone to the granary! Everyone to the granary! Emergency!" /right/

Now the children— Anasi's children and his wife /yes/

are all there in the granary. They've gone to the upper part there. Anasi arrived. Ohh! He grabbed a beam and swung himself up. Oh! Death said, "OK, I've got you now!" He settled in right below them there.

A MAN:
You mean the fire hadn't killed Death—

KASINDÓ:
Are you kidding?!

THE MAN:
—when he rolled him up in the banana leaf and set it on fire?

KASINDÓ:
No way. They were there for some time. /right/

Then one of the children said, "Oh, Father, my arms are getting tired." He said [nasal]: "Well, then, go to your brother-in-law down there!"

OTHERS:
[laughter]

KASINDÓ:
Ohh, the child dropped right down, *babala gwuu.* Oh, the old man clubbed the child, *gwoo.* He put the kid off to one side. Another one's there for a while, and then: "Father, my arm's getting tired!" [Nasal:] "OK, then, just go on down to your brother-in-law on the floor there." / . . . / The child dropped down. The old man clubbed the kid, *gwoo,* and put the kid off to one side. They went on like that, and after a while Weno [Anasi's wife] herself said her arms were tired. He said [nasal:] "Well, see your son-in-law down below you there? You want to go to him?"

OVERLAPPING VOICES:
[laughter and comments]

KASINDÓ:

Oh! Weno dropped right down. He clubbed her, *gwoo,* and put her alongside the children. Well, Anasi was left up there. Mm, mm!

A MAN:

His arms are getting tired.

KASINDÓ:

Right. The way it is with joints, they hold up for just so long and then they give out. /yes/

So he said [nasal]: "Well, Son-in-law, my dear Son-in-law, you know what you should do?

OTHERS:

[laughter]

KASINDÓ:

I realize that you don't want to answer when I talk to you. But you and I have something to straighten out. I already know you won't answer.

OTHERS:

[laughter]

KASINDÓ:

OK. But you are my very dear son-in-law. So go and collect a big pile of ashes. See how fat I am? Collect really a lot of ashes and put them right where I'm going to drop down here." / . . . / Death said, "OK, no problem." / . . . / Death went and collected ashes till he had a lot.

SOMEONE:

He agreed to collect ashes?

KASINDÓ:

He agreed to collect ashes. He brought them back and put them right there where Anasi was going to drop down. Anasi said [nasal]: "Son-in-law, once you've got the ashes all set there, just bend over and examine the ashes carefully. / . . . / Then when I drop, plop! just press me down in.

OTHERS:

[laughter]

KASINDÓ:

Otherwise you'll lose all the fat. So that's all. Death piled up the ashes there. /well/

And then he got down close and looked right at the pile of ashes.
When Anasi dropped, plop! he pressed down. Then Anasi jumped
up. He grabbed some ashes. He threw them right into Death's eyes.

OTHERS:
[laughter]

KASINDÓ:
He said, "You're so lazy, you said you didn't talk. Today you'll
see!"

OTHERS:
[laughter]

KASINDÓ:
Old Man Anasi scrambled off. Death said, "OK, Anasi, it's me and
you. We had problems out there in the forest, and we're still fighting back here in the village." So that's how Anasi went out looking
for him and introduced him to the world. The old man had always just stayed in the forest, scraping away at his reeds. Anasi
went and brought him back. That's all.

OVERLAPPING VOICES:
[discussion of the tale and the possibility of leaving]

SAKUÍMA:
We've really put in a night's worth!

[A bit of a lull, as if people are about to go home, then:]

ADUÊNGI:
Mató! [127]

AMÁKA:
Tòngôni!

SAKUÍMA [to someone else]:
Let them get on with their *tòngôni* and then I'm going to leave.

ADUÊNGI:
Well, Sister, the one I'm going to tell here is pure gold. / . . . / And
it's long.

KASINDÓ:
Well, I've got one too.

A WOMAN:
[gasp]

KASINDÓ:
And I want a chance to tell it tonight. We're going to have to take this matter down to the rocks by the river [to fight it out].

ADUÊNGI:
Well, let's go to the rocks!

OTHERS:
[laughter]

ADUÊNGI:
Well, we came to be there, and at a certain point, /AMÁKA: well, true/

there was a woman there. And she had a child. /right/

She had a daughter. [Correcting himself:] She had a son. So she gave birth to the boy and then, when it was time, she took him off— She was a church person and that means that when you have a child and the time comes, you take him off to have him baptized by someone. That person will baptize the child. /true/

The person who does it becomes a second mother to the child, whether it's a boy or a girl. /well/

That person becomes another mother. /well/

OK, so, well, the mother gave birth to the child, and she cared for him till he was big enough to be baptized, and then she took him off to get baptized.

KÓDJI [breaking in]:
Well, at the time they were baptizing him there—

ANOTHER MAN:
Bullshit!

KÓDJI:
A certain girl was there. That's all. /ADUÊNGI: íya/

Not a day used to pass when she didn't drug for fish in a place that a certain forest spirit owned. /no/

People told her not to over and over again, but she wouldn't listen. /íya/

AKÓBO:
Why is it that in folktales people can never discipline their children?

KÓDJI:
So that's all. She came and got everything ready. /íya/

And then she put the drug in the water. /íya/

She caught all the fish in that one place, and then, well, nothing much. She listened and she heard. She listened and she heard:

Byán-ti-na kí-si fí-si, Byán-ti-na—oo.

Byán-ti-na kí-si fí-si, Byán-ti-na gá-du, tén-te-le

fu tén-te-le, gá-du foón-doo Byán-ti-na-ee.

Byántina kísi físi, Byántina-oo.
Byántina kísi físi, Byántina gádu, téntele fu téntele, gádu
    foóndoo Byántina-ee.
Byántina kísi físi, Byántina-oo.
Byántina kísi físi, Byántina gádu, téntele fu téntele, gádu
    foóndoo Byántina-ee.

["Byántina caught fish, Byántina. / Byántina caught fish, Byántina (exclamation), *téntele fu téntele*, the god amazed Byántina." In the tale this nugget alludes to, people had told Byántina not to go fishing in that place because of the forest spirit who lived there. When she put her fish in the pot, it got bigger and bigger until she was terrified. Her greed had created an avenging spirit for her lineage. This cautionary tale reflects a general Saramaka concern about individual greed versus conservation for the communal good.[128]]

Go on with your story.

ADUÊNGI:

Eh! Well, nothing much. /true/

So she took him off to get baptized. /well/

KASINDÓ:
That girl called Byántina—

ADUÊNGI:
And after she had the child baptized, things went along for a while. /mm/

KASINDÓ:
—she's some hunter!

ADUÊNGI:
Now the child grew and got bigger. /íya/

The child grew and got bigger, and on and on until he was old enough to send to school. So they put him in school. /right/

The woman who baptized him— Well, she was the one who put him in school. /well/

She sent him to school long enough for the child to understand reading and writing just a little. /true/

Now the woman who baptized the child owned a certain book. /íya/

Nothing in the world you'd ever want to know about—

AMÁKA [anticipating]:
—was missing from it.

ADUÊNGI:
—was missing from that book. /not at all/

Every last thing in the world— If it could be said that you might consider wanting it, it would be in that book for you to read. /well/

So the child would go to school till he returned in the afternoon, and the woman would go over that book with him.

AMÁKA:
And have him read it.

ADUÊNGI:
He'd read it. /OK/

He'd read it and read it, every day, until—

KASINDÓ [breaking in]:
Now at the time when the child's mother was pregnant, /ADUÊNGI: íya/

she loaded up her things and headed off on a path into the forest. /íya/

She had a big, full belly. /that's right/

So, well, she went along the forest path, and she knocked her foot on something. / . . . / Now the child who was in her belly there said, "Mother, walk gently!" /íya/

A WOMAN:
[lets out an explosive laugh]

ANOTHER WOMAN:
The child in her belly said, "Mother, walk softly!"

KASINDÓ:
The mother went "Mmm." She turned around to come back /íya/

and she knocked her foot again. The child said, "Mother, walk gently."

A WOMAN:
Ahh.

KASINDÓ:
Then she got back. Go on with your story.[129]

ADUÊNGI:
Well, that's all. So they put the boy in school. /AMÁKA: right/

They kept teaching the boy until— Well, there's a thing that's called schoolchildren's "fakánsi" [Dutch vacantie = "vacation"]. /yes/

You stay in school till a certain day and then it's fakánsi time. /yes/

So when vacation time arrived, the baptizing person— the mother by baptism sends him off to the mother who gave birth to him. /OK/

She said, "Child—" (he replied) She said, "Go off to your mother. Go stay with her overnight for two days and then come back." /well/

OTHERS:
[a lot of loud talking and laughing]

ADUÊNGI:
Hey, everyone! Listen to the tale!! So he went and slept at his mother's. /right/

He stayed at her house for two days, just like the woman told him, /well/

and then he came back. He went along, stayed in school, until vacation time came again. She sent him off again. She said, "Child—" (he replied) "Go stay at your mother's three days, and then come back." /well/

He went off. He went and stayed three days, and then he came back. The boy kept growing up, the boy grew up, got to be like a man, old enough to do adult things. So the mother who gave birth to him /right/

started wanting to have her child. /well/

She started wanting to take the child /that's the way it was/

and get him back from the baptizing one. /that's how it was/

So one day, when it got to be vacation again, the mother who baptized him said, "Child—" (he replied) She said, "Go to your mother. And this time, you know how vacation is a whole month long?" ("yes" he said) "Well, you can stay there for a week—"

A MAN [anticipating]:
  "—and then come back."

ADUÊNGI:
  "—and then come back." The boy went off. He said, "Mother—" (she replied) He said, "Mother said that when I come I should stay for one week /true/

and then go back." She said, "You won't stay for just a week. / . . . / Vacation time has arrived, and you have a whole month of vacation. You're going to stay here for the whole month before you go back. /hm!/

You aren't going to go back before that!" "Mother—" (she replied) He said, "Mother said I should stay for a week and then go back." She said, "I told you, you're not going! I'm the one who gave birth to you."

A WOMAN:
  She's right.

ADUÊNGI:
  (he said "yes")

A MAN:
  There's trouble coming.

ADUÊNGI:
  The boy stayed for a week and then he said, "Mother, I'm leaving today." She said, "You're not going! /no/

I've got something I want you to help me carry to the garden." /right/

So they went along until the day—

KASINDÓ [breaking in]:
Well, just when they went off to the garden— /ADUÊNGI: *íya*/

Who do you think had cleared that garden site?

ADUÊNGI:
Who had cleared it?

KASINDÓ:
OK! Piká-bird was the one who had flown around and cleared the garden. /that's right/

So he cleared the garden till it was all done. /that's right/

But he didn't clear a path [from the river to the garden]. /no/

Well, then, the old man of the forest [jaguar] came along and he made a path to the garden. /*íya*/

Then he set fire to the garden site. /*íya*/

Piká-bird went along there for a while, and then he heard, "Well, who's in my garden there?" /*íya*/

The voice said, "Who's trespassing in my garden?" /mm?/

Piká-bird said, "I cut my own garden. /*íya*/

'You've Come to Cause Problems for Me.' That's what I call this garden of mine." He heard, "Not at all! This garden is the one I call 'You Should Leave Your Thing to Me.'" /hm!/

OTHERS:
[laughter]

KASINDÓ:
Piká-bird said, "No no! I'm the one who cleared this garden. I flew around in the air and cleared my garden. / . . . / And whenever I come here, it's to work in this garden. /*íya*/

It's the one I call 'You've Come to Cause Me Problems.'" / . . . /
The other one said, "No, no! This garden is where I made a path and cleared the underbrush. It's the one I call 'You Should Leave Your Thing to Me.'"

AGUMIÍI:
Can't he see it's not his?!

KASINDÓ:
Go on with your story! That's why the garden Piká-bird made belongs to the old man of the forest. /that's how it is/

Go on with your talking.[130]

Entranceway on path leading to a Saramaka garden, 1967.

ADUÊNGI:
OK, so the boy— The boy stayed on beyond the day the church mother had told him. /AMÁKA: well/

That mother was back there. Finally she said, "How come the boy's staying past the day I told him?" / . . . / They went along till it got to be two weeks. /well, true/ Then she [the natural mother] said, "Go along." She said that, so he left. Then she [the church mother] addressed him and said, "Child—" (he replied) "Why didn't you come back on the day I told you?" He said, "Well, Mother said there was so much work she needed me to help her with, so I was there helping her." They went along until the time came [for another visit], and she sent him off again. /true/

She said "Child—" (he replied) She said, "When you go this time, stay for three days—"

A MAN [anticipating]:
"—and then come back."

ADUÊNGI:
"—and then come back. And tell your mother that I sent you and told you that you should come for three days and then return, but

if your three days are up and on the fourth day you don't come,"
(he said "yes") "I'm going to come to her and we're going to divide you."

OTHERS:
[exclamations and laughter]

SAKUÍMA:
My goodness! They'll divide him up?! They'll kill him, all because
of his mother?!

ADUÊNGI:
(he said "yes") Then she picked up her book /right/

and gave it to him. /true/

She said, "You see this book here, the one that's taught you so
many things?" (he said "yes") "Well, everywhere you go, you can
take your book with you." /OK/

Then the boy went off. But when he left he didn't take the book.
/uh-uh/

He left it there and went off. He left. He told his mother— He
said, "Well, Mother—" (she replied) He said, "The other one, my
godmother [Dutch *pete*] said I should stay three days and then go
back." /true/

She said, "You're not staying for just three days! You're staying
longer!"

SAKUÍMA:
Ohh, they're going to end up killing that child!

ADUÊNGI:
He said, "No. She said that if—" (she said "yes") "If I didn't come
back after three days, she would come to you and have me divided
between the two of you." /hm/

She said, "Let her just come and we'll divide you. Because I'm the
one who gave birth to you!"

OTHERS:
[exclamations of concern]

ADUÊNGI:
The boy slept there three nights. Morning came, /well/

and they stayed till night fell. Early in the morning on the fourth
day, the mother who baptized him showed up. "Good morning,
Woman!" and she replied, "Good morning," and she said, "Yes,

well, you see how I've come to you here? The boy that you gave
me to baptize— Well, he and I have been living together all this
time, I've been raising him all this time, and now you're taking
him away from me, and even telling him bad things about me."
(she said "yes") "So I've come to you today to divide the boy between us. You gave birth to him, and I baptized him. /mm/

And I've come to you to divide him, to see who's going to have
him." /mm!/

She said, "Well, all right. Let's divide him. Because this is a child
that I gave birth to." /yes/

The mother who gave birth to him grabbed him on one leg and
pulled. The one who baptized him grabbed the other leg and
pulled. They split him right apart, *zaa bálán!*

OTHERS:
[exclamations of concern]

ADUÊNGI:
The mother who gave birth to him threw her side down, limp as
could be. / . . . / The baptizing one took her part quickly back to
her village, and she took her book and opened it wide, and she
said, "My book, my book! Let this child of mine be a one-sided
child all his life. Let him be a one-sided child, but let him stay
alive." The boy was a one-sided child, but he was alive.

KASINDÓ:
Well, at the time when he was a one-sided child, /ADUÊNGI: *íya*/

Old Man Anasi was walking along and he saw the one side and the
other side, /*íya*/

and they were wrestling. /that's right/

So he said [nasal]: "What's going on here? Hm, well, that side over
there, come on and attach yourself to this one. /*íya*/

OTHERS:
[laughter]

KASINDÓ [as others laugh sporadically]:
You almost threw that other one down. Ohh, well this is really
serious. Why can't you just get together with the other part of you
here?" The two sides kept wrestling without getting together. /yes/

So Old Man Anasi went and pulled them together. /eh/

So they got to be a whole person. Go ahead with your story.[131]

ADUÊNGI:
Right on, Turtle! / . . . / Well, that's all. So the boy— / AMÁKA: well, true/

The boy's growing up and he— Well, he got to be a full-grown man.

A MAN:
The one-sided boy?

ADUÊNGI:
The one-sided boy.

AGUMIÍI:
Well, can he still talk?

ADUÊNGI:
And what happened— What happened is that they'd already changed his name. / . . . / They called him Katjédenómu.

AKÓBO:
Katjédenómu.

ADUÊNGI:
Katjédenómu. That's all. / . . . / So the child— Well, in the land of the king, things were just like in Dángogó. Every morning people would go upstream to their gardens. /well/

And in that kingdom there was the king's house with the king's children who lived up there in a two-story house, and the boy would pass by the king's doorway on his way to school. /OK/

He had one leg, one arm, one eye, one side of his mouth, one side of his nose. Every single thing that people have, he had just one side of it. /exactly right/

Right. So he had his walking stick, and he got along like that. / . . . / One morning he was going by the king's doorway. One of the king's children was there looking at him: / . . . / "This is really something!! In my whole life, I've never seen such a person, a one-sided person. Never!" /no/

Then she dashed over and called her sister. She said, "Sister—" (she replied) She said, "Come!" It was her older sister. She came and looked. Then she said, "Oh, Child, well, don't say anything. / . . . / Let it be." (she said "yes") Now the king's children knew what time school got out. /well/

She waited till school was out and then she went back and sat down exactly where she had been before. She said, "I'm going to wait for that person, to watch him go by. A one-sided-only person! I've never ever seen such a thing. / . . . / So she'd come back and watch for the child till he passed by. The next day, as soon as it was light, she'd be there waiting. / . . . / After a while, the boy, Katjédenómu— One day he was going by and he stared back at the child. He said to himself, "OK, Princess, I've been going by here for many many days. I go by and you watch me and make fun of me. But I'm not the one who's responsible for the way I am."

SAKUÍMA:
Well, how does he walk if he's only got one leg?!

ADUÊNGI:
"I'll take care of you!" /right/

He went by. The next morning at dawn he came back again, and he brought his book. / . . . / He came along till he arrived there. He addressed the girl. She just stared back at him. He said to his book, "My book, my book, do you see the king's child up above there? Not a single man has ever had her, but I want you to make her pregnant for me. Let it be said that I, Katjédenómu, fathered the child that she'll bear. That's what must happen." / . . . / So they went along as usual. / . . . / After a while, the king's child was in her place up there and her belly starts to swell. / . . . / Her belly keeps on swelling. Finally one day the king called her. He asked her about it. And she said, "Well, Father, I don't have any knowledge of men!" He said, "Don't argue with me. You do!" She said, "I don't!" / . . . / They kept at it like that, on and on. /well/

They called the civil officer, had him brought in, and said, "You've done this to the girl." They interrogated him for a long time. He said, "Not at all! I swear I don't know a thing about this whole business."

KÓDJI:
At that time, I was there.

ADUÊNGI:
Íya. What did you see?

KÓDJI:
Well, they were having a funeral "play" in a certain village. /ADUÊNGI: *íya*/

Now it used to be that when you went to a village for a play, there would be a certain man who'd perform, but he would never stay till dawn. /no/

He'd play awhile and then he'd go off. /íya/

So that's all. People went to a play. /íya/

And on the day when they— When they were going to play, /íya/

everyone wanted to know who this person was who was performing. /that's how it was/

So they asked the people from that village to prepare some fermented sugarcane juice [to get the person so drunk that he couldn't leave while it was still dark, and they would be able to find out who he was]. /that's right/

Then they went to the play there. When they arrived, they asked the young guys to play. Well, that's all. One sang out:

Loon-bi-aa, ___ loon-bi-aa loon-bi-ee, ___ loon-bi-aa

loon-bi-ee, ___ loon-bi-aa loon-bi-ee. ___

Loon-bi-aa, ___ loon-bi-aa loon-bi-ee, ___ loon-bi-aa

loon-bi-ee, ___ loon-bi-aa loon-bi-oo. ___

Loon-bi-aa, loon-bi-aa loon-bi-ee. ___

Tí-o Sód-jo-ee, ___ un mbóu gó-oo. ___

1.
Loon-bi-aa ___ loon-bi-aa. ___

2.
loon-bi-aa-ee. ___

Loonbi-aa, loonbi-aa loonbi-ee, loonbi-aa loonbi-ee, loonbi-aa
  loonbi-ee.
Loonbi-aa, loonbi-aa loonbi-ee, loonbi-aa loonbi-ee, loonbi-aa
  loonbi-oo.
Loonbi-aa, loonbi-aa loonbi-ee.
Tío Sódjo-ee, un mbóu gó-oo. Loonbi-aa loonbi-aa.
Tío Sódjo-ee, un mbóu gó-oo. Loonbi-aa, loonbi-aa-ee.

[In the tale this nugget is extracted from, the mystery performers were howler monkeys. The *dómbi babúnu* (the large male at the head of every troop of howler monkeys) was the one who got drunk. In the song the other howler monkeys are calling to him, their mother's brother, pleading with him to leave. And that's why just before dawn, you still hear the call of howler monkeys. The song translates, "(Roar of howler monkeys) / Uncle Sódjo, come on let's go. (Roar)."]

Go on with your story.

ADUÊNGI:

OK, well, right then I was there too. /AMÁKA: true/

[Referring to Kódji, who had just interrupted Aduêngi's tale:] If a man kicks you, you have to kick him back! Right. Well, Trumpetbird lived in folktale-land then. /true/

And when they had an all-night play, he would go and perform until cock's crow and then he'd leave. No one knew who was doing it. /no one/

So this is what he sang at cock's crow: /right/

Kizáán záán zán kolé bóko kôniman tá límbo búsi welé buntí
  bamutjaanga akí tjololoo.
Kôni angolee, bamutjaanga akí tjololoo.
Kizáán záán zán kolé bóko kôniman tá límbo búsi welé buntí
  bamutjaanga akí tjololoo.
Kôni angolee, bamutjaanga akí tjololoo.

[In this nugget, Trumpet-bird is the mystery performer who always leaves just before dawn. And that's why you always hear Trumpet-bird calling in the early morning. We do not have a persuasive translation of this song; compare it, however, with the song in Kandámma's otherwise quite dissimilar nugget on p. 143.]

Go ahead with your story, Child.

A MAN:
The short-legged turtle!

ANOTHER MAN:
Well, let's get on with it.

ADUÊNGI:
So that's all. They questioned the girl till they were exhausted. /OK/

"Mmm! This whole thing is really amazing to us!" So they went along and the woman got very pregnant. /well/

It was a tremendous belly, and finally she gave birth. /right/

She had a child. She had a boy. /well, true/

Brother, the whole incident was really something. /really something/

They investigated— They interrogated every single man. /well/

There was not a single man /right/

who said he'd been with her. The girl herself— There was no man who she'd point to and say, "That man, that's the one I saw here one day." The civil officer— he had never seen any man go by there, ever, /not at all/

in a secretive way. /no/

The only men who'd come there were those who were on business with the king, and you'd come and sit down and discuss your business and then you'd leave. /that's all/ But not in a secretive way.

No man ever went beyond that. / . . . / Mm! Well, this thing is really something! /hm!/

So then they— Once the woman gave birth to the child, the king took it. They raised him and he grew up very nicely. /well/

They had already had the ritual introduction of the baby to the village. The child had gotten big enough to sit up. /right/

Then he had started walking. /OK/

And word went out that the man who fathered the child— They had to know who he was. /OK/

Every last man in the world, if he lived anywhere within traveling distance to the king's village, should come to the king's village. /right/

Because the child absolutely had to know who his father was. /OK/

So they should all come. / . . . / Ohhh, the day came for them to call a meeting. Well, I can't describe it for you. /no/

They came from Guyába, /right/

all the way up to Sitónúku [from the Middle Suriname River all the way to the southernmost village on the Gaánlío]. /well, true/

Men came. The child walked and walked all around the village until night fell. He didn't see a single person who was his father, and he said that of the ones who'd come, none was his father, that his father wasn't among them. / . . . / Anasi calls him [nasal]: "Child, come on over here!"

OTHERS:
[laughter]

ADUÊNGI:
All those big important white men were calling to him, were caressing him with their hands [in hopes of being named as the father]. As the child would go by, you'd tap him on the ribs, he'd stare back at you, and he'd pass on. / . . . / This went on for days and days. Ohh! And it wasn't Guyába— This wasn't just to Guyába anymore! Now it went as far as what's its name— to Ganzê [a village much farther downstream, and the largest Saramaka village]. /OK/

It happened three times, and then Katjédenómu's mother called him. "Katjédenómu—" (he replied) She said, "Well, you're a man."

(he said "yes") "Well, this is the third day of the big meeting."
(he said "yes") "Well, it's the last day." (he said "yes") "You have to
go. /well/

Because you are a man. /that's exactly how it was/

And every single man is supposed to go." (he said "yes") "So you
should go." /well/

He said, "Well, Mother, I can't go. / . . . / I'm a one-sided person.
What on earth could I have to do with this business?" She said,
"No, no, go!" / . . . / (he said "yes") That's all. Katjédenómu set
out. /true/

He went along and after a while he sat down, with his one side, at
the edge of the forest there. /true/

SAKUÍMA [sympathetically]:
Well, how could he manage?!

ADUÊNGI:
The king summoned the little boy. "Boy—" (he replied) He said,
"Well, today—" / . . . / (he said "yes") "It's the last day for both you
and your mother."

AGUMÍÍI:
He's going to die.

ADUÊNGI:
"You must find out who your father is. /OK/

But here we are today, and there's not a single man left anywhere.
/mm/

Because, well, I've heard of a man known as Katjédenómu. He
was a one-sided child, but now he's a man. So today he should
come too. /OK/

He's the only one who's left, so he has to come today. And if it
turns out that you don't have a father, that he's not among all
those who've come here, we'll kill you and we'll kill your mother,
and that'll be the end of it."

OTHERS:
[exclamations of concern]

ADUÊNGI:
He said "Yes, Father. But if I don't really see my father, I won't say
I have. /not at all/

You'll just have to kill me."

RESPONDER:
And that will settle it.

ADUÊNGI:
"But if I do see him, I will say so. No matter how undesirable a person he may be." /no matter/

No problem. They set up the boy again. Well, then, the boy walked all around. /OK/

He broke through the crowd assembled there [looking for his father] and went right up to where Katjédenómu was sitting on top of a log!

AKÓBO:
And then, Katjédenómu— His heart was ready to split!

ADUÊNGI:
He'd sat down, all crooked and deformed. The boy breaks through the crowd and heads straight for Katjédenómu. He went and sat down on his one-sided lap, *siaan*. / . . . / He said, "Everybody—" (they replied) He said, "This person is my father. /hm!/

For the whole time that people have been coming here, and this is the third day, he hadn't yet come. This is the first time I've seen him here. Today I've seen him. /well/

That's why I'm speaking to you. He's my father, he fathered me." / . . . / Cannons boomed and then they stopped. Cannons boomed and then they stopped. The king said, "Well, the thing that's happened here is really amazing. /OK/

Because I'm an important king, and for my child to come and say that I have to accept a one-sided person, that he must be my son-in-law— Because the two of them will have to be [church] married. /well/

He has to become my son-in-law and live in my royal house. This is really terrible for me!"

KASINDÓ:
How can you get married on one side?

ADUÊNGI:
[The king, addressing his daughter:] "Child, I'm going to send you and Katjédenómu off to sea, and that will be the end of you two. The child— Well, I can raise him myself." /well, right/

So then— Ohh, the king gave out orders to his soldiers. They bailed out a broken old punt of his that was there. They bailed it all out. / . . . / The punt's leaking, drip, drip, drip, so they bailed it all out.

AKÓBO [critically]:
What's going on here is that somebody's being made fun of. That's what's happening!

ADUÊNGI:
They bailed it out till they were all finished. They took the girl and put her in. They took Katjédenómu and put him in. Then they launched it, *zaíín*, way out to sea. / . . . / They took the child. The king kept him. Ohh!

AGUMIÍI:
They're getting thrown out, but maybe they'll go back to his own village.

ADUÊNGI:
The tide came up. The big waves carried them off, were taking them out to sea. The boat, the punt was going drip, drip, drip. It was sinking. / . . . / It kept sinking more and more. The waves would come up, *wòòò*, and crash right into it. They'd come up and crash in some more. Katjédenómu— Ever since they'd left, he'd been trying to talk to the woman, and the woman, well, ever since they'd left, she hadn't said a word to Katjédenómu. She went and sat at the prow of the punt. Katjédenómu was at the punt's stern.

OVERLAPPING VOICES:
[discussion of the situation]

ADUÊNGI:
When the boat started to sink, he called out "Wife!" (she replied) He said— [Then, correcting a slip of the tongue:] He called out "Wife!" / . . . / But she DIDN'T reply. He said, "If you wanted to, you'd answer me. The way things are going for us here, you're going to die. But I will live. /well/

So if you'd like to, you shouldn't refuse to speak to me, Katjédenómu. Great God has declared that I, the one-sided person, and you should be together.

SEVERAL WOMEN:
[sounds of empathy]

ADUÊNGI:
So if you like, why don't you answer me. Let it be that if I can get us out alive, we'll live, and if we're to die, let it be that both of us

died, but we died talking to each other. Well, but if you're going to be like that and we're going to die, well, you will die but I won't." / no /

Mm. The girl just didn't know what to do anymore.

A WOMAN [talking on top of Aduêngi's voice]:
She didn't know whether to believe it.

ADUÊNGI:
She didn't want to answer him. She didn't know what to say. The waves are crashing into the punt. The boat is going under, and then it would come up again. Katjédenómu took that little book of his and opened it up. He said [in the rhetoric and tone of prayer to a god or an ancestor]: "My book, my book, let the punt here stay just the way it is now, all night and all day. Let it not sink any more than it has. And let it not dry out more than this."

SOMEONE:
Hm!

ADUÊNGI:
They went on like that. The boat kept dipping in and out of the water. They kept on going.

A WOMAN:
They were going out to sea.

ADUÊNGI:
They were going out to sea. Without any food! They went along for a while and he said, "Wife, aren't you hungry?" Ohh, it was just as though he was talking to himself. Katjédenómu opened his book, wide open, and he said, "My book, my book, I'm hungry. I want to eat." / . . . / Ohh, Katjédenómu is all set up there, with his big table all laid out in front of him. He ate till his belly was full.

OVERLAPPING VOICES:
[laughter and comments]

ADUÊNGI:
He said, "My book, be closed." /true/

The girl was there just staring at all this.

AKÓBO:
If it had been me, I would've talked to him.

A WOMAN:
I would've too.

OVERLAPPING VOICES:
[discussion of what each would do in the circumstances]

ADUÊNGI:
Now what happened is that when she saw Katjédenómu do that, she was really upset. /well/

She thought about it to herself and then she said, "This thing that's happening, Katjédenómu—" (Katjédenómu replied) She said, "Look, today it's been three days and three nights since we left, and now I'm ready to talk to you." (he said "yes") "The way you used to walk by on the ground while I was in the king's house, way up above—" (he said "yes") "And Great God came there. It was really an amazing thing when that happened. They say you made me pregnant there, and I even gave birth, without my understanding it. It's a truly astonishing thing for me. /well/

So if you, Katjédenómu, know what you have to do so we can stay alive—" (he said "yes") She said, "Do everything you can to save us. But I don't want to have to go back to my mother and father again."

A WOMAN:
Ké! [exclamation of sympathy]

ADUÊNGI:
He said, "Wife, that's just what I wanted you to say to me." /right/

He opened his book wide and said, "My book, my book, I want to be in a dry punt, with its insides dry as a bone, and with food for us and everything we might need, so let us be in a dry, dry punt, but let us be right there in a punt."

AKÓBO:
There's no one else around, so why shouldn't they just make up?

TÍANÊN:
Even if there were other people, they still should make up.

ADUÊNGI [simultaneous with the remarks by Akóbo and Tíanên]:
They were in a dry punt, absolutely not a drop was in it. Their food, everything else they needed was right there. Place to sleep, absolutely everything was in the punt, out there at sea.

AKÓBO:
[indistinct comment, then:] She's decided to start acting flirtatious.

A MAN:
Out at sea?

ADUÊNGI:

Out at sea. [indistinct phrase] right there in the punt. /well/

Ohh, the girl went along for a while and then her mood changed, and she stopped speaking to Katjédenómu. She went back and sat down where she'd been. After a while Katjédenómu opened his book wide and said, "My book, my book, my book, let me sink here, sink the punt for me!" They started sinking swiftly. /hm!/

OTHERS:

[laughter]

ADUÊNGI:

She ran toward Katjédenómu and pressed up against his side.

AKÓBO [laughing]:

My goodness, she's really impossible!

ADUÊNGI:

She called him. (he replied) She said, "Let's make up." (he said "yes") He opened his book wide and said, "My book, my book, let the inside of this punt be dry again."

AKÓBO:

That person is really impossible!

OVERLAPPING VOICES:

[various criticisms of the girl's behavior]

ADUÊNGI:

So they kept on going along and going along. The people back in the king's village there had forgotten about them. They were finished with them. /well/

So they kept going along until finally the woman changed and rejected all those thoughts that she had had. She rejected them completely. And she treated Katjédenómu as her husband. The two of them lived very happily, talked to each other, laughed with each other.

OVERLAPPING VOICES:

[During this whole description, various people add their own versions of what must be happening.]

AKÓBO:

At night they'd sleep.

ADUÊNGI:

At night they'd sleep. Then one day she called him, "Katjéde-nómu—" (he replied) She said, "Well, the way we are, inside this punt here— Is this the way we'll be forever? Without ever trying to change things so our life can be better?"

AGUMIÍI [simultaneously with Aduêngi, and sarcastically]:
So after they split the boy in two, are you sure she got the living half?!

ADUÊNGI:
He said, "Well, Wife—" (she replied) He said, "I don't know. Our life is really up to you. The way it is—" (she said "yes") "There's nothing that's capable of killing me. So our life is up to you. If you really want us to live, we'll live." /well/

She said, "Well, what I say is—" (he said "yes") "Everything you have that could allow us to live—" (he said "yes") "Let's do our very best to live. You and I— Some day, I can tell you, we'll be [church] married."

WOMEN:
[exclamations of astonishment]

ADUÊNGI:
They went along like that for a while.

KASINDÓ:
They're heading right for the land of the dead.

ADUÊNGI:
Then Katjédenómu opened his book wide and said, "My book, my book, this punt that I'm in here, I've been in it too long and I'm suffering, so let me be inside a big ship with my own crew and everyone I need." / . . . / They were in a huge, enormous ship. There were grocery stores in one part. / . . . / There were bananas to eat. / . . . / Every single thing from the modern world that white-folks have was there.

KASINDÓ [breaking in]:
Well, pay attention to your story!

ADUÊNGI:
Íya

KASINDÓ:
Wouldn't he have been clever enough to turn himself into a whole person?!

ADUÊNGI:
Well, no. But that will come later.

KASINDÓ:
[laughs]

AKÓBO:
And the part that got left back with the mother [who gave birth to him]. What had happened to that?

ADUÊNGI:
That part— What happened to it is that it died.

AKÓBO:
Oh!

ADUÊNGI:
That story's finished. So that's all. Their ship was puffing along, *djim djim djim djim*. Then one day he said, "Wife—" (she replied) He said, "We're going back. /true/

You know how we left the king's village?" (she said "yes") "When we'd been gone three days, a war broke out in the king's land. /well, true/

They're fighting." / . . . / (she said "yes") "Now there are three more days of fighting left and then a big ship is going to come destroy the land." /right/

(she said "yes") "So I have to go there."

AKÓBO:
To go get their child.

ADUÊNGI:
"No no, Katjédenómu!" (he replied) She said, "Let's never go back to my father and mother's village. /uh-uh/

Let's go off somewhere where we can manage— Go somewhere and manage to make a life for ourselves. Let's not go back there again." He said, "No, forget that idea. Forget it."

OVERLAPPING VOICES:
[various comments]

ADUÊNGI:
Katjédenómu opened his book wide and said, "My book, my book, this ship of mine here— Well, it's just that we've been heading out to sea and we don't know where we are, but the place where I started out, that's where the ship's prow should be pointed, and the person who's steering the ship, let him know what direction to steer so he can get us there." /right/

Ohh! The white people who were there in the ship— The sailors— The people known as "sailors"—

AKÓBO:
Who's replying for this tale?!

AGUMIÍI:
It's supposed to be Zèngêni ["Swinger," a play name for Amáka ("Hammock")].

ADUÊNGI:
The thing called white people, pale as they could be— They were all over the place. They were the ones steering the ship. /well, true/

The whites were steering the ship, going right along, and then one day Katjédenómu got up very quickly /true/

and went to the bridge of the ship. /well/

Went to the ship's bridge while the woman was still in bed— /right/

TÍANÊN:
She's already found herself a bed?!

ADUÊNGI:
—sleeping. So Katjédenómu went to the ship's bridge there, and he opened his book wide. He went right to the ship's bridge there and opened— He opened his book wide. He said, "My book, my book, don't you see how I've been a one-sided person? /right/

But with the ship arriving here, the time has come for me to turn into a two-sided person, the way people are used to being. /hm!/

So let me change and become just the way I was when my mother and father gave birth to me: a two-sided person. Everything a man has, everything a person has, let me have it." /OK/

OVERLAPPING VOICES:
[a great deal of extraneous conversation over the past several paragraphs]

ADUÊNGI:
Katjédenómu was very still. Then he felt that his body was starting to feel prickly. He saw the side of him that had been all rotted away turn into a real man, *tjéntjén*—

AGUMIÍI:
Well, the side that had been split off— Wouldn't that have been too dried up to be put back on again?

SOMEONE ELSE:
Right, it would have.

ADUÊNGI:
—with two arms, a whole mouth, his whole body— Every single thing a person has. He became a real person, *tjén tjén*.

SOMEONE:
Two legs, two arms.

ADUÊNGI:
Right. He said, "My book, my book, I want to be a real person just like a civil officer, with the full uniform of a civil officer on my body." / . . . / Ohh, it just couldn't be described! His uniform— If you saw Katjédenómu, your eye couldn't take it all in. / . . . / Then he left. He tucked his book into his pants pocket. He left where he'd been and walked out. /true/

Oh! He didn't see his wife there where they used to sit down. She was in bed, in her cabin, sound asleep. /right/

He went and knocked on the door: "knock! knock! knock!" The woman got up, with her nightgown on and pulled on a dress, 'cause she thought the sailors were coming to talk to her. /well/

So she got up, slipped on a dress, and opened the door. / . . . / She saw one of the whites, a really handsome-eyed fellow. He looked like he wanted to enter her room. She said, "What?! Where are you going?" / . . . / He said, "I'm coming in here." She said [in an alarmed tone]: "Not at all! What makes you think you can come here? Katjédenómu is the one in charge of both me and you. He takes care of us. And you come here to my bedroom! What business do you have here? / . . . / Because you've never come here before. You've never come here before, and now that Katjédenómu has gone up to the bridge, you decide to come here?! What business do you have here? If you have a message for me, then out with it!"

AGUMIÍI:
She doesn't realize that it's her husband?

AKÓBO:
How's she supposed to know?

ADUÊNGI:
He said, "No, I've just come to see you here. I've come so that you and I can live together."

A WOMAN [in response to Agumiíi]:
Well, he had been a one-sided person.

ADUÊNGI:
"No!! Go back! Go back! Go back! If you try anything with me,
you'll be in real trouble. If Katjédenómu finds you here with me,
you're as good as dead." / . . . / (he said "yes") He stayed there
with her, so she said, "Get out! Turn around and leave! Katjédenómu will be here any minute." The woman went back, lay down
in her bed, pulled her door tightly shut. He said, "Woman—" (she
replied) He said, "It's me, Katjédenómu himself." "What did you
say?!" He said, "Katjé—" "What do you— Don't try to trick me!"
He said, "Look, here's the book I own." He opened his book wide,
showed her, said, "Here's my book. It's me. Me. Katjédenómu."
The woman threw her arms around Katjédenómu's neck. They
fell into her bed together.

OTHERS:
[laughter]

ADUÊNGI:
. The bed buried them deep inside it, it completely silenced them!

A MAN:
Right, because it had a mattress.

ADUÊNGI:
Oh, it was the kind of thing that can only happen in a folktale!
Katjédenómu had become a man for her the way she wanted.

A MAN:
Folktale-land!

ADUÊNGI:
They were heading for the king's village at that time. /well/

A MAN:
They were going to stop the fighting.

ADUÊNGI:
Oh, they were going to stop the fighting.

AKÓBO:
I'm starting to look at the person who's telling us this tale as if he
were Katjédenómu himself [because it's a really amazing story]!

ANOTHER WOMAN:
Yes, he's just like Katjédenómu!

ADUÊNGI:

They continued on until the big ship touched shore, *patáa*. When the big ship arrived, /true/

well, at that time, big ships would come up to the pier, just the way they do today. A little ship would be sent to ask— /well/

It would go out to the big ship before it could dock /that's indeed how it was/

and throw its anchor *gililili* into the water. A little ship came to it— Came to say— Well, nothing much, just to ask what it was carrying.

AKÓBO:

Of the two people who split up the kid— The one whose side lived is the one who won out.

ADUÊNGI [simultaneous with Akóbo's remark]:

He, Katjédenómu said, well, nothing. He'd heard that the king's village there was being ruined by fighting /OK/

and he'd come to see what was going on. /right/

(he said "yes") The king sent word that the person who was coming in the ship, the person in charge, must come ashore. / . . . / Katjédenómu sent word back that he couldn't come ashore. /no/

He'd heard that the king there couldn't tolerate one-sided people. / . . . / So since the king couldn't tolerate [had a "taboo" against] one-sided people, he couldn't come ashore, because his mother and his father gave birth to him and he was a one-sided person. /well/

He couldn't come ashore. / . . . / The king said, "Ahh! When you go back, tell him that whether he's a one-sided person or not a one-sided person, he's to come ashore." He said he couldn't come. But since he'd heard that the war was ruining the whole place there, he came to help. /true/

He came to tell them— To say that the king's war-horse /right/

and the war officer that he had should be sent out to him in the boat. /well, true/

Let them help him fight against the kingdom that was attacking and ruining their kingdom. / . . . / That's what he'd come to do. /well, true/

"I see," said the king. Mm! The king was enthusiastic right away. He could hardly contain himself.

A MAN:
His kingdom's in trouble.

ADUÊNGI:
He sent his war officer and his war-horse out to him. /well, true/

They got on the ship. Katjédenómu said, "My book, my book, let me be in a warship, and leave the big one I'm in here. Let all my people stay here, but as for me, I want to be in a warship with this soldier and this horse." Right away, they were in a fine warship, equipped with cannons, lots of them. /OK/

Ohh, that's all. The ship was forging right ahead, it was *nafidjé*-ing [from French Guiana creole for "navigate"] really hard. It was really something! They continued on toward the enemy's territory till they could see it, very tiny, and then the king's commanding officer— He said, "Well, OK. The people we're going after, to fight— They're on their way toward us too." /well/

"OK, then, shoot them! Shoot and destroy them right away!" / . . . / Katjédenómu opened his book wide and said, "My book, my book, the way the ship's going, the way I'm going along here— We need to keep going right to the center of the kingdom. To touch right up against the pier, the main pier of the kingdom. We'll be on horseback. We must go right to the center of the kingdom before we start fighting.

AKÓBO:
Are we still involved in the *"nafidjé"* business?

ADUÊNGI:
Let them shoot at us as much as they like, but let us come through unharmed." Mm! They shot at the ship so much that smoke covered it and you couldn't see a thing.

A MAN:
No, it just keeps on *"nafidjé-ing."*

ADUÊNGI:
Nothing but *"nafidjé."* Finally it touched in at the dock. And then the kingdom was really shaking. Because all the war things they had were being used. But it didn't seem to be helping. /no/

Katjédenómu called the officer and said, "Man—" (he replied) "You see how we're doing here? But I don't want to take you off to get killed. /no/

Because you're the king's officer." /true/

(He said "yes") "And it's his horse." (he said "Yes") "So I don't want to take either of you off to get killed. If your grip loosens from the horse, you'll die. /hm!/

But as long as you hold on tightly to the horse— Even if it falls to the ground, just hold on to the horse—" (he said "yes") "And then you can't die. Don't be afraid." / . . . / The officer said, "Well— Uhh— White man—" (he replied) (Well, the man didn't know who Katjédenómu was.) /no/

"White man—" (he replied) He said, "The way things are— Well, the horse—" (he replied) "I won't be thrown off, but I am afraid about their shooting us and killing us." Katjédenómu said, "Don't be afraid." /not at all/

They jumped up on horseback till they were all set. They whipped the horse, *kwíaa*. Nothing to it. They shot at the horses with Katjédenómu and the officer.

AKÓBO:
Was the woman still back there on the other ship?

ADUÊNGI:
They kept shooting at them for a very long time. The horse kept running till it got right to the middle of the village. It stood there, tall and straight. /well/

Katjédenómu opened his book wide. He said, "My book, my book, let this whole area be turned into a sea. /hm!/

But let every person who dies here be reborn in the king's kingdom. /hm!/

But the spot where I am here must remain completely dry, here where the horse is standing, but all the rest of the kingdom must become sea." /hm!/

Then they saw water rushing in toward them, *wòòò*. The officer said, "Uhh— White man, aren't we going to die?" He said, "No, don't worry."

AGUMIÍ [laughing]:
The guy doesn't know what term of address he should use for him.

AKÓBO:
Right. Because he called him "white man."

OTHERS:
[laughter]

ADUÊNGI:

"When it gets right up to where the horse is standing, it will stay dry around his feet." /well/

They were the only ones who stayed dry. The whole kingdom was covered with water as far as the eye could see. They could see the ship, the warship of theirs teeny-teeny-tiny in the distance there.

A MAN:

Out in the sea.

ADUÊNGI:

Out in the sea. That's all.

AGUMIÍI:

This Katjédenómu is something else!

ADUÊNGI:

He said, "My book, my book, let my ship be able to see me. Because when it's so far away the people can't see me. /not at all/

Well, but let them all pay attention to steering the ship till it gets to me." Ohhh! They started the ship up there, *di di di di,* till it came right up to the little dry spot. The horse quickly jumped onto it. As soon as he was safely on the ship, the place turned completely into water.

A MAN:

The kindgom was ruined.

ADUÊNGI:

The kingdom was ruined. All the houses in the kingdom had fallen apart and were "reborn" in the king's kingdom. / . . . / All the people who'd been there were dead, along with their chickens, and everything they owned. If they had been there in that kingdom, they now appeared in the other one. /hm!/

Katjédenómu went back to his big ship. He sent the officer off. He said, "Well, go on ashore, Brother. We're back. Tell the king that I went to war for him, and we won the battle. /well, true/

And now I've returned. /right/

And since I'm back, I'm letting him know, I'm sending you to him. Let him watch over things so they'll be happy the way they were before. /OK/ And I'm sending him my farewell." / . . . / Ohhh! They went and told him. He said, "No, no! The one who's leaving there mustn't leave! He must come ashore!" /right/

He said he couldn't come ashore. / . . . / The woman said, "We certainly can't come. We really can't come ashore." They went on like that until finally the king said, "Well, it's been said that you mustn't come ashore. If I were dead, then you could simply go back. But since that's not so—" (he said "yes") "Why don't you just come and sit down on my royal stool here. And I will be your subject."

A WOMAN:
What are things coming to?

AKÓBO:
He wanted the one-sided person to take over his stool?

ADUÊNGI:
Yes. No problem. Katjédenómu came ashore. His clothes and his wife's were made of gold. /OK/

The king was a real nobody. He was dying of poverty. He was a real king of poverty.

OTHERS:
[laughter]

ADUÊNGI:
Katjédenómu became king. He was on the king's stool there, with his queen right next to him. /true/

The other king who'd been there before, who'd ruled the place before, had his stool on the other side. The other stools were on the other side. They came and sat down. Katjédenómu and his wife sat down gracefully. They became rulers. Cannons boomed and then they stopped. Cannons boomed and then they stopped. They became rulers, and it's their kingdom that we live in here.

A WOMAN:
They must have given them back their child.

AKÓBO:
Well, did they understand what had happened?

ADUÊNGI:
They did. They gave them back their child. They knew! Because he had told them about it. And now we're in Katjédenómu's kingdom here. And the king became a nobody. He became Katjédenómu's subject.

A MAN:
A real nobody.

OVERLAPPING VOICES:
[A little further discussion]

ADUÊNGI:
Yes. That's as far as my story goes.

KASINDÓ [loudly]:
OK! Here in "Bush Negro" land— /ADUÊNGI: yes/

Well, you know how we've been doing things here? /mm/

We've been working along for quite a while already. /eh/

And we've been working hard. /eh/

But we shouldn't just keep on working and working without discussing what we're doing. /no, we shouldn't/

So let's discuss things. /that's how it is/

We've been at this long enough so that we could simply close the book here. /eh/

Except that— I'd like to ask all of you /that's how it is/

if I could add one that I know in here ever so quickly! /right/

OTHERS:
[laughter]

KASINDÓ:
Then, when I finish, /that's right/

if folks want to go home, /that's how it is/

or if they want to listen to one more—

AKÓBO:
Let's listen to this one right now.

KASINDÓ:
—that's OK with me. But I'm not going to tell any more after this. /that's how it is/

That's all.

AKÓBO:
Come on, he's asked us formally to sit down.

A MAN:
OK with us.

ADUÊNGI:
That's fine, we've already agreed.

KASINDÓ:
Well, who's going to be my responder?

ADUÊNGI:
Here I am!

KASINDÓ:
OK.

ADUÊNGI:
But I'm also going to cut it. I'll be cutting in!

KASINDÓ:
Right! Well, then, we came there.[132] /íya/

And Old Man Anasi, /íya/

Brother Brocket [*mbata*, a small species of deer], and Brother Deer [*djangafútu*, a larger species], /íya/

as well as all the other young men /íya/

went off to a certain village. /that's how it was/

They were suffering from a scarcity of ladies. /íya/

So they went to a village in search of ladies, *gbólóó!* /well/

Mm. They went to propose to the ladies, /íya/

and the women agreed. /íya/

They gave them all wives. /that's right/

As soon as they asked. Because they were fine men. /yes/

Anasi asked about gardens first thing, /íya/

because it was the season to clear gardens. /yes/

Mm! They were given gardens to clear. /mm/

So they went off to clear gardens. /íya/

After a while, Anasi returned, *tjálá*, to where the women were. /that's how it was/

He went to tell the women [nasal]: "Women, you know how we've come and begun work here? Well, if you don't know our names so you can call us to come eat, we simply won't come." /not at all/

"Really, Man?" ("yes" he said) They said, "Well, all right." Mm! Then he went right back again, *tjálálá*. /íya/

He'd tricked the others out there by telling them he had belly cramps, /yes/

so he could go off briefly into the forest. But he really dashed back to see the women.

ADUÊNGI:

Well, just when he dashed back to see the women, /KASINDÓ: *íya*/

the chief had prepared a cedar tree to be hauled to the river. /*íya*/

Now he had a child, a daughter, whose name was Ayaánda. /mm/

And the man who could haul the cedar single-handedly and push it into the water /*íya*/

would be allowed to marry Ayaánda. But if you couldn't haul it, then you couldn't have her, and the woman wouldn't ever get married. /uh-uh/

OK, so Mbeinkima— [possibly correcting himself:] The old man known as Hóndima [a large black flying insect, with a painful sting] succeeded in hauling it. /*íya*/

And Anasi jumped out and took his place:

Tjé ku tjé. <u>Kón gó na ósu, Ayaánda, kón gó na ósu.</u>
Tjé ku tjé. <u>Kón gó na ósu, Ayaánda, kón gó na ósu.</u>
Tjé ku tjé. <u>Kón gó na ósu, Ayaánda, kón gó na ósu.</u>
Tjé ku tjé. <u>Kón gó na ósu, Ayaánda, kón gó na ósu.</u>

["*Tjé ku tjé.* / Let's go home, Ayaánda, let's go home." Anasi had been hiding near the river, waiting to jump out so he could get credit for the log that Hóndima had hauled and win the chief's daughter. This is his log-hauling "work" song; it is accompanied by handclapping.]

Continue your story.

KASINDÓ:

OK, so nothing much. He came back. /ADUÊNGI: *íya*/

So he and the other guys were clearing the gardens. They cleared the gardens until a certain point. Now, since he'd already gone back to stop the women from serving the meal, the men's bellies were already starting to rumble. /yes/

The women weren't able to call them [because they didn't know their names]. /mm!/

So after a while, ohhh, [nasal]: "Brother Brocket, Brother Deer! Hey, you two! My belly's killing me."

SAKUÍMA [laughing]:

He's going to pretend to be sick.

TÍANÊN:

He's going to go back to the women.

KASINDÓ:

"My belly, my belly, my belly! I'm going to run off for a moment into the woods."

AKÓBO:

He's going to tell the women how to call the men.

KASINDÓ:

"Be right back." Then he dashed into the forest.

ADUÊNGI:

Well, when he dashed into the forest there, I was there. /KASINDÓ: *íya*/

Now Shrimp and what's his name had gone to drag a dry-season pool. And he was planning on tricking the other one to death. [Chanting:]

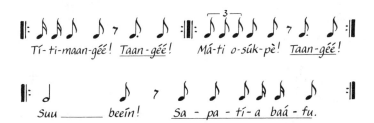

Tí-ti-maan-géé! Taan-géé! Má-ti o-súk-pè! Taan-géé!

Suu _____ beeín! Sa - pa - tí-a baá - fu.

Títimaangéé! Taangéé!
Títimaangéé! Taangéé!
Títimaangéé! Taangéé!
Máti osúkpè! Taangéé!
Máti osúkpè! Taangéé!
Suu beeín! Sapatía baáfu.
Suu beeín! Sapatía baáfu.

[On hearing this recording in 1987, Kalusé claimed that "what's his name" was Jaguar and that in the longer tale Shrimp first benefited from Jaguar's help and then tricked him out of his share of the catch. According to Kalusé, "*títimaangéé*" is Shrimp saying "Every man for himself" and putting all the fish in his basket, and *suu beeín* is the sound of Jaguar blowing smoke to dry up the water. *Taangéé* means "Heave ho!" and *sapatía baáfu* ("sapodilla sauce," a circumlocution for "sweet broth") refers to the fish they will be cooking and eating. Some Saramakas who listened to the recording heard *Mmá dosúkpè!* instead of *Máti osúkpè*, but none knew what either might mean.]

Go on with your story.

KASINDÓ:
OK, so he dashed back to where the women were. He went to talk to them. [Pause, then, reprimanding Aduêngi:] You're supposed to be doing responses!! /ADUÊNGI: *ÍYA!*/

He went to tell the women— /*íya*/

He said, "Well, Women, now that we're here— /yes/

Well, my name is Zanganámikúta. /*íya*/

The other guy out there is Sesíyênga-ayênga, and the other one— he's Koosóánamoi."[133] /*íya*/

They said, "Yes. Mm. Really?" (he said "yes") Then he dashed back to the garden. /*íya*/

[Nasal:] "Mmm! Brother! When I went off to the bushes there, I got a little relief. /*íya*/

So now let's get back to work." Then they really cleared the site. /*íya*/

In other words, he'd gone to set up the women for calling them. /that's how it was/

Ah! In a little while, sure enough, he heard the women calling them, quick as could be. /íya/

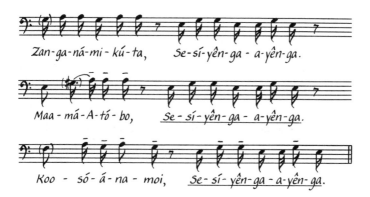

Zanganámikúta, Sesíyênga-ayênga.
Maamá-Atóbo, Sesíyênga-ayênga.
Koosóánamoi, Sesíyênga-ayênga.

[Here the women are calling the three men's names, chorused by "Sesíyênga-ayênga."]

He said [nasal]: "Wait! Well, what—? It sounds as though the women are calling us! Well, wait!" [Over laughter for the next several sentences:] Ohhh, Anasi threw down his forked stick. He threw down his machete.

OTHERS:
[laughter and exclamations]

KASINDÓ:
They ran lickety-split back to where the women were. And, well, the women had already set out the plates. So he said [nasal]: "Well, /íya/

well, Women, we'll eat— But we won't eat quite yet. /íya/

You've set out the plates here and you've called us. Now who was it who told you our names?" /íya/

They said, "No, no one told us. /íya/

We just know on our own." He said, "No, someone told you. /íya/

And if you don't tell us who it was, we won't sit down to eat." Then after a while, Anasi said [nasal]: "Well, Brother Brocket, you! /íya/

You think you're so smart! You're the one who told our names to the women!"

OTHERS:
[laughter]

KASINDÓ:
Brocket said, "Well, Anasi, when we were out clearing gardens there, did you ever see me leave?! /íya/

Did you see me leave even once?" Anasi said, "Yes, it was surely you! /íya/

Don't tell me it wasn't. Or Brother Deer, then it was you! You! Eh, uhh, you!"

OTHERS:
[laughter]

A MAN:
And the women weren't telling?

KASINDÓ:
The way the women were— They said, "No, no one told us your names." He said, "It was someone." Ohh, Anasi said [nasal]: "OK," /íya/

"Well, since we disagree, let's settle it by ordeal!" /íya/

SAKUÍMA:
Aren't they going to eat?

KASINDÓ:
Not at all! They're going to have to go to the ordeal and finish that first.

A MAN:
Anasi wanted to eat all the food by himself!

KASINDÓ:
Ohh, Old Man Anasi— What he did was— He went and spun his web along in a fine line across the river. / . . . / He made a string all across. He said [nasal]: "OK, Brother Deer, you were claiming that it wasn't you. So climb up on the string there and cross the river!"

AGUMÍÍ:
Shouldn't Anasi have gone first?

KASINDÓ:
Ohh! Brother Deer climbed on. /íya/

Zanganámikúta, Sesíyênga-ayênga.
Maamá-Atóbo, Sesíyênga-ayênga.
Koosóánamoi, Sesíyênga-ayênga.

Right across to the other side, quick as could be. /eh!/

Then Brother Brocket got on. Ohh:

Zanganámikúta, Sesíyênga-ayênga.
Koosóánamoi, Sesíyênga-ayênga.
Maamá-Atóbo, Sesíyênga-ayênga.

Brother Brocket, right on over to the other side there! Only Anasi was left.

TÍANÊN [laughing]:
He's as good as dead! [because the two heavier animals have so weakened the web he is sure to break it]

KASINDÓ:
Mmm. The other two said, "OK, Anasi, come on over to this side! We've already done it. /yes/

So come on over quickly. Because we're starving. We want to eat." So Old Man Anasi got up and he said [nasal]: "*Hehn! Hoóohn!*

OTHERS:
[laughter]

KASINDÓ [singing]:
Well, my wives—" [To the crowd:] You should all chorus "Sesíyênga-ayênga."

A COUPLE OF VOICES [very weakly]:
Sesíyênga-ayênga.

KASINDÓ:
I'm telling you to do the chorus!

THE OTHERS:
Sesíyênga-ayênga!

KASINDÓ:
Really do it now!!

THE OTHERS [laughing but louder]:
SESÍYÊNGA-AYÊNGA!

KASINDO [nasal]:

Déé mu-yèè u mi-ee!_____ SE-SÍ-YÊN-GA-A-YÊN-GA,

un duu-mún-du-oo._____ SE-SÍ-YÊN-GA-A-YÊN-GA.

Déé miíi-ee, ____ SE-SÍ-YÊN-GA-A-YÊN-GA, baa-sá mi-oo.____

SE-SÍ-YÊN-GA-A-YÊN-GA. Nòn gô tjè - - ee,

SE-SÍ-YÊN-GA-A-YÊN-GA, wán bó-to u mi dê a

wá-ta-dê, i ya-sé ên dá mi-oo.____ SE-SÍ-YÊN-GA-A-YÊN-GA.

Wán tjé ên pói-éé! SE-SÍ-YÊN-GA-A-YÊN-GA.

Déé muyêè u mi-ee! SESÍYÊNGA-AYÊNGA,
un duumúndu-oo. SESÍYÊNGA-AYÊNGA.
Déé miíi-ee, SESÍYÊNGA-AYÊNGA,
baasá mi-oo. SESÍYÊNGA-AYÊNGA.
Nòngôtjè-ee, SESÍYÊNGA-AYÊNGA,
wán bóto u mi dê a wáta-dê, i yasé ên dá mi-oo. SESÍYÊNGA-
    AYÊNGA.
Wán tjé ên pói-éé! SESÍYÊNGA-AYÊNGA.
Déé pái u mi-éé, SESÍYÊNGA-AYÊNGA,
duumúndu-oo. SESÍYÊNGA-AYÊNGA.
Zanganámikúta, SESÍYÊNGA-AYÊNGA,

Koosóánamoi, SESÍYÊNGA-AYÊNGA,
déé miíi-ee, SESÍYÊNGA-AYÊNGA,
duumúndu-oo. SESÍYÊNGA-AYÊNGA.
Déé mái-ee, SESÍYÊNGA-AYÊNGA,
hói déé miíi búnu-oo. SESÍYÊNGA-AYÊNGA.
Déé pái u mi-ee, SESÍYÊNGA-AYÊNGA,
hói déé muyêè dá mi-oo. SESÍYÊNGA-AYÊNGA.
Nòngôtjè, SESÍYÊNGA-AYÊNGA,
wán bóto u mi dê a wáta-dê, i yasé ên dá mi-oo. SESÍYÊNGA-
    AYÊNGA.
Wán tjé ên pói-éé. SESÍYÊNGA-AYÊNGA.

["My wives, oh! SESÍYÊNGA-AYÊNGA / Good-bye now.
SESÍYÊNGA-AYÊNGA / My little ones, SESÍYÊNGA-
AYÊNGA / hug me now. SESÍYÊNGA-AYÊNGA / Nòngôtjè
[Anasi's favorite son], SESÍYÊNGA-AYÊNGA / a canoe of
mine is there in the water, be sure to finish it for me.
SESÍYÊNGA-AYÊNGA / don't mess it up.[134] SESÍYÊNGA-
AYÊNGA / My fathers-in-law there, SESÍYÊNGA-AYÊNGA /
good-bye now. SESÍYÊNGA-AYÊNGA / Zanganámikúta,
SESIYÊNGA-AYENGA / Koosóánamoi, SESIYENGA-
AYÊNGA / my children, SESÍYÊNGA-AYÊNGA / good-
bye now. SESÍYÊNGA-AYÊNGA / Mothers-in-law,
SESÍYÊNGA-AYÊNGA / take care of the children for me.
SESÍYÊNGA-AYÊNGA / My fathers-in-law, SESÍYÊNGA-
AYÊNGA / take care of my wives for me. SESÍYÊNGA-
AYÊNGA / Nòngôtjè, SESÍYÊNGA-AYÊNGA / a canoe
of mine is there in the water, be sure to finish it for me.
SESÍYÊNGA-AYÊNGA / Don't mess it up. SESÍYÊNGA-
AYÊNGA." During this song of "farewell," Kasindó mimics
Anasi walking across the tightrope. Everyone else is laugh-
ing and joining in the chorus.]

OK, he goes along like that till they say, "Mmm! Anasi, you don't
need to go on anymore. We can already see that it wasn't you."

OTHERS:
Right!

KASINDÓ:
But he'd already gotten to the very middle. And just then, the line
broke right in two, snap! splash! The *yánga-yánga* fish [which eat
spiders] gobbled him right up.

OTHERS:
  [exclamations]

KASINDÓ:
  And if you lie to people, the thing that happened to Anasi might happen to you too. /íya/

  The line snapped right in two! /yes/

OTHER VOICES:
  [laughter and discussion. Then the tape recorder is turned off.]

And with Anasi's tragicomic farewell, which may also serve as the late Basiá Kasindó's final farewell, we too can say

And that's as far as our story goes.

Appendix

The following pages present a transcription/translation of Aduêngi's tale about the "discovery" of the *apínti* drum (pp. 218–43). Commentary and "stage directions" are included only in the English text; capitalization and punctuation have been made maximally compatible between the two texts for easier comparison.

ADUÊNGI:
> *Mató!*
> *Mató!*

A MAN:
> *Tòngôni!*
> *Tòngôni!*

ADUÊNGI:
> *Wè da u saí dê. /íya/*
> Well, there we were. /THE MAN: *íya*/

> *Da u saí dê tééé dóu wán yúu tén. /íya/*
> We were there once upon a time. /*íya*/

> *Nôò hên wè da— Wán tatá dê gbóló. /íya/*
> And, well— There was a man. /*íya*/

> *Nôò hên wè a paí miíi. /íya/*
> And he had some children. /*íya*/

> *A paí dií muyêè-miíi. /íya/*
> He had three daughters. /*íya*/

> *A paí dií ómi-miíi. /íya/*
> And he had three sons. /*íya*/

> *Wè da dí tatá f'u de kái Anáni f'Akísiamáu— /íya/*
> Now the old man called Anáni from Akísiamáu— /*íya*/

> *Nôò a á wán soní tá táki a kóntu táki. /íya/*
> Well, he has something he likes to say when tales are being told. /*íya*/

> *A táa a fésitén, nôò de táki táa wán tatá de kái Donú /íya/*
> He says that in the old days, they would say that a father called Donú /*íya*/

> *paí wán miíi de kái Aduêngi. /íya/*
> had a son called Aduêngi. /*íya*/

OTHERS:
[quiet laughter]

ADUÊNGI:
Sô fésitén, sô de bi na táki kóntu. /íya/
That's the way they told tales in the old days. /íya/

Sô i tá kái dí tatá paí dí miíi nê. /íya/
You'd give the name of the father who had the child. /íya/

Wè ma tidé akí, nôò kôndè gó. /íya/
But today all that sort of thing is getting lost. /íya/

Wán tá sá dee sèmbè nê môò. /íya/
We don't know the people's names anymore. /íya/

Nôò i tá kái táa wán tatá paí wán miíi. /íya/
So you just say that there was a father who had a child. /íya/

Wè da u dê nôò wán tatá dê fèèn nôò a paí dií muyêè-miíi, /íya/
OK, so there we were, and there was a man who had three daughters, /íya/

nôò hên a paí dií ómi-miíi. /íya/
and he had three sons. /íya/

SAKUÍMA:
Ambê tá kandá?
Who's singing? [meaning: "Who's going to cut into this tale with a nugget?" No one responds.]

KASINDÓ:
Sô seéi: "Wán mamá paí wán miíi."
That's like: "There was a woman who had a child."

A MAN:
A kó síkísi.
That makes six.

ADUÊNGI:
Sôò. /íya/
Correct. /íya/

Wè da hên u dê tééé dóu yúu, nôò dêdè yúu u dí tatá dóu. /íya/
Well, so there we were until the time came, and it came time for the old man to die. /íya/

Nôò hên wè a kái de, /íya/
So he called them, /íya/

kó butá, táa, "Wè Miíí—" (de píki) A táa, "Wè mi ó dêdè. /íya/
got them together, and said, "Children—" (they replied) He said,
"Well, I am going to die. /íya/

Wè nôò dí mi ó dêdè— Wè hên mi kái únu kó ákísi— /íya/
Well now, since I'm going to die— Well, I've called you here to ask
you— /íya/

Fá mi ó dêdè akí, unfá ún ó béi mi tjıká? /íya/
When I die, what do you plan to do for my funeral? /íya/

Mbéi mi sábi." /íya/
I want to know." /íya/

(de táki "aái") Di gaán wan táa, "Wèè—" Di gaán ómi-miíí /íya/
("yes" they said) The oldest one said, "Well—" The oldest boy /íya/

táa, "Wè, Taatá—" /íya/
said, "Well, Father—" /íya/

(a píki) A táa, "Wè fá yó dêdè akí—" /íya/
(he replied) He said, "Well, when you die—" /íya/

(a táki "aái") A táa, "Nôò máán soní seéi ó dú tá u m' dú môòsò. /íya/
("yes" he said) He said, "There's only one thing that I'll be doing.
/íya/

Sôsò kèê tô seéi mi ó tá kèê. /íya/
Nothing but crying. /íya/

Kèê tô seéi mi ó tá kèê u té de béi i." /íya/
I'll keep on crying, just wailing and wailing, until they bury you."
/íya/

OTHERS:
  [laughter]

ADUÊNGI:
  (a táki "aái") /íya/
  ("yes" he said) /íya/

  Di gaán muyêè-miíí táa, "Wè, Taatá—" /íya/
  The oldest daughter said, "Well, Father—" /íya/

  (a píki) A táa, "Wè fá yó dêdè akí—" /íya/
  (he replied) She said, "When you die now—" /íya/

  A táki, "Aán soní seéi mi ó dú môô, sôsò pèê tô mi ó tá pèè /íya/
  She said, "The one thing I'm going to do is sing and dance, without stopping, /íya/

u mi béi i." /íya/
for your funeral." /íya/

Dí míndi báa /íya/
The middle brother /íya/

táa, "Wè, Taatá—" (a píki) A táa, "Fá yó dêdè akí—" (a táki "aái") "Nôò mi ó béi i ku gúdu. /íya/
said, "Well, Father—" (he replied) He said, "When you die now—" ("yes" he said) "Well, I'll bury you with grave goods. /íya/

Nôò mi ó mbéi di kési f'i /íya/
And I'll make your coffin /íya/

té mi kabá, béi i ku gúdu, /íya/
so it's really nice, and supply goods for your funeral, /íya/

tjiká fá mi sá butá gúdu a i tjiká, /íya/
just as many goods as you may need, /íya/

fu té i dêdè, sèmbè seéi dí kó a i dêdè kaa, / . . . / mi ó dé ên wán koósu nôòmo." /íya/
so that when you're dead, not a single person will come to your funeral / . . . / without receiving at least a length of cloth from me." /íya/

SAKUÍMA:
A ó tái ên bêè, puaan.
He'll tie their bellies, *puaan.*

ADUÊNGI:
"Sô mi ó béi i tjiká." /íya/
"That's how well I'll bury you." /íya/

Dí míndi muyêè-miíí táa, "Wè, Taatá—" (a píki) A táa, "Fá yó dêdè seéi píí akí—" (a táki "aái") "Nôò mi ó béi i. /íya/
The middle daughter said, "Well, Father—" (he answered) She said, "When you are dead and still as can be here—" ("yes" he said) "I will help bury you. /íya/

Mi ó béi i ku nyanyá. /íya/
I will help bury you with food. /íya/

Nyanyá seéi— Sèmbè án dê dí ó kó té nôò i sá gó ku ángi. /íya/
Talk about food— Not a single person who comes here will leave hungry. /íya/

Íbi wán miíí— Sèmbè dí kó a téla kaa, i sá nyán nôòmo." /íya/
Every child— Every person, once they step ashore here, will have plenty to eat." /íya/

A táki, "Aái Miíi, i béi mi tuú." Dí kabá pikí muyêè-miíi táa, "Wè, Taatá—" (a píki) A táa, "Fá yó dêdè akí—" (a táki "aái") "Nôò ómi seéi dí kó a dí kôndè akí saa—" /íya/

He said, "Yes, Child, you're really helping to bury me." The very youngest daughter said, "Well, Father—" (he replied) She said, "When you die now—" ("yes" he said) "Every single man who slips into this village—" /íya/

OTHERS [who know what's coming next]:
[laughter]

ADUÊNGI:
(a táki "aái") A táa, "Mi tôtò ên nôòmo!"
("yes" he said) She said, "I'll be sure to screw him!"

OTHERS:
[exclamations and laughter]

TÍANÊN:
Dí sèmbè dè béi ên búnu!!
That person is really contributing well to the funeral!!

KASINDÓ:
A ó béi ên wái-wái!
She'll give it all she's got!

TÍANÊN:
Déé sèmbè bi béi ku gúdu naandê, án béi. Hên béi ên búnu.
Those people who helped out with goods didn't bury him all that well. But this one did it just right.

OVERLAPPING VOICES:
[wild laughter and animated discussion]

KASINDÓ:
Dí béi dè, a tá á wái.
That kind of contribution is really fine!

ADUÊNGI:
"Miíi—" (a píki) A táki, "Aái, i béi mi tuú." /íya/
"Child—" (she answered) He said, "Yes, you're really helping to bury me well." /íya/

Dí kabá pikí báa /íya/
The very youngest brother /íya/

táa, "Wè Taatá—" (a píki) A táa, "Fá yó dêdè akí—" (a táki "aái") "Nôò dí soní de kái Doón— /íya/
said, "Well, Father—" (he replied) He said, "When you die now—" ("yes" he said) "Well the thing known as Drum— /íya/

Mi tá yéi nê fèèn, /íya/
I keep hearing its name, /íya/

wè ma, m'án sábi ên. /íya/
but, well, I don't know it firsthand. /íya/

Wè ma, té ka Doón dê, /íya/
But wherever Drum may be, /íya/

mi sá gó téki ên kó pèê a i dêdè nôòmo, pèê apínti a i édi, é dí dáka de béi seéi, té de béi i, aluwási sêbèn dáka f'i seéi, m'músu pèê ên a i geébi édi. /íya/
I'm going to go get it and bring it back to play at your funeral, play the *apínti* drum at the head of your coffin, even if it's not till the day they bury you, even if it's the seventh day of your funeral, I will absolutely play it at the head of your grave. /íya/

Bigá, wè, dí soní de kái apínti— Mi tá yéi a goón líba a dê wán— a dê wán— wán gaán soní fu búsi nêngè kôndè. /íya/
Because, well, the thing that's called *apínti*, I hear people saying that it's, well, that it's a really important thing in Bush Negro land. /íya/

Nôò té ká apínti dê, mi sá gó féni ên, kó pèê NÔÒMO a i édi." /íya/
So wherever *apínti* may be, I'll go find it and be SURE to play it at your head." /íya/

(a táki "aái") "Hên dí béi dê mi ó béi i." /íya/
("yes" he said) "That's the way that I'll help with your funeral." /íya/

"Fá dí dáka seéi i dêdè kaa—" (a táki "aái") "Nôò, mi kabá a dêdè soní f'i, /íya/
"The very day you die—" ("yes" he said) "I'll leave the preparations for your burial, /íya/

hên a dí apínti báka mi ó gó fu té de béi i, é de béi seéi, mi sá pèê ên a i kési geébi édi nôòmo." /íya/
and I'll go off in search of the *apínti* until they're ready to bury you, and even if you've already been buried, I'll still play it at the head of your grave." /íya/

A táki, "Aái Miíi, hên da i béi mi tuú, bigá, wè, apínti dê wán soní fu u búsi nêngè." /íya/
He said, "Yes, Son, you will really have contributed to my funeral, because, well, *apínti* is an important thing for us Bush Negroes." /íya/

Nôò hên de dê dí dií dáka, nôò hên dí tatá dêdè. /íya/
Then three days went by and the old man died. /íya/

OTHERS:
[laughter and exclamations]

ADUÊNGI:
Nôò dí tatá dêdè,
The old man died,

SAKUÍMA [interrupting]:
Ná dêdè-dêdè a bi dê, nô?
Hadn't he been as good as dead already?

ADUÊNGI [simultaneous with Sakuíma's question]:
té a kabá dêdè kêê. /íya/
dead as could be. /íya/

Nôò hên dí sèmbè bi táa a bi ó kèè— /íya/
And the person who said he would cry— /íya/

Nôò a tá kèê té i kó dê nôò i tá fan seéi, de án tá yéi andí i tá táki. / . . . /
Well, he was crying so much that when you came there and tried
to talk, nobody could hear what you were saying. / . . . /

OTHERS:
[laughter]

ADUÊNGI:
Nôò dí sèmbè dí bi táki táa wè a ó béi ên ku pèè— /íya/
And the person who said she would help by singing and danc-
ing—/íya/

Nôò a tá pèê téé.
Well, she's playing and playing.

OVERLAPPING VOICES:
[indistinct comments]

ADUÊNGI:
A tá kandá té tutú fèèn tapá búú, a píi uwíi,
She keeps singing until her throat gives out completely, and then
she prepares an herbal mixture,

A WOMAN [interjecting helpfully]:
bebé,
drinks it,

ADUÊNGI [without missing a beat]:
a dê a kandá. /íya/
and is right back in there singing. /íya/

AMÁKA [speaking very deliberately, in contrast to Aduêngi's excited delivery]:
Nôò, Djeendjé ku Mafendjé bi hásuwa.
Well, Squirrel and Mouse were wrestling.

ADUÊNGI:
Léti sô. Unfá de hásuwa môò?
Right. How was it they were wrestling?

AMÁKA:
I sá fá de hásuwa-u?
You know how they were wrestling?

ADUÊNGI:
Nônô.
No.

AMÁKA [singing]:
Djeendjé ku Adumákaa, Djeendjé woli.
Djeendjé ku Adumákaa, Djeendjé woli.
Djeendjé ku Adumákaa, Djeendjé woli.

a híti ên vúúún. Djeendjé kumútu aá vaaa gbóo. A túwè ên. Djeendjé kísi Mafendjé. A híti ên vúúún. A kaí fèèn, tjálá! / . . . /
Mouse threw him in the air. Squirrel landed with a thud. Mouse pinned him. Squirrel grabbed Mouse. He threw him in the air. He landed right on his feet, *tjálá!* / . . . /

A YOUNG WOMAN [laughing]:
Ku dí gáu u Djeendjé!
Even though Squirrel's so quick!

SAKUÍMA:
Mafendjé wíni Djeendjé.
Mouse beat Squirrel.

AMÁKA:
Aái. Gó i tóli.
Right. Go ahead with your story.

ADUÊNGI:
Wè áán soní. /íya/
So that's all. /íya/

Dí pèêma tá pèê kuma soní. /*íya*/

The performing one is performing like nothing else. /*íya*/

Dí sèmbè dí ó béi ên ku nyanyá— /*íya*/

The one who said she'd help by providing food— /*íya*/

Hòòn, dí dáka de kó wási dêdè dê, híi sèmbè u dí kôndè, híi sèmbè nyán, téé de áán peésa môò. /*íya*/

Ohh, the day they came to wash the corpse there, every person in the village, every single one, ate so much they couldn't take another bite. /*íya*/

KASINDÓ:

Nôò dí yúu tén de bi tá pèê dê, /*íya*/

And while they were "playing" there, /ADUÊNGI: *íya*/

Tatá Anasi bi ên pái wè. /*íya*/

Father Anasi was his son-in-law. /*íya*/

Hên pái wè bi dêdè naandê. /*en-hen*/

It was his father-in-law who'd died there. /uh-huh/

A táa, "Wè, áán soní seéi u béi dí pái môò sô, môò léki pèê," a gó pèê béi ên pái. /*léti sô*/

He said, "Well, the most important thing to do to help at a father-in-law's funeral is to sing and dance," so he went to perform at his father-in-law's funeral. /that's right/

Nôò ên wè a ó gó seeká búka ku wán sèmbè saí éti a sê dê. / . . . / *Ên wè wán fóu saí dê, nôò ên wè a ó kísi kó pèê a kamísa básu.* /*íya*/

Well, he decided to make a private arrangement with someone who was off on the side there. / . . . / Well, there was a certain bird there, and he decided to catch it and perform with it under his breechcloth. /*íya*/

Mm! De dê a dí pèê té wán písi.

Mm! The singing and dancing had been going on for quite a while there.

A MAN:

Ún fóu?

What kind of bird was it?

KASINDÓ:

Wè bóu táa pítawóyo.

Well, let's just say it was a *pítawóyo* [a songbird].

THE MAN:
Mm-hm.
Mm-hm.

KASINDÓ:
Ên a tjèèn kó butá nèèn kamísa básu dê sáápi.
He just took it and slipped it discreetly into the inside of his
breechcloth.

SEVERAL WOMEN:
[laughter]

KASINDÓ:
Nôòmo, de tá pèê té wán písi gwólóó, nôò de pèê gó na Anasi. / . . . / Ên
a djómbo vúún kaí a gandá. / . . . / Nôò áán soní, dí pikí fóu dê a kamísa
básu dê-u:
The singing and dancing went on for a while, and then it got to be
Anasi's turn to dance. / . . . / So he leaped into the center. / . . . /
That's all, the little bird was right there inside his breechcloth:

OTHERS:
[laughter]

KASINDÓ:
Nôò, tjéin tjéin tjééin kína-ee.
Tjéin tjéin tjééin kína-oo.
Tjéin tjéin tjééin kína.
Tjéin tjéin tjééin kína-ee.
Tjéin tjéin tjééin kína-oo.
Tjéin tjéin tjééin.

Nôò de boóko gilili kó na Anasi.
Then people fell all over Anasi to congratulate him.

WOMEN:
[Wild laughter, in the midst of which someone seems to have asked
where the bird was.]

KASINDÓ:
Dí fóu? A kumútu seéi gó kaa.
The bird? It'd already flown away.

A MAN:
Nôò té a ó pèê môò, nôò a ó kó môò?
And when he dances the next time, will the bird come back?

KASINDÓ:
Òn! Únsê a ó féni ên môò?!
Oh! What makes you think he could ever find it again?!

OTHERS:
[laughter]

AGUMIÍI:
Bási-o!
Hey, Bási! [Kasindó]

KASINDÓ:
Yéé?
What?

AGUMIÍI:
Dí tén i sí dí, dí soní bi tá kandá a dí kamísa básu f'adjáansi dê, /íya/
Just when that, when that thing was singing inside Spider's
breechcloth, /KASINDÓ: *íya*/

nôò hên wè dí didíbi bi saí léti dê, /mm-hm/
well, the devil was right there, /mm-hm/

kê nyán dí miíi. /íya/
thinking about eating the child. /íya/

Hên wè a kó dóu. /mm-hm/
He came right up. /mm-hm/

Hên a bái:
He called out:

> *Maanpáya-ee, Maanpáya-eee, m'Towêsinaagooo.*
> *Maanpáya-ee, Maanpáya-eee, m'Towêsinaagooo.*
> *M'zaukúnde-oo, gwôyòtòò. M'zaukúnde-oo, gwôyòtòò.*
> *Madjaáfo m'péneni-ee.*
> *Mi dánsi-oo m'péneni-ee.*

*A bái, "Zángana m'kolóbi, zángana m'koló. A tjiká m'kôndò tjóóhóhó f'i,
Miíi." A púu wán fútu túwè dé ên, tapá dí fáya. / . . . / Wáka i wáka.*
He called out, "Zángana m'kolóbi, zángana m'koló. Now I can claim
my victory, Kid." He took his foot and stamped out the fire. / . . . /
Go right ahead.

OTHERS:
[hooting, noise]

ADUÊNGI:
Nôò, áán sondí.
So that's all.

KASINDÓ:
I tá sí-ó?
You see?

ADUÊNGI [excitedly—a tone that continues into the tale itself]:
Aái, déé muyêê— Mi táki dá i, de tá sá dí soní! /íya/
Yes, it's the women— I told you, they're the ones who know these things! /ADUÊNGI'S RESPONDER: *íya*/

Nôô áán soní. Nôô dí tén dê, nôô dí— nôô dí gúduma, /íya/
So, nothing much. At that point, the one— the one in charge of the goods— /íya/

nôô húi déé sèmbè kó wási dêdè dê—
well, all the people who came for the washing of the corpse—

SAKUÍMA [anticipating]:
Déé túu bêè a tái.
He tied a cloth onto every belly.

ADUÊNGI:
Déé túu bêè a tái. /íya/
He tied a cloth onto every one. /íya/

Nôô a púu wán hôndò gaán koósu, wán hôndò amáka. /íya/
And he provided a hundred cloth sheets and a hundred hammocks. /íya/

Dí pikí koósu, néèn fu u kondá. /íya/
The smaller cloths he gave were too numerous to count. /íya/

A mbéi dí kési ku— ku sédu ku bóóánti môkísi ku apísi, hánso té án sá sí. /íya/
He made the coffin with— with cedarwood and brownheart mixed with canela, more beautiful than you can imagine. /íya/

A WOMAN:
Kóti pópu háti tuúsi.
And inserted some purpleheart too.

ADUÊNGI:
Aái. Sòò, nôô dí tén dê seéi, nôô dí sèmbè dí bi táa wè a ó tá tôtò— /íya/
Right. [He pauses a moment while others finish talking in the background.] OK! And at the same time, the person who said she would be screwing— /íya/

Nôô ósu fèèn dê pááli. /íya/
Well, her house was jam-packed. /íya/

*Híi déé ómi dê kó dê túu a dá de wán wán gaási púu (piimísi f'únu lánti,
a kóntu táki u dê).*
All the men who came there were given a little pussy to enjoy
(please excuse me, folks, but this is tale-telling that we're doing
here).

MANY VOICES:
[laughter, comments]

ADUÊNGI:
Otèli dê kêdêê! / . . . / Nôò áán soní. /íya/
A whorehouse if ever there was one! / . . . / So that's all. /íya/

Nôò dí— nôò dí bi táa bi ó— a bi ó gó súku Doón dê— /íya/
Now the one— the one who said he'd— that he'd go off to find
Drum— /íya/

Nôò fá de wási dêdè kaa, nôò de án sá fá fèèn môò kaa. /íya/
Well, once they'd washed the corpse, he was already out of sight.
/íya/

Nôò hên a gó. /íya/
He'd already gone. /íya/

Nôò hên de béi dí dêdè. /íya/
So they were going ahead with the funeral. /íya/

De tá béi dí dêdè téémm, nôò hên a gó. /íya/
They're going ahead with the funeral, on and on, and he was
gone. /íya/

A nángó tééé a téi wán papákái— díi papákái puúma, /íya/
He went along for a while and then he took a parrot— [correcting
himself:] three parrot feathers, /íya/

díi papámôni, /íya/
three cowrie shells, /íya/

díi keéti dómbo. /íya/
and three balls of kaolin. /íya/

Nôò hên a gó ku de. /íya/
And he set out with them. /íya/

Hên a nángó téééé a dóu a wán lío. /íya/
Then he went along until he came to a river. /íya/

*Nôò dí tén a dóu a dí lío, a tá sí hòngóo gó alá, kamía seéi án dê f'a pasá
môò.*
Now when he got to the river, he sees an endless expanse of
water, and there's no way for him to get across.

TÍANÊN [breaking in]:
I sí dí yúu tén a táa a sí hòngóo dê-ú? /*íya*/
You know when he saw the endless expanse there? /ADUÊNGI: *íya*/

Nôò hên wè a dóu a Makáku. /*léti sô*/
Well, he met up with Monkey. /that's right/

Hên Makáku bái, /*sôtu*/
And Monkey called out, /true/

táa, "Wè u sí sèmbè akí tjiká f'u sá nyán, /*léti sô*/
and said, "Well, we see people here who are good to eat, /that's right/

ma wán ó nyán de." /*nônô*/
but we're not going to eat them." /certainly not/

A túwè:
He sang:

> *Kizáán mi na kasúle záán-oo.*
> *Kizáán mi na kasúle záán-oo.*
> *Kizáán kó lúku a máwè.*
> *Kizáán kizáán-ee.*

Wáka i wáka.
Go right ahead.

ADUÊNGI:
É! Logoso fútu u mi sáti pói!
Eh! My turtle foot is really short!

A WOMAN:
Aái, a sáti!
Yes, it's short!

ADUÊNGI:
Wè áán soní nôò. /*íya*/
Well, so that's all. /ADUÊNGI'S RESPONDER: *íya*/

Nôò, ên a sí hóóó, a bià lúku aá. /*íya*/
As he was gazing out at the void, he turned and looked. /*íya*/

A sí wán soní hópo a míndi wáta aá vááu. Nôò a tá sún dalala, tá kó té a kó dóu a lanpéé— a dí— a dí pási búka, a butá édi dê, gbagba. A sí wán gaán gindi káima. /*íya*/
He noticed something surfacing out there in the middle of the water. It came swimming, *dalala*, toward him and arrived at the sho— at the— at the mouth of the path, and it set its head out right there, and he saw that it was an enormous cayman. /*íya*/

A bígi kuma dí ósu akí. /íya/
It was as big as this house here. /íya/

Dí miíi tá— Dí miíi tá wáka tá kó té a kó dóu. / . . . / *A dé ên "m'Bóto
Saayé, ódi." (a píki "tangí, Miíi")* /íya/ *A táa, "Miíi, únsê i nángó?"
A táa, "M'Bóto Saayé, pasá mi wáta."* /íya/
The boy— The boy walks over till he comes right up to it. / . . . /
He went: "My Boat Saayé, greetings." (it answered "greetings,
Boy") /íya/ It said, "Boy, where are you going?" He said, "My Boat
Saayé, take me across." /íya/

A táa, "Únsê i nángó?" A táa, "Mi nángó a didíbi kôndè gó súku Doón."
/íya/
It said, "Where are you going?" He said, "I'm going to where the
devils live to look for Drum." /íya/

A táa, "Miíi, yása dóu." /íya/
It said, "Boy, you'll never get there." /íya/

A táa, "Taatá, mi sa dóu. /íya/
He said, "Father, I can get there. /íya/

Pasá m'wáta." /íya/
Take me across." /íya/

*A táki, "Aái. Wè, Miíi—" (a píki) A táa, "É u m'pasá i wáta, i músu
paká m."* /íya/
It said, "Yes, well, Boy—" (he replied) It said, "If I take you across,
you must pay me." /íya/

A táa, "Andí mi ó paká i?" /íya/
He said, "What will I pay you?" /íya/

A táa, "Dí soní dí i ábi. /íya/
It said, "Whatever you happen to have. /íya/

Fá a makisá, ma paká m. /íya/
No matter how shoddy it may be— But you must pay me something. /íya/

Hên da, paimá u mi nôòmo i musu dá m." /íya/
I mean, you've got to give me some kind of a payment." /íya/

*(a táki "aái") A téi wán keéti dómbo, wán papákái puúma, wán pa-
pámôni,* /íya/
("yes" he said) He took one ball of kaolin, one parrot feather, and
one cowrie shell, /íya/

hên a dé ên. /íya/
and he gave them to it. /íya/

SAKUÍMA:
Aa, nônô! F'a tjé ên dóu a dí kôndè.
Uh-oh! So it would ferry him over to the village.

ADUÊNGI [interrupting the end of Sakuíma's remark]:
Áán soní, dí miíí djómbo vúú subí a dí káima míndi édi, gwébòò, a táa,
"M'Bóto Saayé, ába m'wáta." /íya/
So that's all. The boy climbed right onto the middle of the cayman's
head, *gwébòò*, and said, "My Boat Saayé, cross me over." */íya/*

A kóti zalalalalalalalala, té a dí sê téla aá djaláa.
It cut right through the water, *zalalalalalalalala*, and up onto the
shore on the other side.

TÍANÊN [breaking in]:
Dí yúuté a bi kóti ên wáta dê, /íya/
At the very time it was cutting through the water, /ADUÊNGI: *íya*/

m'bi dê a pê.
I was standing right there.

ADUÊNGI:
Andí i sí?
What did you see?

TÍANÊN:
A túwè:
It sang:

> *Afúnguyani-ee, afúnguyani-ee, afúnguyani afuumá-ee.*
> *Afúnguyani-ee, afúnguyani-ee, afúnguyani afuumá.*
> *Eé-afuumá, ma di ya yéi-oo anáki kítoonya,*
> *Toonya kíi wanapú-éé, kíyoonya-éé.*

A tjokó ên a lanpéési zalala. Wáka i wáka.
It set him down at the landing, *zalala*. Go right on.

ADUÊNGI:
Hên! Dí soní akí, a tá súti-é!
Oh! This thing is getting really sweet!

A MAN:
A tá súti kuma—
It's as sweet as—

ADUÊNGI:
Hên! /íya/
OK! /ADUÊNGI'S RESPONDER: *íya*/

A tjé ên zalala gó namá gbabáu. / . . . / A táa, "M'Bóto Saayé—" (a píki)
A táa, "Té dí dáka seéi mi dóu, tooná tá kó té m'dóu akí, i músu dê akí."
/íya/

It carried him, *zalala*, right up onto the bank, *gbabáu*. / . . . / He
said, "My Boat Saayé—" (it replied) He said, "The very day I get
back, when I return back to this place, you've got to be here." */íya/*

A táa, "Miíi, ná pantá, mi nyán paimá f'i kaa, ná pená kusumí." /íya/
It said, "Child, don't panic, 'cause I've already taken your payment, so don't even bother to worry about it." */íya/*

A WOMAN:
"Mi ó dê."
"I'll be there."

ADUÊNGI:
A pasá. / . . . /
He went on. / . . . /

A MAN [anticipating]:
Bigá kulé, a ó kulé kó a dí lío!
Because he'll be running when he comes back to the river!

ADUÊNGI:
Aái.
Yes.

OTHERS:
[laughter]

ADUÊNGI:
A nángó téémm.
He kept on going for a long time.

OTHER VOICES:
[more remarks on how fast he'll be running]

ADUÊNGI:
Aái. A tooná nángó té a dóu a wán gaán gindi lío. /íya/
Really. He went on until he got to a really enormous river. */íya/*

A dê píí dê. A táa, "M'Bóto Saayé ódi," a píki, "Tangí, Miíi, unsê i
nángó?" a táa, "Mi nángó a didíbi kôndè gó súku Doón," a táa, "Miíi,
yásá gó." /íya/
Another cayman was there, just waiting. [Aduêngi pauses and
then rattles off the rest of this segment in one breath.] He said,
"My Boat Saayé, greetings," and it answered, "Greetings, Boy,
where are you going?" and he said, "I'm going to where the devils

live to look for Drum," and it said, "Boy, You'll never get there."
/*íya*/

A táa, "M'Bóto Saayé, pasá m'wáta," a táa, "É u m'pasá i, yó paká mi."
/*íya*/
He said, "My Boat Saayé, take me across," and it said, "If I take
you across, you'll have to pay me." /*íya*/

A táa, "Andí mi ó paká i?" a táa, "Yó paká mi dí sán dí i ábi nôò i dá mi,
aluwási fá a makisá, ma dá m."
He said, "What will I pay you?" and it said, "You'll pay me whatever you happen to have, that's what you'll give me, even if it's
something very shoddy, you'll still give it to me."

SAKUÍMA:
Nôò de án dê a béi nô?
Aren't the others busy with the funeral by now?

ADUÊNGI:
De dê a béi aá, tá kéndi. / . . . / Híi déé lô soní dí u bi táki dê kaa, nôò
déé túu dê aá tá pasá.
Back at the funeral there things are really heating up. / . . . / All
those things that we mentioned before, they're all in full swing.

SAKUÍMA:
Mm-hmm.
Mm-hmm.

ADUÊNGI:
Déé soní—
All those things—

SAKUÍMA [interrupting]:
Déé péi péi—
All the different ones—

ADUÊNGI:
Un sábi kaa.
But you know about all that.

SAKUÍMA:
Aái-oo!
Sure do!

ADUÊNGI:
De túu dê alá de tá dú alá.
All of them are back there, doing things.

SAKUÍMA [interrupting]:

Aái-on! Déé woóko hía.

Right! There's really a lot to do!

ADUÊNGI:

Áán soní. /íya/

[a phrase drowned out by Sakuíma's comment, then:] That's all. /íya/

A pasé ên wáta zaa gó butá gbagbaa. / . . . / *A táa, "M'Bóto Saayé—" (a píki) A táa, "I nyán paimá u mi."* /íya/

It took him across, *zaa,* and set him down, *gbagbaa.* / . . . / He said, "My Boat Saayé—" (it replied) He said, "You've accepted a payment from me." /íya/

(a táki "aái") "Nôô té dí dáka mi dóu akí i músu sá pasá m'wáta, soní án musu bígi té yán pasá m'wáta," a táa, "Miíí, ná pantá." /íya/

("yes" it said) "So the very day I get back here you must be ready to take me across, there can't be anything so important that it prevents you from taking me across," and it said, "Boy, don't panic." /íya/

A pasá. / . . . / *A nángó téééé a dóu a wán gaán gindi zèè* /íya/

He went on. / . . . / He continued on and on until he got to a really enormous sea /íya/

hòngóo gó alá pííí. /íya/

that stretched as far as the eye could see. /íya/

A biá lúku, a sí ên seéi, dí wán seéi soní. A dóu gbagbuu. A dé ên ódi. (a píki) A táa, "Únsê i nángó?" A táa, "Mi nángó a didíbi kôndè." A táa, "Wè Miíí—" (a píki) A táa, "Fá i nángó a didíbi kôndè akí—" (a táki "aái") "Nôô yó gó dóu nôô yó sí wán gaán gindi gangása. /íya/

He looked out and saw the same thing again. It came up, *gbagbuu.* He greeted it. (it answered) It said, "Where are you going?" He said, "I'm going to where the devils live." It said, "Well, Boy—" (he replied) It said, "When you go to the devils' village—" ("yes" he said) "You'll arrive there and you'll see an enormous open-sided shed. /íya/

Nôô dí soní de kái Doón— /íya/

And the thing known as Drum— /íya/

sôsô tô dê nèèn! /íya/

Well, that whole place is crammed with them! /íya/

Yó sí lánga doón-é. /íya/

You'll see long drums. /íya/

Yó si mamá doón, yó sí apínti-ee, yó sí agidá, híi déé péi doón túu yó sí.
/íya/

You'll see *mamá* drums, you'll see *apínti*s, you'll see *agidá*s, you'll
see every kind of drum there is. */íya/*

Nôò dí ó tá bái táa, 'Ná panyá mi! Ná panyá mi! Ná panyá mi!' Nôò óto
wan ó tá bái táa, 'Kó panyá mi! Kó panyá m!' Dí sèmbè akí: 'Kó tumá
mi! Kó tumá mi!' Dísi: 'Ná tumá mi!' Nôò dí tá píki táa, 'Ná panyá
mi!'— hên nôòmo i musu téi. /íya/

[In rapid, run-on speech:] Now some will be calling, 'Don't touch
me! Don't touch me! Don't touch me!' And other ones will be calling, 'Come grab me! Come grab me!' The one over here: 'Come
take me! Come take me!' The one over there: 'Don't take me!' [He
draws a quick breath.] Now the one that's calling out, 'Don't touch
me!'— that's the one you must be sure to take. */íya/*

Ma déé sèmbè tá kái i táa i téi de, é i téi de, Miíi, m'áán kôni f'i. / . . . /
Ma dí sèmbè táa ná téki ên, yán musu panyé ên seéi— hên nôò i musu
panyá."

But the ones that are calling out, telling you to take them— If you
take them, Boy, there'll be nothing I can do for you. / . . . / But
the one who's saying you mustn't take it, that you mustn't even
touch it— that's the one you must be sure to take."

OVERLAPPING VOICES:
[laughter and comments]

ADUÊNGI:

A táki, "Aái, áán soní." / . . . / A táa, "Wè áán soní." A téi dí papákái
puúma, dí papámôni, / . . . / a butá nèèn édi a dé ên. /íya/

"OK," he said, "No problem." / . . . / He said, "Well, no problem."
He took the parrot feather and the cowrie shell, / . . . / and he put
them on the cayman's head, gave them to it. */íya/*

A pasé ên wáta zalalalala, tjokó djaa.

It carried him right across, *zalalalala*, and set him down.

SAKUÍMA:

Déé soní fèèn kabá túu.

The things he had were all used up.

ADUÊNGI:

Hòòn, soní kabá nèèn máu kêê. A táa, "Wè m'Bóto Saayé—" (a píki) A
táa, "M'paká i, i nyán m'paimá." (a táki "aái") "Té m'dóu akí, i músu
dê." A táa, "Ná pená pantá, Miíi." /íya/

Ohh! There was nothing at all left in his hands. [Very rapidly:] He said, "Well, my boat Saayé—" (it replied) He said, "I've paid you, and you've accepted my payment." ("yes" it said) "When I come back, you've got to be here." It said, "Don't even bother to worry, Boy." /íya/

(a táki aái) Dí miíi aá, hòn— Nôò hên dí miíi dí subí dí— A subí kúun té a kabá, nôò hên kaí a Bongóótu-písi, djaláa.

(he said OK) That boy there— Then the boy went up— He went up the hill to the top, and he got to Bongóótu-písi, *djaláa.*

SAKUÍMA:

Awáá! Ên hópo wóyo lúku dí gaán gangása alíba aá.

Right! He must have looked up and seen the open-sided shed up there.

ADUÊNGI [continuing over Sakuíma's last several words and still rushing his speech:]:

Aái, nôò hên kaí. Nôò dí fá a kaí alá djaláa, nôò déé doón saí djalala dê. Nôò óto wan tá bái táa, "Kó panyá mi! Kó tumá mi! Kó tumá mi!" Óto wan tá bái táa, "Ná tumá mi! Ná tumá mi! Ná—" Óto wan táa, "Kó tumá mi! Kó tumá mi! Kó—" Hóó! De túu tá fan a dí kamía.

Right. And then he got there. And when he got there, he saw the drums all over the place. Some of them are calling out, "Come grab me! Come take me! Come take me!" Others are calling, "Don't take me! Don't take me! Don't—" Others are saying, "Come take me! Come take me! Come—" Ohhh! They're all talking at once in that place.

SAKUÍMA:

A dí kôndè, yán sá úndi da úndi.

In that village, you couldn't tell what was what.

ADUÊNGI:

Nônô. Dí miíi kó dóu. A kó té kó zúntu dê, a taánpu píi. De tá bái dé ên. De tá bái dé ên tá kondá déé soní dé ên. / . . . / A nángó, dí sèmbè tá bái táa, "Ná tumá mi!" Nôò dí té a tá tèndê máu, nôò dí bái fèèn tá bái té dí miíi fèê. / . . . / A táa, "Ma m'Bóto Saayé bi táki dá mi táa déé sèmbè dê, hên nôò m'musu téi, mi ó téi ên." Tééé a gó panyé ên, lúsu saa. Nôò déé sèmbè tá táki táa, "Kó tumá mi" dê— Nôò kúkútulábu-é! nôò yaakú-é! nôò ndjúwé-ndjúwé! nôò táku tatái! híi déé péi hógi túu dê a de sinkíi, yakaa.

Not at all. The boy got there. He came up till he was very close, and he stood there completely still. They're calling out to him. They're calling out to him to tell him what to do. / . . . / He goes up and one of them calls out, "Don't take me!" and when he reaches out

to touch it, its shouting is so fierce that the boy gets scared. / . . . /
He said [reflectively]: "But my Boat Saayé told me that's the one I
should be sure to take, and I'm going to take it." So he went over,
took it and untied it. Then the ones that had been saying "Come
take me"— Well, scorpions! stinging ants! venomous lizards! poi-
sonous snakes! and every imaginable dangerous thing was crawling
all over them.

KASINDÓ [volunteering helpfully]:
Wasiwási.
And wasps.

ADUÊNGI:
*Aái. / . . . / Nôò áán soní. A gó téi dí apínti, lúsu saa, butá a goón, tem.
/ . . . / "É aa! Dí soní de kái—"*
Right. / . . . / So that's all. He went and took the *apínti*, untied it,
and set it on the ground. / . . . / [In the voice of the boy, marveling
at what he's found]: "Ah! The thing they call a—"

TÍANÊN:
Wè únsê déé sèmbè á dí kôndè dê?
And where were the people who lived in that village?

ADUÊNGI:
*Déé sèmbè á dí kôndè— Ná wán kódó saí dê. De gó a wáka. Wè da a dê
de nángó tá simíti dá Gaán Gádu té sápate nôò de kó. Nôò de kó tá pèè
déé doón. / . . . / Áán soní. Dí miíi lúsu dí doón saká butá. A téi bángi, a
sindó. / . . . / A lúku dí doón té, biá dí doón lúku té a táki, "Aái, dí soní
akí hánso!" Nôò hên a náki ên, "tim! tim! tim! tim!" A yéi:*
The people who lived in that village— Not a single one was there.
They'd gone off. Because they used to go off and do blacksmiths'
work for Great God until evening and then they'd come back. And
then they'd play the drums. / . . . / So, that's all. The boy untied
the drum and set it down there. He took a stool and sat down.
/ . . . / He looked at the drum there, he turned it all around to
look at it, and said, "Yes, this thing is certainly beautiful!" Then he
played it: "*tim! tim! tim! tim!*" He heard:

> *Kaadím, kaadím, mitóóliaa.*
> *Kaadím, kaadím, mitóóliaa.*
> *Sibámalé, sibámalé.*
> *Kaadím, kaadím, mitóóliaa.*

*Déé didíbi dê alá, de táa, "Oló! U dêdè! Sèmbè kó a u kôndè. Dí sèmbè dê,
i dêdè!"*

The devils were out there and they said, "Help! We're dead! Some-one has come to our village. Whoever's there, you've had it!"

OTHERS:

[exclamations]

ADUÊNGI:

Dí miíi hópo dí doón, nôò hên a kulé. A kulé téé a kó zúntu u dóu a lío, a tooná buté ên.

The boy picked up the drum and ran. He ran till he was almost at the river, and then he set it down again.

SAKUÍMA:

Dí ógi ógi miíi!

That boy's really baaad!

ADUÊNGI:

A táa, "Dí soní akí súti túmúsi. Mi ó náki wán máu môò." / . . . / A náki: "tim, tim."

He said, "This thing is just too sweet to resist. I'm going to play it just a little more." / . . . / He played: "*tim, tim.*"

> *Kaadím, kaadím, <u>mitóóliaa.</u>*
> *Kaadím, kaadím, <u>mitóóliaa.</u>*
> <u>*Sibámalé, sibámalé.*</u>
> *Kaadím, kaadím, <u>mitóóliaa.</u>*

Hòòn! Déé didíbi dê tá latjá páu wáá-u, tá kaí gwolou. / . . . / Hên wè, dí miíi kó dóu, a táa, "M'Bóto Saayé, m'dóu." A táa, "Miíi, mi dê kaa." Áán soní.

Oh! The devils were charging through the trees, falling all over themselves. / . . . / Then when the boy got there, he said, "My Boat Saayé, here I am." It said, "Boy, I'm all ready." Nothing to it.

SAKUÍMA:

Aaa. Dí a sí a pasá wáta kaa, nôò a líbi.

Ahh. He knows that once he gets across, he'll be OK.

ADUÊNGI:

Nôò a táa, "Wè Miíi, dí i kó, náki dá mi mbéi mi yéi, bigá m'bi tá yéi Doón nê, mi seéi kê yéi tu."

So he said, "Well, Boy, since you're here, play a little for me to hear, because I keep hearing about Drum, and I'd like to hear what it sounds like too."

SAKUÍMA:

Máa nêngè! Andí kó a mi!

My god! This is getting to be too much for me!

OTHERS:
  [laughter]

ADUÊNGI:
  A táa, "Ma m'Bóto Saayé, pasá mi." A táa, "Nônô, náki doón dá mi."
  He said, "My Boat Saayé, take me across." It said, "No, no, play
  the drum for me."

OTHERS:
  [clucks of concern]

ADUÊNGI:
  Áán soní. A náki dé ên. Hòn, a kandá téé a kóti. A táki, "Aái, Miíi,
  subí." Nôô dí tén dê, déé didíbi dê kuma a lanpéési dê. / . . . / Hòòn! Dí
  véntu dí tá kó! A tuúsi zalala. /íya/
  No problem, So he played for it. It really sang and then it stopped.
  The cayman said, "OK, Boy, climb on." Now by that time, the
  devils weren't any farther than that landing just over there. / . . . /
  Ohhh! The wind was coming up! It slipped into the water. /íya/

A MAN:
  Yán tá píki môò, nô?!
  Hey! What's happened to the responses?!

THE RESPONDER [emphatically]:
  ÍYA!
  ÍYA!

OTHERS:
  [laughter]

AGUMÍÍ:
  A duumí seéi fèèn!
  He'd really gone to sleep!

OVERLAPPING VOICES:
  [more comments]

ADUÊNGI:
  A butá a míndi wáta té a kabá butá a míndi wáta kêê, nôô a dê zengêè a
  míndi wáta dê. /íya/
  It had set out into the water till it was right out in the middle, and
  there it was, bobbing gently in the water. /íya/

KASINDÓ:
  A tá wákiti déé didíbi nô?
  Was it waiting for the devils?

ADUÊNGI:
> *Hòòn! De dóu gwitiii, sô.* /*íya*/
> Ohhh! They all swarmed up. /*íya*/

> *De bái táa, "M'Bóto Saayé, síngi!" A táa, "M'Bóto Saayé, ná síngi, i bi nyán paimá u mi! Ambê táa f'i síngi?" De táa, "Síngi!"* /*íya*/
> They called out, "My Boat Saayé, sink!" The boy said, "My Boat Saayé, don't sink, 'cause you've accepted a payment from me! Who can tell you to sink?" The devils said, "Sink!" /*íya*/

> *Sèmbè tá púu ên tánda vém, súti gímm.* /*íya*/
> One of them pulled out a tooth and flung it through the air. /*íya*/

> *Dèê dí wáta, halala. M'Bóto Saayé táa, "Nônô, ná u mi."* /*íya*/
> It dried up all the water. My Boat Saayé said, "No, no, you can't stop me." /*íya*/

OTHERS:
[laughter and comments]

AGUMIÍI:
> *Hên dí tánda fèèn dê de kái "Azángana mi kolóbi-é"!*
> That's the tooth known as "*Azángana mi kolóbi*"!

ASABÔSI:
> *Fá i kái ên?*
> What did you call it?

AGUMIÍI:
> *Dí tánda fèèn dê a tá púu da Azángana mi kolóbi, azángana mi koló.*
> The tooth he's pulling out is *Azángana mi kolóbi, azángana mi koló.*

[The exchange between Agumiíi and Asabôsi goes on simultaneously with that part of Kódji's tale nugget that precedes his song:]

KÓDJI:
> *Wè, dí tén dí a bi táa "Nônô,"* /*íya*/
> Well, at the moment when it was saying "no, no," /ADUÉNGI: *íya*/

> *wè, m'bi saí dê.*
> Well, I was there.

SOMEONE:
> *Andí i sí dê?*
> What did you see?

KÓDJI:

A dí tén dê, nôò wán mmá ku wán miíi bi gó fón wán ndekú, nôò hên a kísi wán físi fèèn. /íya/

At that moment a woman had gone off with her child to do some fish drugging, and she had caught herself a fish. /íya/

Hên a saí dê tán léti nôò dí físi púu dí bóto dí a tá tjé ên, hên tjé ên gó túwè a fundá. /íya/

So there they were, and the fish pulled the boat and it dragged them down to the bottom. /íya/

> *Mi físi, mi físi, a vènuvèè asidáiloo.*
> *Mi físi, mi físi, a vènuvèè asidáiloo.*
> *Éé mi físi, a vènuvèè asidáiloo.*
> *Dáiloo dáiloo.*
> *Éé mi físi, a vènuvèè asidáiloo.*

Gó i tóli.

Go on with your story.

SAKUÍMA:

Fútu f'i sáti kuma logoso!

Your leg is as short as a turtle's!

ADUÊNGI:

Sòò. /íya/

OK. /ADUÉNGI'S RESPONDER: *íya*/

Áán soní. Hòòn, m'Bóto Saayé tá pasá dí miíi wáta téé a dí sê téla aá badaa. De saí a dí sê téla dê, de án sá fá u dú môô, dú soní té de wéi. Latjá dí písi dê, tjumá dí písi dê-u, mêên. /íya/

That's all. Well, My Boat Saayé is taking the boy over to the other shore, *badaa*. The devils are there on the bank, and they just don't know what to do, and they're doing all kinds of things, but all in vain. Breaking up their houses, burning the whole place down. /íya/

Ná dí— ná dí fèèn môô.

There's nothing left there.

KÓDJI:

Ná u de kaí a wáta?

Couldn't they jump in the water?

ANOTHER MAN:

Heépi án dê.

That wouldn't help.

THIRD MAN:
> *Wè, de án sá bulí.*
> They're stuck there.

ADUÊNGI:
> *Wè, a bi, m'Bóto Saayé, fá u dú dê, a kê síngi tuú!* /*íya*/
> Well, as this was happening, my Boat Saayé really wanted to sink!
> /*íya*/
>
> *Wè déé didíbi sán de táki dé ên, de ku ên tá dê a dí písi dê— Sán de táki dé ên, nôò hên a ó dú.* /*íya*/
> Well, whatever the devils would tell it to do— Since they lived together there— Whatever they would tell it to do, it would do.
> /*íya*/
>
> *Ma a nyán paimá fèèn.*
> But it had accepted a payment from the boy.

TÍANÊN:
> *A nyán dí paimá u dí miíi bigá de bi á búka.*
> It had accepted his payment because they had made an agreement.

ADUÊNGI:
> *Yaa. A tá píki ên táa, "M'Bóto Saayé, i nyán m'paimá, yásá síngi."* /*íya*/
> Yeah. He says to it, "My Boat Saayé, you accepted my payment, so you can't sink." /*íya*/

OTHERS:
> [laughter]

ADUÊNGI:
> *Òòn! Áán soní, a kumútu té a kabá, a táa, "Miíi, náki dá m." A náki dé ên:*
> Ohh! Nothing to it, so the cayman came up on the other shore, and it said, "Boy, play for me." He played for it:
>
> > *Kaadím, kaadím, <u>mitóóliaa</u>.*
> > *Kaadím, kaadím, <u>mitóóliaa</u>.*
> > *<u>Sibámalé, sibámalé</u>.*
> > *Kaadím, kaadím, <u>mitóóliaa</u>.*
>
> *A táki, "Aái, Miíi, a súti. Gó f'i."* /*íya*/
> It said, "Yes, Boy, it's sweet. Go along." /*íya*/
>
> *Òòn! A pasá, tééé a dí óto wan kêdêê.* /*íya*/
> Ohh! He went along till he got right up to another one. /*íya*/

A táa, "M'Bóto Saayé, mi dóu," a táki, "Aái, wè náki dá mi." A náki dé ên, /íya/

He said, "My Boat Saayé, here I am," and it said, "Yes, well, play for me." He played for it, /íya/

té a kabá, a pasá. /íya/

and when he was done he went on. /íya/

A tjé ên zalalala, gó tjokó. /íya/

It carried him smoothly and set him down on the shore. /íya/

AGUMIÍI:

Wè a bi táa a bi ó pèê dí doón a dí geébi hédi fèèn. Gó a nángó pèê dí doón dê.

Well, he said he was going to play the drum at the head of the grave. And he's on his way to play that drum.

TÍANÊN:

Dí kési-hédi-soní a gó súku, a gó súku dê.

The head of the coffin thing is what he'd gone looking for.

[Agumiíi and Tíanên's remarks here overlap with Aduêngi's next few phrases.]

ADUÊNGI:

Tééé a tooná dóu a dí óto wan. A náki dé ên, téé a kabá, a pasá. /íya/

Finally he got to the other one. He played for it, till he was done and he went on. /íya/

A nángó tééé, hòòn. A nángó tééé dí tén— dí tén de púu kési butá a dóu, / . . . / tá paatí, túwè keéti lóntu de tá paatí. Áán soní. Dí miíi dóu. / . . . / Táa, "Lánti, mi dóu." De táki, "Aái, wè u nángó a béi." /íya/

He continued along. He kept on going and going until— the very moment when they were taking the coffin outside, / . . . / performing the ritual separations, sprinkling the kaolin for the separations. So that's all. The boy arrived. / . . . / He said, "Everyone, I'm back." They said, "OK, well, we're just going off for the burial." /íya/

A táki, "Aái, wè heépi án dê. Un haíka mi." /íya/

He said, "Yes, well, let's do what we have to do. But listen to me." /íya/

A hái ên doón kó butá a dí kési édi dê, nôò hên a náki ên. /íya/
He pulled the drum over and set it right at the head of the coffin, and then he played it. /íya/

> *Kaadím, kaadím, mitóóliaa.*
> *Kaadím, kaadím, mitóóliaa.*
> *Sibámalé, sibámalé.*
> *Kaadím, kaadím, mitóóliaa.*

De hópo kési, zengêè, butá a édi. Hên i sí fiká apínti kó fiká, híi péi doón a goón líba, dí doón dí miíi gó téi dê, hên kó fiká doón a goón líba. /aái/
They lifted the coffin up onto the bearers' heads. And so you see that the *apínti* came to stay, and every kind of drum in the world, 'cause the drum that the boy went to get, well, it became the drum for the whole world. /yes/

A fiká apínti fu u búsi nêngè— I tá pèê ên akí, dí sèmbè tá yéi apínti, i táki, "Aái, sô wán soní dí soní dê táki." Nôò ên dí, a didíbi kôndè de gó téi, násô wán bi ó á doón.
As a result, *apínti* for us Bush Negroes— If you play it, people hear the *apínti,* and you say, "Yes, such and such a thing is what it's saying." It was taken from the land of the devils, and if it hadn't been, we never would have had drums.

SAKUÍMA:
Aái, gaán tangí u dí miíi.
Right, let's all give thinks to the boy!

ADUÊNGI:
Adê mi tóli dóu.
That's as far as my story goes.

Notes

1. There has been considerable recent debate about whether the term *oral literature*, because of its etymologically oxymoronic status, deserves to survive (see, for example, Bauman 1986:1). Like discussions of the similarly problematic term *primitive art* (see S. Price 1989), this debate evokes the specters of social Darwinism, racism, and ethnocentrism. Yet this term has an advantage over such alternatives as *oral art* or *spoken art* in that it accords the verbal creations of nonliterate peoples (as well as the oral artistry of the literate) a place in the general body of world literature. In this book we presume the dignity and artistry of Saramaka folktales and do not linger over their more general classification or label.

2. This book is about Upper River Saramaka society in 1968, based on periodic fieldwork conducted there between 1966 and 1978 and supplemented by fieldwork with exiled residents of the region in 1986, 1987, and 1989. Since our last stay there, the military government of Suriname (which seized power in 1980) has waged a devastating war against the Maroon populations, including the Saramakas. Since 1986, a number of Saramakas have been killed by government forces, and many others have died because of war-related food shortages and lack of medicines and medical care. Those Saramakas now in French Guiana, who are cut off from their homeland by the war, often live in poverty alongside slum dwellers of diverse backgrounds (illegal Haitian immigrants, Brazilians fleeing drought in the northeast, other Maroon refugees, and so on). Deprived of access to Saramaka territory since 1986, we remain for the time being unable to assess the ravages caused by the war or the extent to which Saramaka life, as it existed before the war, has been transformed. As we write, efforts are underway to reunite the troubled nation, but the future of the Saramakas, and their Ndjuka brethren, remains cause for serious concern.

In terms of the materials presented in this book, our 1986–89 interactions with Saramakas in French Guiana made clear that wakes of the sort we attended in the 1960s and 1970s still take place (both among exiles in French Guiana and in the villages of Upper River Saramaka), that tale-telling continues to hold a special place in these wakes, and that the antics of Anasi, the scrawny little kid, and the other denizens of folktale-land are as much a part of Saramakas' everyday consciousness as they were at that time.

3. The English word *maroon*, like the French and Dutch *marron*, derives from Spanish *cimarrón*, a term with Arawakan (native American) roots that by the mid-1500s had come to be used in plantation colonies throughout the Americas to designate slaves who successfully escaped from captivity (Arrom 1986; R. Price 1979).

4. It is in part because of such elicitation techniques that a scholar like

Jean Hurault could describe Maroon folktales (which are in fact filled with ribald incidents) as "never of a licentious character" (1961:268).

5. For recent assessments of Saramaccan, see Smith (1987) and Alleyne (1987). Possessing a syntax that emerged from West African progenitors (Alleyne 1980), approximately half of its extensive lexicon derives from one or another of the scores of African languages that were spoken by the seventeenth- and early eighteenth-century maroons; another 20 percent comes from Portuguese (the language of most of the slave masters from whom these maroons escaped), including the word *kóntu* for "folktale"; another 20 percent from English (the language of the original seventeenth-century European settlers of Suriname); and 10 percent from Dutch and Amerindian languages (R. Price 1976).

6. For Saramakas, both *kóntu* and First-Time (historical) knowledge are central cultural resources, important components of their collective identity, but they occupy separate spheres. Though the morals, as well as certain rhetorical devices, of folktales may overlap with those of particular First-Time stories, Saramakas maintain a clear distinction between the two—both in the contexts where they are communicated and in the kinds of characters and incidents they depict.

7. See, for example, the "dilemma tale" about the two brothers and their sister in the riddles presented below.

8. Tales are sometimes (though rarely) told outside the context of wakes—most commonly by children or during a relaxed evening in a horticultural camp; *Mató* and *Tòngôni* are prohibited for such occasions, and the opening for riddles (*Hílíti/Dáíti*) is substituted.

9. Much of the general discussion of Saramaka performance that follows in the next several paragraphs is abstracted from S. Price and R. Price (1980: 167–85), a book devoted primarily to the visual artistry of Maroons.

10. The Herskovitses' penetrating analysis is all the more remarkable given their rudimentary command of Sranan and Saramaccan. They make several egregious claims about Suriname tales—for example, that "there is but little difference between town [Paramaribo] and bush [Saramaka] . . . both in the tales told and in the social setting of the stories" (1936:139). But many of their comparative/historical insights and concerns deserve systematic elaboration: the widespread distribution of antiphonal (and interruptive) patterns in tale-telling; formulaic openings and closings (where one might be able, for example, to link historically the Jamaican "Jack Mandora" to Sranan "Waka i tori"); the use of what Abrahams calls "the intrusive I" (1967:472–74); various "sound effects" (compare, for example, the snoring and feigned snoring of Saramaka devils [pp. 173–76] with the way Bété [West African] dragons snore—"*Kpagogovooun! Kpagogovooun!*" when they are really asleep, "*Kpan! Kpan!*" when they are not [Paulme 1986:3]); voice mimicry; the role of songs; and a host of other features of performance, not to mention specific characters and plots.

11. This English translation was made by English Moravians soon after the original German text (itself translated from spoken Saramaccan) was written down.

A negro from the Upper Country [from upstream] called here [the mission post in Saramaka, in 1804], on his journey to Paramaribo. He said, he came to tell us a story he had heard from his parents, and to ask whether it was true. They had an old tradition, that the great God in heaven, after he had created heaven and earth, made two large chests, and placed them near the dwellings of mankind, on the coast. The black people, on discovering the chests, ran immediately to examine them, and found one locked, and the other open. Not thinking it possible to open that which was locked, they contented themselves with the other, which they found quite full of iron ware[?] and tools, such as hoes, axes, and spades, when each seized as much as he could carry, and all returned home. A little while after, the white people came also, and very calmly began to examine the locked chest, and, knowing the way to open it, found it filled with books, and papers which they took and carried away. Upon which God said, "I perceive, that the black people mean to till the ground, and the white people to learn to read and write." The negroes, therefore, believe, that it thus pleased the Almighty to put mankind to the proof; and as the blacks did not show so much sense as the white people, he made them subject to the latter, and decreed, that they should have a troublesome life in this world.

We heard him patiently, and gave him the needful information concerning the difference of rank and status[?] amongst men, and then described to him the love of God. . . . We told him, that now He invites all men, black as well as white, to come unto Him, that they may obtain the forgiveness of, and deliverance from sin, and life everlasting, through His blood-shedding and death. (Extract . . . , n.d.: 425–26)

We are not aware of the existence of other *kóntu*s that explicitly denigrate Saramakas or other blacks relative to whites, and certainly not of any that justify (as opposed to commenting on) their differential status. During the eighteenth century, as today, Saramaka men drew on a broad gamut of routines designed to please whitefolks while at the same time making clear to other Saramakas who were present their disdain for whites (see, for multiple examples, R. Price 1990), and we suspect that the incident reported here forms part of that pattern. (For other versions of this widespread Afro-American tale, see Giraud and Jamard 1985:83, and also Dance 1985:7–8, which contains additional references. For a number of African versions, see Görög 1968, and for a discussion of a seventeenth-century West African version, see Gates 1988:141.)

12. Once a Saramaka discussing tales with us did, however, volunteer (when we asked specifically about the notion of "lying" in tale-telling) that "if you don't lie [bullshit], you can't tell tales. You have to know how to make things up."

13. Among the relatively few examples in our two evenings of tale nuggets that seem to be related to the tale they interrupt only by general features of plot or theme, we might cite Antonísi's tale nugget about how Dog and Goat courted the same woman (p. 76) in Kasólu's tale about how three animals take human wives; Amáka's nugget about a wrestling match between Squirrel and Mouse (p. 223) during Aduêngi's description of the activities surrounding a funeral—into which a wrestling match fits appropriately; Aduêngi's story about a devil who helped some girls drag a dry-season pool for fish (p. 302) in a tale told by Amáka that centers on this same activity; and Aduêngi's two tale nuggets involving one character tricking another (pp. 348 and 349) in Kasindó's tale about Anasi's (ultimately unsuccessful) attempt to trick two friends.

14. This version of *nóuna* is considerably condensed from two tellings recorded by RP in 1978 and told explicitly for his ears by Kandámma, then ailing and in her hammock. As we have pointed out elsewhere (R. Price 1983 : 159), the rhetorical structure of *nóuna* almost exactly parallels that of a central First-Time historical account—that of the faithful slave/spy, Kwasímukámba, who arrived in Saramaka feigning friendship, who *almost* learned the secret of Saramaka invulnerability, "escaped" back to the whites to lead a giant whitefolks' army against the Saramakas, and in the final battle was maimed by the Saramaka chief in an ultimate act of vengeance.

15. We have examined a number of variants of the Saramaka *nóuna* tale from elsewhere in Afro-America (for references, see Tanna 1984 : 125–28; Bascom 1969 : 134–37). The common elements they draw on seem limited to a monster (witch, bush spirit, animal) becoming a beautiful seductress; her requiring that a vessel be knocked off her head; the old mother tending the dogs back home while the hunter goes off to gather fruit with his changeling lover; the lover calling out helpers to fell the fruit tree; and the dogs eventually massacring her. In none of the variants known to us is the lover a disguised enemy of the people. In none does she try to extract a "secret." And in none is she merely maimed (rather than killed) by the hero, as a way of showing his ultimate disdain. Among the more than twenty variants we have seen from Africa (for references, see Bascom 1969 : 134), only one—from Dahomey—includes an animal in disguise/spy who tries to extract a secret from her hunter-husband (Herskovits and Herskovits 1958 : 186–90).

16. The scrawny little kid contrasts with Anasi not only in his altruistic motives but in his distinctly asexual persona.

17. For details of Saramaka name use, see R. Price and S. Price (1972).

18. For certain kinds of materials (esoteric languages, play languages, hunting calls, some songs, and verbal "transcriptions" and "translations" of *apínti* drumming), we found it possible to make recordings only in an inter-

view setting. Such recordings represent about 15 of the 117 reels that we recorded and placed on deposit.

19. In her translations of Kalapalo tales from Brazil, Basso segments her texts by verbal interruptions not unlike Saramaka *íyas*. But because the narratives were presented in private, explicitly for her tape recorder, it was she herself (following her general knowledge of Kalapalo speech and the silent cues of the speakers) who provided the verbalized interruptions (1987:xv).

20. For technical discussion of the multiple functions of Saramaccan initial particles, see Glock and Levinsohn (1982) and Rountree (1982).

21. The identification of such "unanswered cues" is more subjective (and less easily replicable) than most aspects of our translation process. Pauses, intonation, and sentence structure all contribute, and each speaker's individual idiosyncrasies of pacing and rhythm must also be considered. We have simply done our best, with the help of Saramakas who have listened to the tapes with us.

22. Note that the words and phrases we label as Sranan may in some cases derive rather from Ndjuka (the language of the Ndjuka Maroons, which is closely related to Sranan).

23. We stress that the following paragraphs, and those that introduce our second evening, are not field notes—either raw or tidied up—but rather a highly selective reconstruction/evocation, written twenty years after the fact, based on several-score pages of notes taken at the time.

24. Saramakas have a tribal chief (*gaamá*, which we gloss as "chief"); and villages have headmen (*kabiténis*, "captains") and assistant headmen (*basiás*, which we leave in Saramaccan).

25. Our field notes contain numerous allusions to Sindóbóbi's alleged evildoing. She is said to have performed rites involving the burial of live cocks (to increase her own rice yields at the expense of others), to have magically fixed her own daughter's marriage basket (to prevent the husband from divorcing her), and to have called out curses that brought sickness and death upon her victims. Asipéi once remarked that "Sindóbóbi never washed in simple water even once in her life—all she ever used were *óbia* [magical] leaf baths. Whenever you walked by her house, you could smell the odor of the leaves!" Asabôsi was also implicated by association. People said, "Her only daughter. Of course she taught her everything she knew!" We know of a half-dozen people Sindóbóbi is said to have killed (supernaturally), and many others are said to have escaped only after paying her cloths and other goods so that she would stop sickening them. Her own sister refused to attend her funeral rites because Sindóbóbi had been found years earlier, through divination, to have caused the death in childbirth of the sister's daughter.

Let us stress that Saramakas discussed such accusations openly; Sindóbóbi's alleged activities were fully in the public domain. And such accusations were not rare—few Saramakas go through life without rumors of evildoing occasionally being floated about them. What was special in Sindóbóbi's case was their persistence and, at least after the stroke that rendered her defenseless, their widespread acceptance. Asabôsi, despite all the talk about her involvement in her mother's activities, led a social life largely unaffected by it.

26. Normally a woman in her sixties or seventies would be buried only several weeks after her death. At the other extreme from Sindóbóbi, Kandámma—a much-loved older woman in Dángogó (and a gifted tale-teller, as we will see)—was kept aboveground nearly three months when she died during the early 1980s.

27. Kúnus are avenging spirits of deceased people, or in certain circumstances snake gods or forest spirits or yet other spiritual beings, who affect the well-being of the members of a matrilineage (see R. Price 1973). Sindóbóbi had two such kúnus "in her head"—that is, she served as medium for a snake god and a forest spirit kúnu. Each matrilineage has, in addition, a gaán kúnu ("great kúnu") that is assumed, ultimately, to stand behind each death, even if the proximate cause is found to be some other spiritual being (e.g., a lesser kúnu), sorcery, or something else. It is this "great kúnu" that Aduêngi is asking Sindóbóbi to address on their behalf.

28. After the evening of kóntu-telling, Sindóbóbi's funeral rites continued for several days. The next day, men went hunting for the feast for the ancestors to be held the day after that. On the day of the feast the gravediggers purified themselves and their tools with fire, and that evening kóntu were told again, with Kasindó and Aduêngi the main tellers. At the final libations of the funeral, on 9 May 1968, it was decided that the village of Gaánsééi would hold a "second feast" in honor of Sindóbóbi within a week or two, and tentative plans were made to hold the "second funeral" some months hence in Dángogó. The host villagers presented the gravediggers with cloths and other presents to thank them for their help, and the gravediggers presented the close kin of Sindóbóbi with presents of their own. The funeral—truncated because of the deceased's evil reputation—had nevertheless taken place properly. Sindóbóbi had been buried, even if somewhat grudgingly, "with celebration."

29. This narration draws on a number of common Saramaka plot elements: a forest path along which a devil lives, an óbia-man (sometimes another wise person) knowing the secret of the devil's invulnerability (here, as often, a needle), and the devil's weakness for music (here, as often, the song of a specially forged horn), as well as the magical revival of someone who has been killed and the stated relationship of this act to Saramaka notions about nêséki—see notes 83 and 86.

30. The device of a man overhearing the song by which a woman calls her animal lover appears in other Saramaka tales; for example, we have heard a tale in which Anasi eavesdrops on a woman who is calling to her fish-lover, then imitates her song to call and kill the fish, causing the woman to commit suicide. Saramakas credit the origin of their elaborate rituals for twins to a monkey—in that case a spider monkey rather than a howler monkey—who taught one of their early ancestors how to care for her twin infants (see R. Price 1983:60–61).

31. Although the person telling the main tale usually serves as responder for those who interrupt with tale nuggets, here it is Kasólu, rather than Kandámma, who supplies responses for Akóbo.

32. The theme of "strong-eared children" (*tánga-yési miñ*) turns up frequently in Saramaka tales. Although in this narration Kandámma's tale is phrased in terms of a man with a hunting dog, the song the man uses to taunt the devil (see below) suggests there is another version in which his role is taken by children who disobey their parents. And it is Akóbo's knowledge of that version—even though Kandámma has not yet alluded to it, even in song—that provides the conceptual link between Kandámma's tale and Akóbo's tale nugget.

See, for other examples, the boy who never listened (pp. 208–18), the two girls who refused to take the recommended path (pp. 243–61), the girl who drugged the forbidden pond (p. 315), and the girl who entered the forest on the forbidden day (p. 268).

33. Two of the men we worked with in Kourou had heard other versions of the tale this nugget alludes to. As Samsón had heard it, the children had gone to cut firewood and met the devil, and the boy's horn played a different song. In the version Antonísi knew, it used to be that you couldn't go to cut firewood without getting killed by a devil. A scrawny little kid had been warned not to follow people when they went to cut firewood, but he went anyway. He used a horn fashioned from a root crop (*napí*) to kill the devil. It too played a different song.

34. Kandámma used the word for "boy" rather than "man" here, and during the rest of the tale she alternated the two, seemingly at random. For clarity we have used "man" throughout. (From Kandámma's perspective as one of the oldest women in Upper River Saramaka, it was not unnatural for her to consider almost any man a boy.)

35. Saramakas believe that many dead people "come back" by participating (along with the biological mother and father) in the conception of a child, for whom the dead person thereafter serves as *nêséki*—a kind of tutelary spirit—throughout the child's life. (See also notes 83 and 86.)

36. In his eagerness to take the floor, Kasólu used *Hílíti!* the opening for tales when they are not told in connection with a death. After both Antonísi and Kandámma step in to correct this slip, Kasólu comes back with the appropriate *Mató!* and Antonísi replies *Tòngôni!* thus taking on the role of responder for the tale.

37. This tale itself deals with some heavy themes—the impelling solidarity of siblings, even when they do not know of each other's existence; the emotional costs of virilocal residence, which isolates a woman from her family; the ambivalence of both brothers-in-law and "formal friends," who juggle solidarity and hostility in a precarious balance; the separation of edible foods from those prohibited for human consumption; the division of the world into land, air, and water (here represented by Elephant, Eagle, and Cayman); the alternation of night and day; the relation between body and soul (which allows

the killing of a monster by an attack on his physically separated "heartbeat"); the issue of mortality and rebirth (as the temporary replacement of a severed head brings the reptilian monster briefly back to life); and the delineation of nature and culture (in this case the establishment of a boundary around the territory where an anthropophagous snake has been vanquished).

But at the same time, the ambiance during this narration was consistently light and fun-filled, with comments focusing on the specifics of the story rather than on its cosmological and moral messages. There was real empathy for the mother who watched her last child leave home in search of his sisters, cautious disbelief at the announcement of Jaguar's alleged death, curiosity about where a woman would hold her basket if she had a husband who carried her on his back, joy at the recognition scenes between brother and sister, concern over the appropriate etiquette for those encounters, amusement at the inevitable appearance of Anasi as soon as there was glory to be claimed, nervousness at moments of oblivious relaxation when danger was clearly at hand, incredulity when the tale's hero declared his feelings of affection toward the twelve-headed monster, and some discussion of that monster's gullibility when the boy claimed he was going off to urinate and would be right back.

Abrahams has pointed out the existence, throughout Afro-America, of tales involving "a transformed [animal] bridegroom who has achieved his change by borrowing various parts of the body to pass himself off as an appropriate suitor" and a younger brother who "through snooping or using one of his witching powers, is able to follow the couple and discover that his sister has married an animal or bush spirit" (1985:22). See, for a Vincentian example, Abrahams (1985:108–10); for a Paramaribo example, Herskovits and Herskovits (1936:296–301); for references to similar examples elsewhere in the Caribbean, Flowers (1980:392–405, 601); and for a discussion of this theme among the Mende (West Africa), Cosentino (1982:144–92).

The device of identifying the slayer of a snake (or other monster) by seeing who can produce its severed head(s)—or sometimes tongue(s)—is widespread in Afro-American tales (see Flowers 1980:60–70).

38. Saramaka women, even those who spend the bulk of their time in their husbands' villages, retain strong ties to their matrilineal villages, where they will eventually be buried.

39. Recall that *papá* is the Saramaka music of death, played by specialists on the night before burial and, many months later, on the night before the ghost is chased forever from the village.

40. The tale this song alludes to appears in many variants throughout West and Central Africa as well as Afro-America (see, for examples, Herskovits and Herskovits 1936:174–79; Abrahams 1985:207–9). Note that the song refers to *Father* Jaguar, but that Kandámma seems to have altered the story to mesh more closely with the tale it is interrupting. There is another version, by Kasindó, in our second evening (pp. 203–8). In 1987 in Cayenne, Kalusé told us a related tale that has almost the same song: A king promised his daughter in marriage to the man who could bring him the tails of a twelve-

tailed *makáku* (kind of monkey). Anasi feigned being dead at the side of a creek, with a club in one hand and a machete in the other. From up in the tree the one-tailed *makáku* had seen Anasi walk to the creek and fall "dead" on his back, holding the machete and club. He came down to the ground and said he didn't have the expertise to bury someone who had died holding a club and machete. So he called the two-tailed *makáku* to help (by singing a nearly identical song). The two-tailed *makáku* then called the three-tailed *makáku*, and so on until finally the twelve-tailed *makáku* arrived. Anasi jumped up and killed him and won the king's daughter. (For references to tales from elsewhere in Afro-America about feigning death in order to capture multitailed animals, see Flowers 1980:525–26.)

41. Akóbo's substitution of "underwater work" for "swimming" is an example of a common type of Saramaka speech play.

42. The dramatic device of a boy/man persistently asking his parents—despite their repeated denials—whether they had had other children, until they finally admit the existence of a child who had been separated from them, appears in other Saramaka narrative contexts. See, for example, the moving historical account by Captain Góme of Alábi's quest for his sister Tutúba and her eventual release from slavery (R. Price 1983:9).

43. Here Kasólu shifts from the Saramaccan word for hat, *kaapúsa*, to the Sranan equivalent, *hati*.

44. Upon listening to the recording of this tale nugget in 1987, the Saramaka men in Kourou told us a version of what they thought was the same tale: It used to be that when a man asked for a wife, she would engage him in a dance contest. If she outdanced him (if he got tired and gave up), she'd kill him. In the tale, Anasi seeks the hand of a very beautiful woman named Agangaai, who could outdance any man. As they danced around and around each other, Anasi flattered her with this song of praise. In the end Anasi won the contest. Thanks to him, men since then have not had to undergo this ordeal.

Compare this with the tale nugget told by Aduêngi in Evening Two that uses a nearly identical song but has a different plot—the woman, there named Asíminti, sings this song to a devil named Agangai (p. 298).

45. In Saramaka, tying hammocks side by side and spending the night in each other's company is a gesture of friendship and solidarity among men. By saying that he would not sleep with his wife, Elephant is telling her what a good host he would be for any of her male relatives who might visit.

46. Compare this tale nugget with the similar one told by Asabósi on p. 162.

47. Saramakas say that when a cayman attacks a person, it usually strikes the knee.

48. The *tonê óbia*, one of whose songs Anasi is singing here, controls the rains, through the *tonê* gods that dwell in rivers.

49. In Kourou, none of the men we worked with knew a fuller version of

this tale, but Samsón offered a partial version. The spoken words were: *Kidi-bántá, kidibántá. Dom! Tidé u sá gó na tjóló ukulunyèn,* and the words to the song were:

> *Umá yee, umá yee.*
> *A sidón yoyo.*
> *Gidi umá yee.*

50. When we played this tape to Saramakas in French Guiana in 1987, several responded spontaneously to this phrase by exclaiming, "Bóóta!"—referring to Desi Bouterse, the military strongman of Suriname. Similarly, in her analysis of the French Antillian Ti-Jean tales, Ina Césaire argues that "the beast with seven heads" is the symbol of all oppression, tyranny, and domination imposed from outside (1987:9).

51. *Máti* is a highly charged volitional relationship, usually between two men, that dates back to the Middle Passage—*máti*s were originally "shipmates," those who had survived the journey out from Africa together; by the eighteenth century, *máti* was a lifelong relationship entered into only with caution and when there was strong mutual affection and admiration (R. Price 1990). Today, an often-cited Saramaka proverb holds that *máti ganyá i, án o láfu* (when your *máti* betrays you, he won't be smiling—that is, he'll be dead serious). And for a man, perhaps the most strongly forbidden of all sexual partners is the wife of a *máti*, since between *máti*s there should be absolute trust.

52. Antonísi sang us Agouti's song:

> *A djam zenge zenge, djimbo koo djimbo.*
> *Tjama, boi tjama.*
> *Un fá un de mi tío Aladígwaha?*
> *Tjama, boi tjama.*

Line 3, the only one he could explain, uses an insulting name for Jaguar (Aladígwaha) and means "Well how do you do, Uncle [Mother's Brother] Aladígwaha?"

53. The initial situation was that each boy would bring his plate and food to eat when he went to the garden to chase away birds. But the devil would take it all, plus the boy, and eat everything. The next day another boy would go off to chase birds and suffer the same fate.

54. The term she uses here is *sitááfu bêè*—a "belly of suffering/punishment."

55. Dúnguláli is a "great *óbia*" belonging to the village of Dángogó.

56. For a variant of this tale from St. Vincent, see Abrahams (1985: 260–62), and for references to variants throughout the Caribbean, see Flowers (1980:265–69). Antonísi said he had first heard the tale from another Saramaka working on the Corantijne River (the border between Suriname and Guyana), which may help explain its strong links with the Anglophonic creole

tradition. "Bámbèl," the name of the horse—which Saramaka listeners found hilarious—may possibly derive from "[Yellow] Dander," a magical horse in Anglophone Caribbean tales (see Flowers 1980:105).

57. When a man gets a woman pregnant in Saramaka, he is expected to have frequent sex with her throughout the pregnancy, to nurture the fetus.

58. There is a Sranan story, told by the great Creole raconteur Aleks de Drie during the 1970s, that includes a very similar song (de Drie 1985: 198–200, and for an English version, R. Price 1990, epilogue). Note also that in the final tale of our two evenings, Kasindó sings the song of Anasi in a similar situation—crossing over the river on a tightrope in an ordeal that he knows in advance he will fail; the chorus there is "*sesíyênga-ayênga.*"

59. Upon hearing this fragment in 1987 in Cayenne, Kalusé told us the following version: Women and men used to live in separate villages. Men couldn't go to the women's village and vice versa. The women's village was called Zabwaangáikita. Three brothers said they were going off to get medicine, but their father was ritually astute and could tell what they were up to. They went to an all-night play to meet women. One of the brothers slept with a woman and got her pregnant. Once he'd done that he shouldn't have returned to his village, because it would pollute the *óbia*s. The three brothers returned anyway. The father made them undergo the spear ordeal, and the guilty brother died. The other men all fled from the village and went somewhere else, because of the ritual pollution. The wife discovered her husband stuck on the spear and revived him. But she also warned him that because she had saved his life, he must never take another wife. Later, when he did, the first wife killed herself. The man got in a canoe and went off to Zabwaangáikita.

60. This tale is a Saramaka variant of a fairly standard African/Afro-American "contest tale" about not getting angry (see, for a version from Paramaribo, with references to two others from Nigeria, Herskovits and Herskovits 1936:368–75, and for several other Caribbean variants, Flowers 1980:287–88). But while drawing on similar themes, it also expresses a uniquely Maroon ideological message of great power. In the Saramaka version, plantation slavery and wage slavery are poetically merged, and the secret to survival in such situations is unambiguously spelled out: never accept the white man's definition of the situation. None of the other versions known to us from non-Maroon sources—from Nigeria, the Cape Verde Islands, Puerto Rico, the Dominican Republic, coastal Suriname, and Haiti—contain the same, prototypically Maroon message. These others focus on explicit contests or wagers between a boy and a king (sometimes a boy and a devil) to see who can keep from getting angry the longest. In this comparative context, what is striking about the Saramaka version of the tale is that it describes an ongoing, long-term labor situation—indeed, alienated labor itself—and that, rather than a particular, explicit "contract" about not getting angry, the story hinges on the hero's figuring out (after many of his fellows have already been killed in the attempt) that the only way to triumph is to challenge the very nature of the system itself, to reject the boss's definition of the labor situation, be it slav-

ery or servile wage labor. And today, however hard it may be for Saramaka men to retain their inner strength and dignity while submitting to humiliating work and treatment in coastal wage-labor situations (cleaning out toilets at the French space center at Kourou, for example), the wisdom behind this tale helps them keep going. (For more on this theme and its meaning for Saramakas, see R. Price, n.d.; for more on the relationship of unalienated work, wage labor, and slavery, see Giraud and Jamard 1985; R. Price and S. Price 1989.)

The device the hero uses to trick the white man (or devil)—burying the tails of pigs (or cows or donkeys) in the ground as if whole pigs had burrowed under—appears in other cycles of tales throughout Afro-America (see Flowers (1980:289–90; Jean-Louis 1987:197–98). Note also that as part of the re-definition of the labor situation in the Saramaka tale, the hero shifts—over the course of his relationship with the king-boss—from the role of passive victim (having plants break as soon as he reaches out to harvest their fruit) to that of active aggressor (bludgeoning the king's animals to death).

61. The term used here is *bakáa kôndè woóko*—"whitefolks' territory work," coastal wage labor as opposed to work in Saramaka.

62. The men who listened to this tale with us in 1987, including Kasólu, suggested that the king's name should have been given as Sôndò Háti Boónu (King "Nothing Can Get Him Angry" or, more literally, "Without Anger").

63. The plot of this tale—in which Goat is first victimized by the far more powerful Jaguar and then, by means of magic, beats him at his own game—is widespread in Africa and Afro-America (Herskovits and Herskovits 1936: 302–5). The tale also contains a recurrent Saramaka theme—the ambiguities that inhere in the relationship between wild animals and humans, the conceptual distinction between hunting and murder. Here Goat is forced to butcher his own relatives. In the *nóuna* tale (p. 17), the woman turned Bush Cow sadly contemplated the skulls of her relatives who had been slain by her human husband. And in the tale about Elephant, Eagle, and Cayman, each of their wives expressed anxiety about the possibility that her husband's hunting kills included her own relatives.

64. Saramaka men know a variety of techniques to consult with the god whose place it is before cutting a garden site. The most common involves setting up a small palm-leaf structure (*azang-páu*) in the evening, praying to the god to ask permission to work there, and then returning in the morning to see if the structure is still standing, which indicates divine approval.

65. This appears to be a reference to *opéte*, the vulture or buzzard—a bird considered to be a vehicle for *komantí* spirits and hence extremely powerful.

66. Kandámma here refers to the *deindein* drum, which is beaten with sticks rather than hands (see S. Price and R. Price 1980:180). Two other tales included in our two evenings also revolve around a boy who goes off to the land of devils to bring back Drum—but in those cases it is an *apínti* rather than a *deindein* (see pp. 165–80 and 218–43).

67. Saramakas distinguish two kinds of peanuts or groundnuts—*pindá* and *ndju* (*gobo-góbo*). Kandámma's tale nugget refers to the latter variety.

68. In Saramaccan, a man's *báka dôò* ("back door") is his last resort when he's in trouble, his ultimate power.

69. We translate Saramaccan *pu* as "pond" or "dry-season pool." The technical term would be "oxbow lake." These small bodies of water are formed on the forest floor when the level of the river recedes during the dry season. Saramakas consider them ritually dangerous places.

70. Compare this tale nugget with the one told by Kandámma on p. 89.

71. This tale appears again in our two evenings, in a version by Aduêngi (pp. 218–43). The initial situation of children being interrogated about their intended contributions to a parent's funeral appears elsewhere in Afro-America (see, for example, Herskovits and Herskovits 1936: 166–69).

72. Saramaka listeners would be familiar with other versions of this common folktale that are less delicately euphemistic about the youngest daughter's contribution to the funeral. See, for example, Aduêngi's version in our second evening, where she declares, "Every single man who slips into this village . . . I'll screw every single one of them!" Later on in Kasólu's version, he too becomes more explicit.

73. Compare with Aduêngi's longer version (p. 276).

74. An *atígo* is a ritually prepared object small enough to fit easily into a man's hunting sack. It can take any of numerous physical forms (an egg, a ball of kaolin, a piece of wood, etc.). It appears only in folktales. When it is slammed down, it turns dry land into sea, sea into dry land, an open path into one blocked by a mountain, and so forth. Like a bomb (it was explained to us), each *atígo* can be used only once.

75. Compare this song with the one Aduêngi used in his version of this tale (pp. 218–43).

76. The binding nature of Saramaka contracts, once sealed by a payment, is even more explicitly discussed in Aduêngi's version of this tale (p. 240). For more general discussion of the significance of Maroon "payments," see Vernon (1987).

77. There is a rigid prohibition, dating back to the eighteenth century, against bringing a corpse back from whitefolks' territory: "Dead people can't be brought over Mamádan Falls," says the aphorism (R. Price 1990).

78. We have translated the following text, which was recorded on tape, from the transcriptions made by Adiante Franszoon (a son of Captain Faánsisónu) in the early 1970s, not from the original tape (which is unavailable to us in Martinique as we write). We translate *avó* as "grandfather" (though it can also refer to more distant generations). Saramaka prayers to ancestors have an antiphonal pattern, but with the responder (in the land of the ancestors) "answering" silently in the pauses deliberately left by the person praying. In this translation we have not marked pauses.

79. For those interested in this level of ethnographic detail, we provide here a key, in sequential order, to the ancestors invoked in Captain Faánsisónu's

prayer. (This information is incomplete, since we are without Saramakas to help us out as we write.)

Bongóótu, an important Matjau captain and for a time in the 1880s acting tribal chief, founded Dángogó approximately 110 years ago. Djankusó and Atudéndu were at the time of this prayer the two most recently deceased tribal chiefs, having held the stool from 1898 to 1932 and from 1932 to 1948, respectively; Atudéndu was the mother's father's son of Bèkióo (who called him "older brother"). Kónuwómi was an important captain of the Kasitú clan who nevertheless resided in Dángogó; he was the father of Atudéndu, the son of Bongóótu, and Bèkióo's mother's father. Wabé was Kónuwómi's wife and Bèkióo's mother's mother. (Faánsisónu's use of "wife" as term of address is part of the "*mbéi avó*" pattern—the joking relationship between people separated by two or more generations.) Daída and Bukêtimmá were among Wabé's daughters (hence Bèkióo's mother's sisters). Makoyá and Agáduánsu were two of their brothers. Captain Bitjé[nfóu] was an early twentieth-century captain of Dángogó and the father-in-law of Daída (hence the father's father of Asipéi, the unofficial leader of Bèkióo's kingroup in Dángogó). The remaining people invoked in the paragraph are not known to us, at least by those names.

Captain Gónima, then recently deceased, was a captain of Akísiamáu, the matrilineal village of Bèkióo and his kin. Presumably, Guusé and Fáya are also Akísiamáu people. Captains Saayé and Pótji were Faánsisónu's immediate predecessors on his captain's staff; Amútu and Afaadjé were earlier holders of the same staff. Bitjé[nfóu] and Apeéli were the two most recently deceased holders of another of Dángogó's captain's staffs—that once held by Bongóótu. (We are not sure about the identity of Kwabátatái.)

In the prayer for Alébidóu, Faánsisónu invokes his father Mánpana and then, we would guess, his father's father and perhaps father's father's brother. The string from Captain Abemazóo through Basiá Pólu is not known to us but may refer to Faánsisónu's father's village, Kayána, in Lángu. Mandéa, and Kwênkwên were, with Bongóótu, founders of Dángogó in the 1870s. Amánabentá was Chief Atudéndu's mother's brother.

No new names are invoked until the end of the rum libation, but these are very much of a piece with those who came before. Djúa was a brother of Mandéa, the founder of the part of Dángogó over which Captain Faánsisónu presides. Gidé is another name for (Captain) Apeéli, mentioned earlier. Kositán, an older brother of Tribal Chief Agbagó, was an important elder during Faánsisónu's young adulthood, and Asápampía was another important Dángogó elder, one generation older.

80. The imagery alludes to the ideal—rarely realized during the 1960s— of a man preparing a garden, going off for some months of wage labor on the coast, and then returning for the harvest. Men like Bèkióo, who stayed on the coast for many years at a time (and were called *fikáma* ["men who stay"]) were considered to be depriving their lineages and home villages of numerous benefits.

81. Deceased officeholders play an especially influential role in praying—on behalf of the living—to evil spiritual forces. As we pointed out in note 27, *kúnus* are avenging spirits that affect the members of a matrilineage. The "great *kúnu*" (*gaán kúnu*) of each matrilineage is assumed, ultimately, to be behind each death, even if the proximate cause is found to be some other spiritual being, sorcery, or something else.

82. When Faánsisónu says "those villages never separated" he is stressing the solidarity of two groups that have periodically been at odds for some one hundred years. A little over a century ago, in the wake of a big fight, the ancestors of the people who founded Akísiamáu and Dángogó (after having lived together since the 1690s) *did* in fact separate to found their respective villages.

83. Saramakas believe that every child has, in addition to a biological mother and father, a *nêséki*—a kind of supernatural genitor—who intercedes at conception and plays an important role as tutelary spirit throughout life. Normally the *nêséki* is a deceased relative, but in rare cases it can be a forest spirit or even a dead hunting dog. Divination to determine an infant's *nêséki* goes on during one or another early illness, and once its identity is discovered, the child has obligations to respect the dead person's food taboos and attend to its other personal needs. A person calls on his *nêséki* to intercede with other (particularly, malevolent) powers whenever there is need.

84. This money matter was the most bitter part of the aftermath of Alébidóu's death. In the 1960s life insurance was a foreign notion to Upper River Saramakas, though some men working for companies on the coast, like Alébidóu, became involved as part of their employee benefits. Normally Saramaka inheritance is strongly matrilineal (though certain goods, e.g., a man's shotgun, may be passed to a son shortly before death); in most cases, after death everyone in the close lineage receives a little something, with the closest kin getting most (R. Price 1975:127–29). The idea of assigning rights to a wife and children rather than to one's matrilineage, as Alébidóu seems to have done, thus runs counter to Saramaka principle. Hence the consternation surrounding this case—in which we heard accusations that the widow, in the city, had hidden the key to Alébidóu's "money chest" and so forth. Alébidóu's lineage clearly came up short, and they felt cheated.

85. This rhetoric concerns the special relationship of Bèkióo's matrilineal kin segment to Dángogó. Although they are members of the Wátambíi clan, whose matrilineal village is Akísiamáu, they have lived in Dángogó since Kónuwómi—Chief Atudéndu's father—brought his Wátambíi wife, Wabé, to live with him there. Bèkióo was Wabé's daughter's son. This whole group—the descendants of Wabé—ultimately live in Dángogó because of their connection with Kónuwómi. Faánsisónu is stressing the extent to which Dángogó has treated these people as its own.

86. See note 83. This is a way of asking the *nêséki*—tutelary spirit—to protect the person, to guard him or her against dangers. People who share

tutelary spirits with the deceased always tie their heads with a kerchief while attending such a feast, and a person whose tutelary spirit is particularly threatening often stays away from the feast altogether.

87. The morning after the tale-telling session a final set of libations was poured, lasting four times as long as the first afternoon's libations, which we translated above, though the ancestors invoked were much the same. Now, however, among other messages to the land of the dead were special pleas for protection of the village and the deceased's kinsfolk in the future. Formal thanks to the many individuals who contributed to making the feast (and the evening of tale-telling) a success were an important part of these final libations.

88. This tale, like another that Amáka tells later in the evening (pp. 261–67), deals with the difficulties of being a good parent, of balancing discipline and caring. Its plot also has parallels with Kasólu's tale about Goat and Jaguar (pp. 138–53) in that an unarmed, relatively weak character who is taken hostage manages through a magic aid to instill fear in the more powerful characters by hunting despite his lack of weapons; in both tales, there are scenes in which the feline heavies spy on the hero to see how he manages to hunt and then beg him not to do it to them.

89. The Saramaccan phrase *sondí dê a múndu* could as well be translated "life is full of surprises" or "this is really amazing."

90. Aduêngi's tale nugget is particularly revealing of the inner workings of Saramaka tale-telling, of the art of stitching together diverse fragments and transforming them into a relatively seamless whole. He begins with a very common initial situation ("There was a devil right there in the forest; you couldn't go hunting overnight; if you went hunting overnight, he was sure to kill you"). Then he specifically relates his tale nugget to the tale it is interrupting by inserting into it the same initial action ("There was a boy and an old man who went into the forest, very deep"). He has to do some especially fast footwork to get the boy center stage ("The devil was all set to kill them both; he was getting ready to kill the boy; the man had let the boy go off hunting and the devil was coming to kill him"), in order to set up the song that is the heart of his *kóti*—the boy playing his finger piano to beat the devil. (See also note 91.)

91. Upon hearing this tale nugget in 1987, Lodí told us a tale that uses what he considered to be the same song (though it has a different melody), and he claimed that his tale represented the longer version of this tale nugget—the story Aduêngi remodeled to fit into the current tale-telling session. Lodí told us explicitly that his tale was a "whitefolks' *kóntu*" (and indeed it seems related to the Bluebeard cycle), but Aduêngi here reset it in a fully Saramaka context. As Lodí summarized the original story: A girl who had refused all previous suitors married and went off to live with her husband, telling her scrawny little brother not to follow. The husband turned out to be a devil named Bòkôôzina; he was a headman. The brother did follow her, carrying a spool of thread. When the husband went off hunting, she was left at home. She used his keys to open various rooms of the house and peek in. One

Lodí, 1987.

room was filled with skulls, the next with ribs, the next with balls of blood. She got locked in. The devil and his friends had already decided on a day for killing the girl and eating her. The brother told her to go to the window and escape by lowering herself down the thread. She protested that if she did, she would surely fall and die. He encouraged her to try anyway, since she had nothing to lose. When the devils returned, they began to sing and dance in anticipation of feasting on the girl. The boy told his sister he was going to join his brothers-in-law at their "play." He took his *víva* (a vibrating string instrument, unknown in Saramaka) and played as he approached:

Djeindje kóti djeindje.
Bòkôôdjina, hai Bòkôôdjina.

[The *víva* is saying that the boy is going to cut off the devil's head.]

As the brother drew near the house where the devils were playing, they started to run away. He ran after them and chased them to the river. They dived in and turned into rocks at the water's edge. (Recordings of Saramaka finger piano music are included in R. Price and S. Price 1977.)

92. *Atangani* is the name of the boy's magic.

93. Various kinds of gods, including *vodú* (snake gods), *apúku* (forest spirits), and *komantí* (warrior spirits), are capable of possessing individual Saramakas, with whom they have a special relationship. Spirit possession is one of the primary means through which Saramakas communicate with the unseen world that affects their lives.

94. This is a standard way for a woman to get pregnant in tales. Such a child is called a *kiní édi miíi* ("kneecap child").

95. The tale of the boy going off to the land of the devils to discover Drum is the only one in our two evenings that is told in full twice—first by Kasólu (pp. 165–80) and here by Aduêngi (see also Kandámma's tale nugget, p. 142). Although both tellings are dramatically effective, they stress different aspects of the story and draw on different expressive devices. To mention just a few of the contrasts: Kasólu has the youngest daughter providing a ritual welcome to each male visitor to the funeral, but Aduêngi has her setting up a one-woman "hotel" (whorehouse) to welcome them; Kasólu's includes a single cayman-boat, but Aduêngi's has three and insists more heavily on the sacredness of contracts in Saramaka; Kasólu's expressive devices include the devils feigning sleep and snoring as well as the devils and the boy slamming down magic *atígo*s at each other, and he provides imaginative depictions of the devils' overworked mother and the way they toss her around when they become agitated; Aduêngi builds his peaks of excitement with scenes where the drums call out to the boy cacaphonously and the caymans make the boy play the drum for them before they will carry him back to safety.

96. Later in Aduêngi's tale (p. 238), Agumiíi interrupts with a comment about a certain devil's tooth that was called "*Azángana mi kolóbi, azángana mi koló*" (for which we have no translation).

Upon hearing the recording of this tale nugget in 1986, Rudi Wooje—a young Pikílío Saramaka living in the Netherlands—offered a bare summary of the tale it alludes to: It used to be that babies never lived to grow up. A devil would always kill them. A woman had a son. He went off. She scratched her kneecap again and had a second son. This one asked if he didn't have a brother. "Yes, you had a brother, but a devil ate him." The boy asked his mother to take some reeds and make him a bow, and with that he set off into the forest. He met Awó Mamá—the old woman of the forest. She called to him. She asked him to bring her an egg and a special kind of broom. She told him there was a devil called Anamunagan: "He's the first one you'll meet. He won't want to let you by. He's got a single hair right in the center of his head. If you shoot it, he'll die. Once you've killed him (and he burns up), take the ashes and bring them back to me." The boy arrived at the village of the devil, who smelled him. The devil, a giant, was furious that the boy knew his name. He said, "Let me put you up on my lower lip, and then we'll see if you call my name again!" The boy, standing on the devil's lip, succeeded in shooting the hair on the devil's head with his bow. The devil caught on fire (which is what happens when devils die). The boy took the ashes back to Awó Mamá. She then looked for a *napí* (root crop) and fashioned a horn from it for the boy. She put the ashes inside it. Then she sent him off with the horn and a cock. He met a second devil named Maanpáya (also the name of the devil in Agumiíi's nugget). The cock perched on the top of a large *djuumú* tree while the boy hid at its base, where he played his horn. (This is the song in Agumiíi's nugget.) The devil arrived. The boy tried to shoot him in the face but missed. The devil sang: "*Madjaáfo pénmeni.*" The boy took his last two arrows. (He had to shoot this devil in the forehead in order to kill him.) He missed again. The cock came down and made a fire on the ground between the boy and the devil. The devil stamped out the fire with his foot. The cock then carried the boy onto the devil's head and told him to gouge out the devil's eyes, which the boy did. The cock took one of the eyes and threw it into the horn. The devil caught fire and died. That's why you sometimes come upon ashes in the forest. And that's also why children can now grow up.

97. In 1987 in Kourou, Samsón told us about a *kóntu* concerning *makáku*s that has a very similar song. In it a pregnant woman tells her husband that she has a craving for a twelve-tailed *makáku*. He goes hunting, sees a one-tailed *makáku*, and shoots it. Then he shoots a two-tailed, a three-tailed, and so on, until he gets to a twelve-tailed *makáku* and brings the tails home to her to eat. In the song, the hunter calls to the twelve-tailed *makáku*:

Kizááá, mi da kasú, kizááá-ee.
Kizáá, kizáá, moi-ma záá. Kizáá.

Compare with the rather different story in which Anasi kills a twelve-tailed *makáku* to win the hand of a princess (note 40).

98. Aduêngi here compliments Tíanên's song by deprecating his own skills; compared with her, he sings as awkwardly as a turtle dances.

99. Note that this time Aduêngi does not mention what the payment was, perhaps because Sakuíma distracted him with her question about the funeral.

100. For sketches and discussions of Saramaka drum types, see S. Price and R. Price (1980:178–81).

101. Bongóótu-písi is the part of Dángogó on a hill, where we were all sitting at that very moment telling/listening to tales, in a large open-sided shed. (Bongóótu was the founder of Dángogó, a century ago.)

102. Compare with the similar songs used in other versions of this tale by Kasólu (pp. 165–80) and Asabôsi (p. 169).

103. Recall that Agumíi used this citation in a tale nugget with which she interrupted this tale earlier (p. 227).

104. Sakuíma is teasing Kódji about his singing style by comparing him to a turtle trying to dance on its stubby legs. This conventional image may also be used in tale-telling for flattery via self-deprecation; see note 98.

105. This tale contains many elements familiar from other Saramaka tales—a scrawny little kid who saves his two nubile sisters from certain death at the hands of a lecherous devil; poking a red-hot machete up someone's ass (a theme found throughout Afro-America and possibly related to brutalities practiced historically against slaves [see Stedman 1988]); cooling the devil's instrument of torture by a magic word; bringing the dead sisters back to life by replacing their eyes; deceiving the devil by singing a song; the chase back to civilization with the devil in pursuit; and the explanation of how a particular animal got its coloring.

106. The ceremony of skirt giving, at the matrilineage's ancestor shrine, signals a girl's marriageability. Cutting cicatrizations on her buttocks and thighs, which are an essential part of her being considered sexually mature, begins only at this point (see S. Price 1984). Although in this tale the devil cuts cicatrizations with a machete named Môsòmò, Saramaka cicatrizations are normally incised by a woman using a razor blade.

107. This tale has a wide distribution in Africa and Afro-America; see, for comparative references, Herskovits and Herskovits (1936:254–55) and Flowers (1980:347–49); for an Aluku version, Hurault (1961:279–81); and for a version from Martinique, Laurent and Césaire (1976:234–45).

108. *Piki*[*n*] is the Sranan word for "child."

109. This sentence, which mixes Sranan and Saramaccan along with some added distortions, was described to us as being in "devils' language."

110. This is a fragment of a tale told by Kandámma in the first evening (pp. 111–22). Aduêngi gives a different set of chants/songs from Kandámma, though both mime the way the gluttonous devil moves his mouth.

111. This seems to be a reference—one of the very few direct ones we heard in Saramaka—to the major Congo cult of Lemba that arose in the seventeenth century in response to European incursions (Janzen 1982).

112. Antonísi had heard another version of this tale, in which the girls call (singing) to Fishcatcher:

Mi báki, mi báki, mi báki, gaán tangí tangí kó téki mi.
Seeín seeín seeín.

Ún seéi, na ún seéi.
Bobi ango yego, bobi fíti a bayángo.

[The first line is in standard Saramaccan and means, "My bark, my bark, my bark, please, oh, please, come take me." The second is the sound of the bird's paddling. The third, which means, "Where, oh where?" might also be a continuation of the paddling sound. Antonísi was unable to translate/interpret the last line.]

113. Note that the fishcatcher has white feathers around its neck.

114. Like Amáka's tale earlier in the evening (pp. 208–18), this one evokes the difficulties of being a good parent. For Saramakas, children represent the continuity of their lineage and take on great social and personal value; a standard formula in prayers at the ancestor shrine asks for "wealth, children, and food." But this tale, like the earlier one, stresses the resentment that accompanies parental responsibilities and sacrifice. As Saramakas summarized the story for us, the mother is frustrated by her children's eating all the food in the house and innocently asks help from her friend. But her friend, driven by jealousy because she has no children of her own, wants to reduce her to the same condition and decides to "help out" by killing the children. The moral: *Yán musu kíi déé miíi f'i fu nyanyán édi"* ("You shouldn't kill your children because of [lack of] food"—that is, being a parent demands sacrifices). For a close Ashanti (West African) parallel to Amáka's tale, see Radin (1952 : 36–40).

115. *Síbi* is a relationship of special friendship between two women. As with the *máti* relationship, the reciprocal term of address derives from the Middle Passage itself: *síbi* referred to *ship*mates, those who had experienced the trauma of enslavement and transport together. By the eighteenth century it had already come to signal a rather more playful relationship between two women who had undergone a specific (usually unpleasant) experience at the same time—for example, two women whose husbands had left them simultaneously.

116. In 1987, upon hearing the recording of this tale, Samsón noted that in another version the woman says to the boy (whose name is Akêkèèyánsi), *"Akêkèèyánsi fu dóti"* [Akêkèèyánsi to the ground], to which the child replies, *"Nônô, Mamá. Akêkèèyánsi fu tápu"* [No, Mother. Akêkèèyánsi stays up here]. Note that later on in the version told by Amáka, the boy's name is given as Akêkènyánso (which translates as "He Wants to Eat a Lot").

117. When a tree falls into a large creek, the current deposits various vegetable debris against it, creating a *gánkutu*, under which this species of fish likes to feed.

118. In Saramaka each stretch of forest has at least one particular day of the week when it is ritually dangerous to work there. These prohibitions (which Saramakas call *sabá*, "sabbaths") are historically determined—for ex-

ample, after a hunting or tree-felling death occurred there at some time in the past, divination may have revealed that the gods of the area did not want people to work there on that day of the week.

119. None of the Saramakas we worked with in 1986 or 1987 had ever heard that Kentú is a name for parrot, though that seems to be the clear implication of the tale. The device of a character being swallowed by an animal (often a snake) and then escaping by slitting his belly with a knife is widespread in African and Afro-American tales (see, for example, Abrahams 1985:233; Herskovits and Herskovits 1936:301).

120. This ribald tale has many variants. In one Paramaribo version, Anasi disguises himself as a woman, gets himself hired as nursemaid to the king's overprotected daughters, and teaches them a new "game" (Penard 1924: 339–42; see also Herskovits and Herskovits 1936:384–89 and, for a related Jamaican tale, Dance 1985:68–69). In another Saramaka tale about the discovery of penises, a woman finds a wonderful stick in her garden that "works" for her, until it falls into the hands of her young daughter; enraged that it will no longer work for her, the mother cuts it up and throws the pieces away—where some men eventually find big ones and some find small ones. Note that the initial situation of Kasindó's tale, with men and women living in isolation from each other, also occurs in one of Kandámma's tale nuggets (p. 123).

121. A different version of this encounter between Turtle and Jaguar is transcribed in Saramaccan in Amoida (1987). There was a great famine in the world, during which all the animals in the forest kept alive by eating the palm nuts from a single tree, whose name was Alantavala. One day Turtle gathered all the palm nuts, loaded them into a sack, and went off with them. When Jaguar arrived, he found nothing to eat and cried out:

> *"Huleeeee hule, huleeeee hule,*
> *Ambë njan di alantavala u mi?*
> *Mi a kuku u bani, koo hule*
> *Mi da koobani koo hule."*

Turtle called back with the same song, first from a village far downriver, then from a closer one and then from even closer. When he got to the place where Jaguar was, they fought. Turtle wounded Jaguar with a dagger. Jaguar dealt Turtle a blow that left his paw stuck in Turtle's shell, and he couldn't pull it out. They both died. The lesson is that things intended for everyone to enjoy should not be hoarded as if they were private property.

122. Aduêngi here cuts in with a fragment he had used on the second evening of tale-telling for Sindóbóbi, just three weeks earlier (8 May 1968) in Dángogó, with an audience including many of the same people.

123. Saramakas know Rabbit, whom they call Lapin, only from hearing tales told in French Guiana (where he plays a Brer Rabbit role). The initial activity in Amáka's tale—dragging a pond for fish—is a technique that uses a woven palm-leaf "net." One of the earliest recorded Saramaka *kóntus* (1880s)

also concerns an animal (Jaguar) trying to trick two others (Deer and Brocket) out of their shares after fishing together in a dry-season pond (Schuchardt 1914:41–42); the same general theme recurs in Aduêngi's tale nugget about Shrimp and Jaguar (p. 349); and a Haitian tale is very similar to Amáka's in overall plot structure (Flowers 1980:497–98). The device of Rabbit disguising himself by getting inside Deer's rotting skin occurs in other Afro-American tales (see, for example, Hurault 1961:274–76 and Abrahams 1985:90, and compare Penard 1924:359–60). In coastal Suriname tale-telling, it is more frequently Anasi who makes use of disguises—appearing, for example, as a baby, a white man, a doctor, an American sea captain, and an angel flying around a church (Herskovits and Herskovits 1936:220–21, 228–43, which cites other African and Afro-American parallels). For a Saramaka tale with similarities to that told by Amáka, see Sane (1976:1–14).

124. Compare Asabôsi's tale nugget in the first evening (p. 86).

125. The story of Anasi bringing Death out of the forest to civilization is one of the most widely distributed of African and Afro-American tales. For examples, see Radin (1952:60–61); Abrahams (1985:210–11); Flowers (1980:588–89); and Herskovits and Herskovits (1936:248–51). Other examples from Suriname include Hurault (1961:276–78); Penard (1926:60–63); and Amoida (1974:1–16).

126. Note that *adjáansipái* is a common euphemism for *dêdè* ("death") in normal Saramaccan speech.

127. Aduêngi's complex tale about a boy named Katjédenómu (the Saramaka pronunciation of a French Guiana creole expression, which itself comes from the French *quartier d'un homme,* "quarter of a man") is based on a tale that he had heard while doing wage labor in French Guiana. The closest published version we have seen from French Guiana (Lohier 1960:157–61) has the following story line: A boy is born with only one arm and one leg and is called, derisively, Moitié d'Un ("Half of One"). He is baptized, and the Virgin herself becomes his godmother. In a dream she tells him that because of his handicap, she will give him a magic switch. He tests the switch by asking it to gather firewood for him and then requests that it carry him back home. The princess, seeing him fly by on his bundle of firewood, makes fun of him, and in revenge he asks the switch to make her pregnant, with him as father. When the king discovers her inexplicable pregnancy, he has all the royal physicians decapitated. The child is born holding in his hand a golden apple. The king has summoned all the men in the realm to see which one the child will recognize as its father. The last to arrive, Moitié d'Un, is joyfully greeted by his child, who gives him the golden apple. Totally humiliated, the king and queen put their daughter, her baby, and Moitié d'Un in a leaky boat and send them out to sea to die. With the help of his switch, Moitié d'Un keeps them afloat despite the princess's refusal to speak to him, and eventually he transforms the boat into a luxury yacht. That night he makes himself whole again and appears in her cabin, where she at first takes him for an intruder; but once she realizes the

truth, she throws herself into his arms. They decide to return to see their parents. On arrival, Moitié d'Un invites the king on board and fetes him with champagne. The king invites them back to the palace, where the princess reveals her identity, causing her parents to faint. Regaining consciousness, the king, overcome with joy, offers his throne to Moitié d'Un and they live happily ever after. (For other French Guiana variants, see Jean-Louis 1987:203–6, 386–92. For references to variants from Dominica and Guadeloupe, see Flowers 1980:223–24.)

Aduêngi's wonderfully expressive embellishment of this French Guiana core includes a number of new elements. The boy is born whole but later pulled in two, Solomonically, by his feuding mother and godmother (reflecting—even though Saramakas do not have baptisms or godmothers—important social tensions between women over the right to raise a child). In addition to explaining baptism and godparents, Aduêngi fills in local color by his discussion of the exotic custom known as "schoolchildren's vacation." The magic switch becomes an all-powerful book in this telling, reflecting Saramaka notions about the magic of literacy (and using the widespread Afro-American trope of "the Talking Book" [Gates 1988:127–69]). Anasi puts in a characteristic appearance as one of the men hoping to be identified as the father of the princess's child. Later, when Katjédenómu becomes a whole man again, he also becomes a *white* man, joining a cast of white sailors, officers, and other navigators. War breaks out in the king's land, and Katjédenómu returns to crush the enemy. His triumph includes a worldwide flood, with the Chosen reborn in a dry kingdom, and he gains the throne as reward. Even many of the details appearing in the French Guiana version take on a freshly exotic character in Aduêngi's telling—from mattresses and nightgowns to cannons, horses, and a customs launch.

128. Upon hearing the recording of this tale nugget in Cayenne in 1987, Kalusé told us how he and some others once went hunting on the Upper Pikílío and drugged the river until they killed so many fish it was scary. Then they saw some trees filled with large black birds and shot twelve—far more than they could use. Then a gigantic herd of wild pigs came and stood right in front of them on the river rocks, and they shot many. They ended up leaving much of what they had hunted there, since they couldn't transport it. When they arrived downstream, the chief already knew (supernaturally) what had happened! They were assessed a fine, with each person paying three cloths and five bottles of rum. If they hadn't paid this, the god who owned that stretch of forest and river would have caused their deaths.

A very similar cautionary tale is preserved in Papá language but purports to refer to a late seventeenth-century historical incident (R. Price 1983:50).

129. The Saramakas who worked with us did not know the longer tale from which this tale nugget is extracted—though they all found it hilarious.

130. This tale is understood by Saramakas to illustrate why you should never make a garden without clearing a path to it. The path is what establishes ownership.

131. We remain uncertain whether Kasindó's tale nugget represents a spontaneous embellishment of Aduêngi's tale or an extract from some longer story.

132. In this tale Anasi schemes to set up his two friends (Brother Deer and Brother Brocket), so he can get their share of the food, by having the three of them undergo an ordeal he feels sure of winning. Part of the humor lies in Anasi's (false) confidence that Brocket and Deer, who are much heavier than he, will be the ones to break the spiderweb tightrope he has spun across the river. But in the end the ordeal that Anasi was trying to rig in his favor succeeds in revealing the truth. Understanding the plot line also depends on knowing that a wife's uttering her husband's name has a special valence in Saramaka and that, according to Saramaka etiquette, one should learn others' names discreetly—for example, by overhearing them—rather than asking directly.

Note that one of the tale nuggets earlier in the evening also revolved around Anasi's trying to get his wife to utter his name (p. 274). Many other Afro-American tale plots hinge on the discovery of a personal name (see, for example, Herskovits and Herskovits 1936:228–37, 374–79; Penard 1924: 360–63; Laurent and Césaire 1976:24–37; Flowers 1980:155–60).

133. Kasindó misspeaks himself here. Instead of Sesíyênga-ayênga, he meant to say Maamá-Atóbo, as becomes clear later on in the tale.

134. One of the stages of canoe construction involves leaving the log roughly hollowed out, submerged in the river, before the more delicate procedures of fully hollowing it out, opening it by fire, and finishing it. Anasi's oldest son, known for his cleverness, is Nòngôtjè. For Saramakas, his other children include Táya-mánda ("Taro Basket"), Sé-ofángi ("Sword"), Bakúba-bóngi ("Banana Bunch"), Gadja-édi ("Tall Head"), Fínu-fútu ("Slender Legs"), Gaán-bêè ("Big Belly"), and Lèènlèèn ("Full to Overflowing"?). Lodí once summarized a tale for us in which three of them go to gather maripa palm nuts. Tall Head goes up with a basket and breaks off some nuts. Slender Legs and Big Belly are on the ground. They ask their brother how things are coming along. "Are the maripa nuts sweet?" Tall Head shakes his head, *zénge zénge zénge*, and it breaks off at the neck. Big Belly laughs till his belly splits. Slender Legs runs so hard to get away that he keels over dead. (Compare the Bahamian tale about Big Gut, Big Head, and Stringy Leg in Abrahams 1985:300, the similar one from Marie-Galante in Rutil 1981:55–57, and several from Jamaica in Dance 1985:108–9, as well as the twenty-seven versions from throughout the Caribbean cited in Flowers 1980:57–58.)

References

Abrahams, Roger D.
   1967 The shaping of folklore traditions in the British West Indies. *Journal of Inter-American Studies* 9:456–80.
   1983 *The man-of-words in the West Indies: Performance and the emergence of creole culture.* Baltimore: Johns Hopkins University Press.
   1985 *Afro-American folktales: Stories from Black traditions in the New World.* New York: Pantheon.
   1986 Complicity and imitation in storytelling: A pragmatic folklorist's perspective. *Cultural Anthropology* 1:223–37.
Alleyne, Mervyn C.
   1980 *Comparative Afro-American.* Ann Arbor, Mich.: Karoma.
   1987 *Studies in Saramaccan language structure.* Amsterdam: Centre for Caribbean Studies.
Amoida, Apeninge
   1974 *Anasi ta-pii toobi.* Paramaribo: Instituut voor Taalwetenschap.
   1987 Takumbeti ku logoso. In *Sö de si ku sö de jei,* ed. F. Pansa, 19–25. Paramaribo: Instituut voor Taalwetenschap.
Arrom, José Juan
   1986 Cimarrón: Apuntes sobre sus primeras documentaciones y su probable origen. In *Cimarrón,* ed. Manuel A. García Arévalo, 13–30. Santo Domingo: Ediciones Fundación García Arévalo.
Bascom, William
   1969 *Ifa divination: Communication between gods and men in West Africa.* Bloomington: Indiana University Press.
Basso, Ellen B.
   1987 *In favor of deceit: A study of tricksters in an Amazonian society.* Tucson: University of Arizona Press.
Bauman, Richard
   1986 *Story, performance, and event: Contextual studies of oral narrative.* Cambridge: Cambridge University Press.
Burns, Allan F.
   1983 *An epoch of miracles: Oral literature of the Yucatec Maya.* Austin: University of Texas Press.
Césaire, Ina
   1987 *L'enfant des passages, ou La geste de Ti-Jean.* Paris: Editions Caribéennes.
Cosentino, Donald
   1982 *Defiant maids and stubborn farmers: Tradition and invention in Mende story performance.* Cambridge: Cambridge University Press.

413

Crowley, Daniel J.
  1966 *I could talk old-story good: Creativity in Bahamian folklore.* Berkeley: University of California Press.

Dance, Daryl C.
  1985 *Folklore from contemporary Jamaicans.* Knoxville: University of Tennessee Press.

Dauenhauer, Nora Marks, and Richard Dauenhauer
  1987 *Haa shuká, our ancestors: Tlingit oral narratives.* Seattle: University of Washington Press.

de Drie, Aleks
  1985 *Sye! Arki tori!* Compiled by Trudi Guda. Paramaribo: Ministerie van Onderwijs, Wetenschappen en Cultuur.

Extract . . .
  n.d. Extract of the diary of the missionaries of the United Brethren among the free negroes at Bambey, in South America, from July 1st to December 31st, 1804. *Periodical Accounts Relating to the Missions of the Church of the United Brethren Established among the Heathens* 3:420.

Falassi, Alessandro
  1980 *Folklore by the fireside: Text and context of the Tuscan veglia.* Austin: University of Texas Press.

Flowers, Helen L.
  1980 *A classification of the folktale of the West Indies by types and motifs.* New York: Arno.

Gates, Henry Louis, Jr.
  1988 *The signifying monkey: A theory of Afro-American literary criticism.* New York: Oxford University Press.

Giraud, Michel, and Jean-Luc Jamard
  1985 Travail et servitude dans l'imaginaire antillais: Une littérature orale en question. *L'Homme* 35(4): 77–96

Glock, Naomi, and Stephen H. Levinsohn
  1982 Structure of the Saramaccan folktale. *Languages of the Guianas* 3:31–55.

Görög, Veronika
  1968 L'origine de l'inégalité des races: Etude de trente-sept contes africains. *Cahiers d'Etudes Africaines* 8:290–309.

Herskovits, Melville J., and Frances S. Herskovits
  1936 *Suriname folk-lore.* New York: Columbia University Press.
  1958 *Dahomean narrative: A cross-cultural analysis.* Evanston, Ill.: Northwestern University Press.

Hurault, Jean
  1961 *Les Noirs Réfugiés Boni de la Guyane Française.* Dakar: Institut Français d' Afrique Noire.

Hymes, Dell
1975 Breakthrough into performance. In *Folklore: Performance and communication,* ed. Dan Ben-Amos and Kenneth S. Goldstein, 11–74. The Hague: Mouton.

1981 *"In vain I tried to tell you": Essays in native American ethnopoetics.* Philadelphia: University of Pennsylvania Press.

Jackson, Bruce
1988 What people like us are saying when we say we're saying the truth. *Journal of American Folklore* 101:276–92.

Janzen, John M.
1982 *Lemba, 1650–1930: A drum of affliction in Africa and the New World.* New York: Garland.

Jean-Louis, Marie-Paule
1987 La tradition orale guyanaise: Universalité et spécificité du conte créole. Third-cycle thesis, Université de Provence.

Jones, LeRoi
1967 *Black music.* New York: William Morrow.

Laurent, Joëlle, and Ina Césaire
1976 *Contes de mort et de vie aux Antilles.* Paris: Nubia.

Lohier, Michel
1960 *Légendes et contes folkloriques guyanais.* Cayenne: Imprimerie Paul Laporte.

Naipaul, V. S.
1962 *The middle passage.* London: André Deutsch.

Paulme, Denise
1986 Un conte bété et son narrateur. *Gradhiva* 1:1–8.

Penard, A. P.
1924 Surinaamsche volksvertellingen. *Bijdragen tot de Taal-, Land- en Volkenkunde* 80:325–63.

1926 Surinaamsche volksvertellingen. *Bijdragen tot de Taal-, Land- en Volkenkunde* 82:47–94.

Price, Richard
1973 Avenging spirits and the structure of Saramaka lineages. *Bijdragen tot de Taal-, Land- en Volkenkunde* 129:86–107.

1975 *Saramaka social structure: Analysis of a Maroon society in Surinam.* Rio Piedras: Institute of Caribbean Studies, University of Puerto Rico.

1976 *The Guiana Maroons: A historical and bibliographical introduction.* Baltimore: Johns Hopkins University Press.

1979 *Maroon societies: Rebel slave communities in the Americas.* 2d ed., rev. Baltimore: Johns Hopkins University Press.

1983 *First-Time: The historical vision of an Afro-American people.* Baltimore: Johns Hopkins University Press.

416 · REFERENCES

1990 *Alabi's world*. Baltimore: Johns Hopkins University Press.

n.d. Dialogical encounters in a space of death. In *Death and creation in the New World*, ed. J. Jorge Klor de Alva and Gary H. Gossen. Austin: University of Texas Press. Forthcoming.

Price, Richard, and Sally Price
1972 Saramaka onomastics: An Afro-American naming system. *Ethnology* 11:341–67.

1977 *Music from Saramaka*. New York: Folkways Records FE4225.

1989 Working for the Man: A Saramaka outlook on Kourou. *New West Indian Guide* 63:199–207.

Price, Sally
1984 *Co-wives and calabashes*. Ann Arbor: University of Michigan Press.

1989 *Primitive art in civilized places*. Chicago: University of Chicago Press.

Price, Sally, and Richard Price
1980 *Afro-American arts of the Suriname rain forest*. Berkeley: University of California Press.

Radin, Paul
1952 *African folktales and sculpture*. New York: Pantheon.

Rountree, S. Catherine
1982 Saramaccan personal narrative. *Languages of the Guianas* 3:56–84.

Rutil, Alain
1981 *Contes marie-galantais de Guadeloupe*. Paris: Editions Caribéennes.

Sane, Metson
1976 *Koontu köndë oto*. Paramaribo: Instituut voor Taalwetenschap.

Schuchardt, Hugo
1914 *Die Sprache der Saramakkaneger in Surinam*. Verhandelingen der Koninklijke Akademie van Wetenschappen te Amsterdam 14 (6). Amsterdam: Johannes Müller.

Seitel, Peter
1980 *See so that we may see: Performances and interpretations of traditional tales from Tanzania*. Bloomington: Indiana University Press.

Sherzer, Joel, and Anthony C. Woodbury, eds.
1987 *Native American discourse: Poetics and rhetoric*. Cambridge: Cambridge University Press.

Smith, Norval S. H.
1987 The genesis of the creole languages of Surinam. Ph.D. diss., Universiteit van Amsterdam.

Stedman, John Gabriel
1988 *Narrative of a five years expedition against the revolted Negroes of Surinam*. Ed. Richard Price and Sally Price. Baltimore: Johns Hopkins University Press.

Tanna, Laura
  1984 *Jamaican folk tales and oral histories.* Kingston: Institute of Jamaica.
Tedlock, Dennis
  1972 *Finding the center: Narrative poetry of the Zuni Indians.* New York: Dial.
  1983 *The spoken word and the work of interpretation.* Philadelphia: University of Pennsylvania Press.
Thompson, Robert Farris
  1974 *African art in motion: Icon and act.* Berkeley: University of California Press.
Vernon, Diane
  1987 "Payer n'est pas mourir": La rétribution dans une médecine traditionelle. Manuscript.
Walsh, John, with Robert Gannon
  1967 *Time is short and the water rises.* New York: E. P. Dutton.